A Guide to Ancient Greek Drama

BLACKWELL GUIDES TO CLASSICAL LITERATURE

This series proves concise, authoritative introductions to genres and periods of classical literature. Each volume offers coverage of political and cultural context, brief essays on key authors and historical figures, critical coverage of the most important literary works, and a survey of crucial themes. The series provides the necessary background to read classical literature with confidence.

Published

A Guide to Ancient Greek Drama
Ian C. Storey and Arlene Allan

In preparation

A Guide to Hellenistic Literature
Kathryn Gutzwiller

A Guide to Epic Poetry
Patricia Parker and Brendon Reay

A Guide to Ancient Greek Drama

Ian C. Storey and Arlene Allan

Blackwell
Publishing

BLACKWELL PUBLISHING
350 Main Street, Malden, MA 02148-5020, USA
108 Cowley Road, Oxford OX4 1JF, UK
550 Swanston Street, Carlton, Victoria 3053, Australia

First published 2005 by Blackwell Publishing Ltd

Library of Congress Cataloging-in-Publication Data

Storey, Ian Christopher, 1946–
A guide to ancient Greek drama / Ian C. Storey and Arlene Allan.
    p.   cm. — (Blackwell guides to classical literature)
    Includes bibliographical references and index.
    ISBN 1-4051-0214-4 (hardback : alk. paper) — ISBN 1-4051-0215-2 (pbk. : alk. paper)   1. Greek drama — History and criticism — Handbooks, manuals, etc.   I. Allan, Arlene.   II. Title.   III. Series.

PA3131.S83 2005
882′.0109 — dc22

2004009014

A catalogue record for this title is available from the British Library.

Set in 10 on 12.5 pt Calisto
by SNP Best-set Typesetter Ltd., Hong Kong
Printed and bound in the United Kingdom
by TJ International Ltd, Padstow, Cornwall

The publisher's policy is to use permanent paper from mills that operate a sustainable forestry policy, and which has been manufactured from pulp processed using acid-free and elementary chlorine-free practices. Furthermore, the publisher ensures that the text paper and cover board used have met acceptable environmental accreditation standards.

For further information on
Blackwell Publishing, visit our website:
www.blackwellpublishing.com

Dedicated to all members of the Classics Drama Group
("The Conacher Players")
at Trent University, past, present, and future.

0.1 *Scene from Euripides'* Hippolytos *by the Classics Drama Group, Trent University (1994). Picture by Martin Boyne: Craig Sawyer (attendant), James Laing (Hippolytos), William Robinson (Theseus).*

Contents

Preface

In this Guide we have attempted to provide an introduction to all three of the genres that comprised ancient Greek drama. Many critical studies focus solely on tragedy or on comedy with only a nodding glance at the other, while satyr-drama often gets lost in the glare of the more familiar genres. We begin with a consideration of the aspects and conventions of ancient Greek drama, so like and at the same time different from our own experience of the theater, and then discuss the connections that it possessed with the festivals of Dionysos and the *polis* of Athens. Was attending or performing in the theater in the fifth and fourth centuries a "religious" experience for those involved? To what extent was ancient drama a political expression of the democracy of the Athenian *polis* in the classical era?

We consider first tragedy, the eldest of the three dramatic sisters, both the nature of the genre ("serious drama") and the playwrights that have survived, most notably the canonical triad (Aeschylus, Sophokles, Euripides), but also some of the lesser lights who entertained the spectators and won their share of victories. We have given satyr-drama its own discussion, briefer to be sure than the others, but the student should be aware that it was a different sort of dramatic experience, yet still part of the expected offerings at the City Dionysia. As Old Comedy is inextricably bound up with Aristophanes, much of the discussion of that poet will be found in the section on Old Comedy proper as well as the separate section devoted to Aristophanes. A short chapter addresses how one should watch or read (and teach) Greek drama and introduces the student to the various schools of interpretation. Finally we have provided a series of one-page synopses of each of the forty-six reasonably complete plays that have come down to us, which contain in brief compass the essential details and issues surrounding each play.

We would thank our students and colleagues at Trent University, who over the years have been guinea-pigs for our thoughts on ancient Greek drama. Martin Boyne, in particular, gave us much useful advice as the project began to take shape. Kevin Whetter at Acadia University read much of the manuscript and provided an invaluable commentary. Colleagues at Exeter University and the University of Canterbury in New Zealand have also been sources of ongoing advice and support. Kate Bosher (Michigan) very kindly gave us the benefit of her research into Epicharmos. Karin Sowada at the Nicholson Museum in Sydney has gone out of her way to assist in providing illustrations for the book. We have enjoyed very much working with the staff at Blackwell. Al Bertrand, Angela Cohen, Annette Abel, and Simon Alexander have become familiar correspondents, responding unfailingly to our frequent queries.

Drama is doing, and theater watching. We both owe much to the Classics Drama Group at Trent University, which since 1994 has sought to bring alive for our students the visual and performative experience of ancient drama. This volume is dedicated to them, with admiration and with thanks.

Figures

Maps

Abbreviations and Signs

IG i³   D. M. Lewis & L. Jeffrey, *Inscriptiones Graecae, i³. Inscriptiones Atticae Euclidis Anno Anteriores* (2 vols.; Berlin: de Gruyter, 1981–94)

IG ii²   J. Kirchner, *Inscriptiones Graecae: voluminum ii et iii editio minor* (2 vols; Berlin: Reimer, 1916–35)

PCG   R. Kassel & C. Austin, *Poetae Comici Graeci* (Berlin/New York, 1983–)

Σ   Scholia, ancient commentaries that have been transmitted along with the ancient texts themselves

POxy.   The Oxyrhynchos Papyrus

TrGF   B. Snell, R. Kannicht, & S. Radt (eds.), *Tragicorum Graecorum Fragmenta* vol. 1 (Gottingen: Vandenhoek & Ruprecht, 1971–)

Fragments of the lost dramatists are cited from *TrGF* for tragedy, apart from Euripides, whose fragments are cited from the edition by A. Nauck, supplemented by B. Snell, *Tragicorum Graecorum Fragmenta* (Hildesheim: Olms, 1964). Fragments of the comic poets are cited from *PCG*.

All dates are BC, unless otherwise indicated. Except for some names which have become too familiar to alter (Homer, Aeschylus, Plato, Aristotle, Menander ~ more properly Homeros, Aischylos, Platon, Aristoteles, Menandros), we have used Hellenized spellings ("k" to represent Greek kappa, endings in "-os" rather than the Latinate "-us"). Among other things, it does help the student distinguish a Greek author (e.g., Kratinos) from a Roman one (e.g., Plautus).

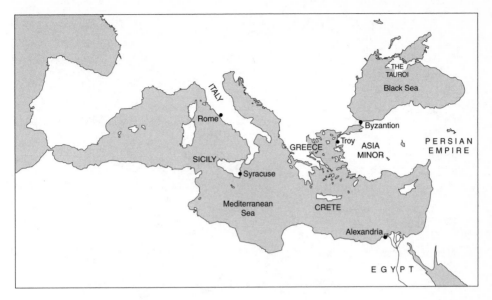

Map 0.1 *Map of the Eastern Mediterranean*

Map 0.2 *Map of Greece*

1

Aspects of Ancient Greek Drama

Drama

The history of Western drama begins in the mid-sixth century at Athens. The high period of Greek drama runs from the sixth to the mid-third century, with special attention paid to the fifth century, when most of the plays that we possess were produced. We shall be concerned with the three distinct genres of Greek drama: serious drama or **tragedy** (instituted traditionally in 534), **satyr-drama** (added ca. 500), and **comedy** (which began formally at Athens in 486, but which flourished at the same time in Syracuse also).

Drama is action. According to Aristotle (*Poetics* 1448a28), dramatic poets "represent people in action," as opposed to a third-person narrative or the mixture of narrative and direct speech as done by Homer. We begin, then, appropriately enough with a Greek word, δρᾶμα (*drama*), which means "action," "doing," "performance." According to Aristotle, the verb *dran* was not an Attic term ("Attic" being the dialect spoken at Athens), Athenians preferring to use the verb *prattein* and its cognates (*pragma, praxis*) to signify "action" or "performance." Whether this was true or not does not matter here – that *dran* is common in Athenian tragedy, but not in the prose writers, may support Aristotle's assertion. For both Plato and Aristotle, the two great philosophers of the fourth century, drama is an example of *mimesis*, "imitation" or "representation," but each took a different view of the matter. (*Mimesis* is not an easy word to render in English. Neither "imitation" nor "representation" really gets the point. We have left it in Greek transliteration.) For Plato *mimesis* was something to be discredited, something inferior, which the ideal ruler of an ideal state would avoid. It meant putting oneself into the character of another, taking on another's role, which in many Greek myths could be a morally inferior one, perhaps even that of a slave or a woman. Plato would have agreed with Polonius in *Hamlet*, "to thine own self be true." But Aristotle found in *mimesis* not only something natural in human nature but also something that was a pleasure and essential for human learning (*Poetics* 1448b5–9):

to engage in *mimesis* is innate in human beings from childhood and humans differ from other living creatures in that humans are very mimetic and develop their first learning through *mimesis* and because all humans enjoy mimetic activities.

Drama then is "doing" or "performance," and in human cultures performances can be used in all sorts of ways. Religion and ritual immediately spring to mind as one context: the elaborate dances of the Shakers; the complex rituals of the Navaho peoples; the mediaeval mystery plays, which for a largely illiterate society would provide a venue for religious instruction and ritual reenactment, as well as for entertainment. Drama can also encompass "science" – the dances of the Navaho provide both a history of the creation of the world and a series of elaborate healing rituals. Drama and performance will often keep historical events alive – here "legend" is a better term than "myth," for legend is based on some real "historical" events, elaborated admittedly out of recognition, but real nonetheless. Greek tragedy falls partly into this category, since its themes and subjects are for the most part drawn from the heroic age, an idealized time about a thousand years before the classical age. The Ramlila play-cycles of northern India were a similar mixture of myth and history, and provided for the Hindus the same sort of cultural heritage that Greek myths did in classical Greece. An extreme example of the history-drama is the history-plays of Shakespeare, in particular his *Richard III*, which is based on the Tudor propaganda campaign aimed at discrediting the last of the Plantagenets. Drama can be used to provide moral instruction. The Mystery Plays in part reiterated the message of the Christian gospel, while the Ramlila plays celebrate the triumph of love and loyalty over evil and lust. And finally humans enjoy both acting in and watching performances. Aristotle is quite right to insist that *mimesis* is both innate to humanity and the source of natural pleasure. We go to the theater or watch formal performances because they give us pleasure, a diversion from the routine, the enjoyment of watching a story-line unfold and engaging with the characters, and the emotional experience involved.

Above all we enjoy hearing or watching a story unfold. The child will ask, "And then what happened?" Indeed Aristotle (*Poetics* chapter 6) will insist that *mythos* ("plot") is the most important part of a Greek tragedy. For the Greeks drama (performance) came later than the purely narrative relation of a story. The sequence would seem to have been purely oral narrative by the bards; the Homeric epics (eighth century), which, as Aristotle points out (*Poetics* 1448a21), do not provide pure narration, but a mixture of narration and direct speech; finally actual dramatic performance.

Another crucial term is "theater." *Thea-* in Greek means "observe," "watch" (related also to "theory" as the result of mental contemplation), and while we speak of an "audience" and an "auditorium" (from the Latin *audire*, "to hear"), the ancients talked of "watchers," "spectators," and the "watching-place." The noun *theatron* ("theater") refers both to the physical area where the plays were staged, more specifically here to the area on the hillside occupied by the spectators, and also to the spectators themselves, much as "house" today can refer to the theater building and the audience in that building. Comedy, which was fond of breaking the dramatic illusion, refers directly to *theatai* ("watchers") and a related term *theomenoi* ("those watching").

In modern critical discussions a distinction is made between the academic studies of "drama" and "theater." A university course or a textbook on "Drama" tends to concentrate more on the text that was performed, that is the words of the text that are recited or read. This approach takes the plays as literature and subjects them to the various sorts of literary theory that exist, and often runs the risk of losing the visual aspect of performance in an attempt to "understand" or elucidate the "meaning" of the text. The reader becomes as important as the watcher, if not more so. Greek drama becomes part of a larger literary approach to drama, and can easily become part of a course on world drama, in which similar principles of literary criticism can be applied to all such texts.

But the modern study of "Theater" goes beyond the basic text as staged or read and has developed a complex theoretical approach that some text-based students find daunting and at times impenetrable. Mark Fortier writes well:

> Theater is performance, though often the performance of a dramatic text, and entails not only words but space, actors, props, audience, and the complex relations among these elements . . . Theater, of necessity, involves both doing and seeing, practice and contemplation. Moreover, the word "theory" comes from the same root as "theater." Theater and theory are both contemplative pursuits, although theater has a practical and a sensuous side which contemplation should not be allowed to overwhelm.*

The study of "theater" will concern itself with the experience of producing and watching drama, before, during, and after the actual performance of the text itself. Theatrical critics want to know about the social assumptions and experiences of organizers, authors, performers, judges, and spectators. In classical Athens plays were performed in a public setting, in a theater placed next to the shrine of a god and as part of the worship of that god, in broad daylight where spectators would be conscious of far more than the performance unfolding below – of the city and country around them and of their very existence as spectators.

This is meant to be a guide to Greek *Drama*, rather than to Greek theatrical practice. There have been many first-rate studies over the past twenty years that have called our attention to much more than the words on the stage (or page) to be understood. Our principal concern will be the texts themselves and their authors – and, although such an approach may be somewhat out of date, to the intentions of the authors themselves. But we do not want to lose sight of the practical elements that Fortier speaks of, especially the visual spectacle that accompanied the enactment of the recited text, for a picture is worth a thousand words, and if we could witness an ancient production, we would learn incalculably more about what the author was doing and how this was received by his original "house." Knowing the conventions of an ancient theatrical experience can also assist with understanding the text, why certain scenes are written the way they are, why certain characters must leave and enter when they do, why crucial events are narrated rather than depicted.

---

* M. Fortier, *Theatre/Theory* (London 1997) 4–6.

Drama and the poets

Homer (eighth century) stands not just at the beginning of Greek poetry, but of Western literature as we know it. His two great epic poems in the heroic manner, *Iliad* (about Achilles, the great Greek hero of the Trojan War) and *Odyssey* (the return of Odysseus [Ulysses] from that war), did much to provide standard versions of the myths of both gods and men. Homer is the great poet of classical Greece, and his epics (along with those that we call the "epic cycle" – in addition to Homer's *Iliad* and *Odyssey*, which we possess, there were several other poems [certainly later than Homer] that completed the story of the Trojan War as well as another complete cycle relating the epic events at Thebes) formed the backdrop to so much later Greek literature, including the dramatists. They would take much of the language, characters, and plots from Homer – Aeschylus is described as serving up "slices from the banquet of Homer," and the dramatic critic needs to have one eye on Homer at all times, to see what use the poets are making of his seminal material. For example, Homer created a brilliantly whole and sympathetic, if a somewhat unconventional, character in his Odysseus, but for the dramatists of the fifth century Odysseus becomes a one-sided figure: the paragon of clever talk and deceit, the concocter of evil schemes, and in one instance (Sophokles' *Ajax*) the embodiment of a new and enlightened sort of heroism. Homer's Achilles is one of the great explorations of what it means to be a truly "tragic" hero, a man whose pursuit of honor leads to the death of his dearest friend and ultimately his own, but when he appears in Euripides' *Iphigeneia at Aulis*, we behold an ineffective youth, full of sound and fury, unable to rescue the damsel in distress. Of the surviving thirty-three plays attri-buted to the tragedians, only two directly overlap with Homer's *Iliad* and *Odyssey* (Euripides' satyr-drama *Cyclops* and *Rhesos* of doubtful authenticity), but we know that several of the lost plays did dramatize Homeric material. Homer may be three centuries earlier than the tragedians of the fifth century, but his influence upon them was seminal. Homer himself was looking back to an earlier age, what we call the late Bronze Age (1500–1100), a tradition which he passed on to the dramatists. Both Homer and the tragedians depict people and stories not of their own time, but of an earlier, lost, and idealized age of heroes.

In the seventh and sixth centuries, heroic epic began to yield to choral poetry (often called "lyric," from its accompaniment by the lyre). These were poems intended to be sung, usually by large groups in a public setting. Particularly important for the study of drama are the grand poets Stesichoros (ca. 600), Bacchylides (career: 510–450), and Pindar (career: 498–ca. 440), who took the traditional tales from myth and retold them in smaller chunks, with an effort to vary the material that they had inherited. And they used a different meter from Homer, not the epic hexameter sung (chanted?) by a single bard, but elaborate "lyric" meters, intended to be sung by large choruses. None of Stesichoros' poems has survived intact, but we know of a poem on the Theban story, one of the favorite themes of tragedy; an *Oresteia* (with significant points of contact with Aeschylus' *Oresteia*); and a retelling of the story of Helen that Euripides will take up wholesale in his *Helen*. One poem by Bacchylides tells the story of

Herakles' death at the hands of his wife in much the same fashion that Sophokles dramatizes in his *Trachinian Women* (it is not clear whether Bacchylides' poem or Sophokles' tragedy is the earlier work) and Pindar in *Pythian* 11 (474) will anticipate Aeschylus' *Agamemnon* (458) by speculating about the various motives of Klytaimestra for killing her husband.

Drama and Athens

We shall be concerned principally with the dramas that were written and performed at Athens, for us the best-known city of the ancient Greek world. But theaters were not exclusive to Athens. A reasonably sized theater of the fifth century can be seen at Argos, and Syracuse, the greatest of the Greek states on Sicily, certainly had an elaborate theater and a tradition of comedy in the early fifth century. In the fourth century a theater was a *sine qua non* of every Greek city-state, however small, and the production of plays was an international practice throughout the Greek, and later through the Roman world. During Alexander's great expedition to the East, we know of theatrical performances staged for the entertainment of his army. But it was at Athens in the late sixth and early fifth centuries that the three genres of drama were first formalized in public competitions.

Why did formal drama develop at Athens and not, say, at Corinth or Samos, both major city-states of the sixth century and centers of culture? It is important to remember that during the sixth century Athens was not the leading city of the Greek world, politically, militarily, economically, or culturally, that she would become in the fifth century. The leading states of the sixth century in the Greek homeland were Sparta, Corinth, Sikyon, and Samos. Athens was an important city, but not really in the same league as these others. By the early sixth century Athens had brought under her central control the region called "Attica" – the actual Greek is "the Attic (land)." This is a triangular peninsula roughly forty miles in length from the height of land that divides Boiotia (dominated by Thebes) from Attica to the south-eastern tip of Cape Sounion, and at its widest expanse about another forty miles. Athens itself lies roughly in the center, no more than thirty miles or so from any outlying point – the most famous distance is that from Athens to Marathon, twenty-six miles and change, the distance run by the runner announcing the victory at Marathon in 490 and that of the modern Marathon race today. Attica itself was not particularly rich agriculturally – the only substantial plains lie around Athens itself and at Marathon – nor does it supply good grazing for cattle or sheep. But in the late sixth century Athens underwent an economic boom, through the discovery and utilization of three products of the Attic soil: olives and olive oil, which rapidly became the best in the eastern Mediterranean; clay for pottery – Athenian vase-ware soon replaced Corinthian as the finest of the day; and silver from the mines at Laureion – the Athenian "owls" (figure 1.1) became a standard coinage of the Eastern Mediterranean.

Coupled with this economic advance was the political situation in the late sixth century. The Greeks of the seventh and sixth centuries experienced an uneasy mix of hereditary monarchy, factional aristocracy, popular unrest (at Athens especially over

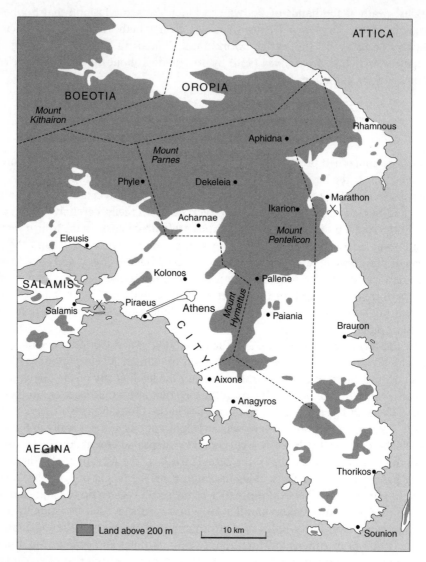

Map 1.1 *Map of Attica*

debts and the loss of freedom), and what they called "tyranny." To us "tyrant" is a pejorative term, like "dictator," but in Archaic Greece it meant "one-man rule," usually where that one man had made himself ruler, often rescuing a state from an internal *stasis* ("civil unrest"). In some versions of the "seven sages" of ancient Greece, the traditional wise men, as many as four tyrants were included. At Athens the tyrant Peisistratos seized power permanently in the mid-540s. He ruled to his death in 528/7, and was succeeded by his son Hippias, who was expelled from Athens in 510 by an alliance of exiled aristocrats and the Spartan kings.

Figure 1.1 *Obverse (Athene) and reverse (owl) of two Athenian tetradrachms, ca. 480. In the collection of the Department of Ancient History & Classics, Trent University. Photo by Mike Cullen, Trent Photographics.*

In the fifth century "tyrant" was a dirty word, used in political in-fighting as an accusation to pillory an opponent, and the first use of the practice of ostracism (a state-wide vote to expel a political leader for ten years) in 487 was to exile "friends of the tyrants." But in the fourth century the age of the tyrants (546–510) was remembered as an "age of Kronos," a golden age before the defeat of Athens during the democracy. The tyrants in fact set Athens on the road to her future greatness in the fifth century under the democracy. They provided political and economic stability after a period of particularly bitter economic class-conflict in the early sixth century, attracted artists to their court at Athens, including the major poets Anakreon, Simonides, and Bacchylides, inaugurated a building program that would be surpassed only by the grandeur of the Acropolis in the next century, established or enhanced the festival of the Panthenaia, the great celebration of Athene and of Athens, and instituted contests for the recitation of the Homeric poems, establishing incidentally the first "official" text of Homer. What the tyrants did was to quell discontent and divisions within the state and instill a communal sense of ethnic identity that paved the way for Athens' greatness in the next century. One other act of the tyrants was the creation of a single festival of Dionysos at Athens, the City Dionysia, which overrode all the local festivals and created one official celebration for the people of Attica. It was at this festival that tragedy was first performed.

In this place and against this background drama develops, tragedy first of all, traditionally dated to 534 and thus part of the cultural program of the tyranny, later satyr-play, and finally comedy. We shall see that drama evolved from some sort of choral performance, a melding of song and dance, allegedly the dithyramb for tragedy, dancing satyrs for satyr-drama, and perhaps animal-choruses, phallic dancers, or padded dancers for comedy. The exact details of this development remain obscure, and we can give no firm answer to the question: why Athens? Corinth, for example, was an even more prosperous city in the sixth century and had flourished under its tyranny. Samos under the tyrant Polykrates in the 520s enjoyed a brilliant artistic life, but it was at Athens that drama first emerged as a distinct art-form.

The time-frame

The traditional date for the formal introduction of a dramatic form (tragedy) is given as 534 and linked with the shadowy figure of Thespis. For some the evidence for this date is not compelling and a rather lower date (ca. 500) is preferred – the matter will be discussed more fully later. Clearly tragedy was not "invented" overnight and we should postulate some sort of choral performances in the sixth century developing into what would be called "tragedy." Thus we begin our study of drama in the sixth century, even though the first extant play (Aeschylus' *Persians*) belongs to 472. Like any form of art, drama has its periods, each with its own style and leading poets. The period we know best is that which corresponds with Athens' ascendancy in the Greek world (479–404), from which we have thirty tragedies, one satyr-drama, one quasi-satyr-drama, and nine comedies, as well as a wealth of fragments and *testimonia* about lost plays and authors. But drama continued through the fourth century and well into the third. New tragedies continued to be written and performed in the fourth century, but along with the new arose a fascination with the old, and competitions were widened to include an "old" performance. In the third century tragic activity shifted to the scholar-poets of Alexandria, but here it is uncertain whether these tragedies were meant to be read rather than performed, and if performed, for how wide an audience.

The evidence suggests strongly that satyr-drama is a later addition to the dramatic festivals; most scholars accept a date of introduction of ca. 501. Thus satyr-drama is not the primitive dramatic form from which tragedy would develop. In the fifth century satyr-drama would accompany the performance of the three tragedies by each of the competing playwrights, but by 340 satyr-drama was divorced from the tragic competitions and only one performed at the opening of the festival. Thus at some point during the fourth century satyr-drama becomes its own separate genre.

Comedy began later than tragedy and satyr-drama, the canonical first date being the Dionysia of 486. The ancient critics divided comedy at Athens into three distinct chronological phases: Old Comedy, roughly synonymous with the classical fifth century (486 to ca. 385); Middle Comedy (ca. 385–325, or "between Aristophanes and Menander"); New Comedy (325 onward). We have complete plays surviving from the first and third of these periods. The ancients knew also about comedy at Syracuse in the early fifth century and about something from the same period called "Megarian comedy."

Dates in the history of Greek drama

ca. 600 – Arion "invents" the dithyramb
534 – first official performance of tragedy at Athens (Thespis)
ca. 501 – reorganization of the festival; first official satyr-drama

Continued

498 – début of Aeschylus
486 – first official performance of comedy
468 – début of Sophokles
456 – death of Aeschylus
455 – début of Euripides
ca. 440 – introduction of dramatic competitions at the Lenaia
427 – début of Aristophanes
407 – death of Euripides
406 – death of Sophokles
ca. 385 – death of Aristophanes
ca. 330 – building of the stone theater at Athens
325 or 321 – début of Menander
290 – death of Menander

The evidence

We face two distinct problems in approaching the study of Greek drama: the distance in time and culture, and the sheer loss of evidence. In some instances we are dealing with texts that are nearly 2,500 years removed from our own, in a different language and produced for an audience with cultural assumptions very different in some ways from our own. "The past is a foreign country: they do things differently there," wrote L. P. Hartley, and we should not react to reading (or watching) an ancient Greek drama in the same way that we approach a modern "classic" such as Shakespeare or a contemporary drama.

The actual evidence is of four sorts: literary texts, literary *testimonia*, physical remains of theaters, and visual representations of theatrical scenes. The manuscript tradition and discoveries on papyrus have yielded to date as complete texts: thirty-one tragedies, one satyr-drama, one quasi-satyr-drama, and thirteen comedies. But these belong to only five (perhaps six or seven) distinct playwrights, out of the dozens that we know were active on the Greek stage. We would like to think that Aeschylus, Sophokles, and Euripides (for tragedy), and Aristophanes and Menander (for comedy) were the best at their business, but were they representative of all that the Athenians watched during those two centuries? Within these individual authors we have six or seven plays out of eighty or so by Aeschylus, seven out of 120 by Sophokles, eighteen out of ninety by Euripides, eleven comedies out of forty by Aristophanes, and only two comedies by Menander out of over a hundred. On what grounds were these selections made, by whom, for whom, and when? Are these selected plays representative of their author's larger opus? In the case of Euripides we have both a selected collection of ten plays and an alphabetical sequence of nine plays that may be more indicative of his work as a whole.

We do not possess anything at all resembling the folios and quartos of Shakespeare, nor anything remotely close to the scripts of the original production or to the "official" texts that were established by Lykourgos ca. 330 and which then passed to the

Library in Alexandria. We have some remains preserved on papyrus from the Roman period (most notably Menander's *The Grouch*, virtually complete on a codex from the third century AD), but the earliest manuscripts of Greek drama belong about AD 1000. Dionysos in *Frogs* (405) talks blithely of "sitting on his ship reading [Euripides'] *Andromeda*" and we do know of book-stalls in the fifth century, but these would not have been elaborate "books" in our sense of the word, but very basic texts allowing the reader to re-create his experience in the theater. The manuscripts and papyri present texts in an abbreviated form, with no division between words, changes of speaker often indicated (if at all) by an underlining or a dicolon, no stage directions – almost all the directions in a modern translation are the creation of the translator – and very frequent errors, omissions, and later additions to the text. But they are what we have, and we must make the most of them.

In addition to the actual play texts, we have a considerable amount of literary *testimonia* about the dramatic tradition generally and about individual plays and personalities. Most important is Aristotle's *Poetics*, a sketchily written treatise dating from ca. 330, principally on tragedy and epic, but with some general introductory comments on drama. Aristotle was himself not an Athenian by birth, although resident for many years there, and was writing a hundred years after the great period of Attic tragedy. The great question in dealing with *Poetics* is whether Aristotle knows what he is talking about, or whether he is extrapolating backwards in much the same manner as a modern critic. He did see actual plays performed in the theater, both new dramas of the fourth century and the old dramas of the masters, and he did have access to much documentary material that we lack. An early work of Aristotle's was his *Production Lists*, the records of the productions and victories from the inception of the contests ca. 501. He would have known writers on drama and dramatists, the anecdotes of Ion of Chios, himself a dramatist and contemporary of Sophokles, Sophokles' own work *On the Chorus*, and perhaps the lost work by Glaukos of Rhegion (ca. 400), *On the Old Poets and Musicians*. Thus his raw material would have been far greater than ours. But would this pure data have shed any light on the history of the genre? Was he, at times, just making an educated guess? When Aristotle makes a pronouncement, we need both to pay attention but also to wonder how secure is the evidence on which he bases that conclusion.

His *Poetics* is partly an analytical breakdown of the genre of tragedy into its component parts and partly a guide for reader and playwright, and contains much that is hard to follow and also controversial: the "end" of tragedy is a *katharsis* of pity and fear, one can have a tragedy without character but not without plot, the best tragic characters are those who fall into misfortune through some *hamartia*. (*Hamartia* is another battleground. When mistranslated as "tragic flaw," it tends to give Greek tragedy an emphasis on character. It is better rendered as "mistake," and as such restores Aristotle's emphasis on plot.)

Other useful later sources include the Attic orators of the fourth century, who often cite from the tragic poets to make a rhetorical point. For example, Lykourgos, the fourth-century orator responsible for the rebuilding of the theater at Athens ca. 330, gives us fifty-five lines from Euripides' lost *Erechtheus*. The fourth book of the *Onomasticon* ("Thesaurus") by Pollux (second century AD) contains much that is useful about the ancient theater, especially a list and description of the masks employed to designate certain type characters of comedy. The Roman architectural writer, Vitruvius (first century AD), has much to say about theatrical buildings especially of the Hellenistic period. Much of what we possess of the lost plays comes in quotations from a wide variety of ancient and mediaeval writers. Two in particular are useful for the student of drama: the learned Athenaios (second century AD), whose *Experts at Dining* contains a treasury of citations, and Stobaios (fourth–fifth century AD), a collector of quotable passages. The first-century AD scholar, Dion of Prusa, has shed light on the three tragedies on the subject of Philoktetes and the bow of Herakles, by summarizing the plots and styles of all three – we possess only the version by Sophokles (409).

Inscriptions provide another source of written evidence. The ancients loved to post publicly their decrees, rolls of officials, and records of competitions. One inscription contains a partial list of the victors at the Dionysia in dithyramb, comedy, and tragedy (*IG* ii^2 2318), while another presents the tragic and comic victors at both festivals in order of their first victory (*IG* ii^2 2325), and a Roman inscription lists the various victories of Kallias, a comedian of the 430s, in order of finish (first through fifth). Another group of inscriptions gives invaluable details about the contests at the Dionysia for 341, 340, and 311, including the information that satyr-drama by 340 was performed separately at the start of the festival. Another inscription from the second century records a series of productions starring an individual actor.

On the purely physical front, remains of hundreds of Greek and Roman theaters are known, ranging from the major sites of Athens, Delphi, Epidauros, Dodona, Syracuse, and Ephesos to small theaters tucked away in the backwoods and barely known. The actual physical details of a Greek theater will be discussed later, but some general comments are appropriate here. Most of the theaters are not in their fifth-century condition – major rebuilding took place in the fourth century, in the Hellenistic period (300–30), and especially under Roman occupation. When the tourist or the student visits Athens today, the theater that he or she sees (figure 1.2) is not the structure that Aeschylus or Aristophanes knew. We see curved stone seats, individual "thrones" in the front row, a paved *orchestra* floor, and an elaborate raised structure in the middle of the *orchestra*. The theater of the high classical period had straight benches on the hillside, an *orchestra* floor of packed earth (an *orchestra* that may not have been a perfect circle), and a wooden building at the back of the *orchestra*. We have been spoiled by the classical perfection of the famous theater at Epidauros (figure 1.7). At Athens and Syracuse the new theater replaced the old on the same site, while at Argos the impressive and large fourth-century theater (figure 1.9) was built on a new site, the fifth-century theater being more compact and straight rather than circular.

The theaters that we do have, from whatever period of Greek antiquity, do, however, shed invaluable light on the mechanics of production. Audiences were large and sat as a community in the open air – this was not theater of the private enclosed space. Distances were great – from the last row of the theater at Epidauros a performer in the *orchestra* would appear only inches high. Thus theater of the individual expression was out – impossible in fact since the performers wore masks. But acoustics

Figure 1.2   *Theater of Dionysos from above. Photo by Ian Vining.*

were superb and directed spectators' attention to what was being said or sung. Special effects were limited – the word and the gesture carried the force of the drama. The prominence and centrality of the *orchestra* reflect the importance of the chorus – Greek audiences were used to seeing more rather than fewer performers before them.

Most of the visual representations are found on Greek vases. This particular form of Greek art begins to reach its classical perfection with the black figure pottery of the late sixth century (figures appear in black against a red background), and continues with the exquisite red figure (the reverse) of the fifth and fourth centuries. About 520 we start to get representations of performances, usually marked by the presence of an *aulos*-player, and later scenes from tragedy, satyr-drama, and comedy.

There are not many scenes showing a self-conscious performance of tragedy; one vase ca. 430 does show a pair of performers preparing to dress as maenads (figure 1.11). But from 440 onward vases depict scenes clearly influenced by tragedy: the opening-scenes of *Libation-Bearers*, a series of vases depicting Sophokles' early tragedy *Andromeda*, another series reflecting Euripides' innovative *Iphigeneia among the Taurians* (figure 2.3), the Cleveland Medea (figure 2.4), and a striking fourth-century tableau illustrating the opening scenes of *Eumenides* (figure 1.3). One or two of these do show a pillar structure, which some interpret as an attempt to render the *skene* front. But these are not depicting an actual tragic performance. The characters do not wear masks, males are often shown nude (or nearly so) instead of wearing the elaborate costume of tragedy, and there is no hint of the *aulos*-player, a sure sign of a repre-

Figure 1.3 *"Orestes at Delphi," influenced by the opening scene of Aeschylus'* Eumenides, *on an Apulian red-figure volute-krater, ca. 390–370. Reproduced courtesy of the Museo Nazionale, Naples (H 3249).*

sentation of performance. For satyr-drama there is the superb Pronomos Vase (figure 3.1) from the very end of the fifth century, the equivalent of the modern movie poster, the performers of a satyr-drama by Demetrios in various degrees of their on-stage dress, accompanied by the *aulos*-player, Pronomos.

For comedy the vases show various sorts of performers of something which may have been the predecessor to what would become comedy, principally padded dancers in a celebration (*komos*) and men performing in animal-choruses. There is not much direct evidence from the fifth century. A vase (ca. 420) showing a comic performer on a raised platform before two spectators may or may not reflect a performance in the theater; it might equally well reflect a private performance at a symposium. But there is a wealth of vases from the fourth century, principally from the south of Italy, which show grotesquely masked and padded comic performers with limp and dangling *phalloi* in obviously humorous situations. For a long time these were thought to be representations of a local Italian low comedy called "phlyakes," but it is now accepted that these reflect Athenian Old Comedy which, contrary to established belief, did travel and was reproduced in the Greek cities of southern Italy. Some of these vases show a raised stage with steps and the double door of drama, and are plainly illustrating an actual stage performance. The most famous of these are the Würzburg Telephos (figure 4.3), a vase from about 370 which depicts a scene from Aristophanes' *Women at the Thesmophoria* (411); a vase by Assteas (ca. 350) showing a scene from Eupolis' lost comedy, *Demes* (417); and the *Choregoi* vase (figure 4.2), which seems to show figures from both comedy and tragedy.

Sculptural representations of drama are much less common, but we do have a relief from the late fifth century featuring three actors holding masks before Dionysos and consort – some have conjectured that this is the cast of Euripides' prize-winning *Bacchae*. One rich source of visual evidence is terracotta masks from various periods that shed valuable light on the nature of comic masks. Scenes from the comedy of Menander (career: 325–290) were often part of the decoration of ancient houses, most notably the so-called "House of Menander" in Pompeii (destroyed in AD 79 by the eruption of Vesuvius) and a third-century AD house in Mytilene on Lesbos, where eleven mosaics remain, with named characters that allow us to identify the exact scene in at least two comedies.

The Dramatic Festivals

At Athens drama was produced principally at two of the festivals honoring the god Dionysos, the Lenaia and the City Dionysia. We shall consider below the extent to which drama (in particular, tragedy) was a form of "religious" expression and what, if anything, Greek drama had to do with Dionysos. We are concerned here with the details and mechanics of the festivals and the place of drama within them. While the festivals honored the god Dionysos and the plays performed in a theater adjoining his sacred precinct, they were also state occasions run by the public officials of Athens, part of the communal life of the city (*polis*). We shall need to consider also the extent to which drama at Athens was "political," in the various senses of the word.

Dionysos was honored at Athens with a number of celebrations: the Rural Dionysia (festivals held in the various local communities around Attica); the Lenaia in late January; the Anthesteria ("Flower Time") in mid-February; and the City Dionysia in late March or early April. There is some evidence that previously performed plays could be restaged at the various celebrations of the Rural Dionysia around Attica, but the two principal festivals for the performance of drama were the Lenaia and the City Dionysia at Athens.

The City Dionysia occupied five days in the Athenian month of Elaphebolion ("Deer Hunt"), which corresponds to our late March or early April. It was one of the developments fostered by the tyrants, who ruled from the mid-540s to 510, a splendid festival of the city in honor of the god Dionysos, uniting all the rural festivals into one to be held within the city of Athens. The tyrants were clearly endeavoring to create a sense of national unity and cultural identity with such centralized institutions. For the City Dionysia, a myth was developed to document the progress of the god Dionysos from Eleutherai, a community on the northern border of Attica, to Athens itself. Eleutherai had recently been joined to Attica, and thus would have been also an element of political propaganda. The festival was a holiday from normal civic business – the *ekklesia* (assembly) did not meet, legal proceedings were stayed (at least for the first day), prisoners were released from prison, and in the fourth century a fund was established to pay the admission charge of two obols for those who could not afford it.

Preliminaries to the actual festival included a *proagon* ("precontest") on 8 Elaphebolion, at which the poets would appear with their actors and chorus and give hints about their forthcoming compositions, and the "introduction" of Dionysos on 9 Elaphebolion, the taking of Dionysos' statue from the precinct of his temple to the Academy, on the north-west outskirts of Athens, where the road from Eleutherai approached the city. The actual details and order of events at the festival is not established with certainty, but the following scheme is a probable one for the 430s:

The City Dionysia, ca. 430

Preliminaries:	8　　Elaphebolion	Proagon
	9　　Elaphebolion	"Introduction" of Dionysos
Events:	10 Elaphebolion	Parade (*pompe*)
		Dithyrambic contests (men & boys)
	11 Elaphebolion	Comic contest (5 poets, 1 play each)
	12 Elaphebolion	Tragedian A (3 tragedies, 1 satyr-drama)
	13 Elaphebolion	Tragedian B (3 tragedies, 1 satyr-drama)
	14 Elaphebolion	Tragedian C (3 tragedies, 1 satyr-drama)
		Awarding of the prizes, parade of the victors

At some point after the festival, a special session of the *ekklesia* was convened within the theater, rather than in its usual meeting-place on the Pnyx, to discuss the conduct of the festival for that year.

There has been considerable critical debate whether the number of comedies was cut from five to three during the Peloponnesian War (431–404) and whether the three remaining comedies were moved, one each to follow the satyr-drama on each of three days devoted to tragedy, thus shaving the festival to four days. In the hypotheses to Aristophanes' *Clouds* (423-D), *Peace* (421-D), and *Birds* (414-D), only three plays and poets are given, whereas a Roman inscription records fourth- and fifth-place finishes for Kallias in the 430s and five plays are also attested for the Dionysia in the fourth century. Aristophanes' *wealth* was part of a production of five comedies in 388, but it is not known at what festival it was performed. A passage from *Birds* (414-D) is crucial here:

> *There is nothing better or more pleasant than to grow wings. If one of you spectators had wings, when he got hungry and was bored with the tragic choruses, he could fly off, go home, and have a good meal, and when he was full, fly back to us.* (785–9)

If the "us" means "comedy," which is the natural flow of the passage, then in 414 comedy was performed on the same day as tragedy. Those who deny that comedy was reduced from five to three must argue that "us" means the theater generally, that the now refreshed spectator would be returning for a later tragedy. But any time that a comic chorus uses "us," it is referring to its identity as a comic chorus and not as part of the general theatrical ensemble. It is usually assumed that comedy was reduced because of

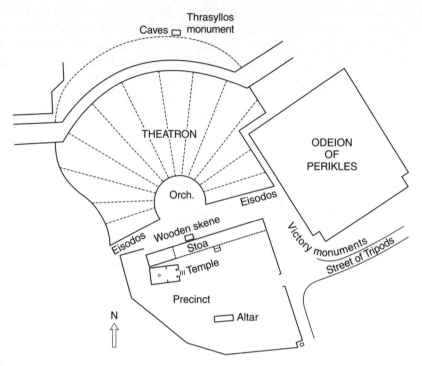

Figure 1.4 *The theater of Dionysos in the classical period*

the economic impact of the War, but comedy was a controversial genre in the 430s and 420s – we know of one decree forbidding personal humor in comedy from 439 to 436, and of two personal attacks by Kleon on Aristophanes in 426 and 423. The reduction may have had as much to do with the now dangerously topical nature of comedy as with economic savings. Comedy also employed more chorus-members and to remove two plays was to free up fifty more Athenians for military service.

The dramatic competitions changed and developed over the next century, and an assortment of inscriptions yields valuable information about the dramatic presentations around 340, about which time the festival was being reorganized. By 340 the satyr-drama had been divorced from the tragic presentations and a single such play opened the festival (Timokles' *Lykourgos* in 340 and someone's *Daughters of Phorkos* in 339). In 386 an "old tragedy" was introduced into the festival – we know of Euripides' *Iphigeneia* in 341, his *Orestes* in 340, and another of his plays in 339. In 341 the three tragic poets each presented three tragedies, employing three actors, each of whom performed in one play by each playwright, but in 340 the tragedians are reduced to two plays each and only two actors. Sharing the lead actors among all the competing poets would presumably have allowed each to demonstrate their abilities irrespective of the text that they had to interpret and the abilities of the dramatist whose plays they were performing. In 339 we are told that "for the first time the comic poets put on an 'old' comedy." Another inscription shows that dithyrambs for men and boys were still part of the Dionysia in 332–328 and lists the victors in the order: dithyramb, comedy, tragedy. We should conclude that that order remained the same in the fourth century, but with certain changes made to the dramatic productions.

Dionysia in 340

satyr-drama: *Lykourgos* by Timokles

"old" tragedy: Euripides" *Orestes*, presented by Neoptolemos

first prize: Astydamas, with *Parthenopaios* (lead actor: Neoptolemos) and *Lykaon* (lead actor: Thettalos)

second prize: Timokles, with *Phrixos* (lead actor: Thettalos) and *Oedipus* (lead actor: Neoptolemos)

third prize: Euaretos, with *Alkmaion* (lead actor: Thettalos) and . . . *Je* (lead actor: Neoptolemos)

actor's prize: Thettalos

The Lenaia took place in the Athenian month of Gamelion ("Marriage"), which corresponds to our late January. It was an ancient festival of the Ionian Greeks, to which ethnic group the Athenians belonged. We know little about the purpose and rituals of the Lenaia – mystical elements have been suggested, a celebration of the birth of Dionysos, or the ritual of *sparagmos* (eating the raw flesh of the prey). A parade on this occasion is attested with "jokes from the wagons," that is, insults directed at the spectators, and a general Dionysiac sense of abandon. The evidence suggests that the celebrations of the Lenaia were originally performed in the *agora*, rather than at the precinct of Dionysos at the south-east corner of the *agora* ("Dionysos-in-the-Marshes"), where the theater itself would be located. Whereas the City Dionysia was under the control of the *archon eponymous*, once the leading political official at Athens, the Lenaia was handled by the *archon basileus*, who had taken over the traditional religious role of the early kings.

Competitions for tragedy and comedy were introduced to the Lenaia around 440. This seems to have been the lesser festival, and it is sometimes assumed that newcomers would try their hand first at the Lenaia before producing at the more important Dionysia. Eratosthenes, a scholar at Alexandria in the third century, seems to suggest that the Lenaia was not considered on the same level as the Dionysia and that a relegation system was in operation *(POxy. 2737. ii. 10–17)*:

> *The thea[trical productions] were [of two types]: the Lenae[an appear not to have been equ]ally reputable, perhaps also because of the fact that in s[pring the al]lies had already c[ome from abroa]d to see [the performances and do b]usiness. With "t]o the city" the Dionysia is indicated. Eratosthenes also says of Plato (the comic poet) that as long as he had his plays produced by others, he did well; but when he first produced a play on his own,* Theater Police *(Rhabdouchoi), and placed fourth, he was pushed back to the Lenaea.* (This is part of a second-century commentary on an Old Comedy. The translation given here is that of Csapo and Slater (1995) nr. 71, p. 135. The Plato mentioned here is not the philosopher, but the comic poet, active 424–380, usually spelled "Platon" to prevent confusion.)

But this may just be the conclusion of Eratosthenes, based on the *didaskalia* ("production records"), which may have shown Platon finishing fourth at a Dionysia of one year and then producing only at the Lenaia of the next year.

In *Acharnians* (425) the main character declares that "this is the contest at the Lenaia, and we are by ourselves," that is, only Athenians and resident foreigners (*metoikoi*) were present, while the Dionysia marked the reopening of travel by sea, the arrival of embassies, and the bringing of the tribute by the allies to Athens and would thus have had a more international audience. At the Lenaia non-Athenians could perform as dancers and act as *choregoi* (see below), something that was not allowed at the more formal Dionysia.

There is no evidence in the classical period for either dithyramb or satyr-drama at the Lenaia; the formal entertainment seems to have been tragedy and comedy only. We have no firm evidence for the number of plays produced. An inscription of 418 shows that two tragedians produced two plays each, while another of 363 gives the number of tragic poets as three. For comedy the hypotheses to *Acharnians* (425-L), *Knights* (424-L), *Wasps* (422-L), and *Frogs* (405-L) record only three plays. Evidence from two Roman inscriptions suggests that five comedies were performed at the Lenaia before and after the Peloponnesian War (431–404).

The Rural Dionysia was celebrated in the various local communities ("demes," 139 in the classical period) of Attica, and there is considerable evidence for the performance of dithyramb, tragedy, and comedy in at least fifteen of the demes, principally the larger of them such as Acharnai, Eleusis, and Ikarion. A small deme theater is extant at Thorikos (map 1.4) in the south-east of Attica, and the port city of Peiraieus is known to have had an important theater, where Euripides produced and Sokrates attended. Plato tells of the theater-mad spectator, who is able to attend one Rural Dionysia after another. In 405 both Aristophanes and Sophokles are recorded as producing drama at a celebration of the Dionysia in Eleusis. One suspects that these productions would be revivals or repeats of earlier plays produced at the major festivals at Athens, to allow those unable to travel to the city to see the plays that they had missed. These were, like the festivals in the city, competitions. The evidence suggests that various deme-theaters preferred one genre or another: Aixone, Rhamnous, and Anagyros seem to have staged only comedy, while Paiania was restricted to tragedy. All three competitions (dithyramb, tragedy, comedy) are known for Eleusis. A particularly interesting inscription from Eleusis comes from the last decade of the fifth century, which attests to a double *choregeia* (see below) and the victories of Sophokles and Aristophanes:

> *IG* ii² 3090: *Gnathis son of Timokedes, Anaxandrides son of Timagoros won the victory as* choregoi *for comedy. Aristophanes was* didaskalos. ⟨*They also won*⟩ *another victory in tragedy, for which Sophokles was* didaskalos.

(The word *didaskalos* means "teacher" and is applied to the person who brings on the play, usually [but not always] the author. "Director" comes closer than "producer," but is misleading since modern plays and movies are rarely directed by their author.)

We know from Aristophanes that the official command to start the performance was "Bring on your chorus." Aspiring playwrights would apply to the official in charge of the festival months in advance for a chorus and the technical term for acceptance was "to be granted a chorus." The officials, the *archon basileus* for the Lenaia and the *archon eponymous* for the Dionysia, took up their positions at the start of the Athenian institutional year, which corresponds to our beginning of July, and would presumably have begun immediately on their preparations for the festivals which were only months away (in the case of the Lenaia just seven). We are not certain how much of a play (or plays) an aspiring comic or tragic poet would submit to the archon, or the extent to which past reputation, youth, or personal connections played a role in the selection. A successful tragic poet seems to be staging a production every two years; thus a playwright might be well advanced on a group of plays by the time of the selection of poets. Comedy speaks harshly of one archon who turned down Sophokles in favor of the inferior Gnesippos:

> [the archon] *who wouldn't give Sophokles a chorus, but did grant one to the son of Kleomachos* [Gnesippos], *whom I wouldn't consider worthy to put on plays for me, not even at the Adonia.* (Kratinos fr. 17)

The speaker here could be a *choregos*, another archon, or just possibly Tragedy herself.

When the poets were selected, the next duty of the archons was to find twenty *choregoi* for the twenty dithyrambic choruses, three *choregoi* for tragedy (one for each playwright), and five for comedy (again one for each competitor). The word *choregos* (plural: *choregoi*) means "chorus bringer," and these were wealthy Athenians whose job it would be to recruit choristers, hire a trainer, provide a training-space, maintain these choristers, provide the costumes and masks and any "special effects" that would be needed. Thus the *choregos* was both providing the chorus and providing for its members. Providing a chorus was a duty (technical term: *leitourgia*, "liturgy") of the very richest of Athenians, considered a patriotic duty as important as outfitting a warship in the navy. There is an interesting tension here between the demands of the state to provide this popular entertainment and the self-glorification of the *choregoi* as the splendid individuals who provided that entertainment. Peter Wilson puts it well (2000: 54), "For the performance of a *leitourgia* was an act of *giving* to the demos, with all the implications of reciprocal obligation that the gift brings." In the law-courts speakers would point to their services as a *choregoi* as evidence of their good character and democratic sentiments. One such example occurs at Antiphon I.β.12 (ca. 420):

> *When you look at the deeds of my life, you will realize that I have never plotted against anyone nor sought what was not mine. On the contrary, I have paid large property-taxes, often served as a trierarch, sponsored a splendid chorus, loaned money to many people, put up substantial guarantees on others' behalf. I acquired my wealth, not through the law-court, but through my own hard work, being a god-fearing and law-abiding person. Being of such a nature, then do not convict me of anything unholy or shameful.*

Lysias 21 shows us a young man recording with pride that in his frequent service as a *choregos* he has spent almost four times what a normal *choregos* might lay out.

Not all would-be *choregoi* participated with enthusiasm, however. It was possible to be exempted from liturgical service, and we know also of a mechanism, called the *antidosis*, where a person designated to perform a "liturgy" could challenge another whom he thought wealthier than himself to take on that role. Aristophanes in his *Acharnians* (425-L) blasts a *choregos* named Antimachos for some sort of unfriendly behavior after the festival, and at *Peace* 1020–2 implies that the particular *choregos* of this comedy is somewhat less than generous. At Eupolis fr. 329 someone exclaims, "Have you ever met a more stingy *choregos*?" We can detect a comic stereotype here, the less than generous sponsor.

A *choregia* provided an opportunity for the *choregos* to revel in the splendor of his position. Such a moment of glory was part of their return for undertaking the expensive matter of sponsoring a dramatic performance. We know that Alkibiades (451–403) wore a special purple robe when he served as *choregos* and that Demosthenes in the 340s had prepared gold crowns and a tunic sewn with gold for his service as a dithyrambic *choregos*. In the victory-lists the name of the victorious *choregos* is given before that of the winning poet:

> [for 473/2] comedy: Xenokleides was the *choregos*, Magnes the *didaskalos*; tragedy: Perikles of Cholargai was the *choregos*, Aeschylus the *didaskalos*.

Perhaps a modern equivalent is the announcement of the award for Best Picture at the Academy Awards, where the producer (often virtually unknown) accepts that award, rather than the high-profiled director or the leading actors. But in the public atmosphere at Athens the *choregos* was someone whom everyone would know – the *choregos* himself would see to that. After the announcement of the results an exuberant procession led the victors to a sacrifice and celebration of the victory. Plato in his *Symposium* shows us the company of revelers at a victory-party for Agathon much the worse for wear on the next day.

A visible sign of a *choregos'* triumph was the erection of a permanent memorial to display the bronze tripod awarded to the winning *choregos*. These tripods were large (some over three meters high) and expensive (costing over 1,000 drachmas), and were dedicated by mounting them on a stone base, with an inscription commemorating the event. We know that the main street leading from the *agora* around the north-east slope of the Acropolis to the east (main) entrance of the theater was called "Street of the Tripods," and that it was one of the most prominent and favored walking areas of Athens. One of these monuments has survived in quite reasonable shape, that commemorating the victorious *choregos*, Lysikrates, in 334, and remains a popular tourist attraction just off Vironos Street in modern Athens. The monument of Thrasyllos (319) was an enclosure set into the hillside above the theater and closed with elaborate gates (figure 1.5).

Of the three genres of performance at the Dionysia it is the sponsorship of tragedy that seems to have held the most prestige, although Demosthenes (21.156) insists that sponsoring a dithyramb was more expensive than tragedy. But here he is contrasting his own *choregia* with a dithyramb with the sponsorship of tragedy by his opponent Meidias. It is the sponsorship of tragedy that formed the highest rung of the liturgical ladder. At the City Dionysia of the year 406/5 two *choregoi* shared the expense of sponsoring the productions on that occasion. This was a time of financial hardship for Athens because of the loss of income from the silver mines, the need to import food

Figure 1.5 *Theater of Dionysos, looking toward the Acropolis; the square recess is the Thrasyllos Monument. Photo by Ian Vining.*

due to the enemy's ravaging of the fields of Attica, and the tremendous expense of rebuilding and outfitting the Athenian navy, and rather than stint on the splendor of the festival, the Athenians preferred to maintain standards by doubling the *choregia*.

We do not know how *choregoi* and poets were matched. For the dithyrambs the *choregos* would come from the tribe whose men or boys were competing, but for drama we cannot say whether the *choregos* had any say in the assignment. Some good evidence for the Thargelia, where dithyrambs were performed, informs us that the *choregos* received his poet by lot, but this may just mean that the *choregos* won the lot and was able to choose first. In some cases there does seem to be a close relationship between dramatist and *choregos*. In 476 Themistokles, the architect of the victory over the Persians in 480, acted as sponsor for the productions by Phrynichos which included his *Phoenician Women*, a tragedy that dramatized the story of the Athenian defeat of the Persians. In 472 the *choregos* for Aeschylus' *Persians*, which covered much the same material as Phrynichos, was the young Perikles, who would become heir to Themistokles' politics. We wonder about Xenokles of Aphidna who was *choregos* for Aeschylus' *Oresteia* in 458. In the third play of that trilogy Aeschylus brings in contemporary political attitudes and issues. What was Xenokles' stance on these issues? In his *Trojan Women* of 415 Euripides seems to allow the preparations for the Armada against Sicily to intrude into his dramatization of the fall of Troy. Did Euripides' *chore-*

gos share his hostility to aggressive war? How would a *choregos* from the *nouveaux riches* react to sponsoring a conservatively minded political comedy by Aristophanes or Eupolis?

The dramatic presentations were competitions. This should not surprise us since today some of the most popular worldwide cultural events are awards ceremonies (the Academy Awards, the Palme d'Or in Cannes, the Emmy Awards for television, the Grammys for popular music, the Booker Prize for fiction etc.). We know also the ancient Greeks were an intensely competitive people, for whom the great cycles of competitions were major events in the life of that society. The Pythian Games at Delphi in fact began as competitions in music and poetry before the athletic competitions were added, and "music" loomed large in the four-yearly festival of the Panthenaia ("All-Athenian") at Athens. When the Athenian populace was divided into ten tribes in the last decade of the sixth century, each tribe performed a dithyramb, the large-scale choral song, one for fifty men and one for fifty boys. It must have seemed natural to them that these performances would be judged and prizes awarded.

There were ten judges, one from each of the ten tribes, appointed or selected in some manner that we do not know. Plutarch tells a story about the Dionysia of 468, when the ten *strategoi* ("generals" – the ten political and military leaders of Athens, elected yearly) were compelled by the archon to judge the contest for tragedy and awarded the prize to the young Sophokles, competing for the first time. But the story is late (ca. AD 100, nearly 500 years after the event) and sounds rather too romantic to be true. The judges would take an oath to judge fairly – as do the two officials at the opening of the modern Olympics – and each judge would cast his vote for the winning entry, be it in the dithyramb for boys and for men, tragedy, or comedy. Of these ten votes only five were selected by lot – lot being used in Athenian practice to forestall bribery of public officials – and the prizes awarded on the basis of these five votes. The speaker of Lysias 4 states clearly that his adversary had been a judge at the festival, and that "he wrote his vote on his tablet, but was excluded by the lot" (4.3).

Obviously there could be problems. One that springs quickly to mind is that a particular playwright could have the support of seven of the ten judges, but if the five unused votes were all for him, he would lose by three votes to two – assuming that the other three all voted for the same rival. How were ties broken? Suppose a particular tragic competition resulted in two votes for A, two votes for B, and one vote for C. Was the judge for C pressed to break the tie, or was the vote of a sixth judge employed? Results, one suspects, could have been controversial and perhaps even made an item on the agenda of the *ekklesia* that examined the conduct of the competition.

Comedy, as befits its tendency to break the dramatic illusion and call attention to itself, often mentions and even addresses the judges (*kritai*) directly. The choruses of both *Clouds* (423 – lines 1115–30) and *Birds* (414 – lines 1102–17) chant briefly to the judges within their dramatic role on why they should award their play first prize and threaten the dire consequences of a negative decision. At the end of *Assembly-Women* (392 – lines 1154–62) the chorus of women appeal openly to the judges for the poet – note the singular "me":

I wish to give the judges a bit of advice: to the clever among you remember the clever bits and vote for me, to those among you who like to laugh vote for me because of the jokes. I'm asking just about everyone to vote for me. And don't let the order of the draw tell against us, because I was drawn first. Keep this in mind and don't break your oaths, but judge all the choruses fairly, and don't behave like second-rate whores who remember only their last lover.

This is a significant passage for the study of ancient drama (in particular, comedy) since it provides evidence for the existence of different sorts of audience, the oath of the judges, that the order of the plays was determined by lot, and that a poet could make last-minute changes to his play once he knew the order of production.

Did the judges take the reaction of the spectators into account? Today at the Academy Awards it is almost automatic that the highest grossing or most popular movie of the year will not do well in the awards, but one wonders if the judges could have ignored a popular groundswell of approbation or disgust. Comedy does appeal directly to the judges, but also to the spectators. In fact it is significant that Aristophanes blames the failure of his first *Clouds* (423-D) not on the judges but on the spectators at large, at *Clouds* 518–62 and again at *Wasps* 1043–59:

And furthermore he swears by Dionysos over many libations that you never heard better comedy than this [first *Clouds*], *and it is to your shame that you did not realize it at once. But our poet is no less recognized by the clever ones among you . . . so, my good friends, in the future love and cherish those poets who seek to say something new.*

Again the poet suggests that there may be different tastes among the spectators, although the appeal may just be an attempt to flatter every spectator to consider himself "clever." Aristophanes seems to be appealing to the general theater-going public in his quest to redefine comedy. Aelian (in the early third century AD) records that at the production of the first *Clouds* of Aristophanes the audience shouted down to the judges to award first prize to that comedy – the play finished third.

Crowns of laurel or ivy or roses were symbolic of celebrations and triumphs in ancient culture. Winning athletes, victorious poets, participants at sacrifices, guests at dinner-parties and symposia, messengers announcing victories wore crowns (*stephanoi*) as symbols of their special situation. The winning dramatic poet, as well as the *choregos*, would have been awarded such a crown after the final production. We do not know whether the proclamation was made in the name of the winning chorus, poet, or *choregos*. Private celebrations clearly followed the public occasion; Plato's *Symposium* purports to be an account of the party following the actual victory-party. Some comic by-play between Aristophanes and a fellow comic poet suggests that victorious poets might appear in triumph, as it were, at the gymnasia. Aristophanes implies that their motive was to pick up impressionable boys, but we do know that the gymnasia were places where the community might gather and where an exuberant victor might well appear.

At *Frogs* 366–7 (405-L) the comic chorus declare certain individuals to be anathema and order that they be excluded from the festival. These include traitors to the state, those who like bad jokes, and:

the politician who nibbles away at the poets' pay, just because he was made fun of in the ancestral rites of Dionysos.

Clearly the politician in question (identified by the scholiast as Archinos or Agyrrhios) had proposed reducing the *misthos* ("pay") of the poets, no doubt because of economic constraints. The comic poet interprets this proposal as motivated by personal reasons, but it is an unequivocal statement that the poets did receive some financial support from the state. After all, putting on a play or group of plays would be a task of several months and would involve "hands on" training of the actors and chorus. A poet or director would need to have recompense for the time required to stage the production. Again this raises the question of the extent to which drama was "political" in that it was sponsored by the state.

Drama and Dionysos

"Religion" is probably not the best word to use when referring to the beliefs and worship of the ancient Greeks. To the modern ear the word conjures up organized systems of formal rituals and creeds, a hierarchy of officials ("hierarchy" means literally "rule of the sacred"), or the sort of entry one checks off (or not) on a census form. In the ancient world the lines were not distinctly drawn between "religion" and "philosophy" or "morality" or "ethics." Greeks worshiped their gods not from any sense of personal guilt or fervent belief or in an attitude of humility, but because the gods of their myths represented forces beyond humanity in the universe, forces which had control over mortals, and which (it was felt) could be influenced by human worship and offerings. The principle of *do ut des* ("I give so that you may give") lay behind the offering of sacrifices to the gods. We see this clearly in Aeschylus' *Agamemnon* where Agamemnon must give his daughter in sacrifice to Artemis so that he may get the winds that will take his army to Troy. This was a sacrifice accepted and the request answered, although with tragic results. We may see the opposite at Sophokles' *Oedipus Tyrannos* 911–23, where Jokaste enters with offerings for Apollo, the god of light and knowledge who operates beneath the surface of the play, and asks for a happy outcome for Oedipus and for the people of Thebes. This will be a sacrifice not accepted and a prayer unanswered.

At Athens dramatic competitions were part of the festivals of Dionysos, particularly (as we have seen) at the Lenaia in late January and the larger City Dionysia in late March or early April. Aristotle (*Poetics* 1449a10) tells us that tragedy developed "from those who led the dithyramb," and as we know from a couplet from Archilochos (700–650),

> *for I know how to lead Lord Dionysos' dithyramb*
> *when my wits are thunder-blasted with wine,*

that the dithyramb was connected with Dionysos, it has become traditional to seek the origins of tragedy in the rituals of Dionysos. The introduction of satyr-drama was connected by certain ancient sources with a saying, "nothing to do with Dionysos," and explained by some as an attempt to retain the presence of Dionysos within drama. Aristophanes himself at *Frogs* 367 claims comedy as part of "the ancestral rites of Dionysos." We may be uncertain how far to trust Aristotle or other later sources, but the fact remains that in the fifth and fourth centuries drama *was* performed as part of the festivals of Dionysos and in the fourth century actors would describe themselves as "artists of Dionysos." A number of questions immediately suggest themselves at this point:

- What sort of god was Dionysos and why should he have been the patron of drama?
- Did the writers, performers, and audience see themselves as engaging in a religious rite?
- Were the ancient dramas (especially tragedy) equivalent to the medieval mystery plays?
- Do these dramas have anything to do with formal religious rituals?
- Were these festivals the excuse for a popular entertainment that was essentially "secular," in the way Christmas (properly the birth of Christ) has become the season for pantomimes and big box-office movies?
- Is there anything "religious" about Greek drama?
- Does Greek drama in fact have "anything to do with Dionysos"?

One's first reaction on hearing the name "Dionysos," or even more so with "Bacchos," one of his titles, is to imagine a god of wine and unrestrained revelry. In Mozart's opera, *The Abduction from the Seraglio*, Pedrillo and Osmin sing a boisterous drinking-song, "Vivat Bacchus! Bacchus lebe, der den Wein erfand!" ("Hail to Bacchos, long live Bacchos, Bacchos who discovered wine!"), which sums up well the prevalent modern attitude to him. But Dionysos is far more than a god of wine and the unrestrained party, he is an elemental force in the life of creation. In *Bacchae* Teiresias considers him as the principle of the "wet," as opposed to the "dry" of Demeter, the goddess of agriculture, and he is very much a god of the liquid life force, not just the grape and wine, but of all plants (his titles include *dendrites*, "of trees," and *anthios*, "of flowers") and of the life force of animals. He is a god of growth and the power of youth.

Dionysos is a notoriously difficult deity to apprehend. He does go back to the late Bronze Age – his name has been found on the Linear B tablets ca. 1300 – and Homer does know the story of his encounter with Lykourgos (*Iliad* 6.130–40), but he was always the outsider in the world of the Olympians. In the standard version of his birth (told in Euripides' *Bacchae*), he was the product of a divine father, Zeus, and a mortal princess, Semele of Thebes, and such an offspring of divine and human is usually a human hero (such as Perseus or Helen or Herakles). But Dionysos was "twice-born." Semele was consumed by the thunder-bolt of Zeus and the embryo, taken at six months from his mother's womb, was placed in the thigh of Zeus and born three months later – compare the birth of Athene (associated with wisdom) from the head of Zeus and the birth of Dionysos (a god of growth) from his genital region. Fathered by and born from Zeus, Dionysos thus becomes a god himself, but his myths tell a repeated story of the need for acceptance. His existence was hidden from Zeus' jealous wife, Hera, who would eventually drive the young god mad and send him on wanderings far beyond the Greek world. He returns to Greece from the East, followed by his Eastern devotees, and must win his place as a new deity, bringing new rites for mankind.

Although a traditional Greek god with an impeccably Greek pedigree, he is almost always seen as a foreigner from the East. His name "Dionysos" seems to combine the Greek "Dio-" (the root of Zeus) and -nysos, which may relate to the eastern mountain Nysa, of which his followers sing at *Bacchae* 556. The *thyrsos* (see below) has been connected with the Hittite word *tuwarsa* ("vine") and his other name, Bacchos, with a Lydian name *bakivali*. There was thus something different about Dionysos, which made him partly "unGreek."

He is a confusing god, one who cannot be easily put in his place. He has often been set against Apollo, most notably by Nietzsche in his antithesis of the Apollonian (order, structure, light, intellect) and the Dionysian (chaos, darkness, emotion, instinct), and is associated with disguise and transformation. He is the god who breaks down boundaries (youth/age, male/female, human/animal, emotion/intellect), who confounds the norms, who drives women from the city to the mountain (in *Bacchae*), and who brings his own wildness and wild followers into the heart of the city. His associations are with the animal – the possessed Pentheus in *Bacchae* sees Dionysos as a bull and he is frequently shown on art with the panther or leopard. Those who encounter and resist Dionysos find themselves transformed into animal guise. His followers are the maenads ("the mad women"), who dress in fawn-skins and carry the *thyrsos* (a branch tipped with ivy), and the male satyrs, half-human and half-animals, creatures that are more and less than human. In their wilder celebrations the worshipers of Dionysos ran berserk on the mountainside (*oreibasia*), filled with wine and the intoxication of the group experience, catching and rending their prey (*sparagmos*) and eating the raw flesh (*omophagia*). In *Bacchae* the messenger describes the women on the mountain, both in harmony and in control of nature. They nurse the young of wild animals, and with their *thyrsoi* produce milk and honey from the earth.

Dionysos is a god of the wild, the mountain as opposed to the city, a god of release from the normal routine (two of his most important titles are *eleuthereus*, "freer," and *lyaios* "releaser"). "City Dionysia" seems like a contradiction in terms, since Dionysos is a deity of the wild rather than the city, a god of the release from cultural constraints, but perhaps a "City Dionysia" was an attempt to rein in this potentially dangerous god and drama a means of channeling the emotional experience involved in his worship. The Athenians may well have been trying to temper and tame the wilder aspects of this god by organizing his rites within a City Dionysia, rites that included the performance of dithyrambic choral songs and of drama.

The myths about Dionysos reveal an interesting tension. Some show his power and devastating effect, often on those who reject his worship. Pentheus at Thebes is the best-known example (the theme of Euripides' *Bacchae*), while Aeschylus wrote a tetralogy about Lykourgos of Thrace, who also opposed Dionysos and was destroyed. The daughters of Minyas in Orchomenos and of Proteus in Argos refuse to accept the rites of Dionysos and are punished with madness, made to kill their own children, and are transformed into animal guise. The *Homeric Hymn to Dionysos* tells how pirates attempted to kidnap the god, thinking him a prince worthy of ransom, and how the god transformed their ship into vines and the sailors into dolphins. The vine (*ampelos*) gets its name in one version from Ampelos, a beautiful youth and beloved of the god, who dies accidentally at Dionysos' hands, and from the god's tears falling on the boy's body grow the first vines and grapes. His cult was fundamentally opposed to the organized city and the rational order of the mind, two of the stereotypes that we associate with the ancient Greeks. Perhaps we can see why he was an outsider to the usual Greek way of looking at the world; he represented emotion and instinct as against intellect and conditioned behavior.

But for all these tales of destruction, Dionysos promises blessings to his followers: not just wine – Dionysos is far more than "jolly Bacchos" – but release from toil and the structures of daily routine, from the miseries of age and responsibility. The chorus in *Bacchae* sings (417–23):

> *This god, the son of Zeus, is friends with Peace, the goddess that bestows wealth and raises boys to men. To rich and poor alike he has given an equal share of the delight from wine that banishes pain.*

He is associated with Aphrodite, the goddess of love, and as the messenger in *Bacchae* puts it, "without wine there is no Love nor anything pleasant for men" (773–4). His myths may depict the death of his victims, but he did also bring his mother Semele back from the dead and install her as a goddess among the Olympians. Hermes may cross the boundary between life and death, as he escorts the dead to the underworld, but only Dionysos can dissolve that boundary.

An alternative version of the birth of Dionysos makes him "twice-born" in a different sense. Born of Zeus and Persephone (queen of the Underworld), he was to be the god to succeed Zeus and unite the upper celestial world of light and life with the lower world of death and darkness. Zeus' ever-jealous wife, Hera, incited the Titans to tear Dionysos to pieces and devour his flesh. Athene saved the heart, which she gave to Zeus, who swallowed it, thereby taking the essence of Dionysos to himself. He subsequently makes Semele pregnant with Dionysos and the story continues as we know it. The Titans were destroyed by the fire-bolts of Zeus, and from their ashes came the race of human beings, thus possessing both the rebellious spirit of the Titans and the godhood of Dionysos. This was the Dionysos of the Orphics, a cult like that of the Mother and Daughter at Eleusis, which promised its followers "salvation" in the next world, through initiation in this world as well as a moral life. The chorus of initiates in *Frogs* may well be devotees of this cult of Dionysos. He is often seen as the Greek equivalent of the youthful consort of the Eastern Mother-Goddess (Adonis or Tammuz), whose death and rebirth both explains and enables the yearly cycle of agricultural fertility.

In the wild rituals described above, the worshipers would lose their own identity, become possessed by the deity they worshiped, and thus achieve a sort of group mentality with one another. But here too lies the dangerous side of Dionysos, for he is essentially hostile to the concept of the individual and conducive of the collective. Although Dionysos was a dangerous pagan god in the official view of early Christianity, the parallels between his mythology and the experience of the early church are striking:

Born of the Sky-Father god and a human woman.
Experienced a marvelous birth.
Died and returned to life.
Through the eating of flesh and drinking of wine, followers become *entheos* ("god within") and achieve a "communion" with each other.
Followers are promised happiness in the next life, by initiation and by behaving in an ethically proper fashion in this life.

Scenes from the myths of Dionysos appear on Christian sarcophagi, and in the Byzantine period an anonymous writer put together a *Christus Patiens* ("The Suffering Christ") by using extensive material from *Bacchae*, to the extent that we can restore part of the missing scene at the end of *Bacchae* from the *Christus Patiens*. Not without cause has Christ been spoken of as "Dionysus' successor."

So this was the god for whom drama was performed, who is shown in art as presiding over the festival, as on the Pronomos Vase (ca. 400) or a stone relief from the same period. But the questions posed above remain. Put generally, was the experience in the theater perceived by the performers and spectators as a "religious" experience? When the actors called themselves "artists of Dionysos," did they see themselves as conscious devotees like the maenads and the satyrs? In the front row of the stone theater that survives the seats are inscribed "of the priest of . . ." As drama was under his patronage, the priest of Dionysos occupied a significant place in the *theatron* – at *Frogs* 297 the frightened character of Dionysos exclaims, "protect me, my priest, so I can have drink with you afterwards." The dramatic productions at the Lenaia festival fell into the jurisdiction of the *archon basileus*, who had control of the religious functions of the state. When the chorus at *Frogs* 686 describes itself as a "holy band," it is speaking in more than its character as *mystai* (initiates), it is placing itself in the context of the religious occasion. The theater intruded upon the sacred precinct of Dionysos, and his temple stood closely beside and behind the *skene*, in full view of the spectators in the *theatron*.

But few of the plots of tragedy have much to do with Dionysos. We have Euripides' *Bacchae*, of course, and know of other plays with this title, and Aeschylus' *Lykourgeia* will have dramatized Dionysos' encounter with Lykourgos in Thrace. Dionysos seems to appear more often in comedy and satyr-play than in tragedy, and while gods do appear on stage in Greek drama, the principal interest of the dramatists (especially Sophokles and Euripides) is with humanity, the greatness of human heroes, their sufferings and their place in the universe. Simply put, Greek tragedy, indeed much of Greek myth, does not have much to do directly with gods. Aeschylus' *Eumenides* (458) and the Prometheus-plays attributed to Aeschylus are unusual in the domination of the action by gods rather than humans. In 1978 Taplin stated decisively: "there is nothing intrinsically Dionysiac about Greek tragedy." In his view tragedy had passed from whatever initial connection it may have had with the god and his cult to a "political" (in the sense "of the *polis*") experience. People went to the theater as a communal activity and for an esthetic entertainment, which in the case of tragedy was "serious" (*spoudaios*) and raised great issues, but there was no longer any sense of the "religious" or the cultic about the event.

Critics were quick to respond, to insist upon an intrinsic connection between tragedy (in particular) and the god. For Vernant Dionysos was the god who crosses the boundaries and confuses reality and illusion, who makes us lose in his collective our self-consciousness and identity of self. Tragedy is appropriately Dionysiac when we suspend our disbelief in watching the drama and enter a world of fiction and *mimesis* (representation), a world presided over by the mask behind which individual identity is hidden. Simon Goldhill among many other modern critics saw the essence of tragedy as political, as part of a civic discourse in the fifth century, where one's assumptions and ideas are challenged. What better patron, he argues, than the god of subversion himself? Richard Seaford, on the other hand, regarded Dionysos as essentially a democratic god, one who removes the barriers between city and country, between rich and poor, between privileged and ordinary citizens. In the collective of Dionysos, "all shall equal be." Many of the stories of tragedy depend on an opposition between the claims of the *oikos* ("house") and the claims of the *polis* ("city"). Great individuals may suffer or die (Oedipus or Pentheus) but the larger collective lives on, and in the case of Thebes in *Bacchae*, will be "saved" by Dionysos. Both tragedy and Dionysos are symbols or products of the Athenian democracy, and hence the performance of drama at the festival of this "democratic" deity.

On the other side of the ledger we must reiterate that the plays as we have them have little to do with Dionysos. Scott Scullion (2002) estimates that only about 4 percent of the plays we know about were concerned with Dionysos. He is not the god most often mentioned in the plays – that honor belongs to Zeus. He is at times invoked by the chorus in their songs, but so too are other gods. The evidence for dramatic production in other cities shows that drama was not elsewhere restricted to the worship of Dionysos. The plays were part of the cult of Dionysos at Athens, but is the connection an intrinsic one? Masks are not restricted to his cult – we know that heads of Dionysos were carried on a pole at the Lenaia, but there is no hint that these were meant to be worn. When the satyrs in Aeschylus' *Spectators* encounter life-like masks of themselves, they intend to put them up on the temple, not wear them. If we accept the etymology of tragedy ("goat-song") as "song at the goat," that is, accompanying the sacrifice of a goat, the goat is not in itself a Dionysiac creature. Goats were sacrificed to Apollo, the Muses, Pan, and Artemis. To put the matter another way: if we did not know that Greek drama (in particular, tragedy) was performed at the festivals of Dionysos, would we have been able to deduce that from the texts of the plays

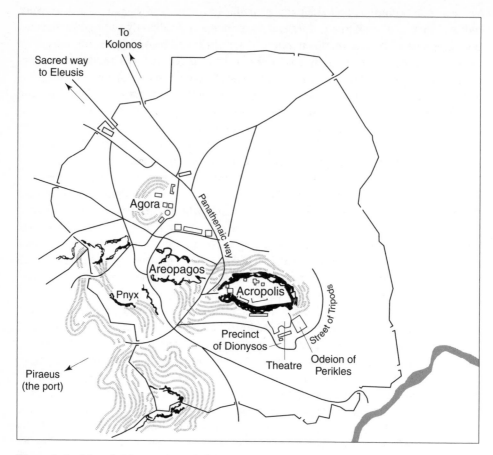

Figure 1.6   *Map of Athens at the end of the classical period*

themselves? If the answer seems to be no, then perhaps we are forcing drama into a Dionysiac box.

Greek drama, especially Greek tragedy, is eminently emotional and entertaining. In a world of small cinemas and contained theaters, we cannot realize what the experience of the ancient outdoor civic theater was like. Aristotle states that the "end" of tragedy is to elicit pity and fear and to achieve a *katharsis* of these emotions, and an audience of some 15,000 people must have responded to a particularly effective drama (be it tragedy or comedy) with a collective and emotional response. But was that response one that they would have associated with Dionysos? One of the results of the worship of Dionysos was the achieving of ecstasy (in Greek, *ekstasis* or "standing out"), and some might assume that the esthetic experience of attending the theater, suspending disbelief, and becoming involved in the sufferings of another was in some sense an *ekstasis*. But how different was this from listening to the epics about Odysseus and Achilles, which are certainly not Dionysiac?

The festival of Dionysos may have been the formal setting, but is it a case of cause and effect? Scullion (2002) suggests plausibly that the theater was located near the temple of Dionysos by accident, that the natural place to locate a *theatron* was on the south-east slope of the Acropolis, in the area traditionally associated with the cult of Dionysos at Athens, and that this is all the connection there is. Perhaps when the dramatic festivals were established, or reestablished in ca. 500 or after the Persian invasion and leveling of the city (480), officials wanted to develop that part of the city, on the other side from the *agora*. In the 440s Perikles has the *odeion* erected beside the theater, in fact jostling into it. The main entry to the theater from the *agora* was around the north and east slopes of the Acropolis, along the Street of the Tripods, the tripods being the monuments erected by victorious dramatic *choregoi*. By this point that area is now a theater district, and we may want to stress that association rather than the presence of the temple of Dionysos. By the late fifth century, one hundred years or so into the history of tragedy, perhaps one went to the theater to be entertained, to be part of the group experience, yes, but not one that had much of the formally religious about it.

One thing we can be sure of, that Greek drama was not a presentation or enactment of ritual. The school of the Cambridge anthropologists explained myth as developing out of ritual. We worship a certain way, do and say things in a certain ordered and repeated pattern, often for reasons unknown, and myths were told to explain the details of that ritual. Beneath the form of a Greek tragedy Murray detected a supposed pattern of ritual, the rites of spring for the "spirit of the year," a cycle of death and rebirth, where the death is a sacrificial death of the *pharmakos*, the scapegoat for whom "it is expedient that one man should die for the people." Characters such as Oedipus (*Oedipus at Kolonos*), Pentheus (*Bacchae*), Eteokles (*Seven*) do die at the end of their dramas, but that does not make them into the scapegoat of Greek society. In fact no play that we possess fits this theoretical model at all. For comedy, Cornford* replaced the death in tragedy with ritual combat and a sacred marriage with overtones of fertility, but although some comedies end with the marriage of the hero with a divine or quasi-divine being (Trygaios with Harvest-time in *Peace* and Peithetairos with Princess in *Birds*), that does not turn Aristophanes' extraordinarily witty and sophisticated comedies into a fertility union. There are too many variations in the plot, characters, and tone of Greek tragedy for it to have come from ritual. By its very nature ritual is performed in the same way again and again. What matters for tragedy in particular is the variation from the pattern, not the pattern itself.

Drama may certainly use ritual, however, and more recent criticism has concentrated on how various rituals, familiar to and taken for granted by the audience, may impinge upon the drama and contribute to our understanding of them. Plays often end with the establishment of a cult or ritual, such as the worship of Artemis near Athens (*Iphigeneia among the Taurians*) or the honors paid to the dead Hippolytos, or on a grander scale the worship of Dionysos himself (*Bacchae*) or the fact that the Furies will be established beneath the Acropolis as Eumenides ("kind ones"). The dramatic impact gains when the reader comes to understand what the ancient spectator knew

---

* F. M. Cornford, *The Origin of Attic Comedy* (Cambridge 1914).

as part of his cultural heritage. For example, the choral ode at *Hippolytos* 1104–50 is unusual in that the principal chorus of serving-women sings with the subsidiary chorus of young huntsmen, first alternately and perhaps together in the last strophe. This is a play very much about love and the relations between male and female, and this song may well relate to the ritual songs by men and women at weddings, ironic in that Hippolytos wants no part in Love, even more ironically so in that Hippolytos will be honored by brides on their wedding eve. Antigone sees her fate of being walled up in a tomb as a sort of marriage to Death, and her song with the chorus at 801–82 is full of the language and symbolism of marriage. In fact the fate of women in tragedy is frequently presented in terms of a marriage to death. Seaford (1987) has seen in the fate of Pentheus in *Bacchae*, who will find not new life and "salvation," but death, an inversion of the initiation-ritual of the devotee of Dionysos. Thus while Greek drama is not the playing out of the same basic ritual in different forms, the dramatists can exploit familiar rituals for effect. In *Wasps* we have the comic spectacle of the genera-tions reversed, the conservative son trying to control and educate his willful father. Here the details of the Athenian rite-of-passage, the *ephebeia*, would have illuminated the humor of that play. In passing, one should note that the ritual of the sacrifice is never performed on stage. Aristophanes makes good comedy out of preparing and then delaying the ritual sacrifice in both *Peace* and *Birds*, with the exasperated hero doing the job off stage.

Dionysos himself is a character in Greek drama, but as we have pointed out above, not all that common in tragedy. If tragedy did develop from the choral songs accom-panying his rituals, it may have been the case that there were not all that many myths about Dionysos that could become good drama. Early Greek myth was an incredibly fertile source of stories, of all kinds about all sorts of heroes. Homer had made the Greek war against Troy part of the common heritage of Greece; other song-cycles had arisen over the troubles at Thebes, the early history of Athens, and the boar-hunt at Kalydon. A good dramatist and an eager audience will have expected tragedy to do more than relate the adventures of Dionysos, which would have perhaps a mono-tonous pattern: the advent of the god, rejection by others, and the god's eventual triumph and reception. Of the thirty genuine tragedies that we possess from the fifth century, only one (Euripides' *Bacchae*) has anything to do with Dionysos. Two lost presentations by Aeschylus did dramatize two separate incidents in Dionysos' career (a possible trilogy set at Thebes and the *Lykourgeia*), but we do not have any hints of a dramatic treatment of the story of the daughters of Minyas or the death of Ikarios, both of whom encountered Dionysos with appropriately "tragic" results.

Dionysos appears more often in satyr-play and in comedy. The satyrs are his fol-lowers, and in the first and last lines of Euripides' *Cyclops* they invoke Dionysos under his title *Bromios* ("the roaring one"). If satyr-play was introduced into the festival for the sake of a Dionysiac association, it is not surprising that this god would appear in satyr-drama. He appeared in Aeschylus' *Spectators*, berating his satyrs for abandoning his *choros* for the life of an athlete:

> no-one, young or old, can resist the appeal of my dances in double rows,
> but you lot want to be an Isthmian athlete, and crowned with boughs of pine
> you pay no honour to the ivy.

He must have been a character in Sophokles' *Young Dionysos*, where the discovery of wine was dramatized, and in Achaios' *Hephaistos* he was responsible for the return of Hephaistos to Olympos. Again the sensual delights of Dionysos are presented to Hephaistos:

Dion.:   *First we will delight you with dinner – and here it is!*
Heph.:   *And then how will you bewitch me?*
Dion.:   *I shall anoint your entire body with fair-smelling perfume.*
Heph.:   *Won't you first give me water to wash my hands?*
Dion.:   *Oh yes, as the table is being removed.*

But it is in comedy that Dionysos appears most often, and he does so, in Alan Sommerstein's phrase (1996: 11), in the role of "Dionysos as anti-hero." Comedy felt free to laugh at and make fun of its gods, even (especially) the deity for whom it was being produced. Comedians would put Dionysos in the most unlikely situation possible and then watch the fun emerge as this essentially unheroic and pleasure-loving god tried to live up to his situation. Two slaves in *Frogs* describe Dionysos well:

Slave: *Your master is a very noble fellow.*
Xanthias: *Of course he is – all he knows is drinking and fucking.*

This last carries in the Greek the nice aural ring of *pinein* and *binein*. In Kratinos' mythical burlesque, *Dionysalexandros* (437?), Dionysos fills in for Alexandros (Paris) to judge the famous beauty-contest of the goddesses. It is he that wins Helen and a thousand ships of very angry Greeks. At the end of the comedy the real Paris keeps Helen and hands Dionysos over to the mercies of the Greeks. In Aristophanes' *Babylonians* (426), Dionysos arrives in Athens with his Eastern followers and encounters for the first time a demagogue, who extorts money from him and threatens legal action. In Eupolis' *Officers* (415), Dionysos joins the navy and is taught the arts of war by the Athenian admiral Phormion. The fragments show us the effete and ineffectual Dionysos trying to adapt to the rigors of army life. And, of course, in *Frogs* (405) he disguises himself as Herakles for his descent to the underworld to bring back Euripides.

Disguise and confusion of identity seem to be very much part of the dramatic *persona* of Dionysos. In Aeschylus' *Edonians* Lykourgos is puzzled by this figure which appears to be both male and female. One of the boundaries that Dionysos dissolves is that of gender. In *Bacchae* Pentheus is both confused and attracted by the delicate hair and smooth white skin of the "priest," who is Dionysos in disguise. In Eupolis' *Officers* someone mistakes him for a "she" and threatens to sell "her" as soon as possible. In *Dionysalexandros* he appears as Paris, either in the guise of a Trojan prince or more likely as a rustic shepherd, and we are told that the chorus of satyrs laugh and jeer at him. In *Frogs* (38–46) Herakles breaks out laughing at the sight of Dionysos in his usual saffron robe, covered by a lion-skin, wearing soft boots and carrying a club. Later in the comedy his slave calls him first "Herakles" – "don't call me that or use that name" – and then "Dionysos" – "that's even worse." Disguising Dionysos and then penetrating that disguise was part of his role in drama.

Drama then does have a religious dimension. Its origins are traditionally assigned to the formal worship of the god Dionysos. Plays were produced as part of the festivals in honor of Dionysos, when the normal life of the city stopped and the life of carnival took over. Centuries later, Plutarch records an anecdote about Sokrates' reply to a question about whether he was worried about comedy's unfair caricature of him (*On the Education of Children* 10c–d):

> When Aristophanes produced his Clouds and piled abuse of every kind on him, one of those present said, "Aren't you angry, Sokrates, for making fun of you in that way?" "Hardly," replied Sokrates, "for in the theater I am made fun of as if I were at a great party."

Lucian (*Fisherman* 14) has Philosophy demonstrate to her devotees that she at least can take a joke:

> You got hot and bothered because someone was being rude to you? And yet you know that although Comedy treats me badly at the Dionysia, I still consider her a close friend. I've never taken her to court or even had a word of private complaint to her. I just let her make her usual jokes that belong to the festival. For I know that no harm can come from a joke.

At various places in the plays the gods and rituals of fifth-century Athens can be seen behind and beneath the texts, and one of the great issues of tragedy is the relationship between humans and gods. But Greek drama, like Greek myth in general, is more about human men and women. Gods appear on stage, intervene and influence the action, interact (often violently) with the human characters, but what interests the playwrights (particularly Euripides) is the human reaction. What do humans believe and expect from their gods, how do these gods live up to human expectations, can one really imagine a divine force or entity behaving in the very anthropomorphic manner that traditional myth (especially Homer) depicts them? Gods are immortal, gods have power, gods exist and are responsible in some way for the ways of the world. Greek tragedy sets out before its spectators instances of this interaction, not with the purpose of providing comforting answers, but of raising uncomfortable questions. Perhaps, after all, a festival of an ambiguous and discomfiting deity was not a bad place to attempt to explore the meaning of life.

The Theatrical Space

Almost anyone with a smattering of knowledge about ancient drama will know the theater at Epidauros (figure 1.7). Set in an isolated part of the Peloponnese against a stunning natural backdrop, and about 90 percent intact, this theater invariably appears in the standard guides and handbooks of the ancient theater. We admire the ornate entrance-ways, the perfectly round *orchestra* (especially when viewed from the air), the mathematical precision of the wedges and rows where the spectators sat, the elaborate and perfectly curved stone benches, and the acoustics by which those in the last row can hear clearly what is said or sung in the center of the *orchestra* (which

Figure 1.7   *Theater at Epidauros. © Archaeological Receipts Fund.*

the modern guide is happy to demonstrate). But this was not the sort of theater that Aeschylus or Aristophanes had at their disposal at Athens in the fifth century. The theater at Epidauros was built in the fourth century and was intended to be a state-of-the art construction. Comparing the theater at Epidauros with that in fifth-century Athens is like a putting a modern domed stadium beside an ivy-clad baseball park or terraced football ground.

Even when we go to Athens, the remains of the later structures dominate what we see and it is with difficulty that we make out the layout that playwrights, performers, and spectators had to work with in the fifth century. Today (figure 1.2) we see a round *orchestra*, nicely paved with marble flagstones and surrounded by a stone drainage ditch, curving rows of stone benches with cross-ramps and aisles, elaborate thrones in the front row for the priests of various civic cults, and a massive elevated platform with steps halfway across the *orchestra*. All of this postdates the fifth century. It was in the 320s the Athenian statesman Lykourgos rebuilt the theater in stone and added the lavish touches that we see today. The backdrop of the modern theater is the bustling and busy twenty-first century metropolis of modern Athens – in classical times the fields and mountains around Athens would have made this a setting surrounded by nature. We have to exercise our imagination to see what was there when the great tragic poets competed in the fifth century.

A "theater" was a "watching area," and in its simplest form consisted of a slope on a hillside with a flat area at the bottom where the performers sang and danced. This flat space was called an *orchestra* or "dancing place." In modern theatrical usage this term denotes the lower part of the house or the collection of musicians before or beneath the playing area, but to the Greeks it was the "dancing place." Scholars assuming a rustic origin for drama used to think that this *orchestra* developed from the round threshing-floor, on which, it is suggested, country songs and dances were performed after the harvest and threshing were complete. But not all early "dancing floors" were perfectly round and drama seems to have evolved in the urban environment at Athens. The theater was located on the south-east slope of the Acropolis, on the opposite side from the *agora* ("marketplace"), the center of Athenian daily life. It was next to, but not part of, the area sacred to Dionysos, and we have discussed already the debate whether drama (especially tragedy) was in any way intrinsically Dionysian, or merely linked by an accident of geography.

Any evidence (albeit late) that we have for the Lenaia festival in late January suggests that performances on that occasion were originally held in the *agora*, where an *orchestra* and benches were located. When the production of comedy and tragedy at the Lenaia became a formally state-sponsored competition about 440, these will have been moved to the theater, although some will argue that production continued in the *agora* through to the end of the fifth century. On this theory at least four of Aristophanes' extant eleven comedies were produced in a venue different from that of the comedies at the Dionysia, and indeed some scholars believe that they can detect differences in staging between comedies at the Dionysia and those at the Lenaia.

The perfectly circular *orchestra* at Epidauros and its nice semi-circle with elegantly curved stone benches for the spectators have overly influenced our view of the ancient Athenian theater. The hollow on the south-east slope of the Acropolis was not a neat semi-circle to begin with, although by the Hellenistic and Roman eras such a semi-circle had been created (figure 1.6). A perfect semi-circle provides the best sight-lines for the greatest number and is thus naturally "democratic," and although the lower part of the *theatron* at Athens did surround the *orchestra* by a little more than 180 degrees, the vast majority of the spectators were sitting in front of the playing area. On the western side (audience's right) the rows of the *theatron* did not extend to any great degree, and on the audience's left intruded the large Odeion ("Concert-hall"), built by Perikles around 440. Thus in the fifth century dramas would be played more frontally than in a perfectly semi-circular theater.

At *Women at the Thesmophoria* 395 the men are described as "coming straight home from the benches (*ikria*)." Ancient sources suggest that dramas were originally performed in the *agora* before spectators seated on *ikria*, before performances were moved to the south-east slopes of the Acropolis. While it is possible that "benches" was a term carried over from the early performances in the *agora* and that spectators sat merely on the ground itself, we should imagine the spectators of the fifth century seated on something that would have resembled the bleacher seating in high-school gymnasia or beside football fields. Obviously the benches could be arranged in some sort of roughly angled pattern, but the neatly curved rows of seating must await the rebuilding of the theater in stone by Lykourgos in the 320s. At both Thorikos, a regional deme-theater in the south-east of Attica (figure 1.8), and the fifth-century theater at Argos the evidence reveals for the most part rows of front-facing seating.

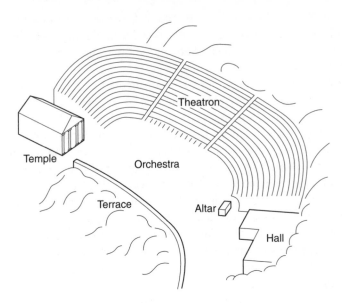

Figure 1.8 *The deme-theater at Thorikos*

Below the spectators extended the *orchestra*. Most of the Greek theaters that have survived are heavily altered by later developments, one of which was the perfectly circular *orchestra*. Dörpfeld, the German archaeologist who excavated the area of the Athenian theater in the 1880s, called attention to a series of seven stones arranged (in his view) in an arc. These, he insisted, formed the ring of a circular *orchestra* some twenty-four meters across, slightly to the south and east of the present *orchestra*. Some have challenged the findings of Dörpfeld, wondering if the arc existed at all, and argue that the *orchestra* in theaters of the fifth century was more rectangular or trapezoidal than circular. Certainly the *orchestra* in the regional deme-theater of Thorikos is anything but circular. But one should remember that the original songs and dances, the dithyrambs which were still part of the Dionysia in the classical period, were in fact called the "circular choruses." These employed choruses of fifty men or boys, and the words "circular chorus" seem to demand a circular performance space. Tragedy and comedy came later and would have adapted themselves to the traditional space. That a local deme-theater such as that at Thorikos did not have the same features as the theater at Athens is not surprising. Touring companies have always had to adapt down to the local space.

When one enters an ancient theater today, one is drawn, almost magnetically, to the center, and at Epidauros and Athens this central spot is marked out by a significant stone. It is often assumed that an altar stood here, although at Thorikos what seems to be the altar lies on the audience's left of the *orchestra*. More likely this central point could be used as the focus of the dramatic action, and there are several places where characters gather around a central point: the tomb of Agamemnon in the first half of *Libation-Bearers*, the statue of Athene in *Eumenides*, the altar of Zeus in *Children of Herakles* around which the sons of Herakles take refuge. This would allow a significant interaction between characters and chorus, the latter circling the central tableau in their dances.

The earliest theatrical space seems to have consisted of spectators on the slope of the hillside and the playing area below (the *orchestra*). Indeed the earliest three plays that we have, Aeschylus' *Persians*, *Seven*, and *Suppliants*, can be staged in only this space. There is no hint of or need for a building in the background – all exits and entrances are made from the sides. To be sure in *Persians* the tomb of the dead king is a physical and visible entity, and at line 681 the ghost of Dareios appears above this tomb, but this can be handled in a number of ways – perhaps by a temporary structure at the back of the *orchestra* near the drop to the terrace below. Actors and chorus originally shared the same performing space, with no area reserved for or associated with the actors separate from the chorus, or with any formal structure at the rear. The hillside drops from the level of the theater to that of the precinct of Dionysos, and there was very likely a terrace wall on the south side of the *orchestra*, marking that boundary of the playing space.

Characters and chorus would enter the *orchestra* from either side. At Epidauros and in other later theaters these entrances (*eisodoi*) are formal structures, with a framed doorway on either side. But in the earliest theater they must have just walked into the playing-space. At *Clouds* 327 (423 or ca. 418) Aristophanes has a character point out the chorus arriving, "there by the *eisodoi*," which should imply more than just a general location but an actual structure. Clearly characters take a while to make their entrance, and would have been visible for some time before they actually set foot in the *orchestra*. Thus arrivals are generally announced by the chorus or another character on stage:

> Chorus: *But here is Haimon, last-born of your children. Does he come here upset over the fate of Antigone, his destined bride, grieving for the loss of his marriage?* (*Antigone* 626–30)

> Orestes: *Look, there I see my best of friends, Pylades, running here from Phokis, a welcome sight.* (*Orestes* 725–7)

There must have been some dramatic tension between spectators who saw these characters about to enter and the players on stage who remained theatrically unaware of their approach.

But by 458 the third element of the Athenian theater has emerged, the *skene* building at the rear of the *orchestra*. The word *skene* just means "booth" or "tent," and here we should imagine not the pup tent familiar from camping, but a pavilion-style affair. It would have been a useful place to store properties and to allow the actors to change costumes, and may have already existed as a temporary structure. But in Aeschylus' *Oresteia* of 458 we become aware of a formal structure on the far side of the acting area, and in particular of its door and roof. Characters come and go as before by the *eisodoi* on either side of the *orchestra*, but now the door in the *skene* building provides a third entrance, which is used to great effect in *Agamemnon*. As Taplin (1978: 33) puts it well, Klytaimestra in that play "controls the threshold," and the entrances from and exits to the unknown space beyond the door form a major dramatic device of the first

Figure 1.9 *Fourth-century theater at Argos. Photo by Ian Vining.*

two plays of *Oresteia*. In two versions of "Orestes' revenge" (*Libation-Bearers*, Sophokles' *Elektra*) the whole plot turns entirely on how to get into the palace.

Look at the elaborate backdrop to Hellenistic and Roman theaters and the observer sees multi-storied structures in stone with lavish decorations, but at Athens in the fifth century, there was only a wooden building on the opposite side of the *orchestra*. Such a structure would have been a temporary one, for it would not be needed for the "circular choruses" of the opening day of the Dionysia, and the very term *skene* ("booth," "tent") suggests something non-elaborate and non-permanent. In fact the *odeion* of Perikles was said to have been modeled on the tent of the Great King, Xerxes, when he occupied Athens in 480.* At the fourth-century theater in Megalopolis we can see the remains of an alcove on the side, from which the *skene*-building was rolled into place when needed. At some point at Athens in the classical period a small stoa (colonnade) was constructed behind the *skene*-building with its back to the theater and would have provided a permanent backdrop for the action. This stoa is usually dated to the rebuilding by Lykourgos in the 320s, but might be as early as 400.

At Epidauros or at the fourth-century theater at Argos (figure 1.9) one will see the remnants of the stone foundations outside the *orchestra*, but the evidence for the earlier theaters suggests that the *skene*-building lay partly within the circle of the *orchestra*.

---

* In Euripides *Ion* (lines 1128–66) we get a description of the formal pavilion (*skenai*) in which Xouthos holds a celebration to introduce his newly found son.

Otherwise there could be a problem of distance from the spectators and a disjunction of the playing spaces, if the *skene* were removed completely from the *orchestra*. The presence of the *skene*-building allows for different *foci* for the action — this is especially true in *Libation-Bearers* (458), where the first half of the drama is played about the tomb of Agamemnon, located in the center of the *orchestra*, and the second half around the central door in the *skene*. As in *Agamemnon*, control of this doorway is of essential dramatic importance. Even in a much later comedy such as *Frogs* (405), the first part of the play, the adventures of Dionysos en route to the Underworld, is played in the *orchestra*, with the action shifting to the door to Plouton's palace in the second. In both tragedy and comedy do we find formal mini-scenes where a character knocks at a door to gain admittance (in tragedy the disguised Orestes at *Libation-Bearers* 653–67, in comedy at *Frogs* 460–78). Often this request is refused or delayed, with dramatically humorous or suspenseful results.

As the fifth-century *skene*-building was of wood, we cannot determine its appearance with any accuracy. The dramatic texts themselves are pressed into service to shed light on what the spectators saw and the performers employed. Although there may have been a tent or booth there in the earliest years of tragedy, an actual structure as part of the performance seems to have been first used around 460. As the watchman who opens *Agamemnon* (458) calls attention first to the palace and then to his position on the roof, it is an attractive conclusion that Aeschylus is highlighting this new aspect of the Athenian theater, perhaps on its very first occasion:

> *The gods I ask for release from my labors, this year-long watch that I keep lying on top of the palace of Atreus.*

Further on in the play Klytaimestra will insist that her husband enter the palace walking on a blood-red carpet, and later she will reappear to compel Kassandra to enter as well. Thus by 458 we can infer for the *skene* both a major door and a usable roof and we may add two further playing areas to the *theatron*: the area before the door, and the roof of the *skene*.

Evidence from vases in the fourth century reveals that this door was in fact a pair of panels opening inward, and in several plays the door marks out different worlds for the dramatic action. In *Oresteia* the door hides an unknown area, where characters go to die, while in *Antigone*, the world of death lies off-stage down one of the *eisodoi*, leaving the door as the entrance to the secure and ordered world of daily life. In *Ion* the *skene* represents the temple of Apollo and characters enter and leave the world of that god of wisdom, although there is an uncomfortable feeling that all is not well inside that temple. In Aristophanes' *Lysistrate* the barred doors represent the gates of the Acropolis behind which the women have sealed themselves. The *skene* can represent a variety of physical structures: temples (that of Zeus in *Children of Herakles*, of Demeter in *Suppliant Women*), palaces (the house of Atreus in *Agamemnon* or Sophokles' *Elektra*, or that in Thebes in *Oedipus Tyrannos* and *Antigone*), private houses (Herakles' in *Herakles* or that of his guest friend in *Trachinian Women*), a tent (as in *Hecuba* or *Ajax*), a cave (as in *Philoktetes* or *Cyclops*). Perhaps the most unusual physical settings occur in *Oedipus at Kolonos*, where the door marks the entry to the sacred grove of the Eumenides, and in Euripides' *Elektra*, where Elektra and her "husband" dwell in a country shack, "worthy of some farm laborer or a cow-herd" (252).

How many doors did the *skene* have? In Menander's comedy *The Grouch* (316) the speaker of the prologue, the god Pan, identifies three distinct dwellings behind three doors: his own in the middle, that of Knemon (the principal center of the action), and that of Gorgias. Clearly in the rebuilt theater of the late fourth century there were three distinct doors of roughly equal importance. But almost all tragedies of the fifth century can be played with only one door, an entrance that we have seen can attain an almost metaphysical significance. But there are instances in fifth-century comedy where more than one door seem to be necessary. In *Clouds* Strepsiades and his son are sleeping outside the house, from which a slave emerges with various items and into which the son departs at line 125. In the midst of all this Strepsiades points out the "reflectory" of Sokrates (93):

Do you see that little door and that small house over there?

This can be played with only one door, used as both Strepsiades' house and the "think-shop" of Sokrates, but some prefer a second smaller door for Strepsiades' house – the same problem will occur again at 790–815, where Sokrates reenters his "think-shop" and Strepsiades his own house. The scene plays more easily with more than one door. In *Peace* the goddess is shut up in a cave from which she must be drawn out — this is surely the central door of the *skene* – but Trygaios has his own house to which he returns at line 800. In a fragment of a comedy (420) by Eupolis we hear that "the three of them live here, each in his own shack." The natural conclusion is that this comedy had three distinct and operative doors.

But if comedy allowed for and did in fact use three doors, why does none of the tragedies that we possess seem to employ these side doors? Does it have something to do with the ethos of the genres? We know that there was a gulf in popular and artistic perception between the two. Tragedy almost invariably maintains the dramatic fiction and rarely, if ever, calls attention to itself as an artistic construct, while Old Comedy, at least, regularly punctures the dramatic illusion and involves the spectators in the action unfolding before them. No tragic poet in the fifth century is ever known to have written comedy, and vice versa. Was the use of one door somehow more solemn or distinguished than the use of three, or the three-door *skene* somehow seen as more "comic"? The comedies of the fifth century can, with difficulty, be played with one door, and there are places in the surviving tragedies where more doors than one could be used. In *Trojan Women*, for instance, the unallotted captives are described as confined "in these buildings," and "with them Helen." A single door could suffice for the entries of the chorus (at line 151) and subsequently that of Helen (line 895), but if there were another door available, it might have made good drama to bring Helen out from a different door.

Sophokles is said by Aristotle (*Poetics* 1449a18) to have developed *skenographia* ("painting of the *skene*"). Since the settings would change from play to play within a particular production, this term should suggest something like portable panels that could be changed as the setting changed from palace to temple to cave to house.

Certain comic texts suggest strongly that the *skene*-building had windows, at which characters could be seen and interact with those in the *orchestra*. At *Wasps* 317–32 the imprisoned Philokleon sings a song of lament "through the opening" to the chorus of elderly jurors gathered below. In *Lysistrate* the semi-chorus of women have barricaded themselves in the acropolis (i.e., the *skene*-building) against the assault of the semi-chorus of old men. At lines 352–462 the two choruses engage in a comic confrontation, culminating at line 420 with the women pouring jugs of water and chamber pots over the old men. This could be done with both choruses on the level out in the open, but it would gain dramatically if the women were above emptying their pots onto the men below. The roof would be good for this purpose but also the windows would do equally well. Finally, at *Assembly-Women* 951–75 a young woman inside the house sings a love duet with her boyfriend outside. Again a window is ideal for the young woman to be seen and heard.

One of the more hotly debated matters is whether a low platform or "stage" lay between the *orchestra* and the *skene*-building. Modern productions at the theater of Epidauros routinely employ such a raised platform, with wide steps leading up from the *orchestra* to the *skene* itself. In both tragedy and comedy we may detect an increasing role for the actor at the expense of the chorus, and in the fourth century actors become "stars" in the sense that we understand them. A raised platform, it is argued, reflects that increased role of the actors and creates their own space apart from that of the chorus for whom the "dancing place" was their natural terrain. But a raised platform against the *skene* would hardly have served actors in a theater where the great majority sat above and looked down. We are too used to looking up at a raised playing area, but at Athens most of the spectators looked down to the *orchestra*. Nor do the dramas of the fifth century reveal a marked distinction between actors and chorus; in fact they interacted as much as they were separated. In *Agamemnon* the chorus approach the *skene*-door when they hear the death-cries from within; in *Eumenides* and *Oedipus at Kolonos* the chorus surround a figure taking refuge at the center of the *orchestra*. In *Eumenides* and *Trojan Women* the chorus enter from the *skene*-building, rather than from the side. In *Frogs* Dionysos can race across the *orchestra* to appeal to his priest in the front row for protection from the monsters.

There are some places in comedy where a character is invited to "come up." In *Knights* the Sausage-Seller has just entered by one of the *eisodoi* and has attracted the attention of the slaves across the *orchestra* (147–9):

> *O wonderful sausage-seller, come here, come here, my friend. Come up and show yourself as savior to us and to the city.*

It is argued that this means to rise from the *orchestra* to a raised playing area, and on vases of the fourth century comic scenes are shown with steps leading up to what is clearly a stage, beyond which there is the double door of the *skene*. If there was a separate raised playing-area at the rear of the *orchestra* and before the *skene*, the steps were few enough and sufficiently wide to allow easy interaction between chorus and actors. On the other hand, "up" may mean only dramatically "up." "Come up" can work equally well as "come up onto this platform where we are" or just "come forward to the central point of attention."

Recent studies in theater production have shown that the crucial area for perform-ance in an ancient theater, either by a chorus or by an actor, was the line that con-nects the center of the *orchestra* to the central door of the *skene*. An actor in the front half of the *orchestra* does not command the *theatron* visually or audibly as effectively as one farther back. This is precisely the area that a raised stage, if one existed in the fifth century, would have occupied, but modern theorists insist that such a stage is not necessary for effective production.

The roof of the *skene* was called the *theologeion* ("god-speaking"), from which one might assume that its primary use was for the advent of deities, either at the start or close of the drama. But the first character that we know of to appear on the roof is a humble watchman at the start of *Agamemnon*, and other scenes show the presence of humans on the roof:

> Menelaos: *Look. What is this? I see the glow of torches, and these people taking refuge on the roof, and a sword held at my daughter's throat.* (*Orestes* 1573–5)

In this scene at least four people are gathered on the roof, which tells us something about the size of the *skene*-building in 408. We should not assume automatically that all gods in drama will have appeared on the roof, but when a character tells others to "look up" at an apparition, the natural conclusion is that this apparition is on the roof of the *skene*:

> Chorus: *Look. Do you feel the same pulse of fear, seeing such an apparition above the house?* (*Herakles* 816–7)

Obviously, then, the roof was accessible from the rear by a ladder or wooden stairs, but since so many of the spectators would be looking down on the dramatic tableau, the advent of a character on the roof would take only the players and those in the lower rows by surprise. Such a suspension of realism was part of the dramatic con-ventions of the Athenian theater.

The Athenian theater may have possessed two other features that would have affected production. Elsewhere we know of something called the "steps of Charon," which allowed an actor to pass underground beneath the *orchestra* and appear in the crucial central position. These may be seen at the Hellenistic theater at Eretria and would have been perfect for the appearance of the ghost of Dareios in *Persians* or that of Klytaimestra in *Eumenides*, but there is no evidence for their existence at Athens in either the fifth or fourth century.

Then there is "Hammond's Rock." In the 1970s N. G. L. Hammond called atten-tion to a rocky outcrop on the east side of the *orchestra*, about five meters square. As this would have been partly inside the *orchestra*, it was assumed that this had been removed early in the fifth century when the *orchestra* was created. Hammond's thesis was that this outcrop still existed in the time of Aeschylus and was used in the staging of his dramas, for the tomb of Dareios in *Persians* or the rock to which Prometheus was chained, and even the human jurors in *Eumenides* – these representing the Council of the Areopagos ("Ares' Hill" or "Crag"). But the evidence for its presence is shaky at best, and such a feature would have provided a lop-sided playing space and blocked the view of spectators on that side of the *theatron*.

The ancient theater was not suited for or given to what we would call "special effects" or the creation of reality in its productions. But there were two devices, attested for the fifth century, whose use can be documented in the existing plays. First there was what is commonly called the *ekkyklema* ("roll out," "wheel out" – *kyklos* = "wheel"), although that term is not found until very late sources. When comedy refers to such a scene, it is the verb *ekkyklein* that is normally found. This was some sort of wheeled device that could be rolled through the double doors in the *skene*, on which could be represented interior scenes *en tableau*. An ancient source describes its purpose as follows:

> It would show things which appear to be happening indoors, e.g., in a house, to those outside as well (I mean the spectators).

One of its primary uses was to display those who had died within the *skene*-building. One such instance is found at *Hippolytos* 808–10 where Theseus calls for the doors to be opened:

> Theseus: *Servants, release the bars of the gate, unfasten the locks, so that I may see the bitter sight of my wife, who in her death has destroyed me.*

Another occurs at *Herakles* 1028–30:

> Chorus: *Ah, ah, look. The double doors of the high-roofed house are opening. See the poor children lying in front of their ill-starred father.*

It seems then that the use of the *ekkyklema* was announced and that the spectators would put themselves in the proper frame of mind to accept this fairly blatant stage convention. Modern critics suggest all sorts of scenes that could have been staged with the *ekkyklema*, but unless we are alerted in some way by the text, it seems safer to restrict its use.

Aeschylus' *Oresteia* (458) presents an interesting problem in this respect. Two display-scenes occur in Aeschylus' *Agamemnon* (1372) and *Libation-Bearers* (973), where first Klytaimestra and then Orestes stands over the bodies of their victims. Here it is often assumed that these tableaux were staged by the *ekkyklema*, while in *Eumenides*, the third play of this trilogy of 458, it has been suggested that some or all of the chorus of sleeping Furies enter through the *skene*-door on the *ekkyklema*. This would mean that the *ekkyklema* would have been part of the *skene*-building from the start, since the *skene*-building itself seems to have been added around 460. Some doubt that the *ekkyklema* existed so early and observe that we get no advance warning of an interior scene as we do in the examples cited above. Perhaps announcing the use of the *ekkyklema* was a convention that developed later in the century. If the chorus in *Eumenides* did enter in this fashion through the *skene*-door, then the wheeled platform was large and solid enough to carry twelve choristers plus the chairs on which they were slumped.

Comedy made great fun out of the *ekkyklema*. Tragedy required the spectators to suspend their disbelief and enter willingly the dramatic illusion, especially when a potentially noisy device such as the *ekkyklema* was employed. Comedy, on the other hand, reveled in disrupting the dramatic illusion, and would call attention to the technique which, in tragedy, would be part of the accepted illusion. Thus in *Acharnians* and *Women at the Thesmophoria* a tragic poet will be "rolled out" on the *ekkyklema* in a self-conscious piece of theater:

Dikaiopolis: *Euripides, dear sweet Euripides, hear me, if you have ever listened to any man. It's me, Dikaiopolis of Cholleidai, calling you.*
Euripides: *I don't have time.*   Dikaiopolis: *So wheel yourself out.*
Euripides: *No, I can't.*   Dikaiopolis: *Please.*
Euripides: *All right, I'll wheel myself out.* (*Acharnians* 403–9)

What better way to call attention to the fact that the *ekkyklema* is but an accepted convention than to bring a tragic poet on stage by that means?

The other piece of stage equipment is known as the *mechane* ("machine"), also known as the *geranos* ("crane") or *krade* ("branch"). This was a device firmly anchored behind the *skene*-building, with a system of winch and pulleys, a wooden beam, and a harness by which characters could be presented as though flying through or hovering in the air. It is this device that has given birth to the much-used phrase *deus ex machina* ("god from the machine"). A variety of suggestions has been offered to explain how the *mechane* worked. One ancient source talks of raising the *mechane* like a finger, and from the comic evidence (*Peace*, *Birds*) it is clear that a character could be raised from behind the *skene* to land in front. Thus the *mechane* could both raise and swivel. To modern eyes such a device with its visible cables and creaking machinery might seem hostile to the ethos of tragedy, but, as with the entire nature of Greek tragedy, spectators were willing to participate by suspending belief, and those who enjoyed spectacle would eagerly await such a dramatic end to the play.

As we might expect, comedy has fun with this dramatic device as well. *Clouds* has a famous scene in which Sokrates enters suspended from the *mechane* – "I am treading the air and looking down on the Sun" (225). In *Peace* the main character Trygaios is carried to heaven on the *mechane* riding on a giant dung-beetle – a clear parody of Euripides' lost tragedy *Bellerophon*. In *Women at the Thesmophoria*, itself a play-length parody of Euripidean tragedy, Euripides himself enters at line 1098 on the *mechane* disguised as Perseus (from his recent *Andromeda*), while at *Birds* 1199 Iris flies in on the *mechane* to land at the newly founded city of Cloudcuckooland. Comedy thus uses the *mechane* to puncture the bubble of seriousness that surrounded its use in tragedy.

How large a load could the *mechane* bear? Usually one person only appears, and in cases where two deities appear (Poseidon and Athene in *Trojan Women*, Iris and Madness in *Herakles*), an equally good case can be made for their epiphany on the roof. But in *Orestes* (see below) Apollo and Helen certainly appeared on the *mechane*, and the two Dioskouroi were swung onto the *skene*-roof in Euripides' *Elektra*. The certain uses of the *mechane* for Pegasos, the world's largest dung-beetle, and a chariot for a god (in *Medea*) show that the device could be dressed up to accommodate more than a single human figure.

The *mechane* seems to have been a later development. Its first certain use is in Euripides' *Medea* (431). It was used principally at the close of dramas, often for the appearance of a deity to resolve or pronounce upon the action down below. But humans could and did appear on the *mechane* – Bellerophon entered upon Pegasos in two lost plays of Euripides, and at the end of *Medea* the heroine appears on the chariot of the Sun to spirit herself and the bodies of her children away. It is not always easy to determine whether a god at the end of a tragedy appears on the *skene*-roof or on the *mechane*. The presence of a chariot or the associations of motion should suggest an appearance on the *mechane*. Thus at *Andromache* 1225–30:

> Oh, oh, what is moving? What divinity is it I see? Look, see! This is a god that is carried through the bright sky and is landing on the horse-rearing plains of Phthia.

we may plausibly conclude that Thetis enters on the *mechane* and lands on the roof. So too the Dioskouroi at *Elektra* 1230 move toward and light upon the palace. At times the deity might appear either on the *mechane* or upon the roof, for example those of Athene at the end of *Ion*, *IT*, and *Suppliant Women*, and the arrival of the Dioskouroi in *Helen*. Perhaps when no attention is called to the arrival, we might infer an appearance on the roof rather than on the *mechane*.

One extraordinary scene in tragedy from the very late career of Euripides demonstrates the simultaneous use of four performance-spaces. At the end of *Orestes* (1549–693), a brilliantly iconoclastic tragedy in a number of ways, the ancient spectators would have seen the chorus in their usual area (*orchestra*), Menelaos and his followers hammering at the door of the *skene*-building, Orestes and others on the roof, and then on the *mechane* Apollo and the now-deified Helen. All four possible areas of performance were in use at the same time, and in the brief space of fifteen lines someone from each area will speak.

The Performance

We shall concentrate principally on the performances at the Dionysia, since it was the earliest dramatic competition, the one that carried the greater prestige, and the one about which we are best informed. The Dionysia was a five-day holiday that was both religious (ostensibly in honor of the god Dionysos with appropriate parades and festivities) and civic, as it involved the ancient city as a whole in its observation. As mentioned above, the assembly would not meet, nor was normal business conducted, at least for the first day – indeed if the theater held at least 15,000 spectators (as we estimate), a good proportion of those engaged in daily business would be at the theater rather than in the *agora*. Thus the spectators were in one sense worshipers of Dionysos (a god honored by wine and a general sense of release), members of the male citizen-body of Athens (there were also metics, foreign visitors, boys, and probably slaves and women – see below), all full of the sense of the occasion and in search of entertainment and emotional diversion. One of the principal problems in the modern study of Greek drama is assessing the extent to which drama was a religious offering, an exploration of political identity, or an engaging piece of popular entertainment.

Plato at one point speaks of dramas performed before 30,000 spectators, but even the largest of the ancient theaters (those at Megalopolis, Syracuse, and Ephesos) do not seem to have held much more than 20,000. But even 12,000–15,000 spectators is an audience on a large scale, and the modern counterpart to the ancient theater is not the enclosed interior box with a darkened hall, but the outdoor football stadium with all the dynamics of the large crowd. The usual entrance to the theater was from the east along the Street of the Tripods, which wound its way from *agora* around the north and east slopes of the acropolis, past the Odeion of Perikles into the *theatron*. At *Acharnians* 26 the main character (Dikaiopolis) imagines the arrival of citizens in the assembly as filling up that space (the Pnyx, on a hill west of the Acropolis) from the top down, but unless there was a separate route around the north side of the Odeion, spectators would enter and fill the *theatron* from the bottom up. Spectators would thus enter the theater by the same *eisodos* that the players themselves would use.

In the later theaters of the Hellenistic and Roman periods the *theatron* was divided by vertical aisles and at least one horizontal walkway (*diazoma*), creating the nice regular wedges of seating (*kerkides*) that are the hallmark of the ancient theater. But in the fifth century, spectators sat in benches on the hills and the arrangements must have been far less formal. We know from a passage in Aristophanes' *Frogs* (405) that the priest of Dionysos sat in a prominent location and that the character Dionysos was able to approach him and beg his protection. In the theater as we see it, the front row is marked by a series of elaborately carved stone thrones, inscribed with "⟨seat⟩ of the priest of . . ."

The audience was essentially composed of citizen males – comedy regularly addresses the spectators as *andres* ("men"), and on a couple of occasions the spectators are subdivided into classes of males:

> Now that you've enjoyed our triumph over that troublesome old man, youths, boys, men, applaud generously. (*The Grouch* 794)

> . . . while I explain the plot to the boys, the young men, the grown men, the older men, and the very old men. (*Peace* 50–3)

Elsewhere a character in Eupolis (fr. 261) complains of a "frigid joke, only the boys are laughing," and in *Clouds* Aristophanes accuses his vulgar rivals of bringing characters on stage with dangling red *phalloi* "so as to get a laugh out of the boys" (538–9). Thus we may assume with confidence that boys did attend the theater.

Some passages from Aristophanes' *Acharnians* (425) shed light on the presence of foreigners at the theater. According to the main character, Kleon (a leading political demagogue) claimed that in a play at the Dionysia of the previous year (usually identified as his *Babylonians*) Aristophanes had "said bad things about the city of Athens in the presence of foreigners (*xenoi*)." But now at *Acharnians* 504–6:

> the contest is that at the Lenaia, and foreigners *(*xenoi*)* are not yet present – here we are then, clean-hulled (so to speak), for I consider the metics to be the bran of our population.

We know also that metics were allowed to act as *choregoi* at the Lenaia and to perform in the choruses. But these were resident aliens and permanent members of the Athenian community, not full citizens admittedly, but men with a real stake in the life and prosperity of the city. As one of the preliminaries at the Dionysia was the presentation of the *phoros* (tribute), we may imagine that at that festival there would be a considerable number of visitors from the cities of the empire in attendance. By the end of March the sailing season had resumed and people would be able to travel to Athens.

But what about women? Could (did) women attend the theater in the fifth century? The issue has been debated constantly but with no accepted conclusion. It is true that ancient Athens was a male-dominated society – only males could vote in the *ekklesia* and hold political office within the state – and much of the evidence (principally, however, from upper-class sources) suggests that women lived in a sort of seclusion like that we associate with certain Middle Eastern societies today. But women did have a public role within the state, both as tradespersons in the *agora* and principally in the area of what we would call "religion." Women held priesthoods, attended festivals – the Thesmophoria was a women's only festival, the Adonia very much a women's celebration, and the main character in *Lysistrate* complains (1–3):

> If they'd invited the women to the shrine of Dionysos, to that of Pan or one of the gods of love and passion, no-one could have got through the streets – tambourines everywhere.

If then the dramatic competitions were part of a religious festival (that of Dionysos), why should women have been excluded or felt excluded from what was in part a religious observance? On the other side of the coin is the argument that the dramatic festivals were more civic and "political" occasions than religious festivals, at which women would be inappropriate visitors.

Plato, writing admittedly in the fourth century after the heyday of the fifth century, talks of tragedy as "a kind of rhetoric addressed to boys, women and men, slaves and free citizens without distinction" (*Gorgias* 502d), and imagines in his ideal state that "people will not be eager to allow tragic poets to put their stages in the marketplace and perform before women and children and the public at large" (*Laws* 817c). Elsewhere he argues that older children prefer comedy, while adult males and women of culture would choose tragedy (*Laws* 658d). These passages suggest that in Plato's time women were a natural and substantial part of the audience. On the other hand, the comic passages mentioned above address only the males. If women were present in the fifth century, either they were present only in small numbers or, in Henderson's phrase, "the audience was notionally male."

Other evidence comes from comedy and is susceptible of opposing interpretations. In *Women at the Thesmophoria* (389–91, 395–7) a woman complains about Euripides' treatment of women in his tragedies:

*Where has he not slandered us women, in any venue where there are spectators and tragic choruses.
. . . as soon as our husbands come home from the benches they give us searching looks and immediately start looking for our secret lovers.*

On the surface this should imply that women were not normally at the theater; on the
other hand the women seem awfully well informed about how Euripides treats women
in his plays. We should probably not treat this as an actual "window" into Athenian
life, but rather a contrived situation for comic effect. Another passage from Aristophanes' *Peace* (962–7) has been used both to support and reject the presence of women
among the spectators:

Trygaios: *Toss some barley-corns* (krithai) *to the spectators.*   Slave: *Okay.*
Trygaios: *You've already given them out?*   Slave: *By Hermes, yes, I have. And there's no
spectator who doesn't have a barley-corn* (krithe).
Trygaios: *The women don't have any.*   Slave: *But the men will give them some tonight.*

This passage is often interpreted that the women were sitting at the back of the *theatron*, where the barley-corns thrown by a slave would not have reached. But the word
krithe ("barely-corn") is also a slang term for the male penis, and the passage might
read:

Trygaios: *Toss some barley-corns* (krithai) *to the spectators.*   Slave: *Okay.*
Trygaios: *You've already given them out?*   Slave: *By Hermes, yes, I have. And there's no
spectator who doesn't have a barley-corn* (krithe).
Trygaios: *But women don't have any.*   Slave: *But the men will give them one tonight*
(nudge, nudge; wink, wink).

The whole business is a set-up, then, for the double meaning of *krithe* and is not necessarily solid evidence for the presence of women in the theater.

There is some evidence that the spectators were given treats during the play – see
the passage from *Peace* quoted above, as well as the prologue of *Wasps* where Aristophanes announces that his play will not have a pair of slaves throwing nuts out to the
audience – the point being that his comedy will succeed on its dramatic merits, not
through a largesse from the *choregos*. In *wealth* (388) a pair of characters toy with the
spectators, first promising to toss out fruit and nuts and then refusing on the grounds
that such behavior "is not proper for a comic poet" (797–8).

We know from the orators that the Athenian court-room was a noisy and con-
tentious group atmosphere, and we can imagine that the Athenian theater was much
the same. There is evidence from the fourth century of spectators hissing and cluck-
ing at unpopular actors or poor performances, perhaps even of hurling food to express
discontent, and applauding wildly when pleased. One anecdote records that a controversial line from Euripides' lost *Aiolos* had aroused the spectators' wrath, another
that his *Danae* was stopped by an outraged audience and only resumed after the playwright urged them to see what would happen to the offending character. These may,
however, just be fictions created after the fact as part of the stereotypical picture of
Euripides as the *enfant terrible* of the Athenian stage. But the theater was a communal
experience, with spectators sitting in close proximity, able to pick up and transmit the
emotional impulses that the performances would generate, be they the sadness and

grief from tragedy or the exuberance and laughter of comedy. For Aristotle (*Poetics* chapter 6) the end of tragedy was the creation and *katharsis* of pity and fear, and we need to be reminded that the theater in classical Athens was not a detached cerebral exercise, but a shared emotional experience. We do know of a theatrical security force, called the *rhabdouchoi* ("theater police," literally "rod-bearers") whose duties seem to have included keeping order in the *theatron*.

By the middle of the fourth century the Athenians had established the "Theoric Fund" (clearly related to the *thea-* root, "spectate") that allowed poorer Athenians to attend the theater by paying the two-obol admission fee. When this was introduced is a matter of controversy. It was clearly in place by the 340s when Demosthenes refers directly to the fund, but some of the sources attribute its introduction to Perikles in the third quarter of the fifth century, and another to the politician Agyrrhios in the 390s (although this last is probably a confusion with Agyrrhios' institution of pay for attendance at the assembly).

Two obols was a reasonably high cost to attend the theater. Some recent critics have argued that in the fifth century this high cost of admission would have affected the composition of the audience, so that only those sufficiently well off could attend. It is this, it is suggested, that explains the right-wing bias of Old Comedy – they were performing for the elite and not for a representative general public. There was some reserved seating (*proedria*): for public officials such as the *Boule* (the council of 400 Athenians; at *Peace* 887, 905–6 and *Birds* 794 specific reference is made to separate seating for the members of the *Boule*), the archons, the ten generals, and the *nomo-phylakes* ("guardians of the laws"), for those being specially honored, and the *epheboi* (young men doing their military service).

Conventions of the space

First, it was a large space. David Wiles estimates that from the central door in the *skene* to the furthest row in the *theatron* was a distance of about 100 meters. Thus the sort of intimate performance that we associate with small theaters or even the close-up of the movie camera was not possible in the ancient theater. For a spectator seated in the last row the performers down below would seem only a few inches high. Thus there could not be a vast horde of players and the actors would need to be dressed distinctively to make them and their roles stand out.

The theater was also a large communal space. There were at least ten thousand spectators crowded into a restricted space, either on benches or on the later marble rows. The experience of attending the Greek theater was not one of individuals responding as individuals to the performance set before them, but of a community of spectators reacting *en masse* to the horror or the humor played out for them. Wiles (2002: 112) puts it powerfully:

> The spectator 100 metres away was part of a single crowd, bounded by a space that created no vertical or horizontal boundaries, and concealed no group from the rest. If all 15,000-plus tightly packed people were listening to the same words at the same time, and

Figure 1.10 *Theater at Delphi. Photo by I. C. Storey.*

shared the same broad response, the power of emotion generated would have been quite unlike that created today in a studio theatre. Communication was effected not simply via light and sound waves but via an osmosis passing through the bodies of the spectators.

It was also an open space. Performances took place in the daytime, probably not long after daybreak – several plays call attention to the rising of the sun (e.g., *Antigone*, a poignant touch if this play were the first play of its group). One would be aware of both the natural surrounding, the view over the south-east part of the city and thence out to the hills of the Mesogaia, and of the other spectators, the citizen-body of Athens. Modern outdoor stadia are usually built to direct the spectators' view inward toward the playing area and do not distract with a view of the natural setting (the baseball field at San Francisco is an exception), but in the Greek theater *theatron* and natural setting formed a harmony of setting and took the spectator from the individual drama unfolding below to the larger world of the natural environment. When gods appear at the end of a Greek play, their arrival seems quite natural in light of the larger universe that surrounded the theater. In *Clouds* the spectators' attention is specifically directed out to the mountains and then back to the *theatron*.

The theatrical space formed also a community of the audience. Actors come into and go from the common space in front of and surrounded by the spectators and very often announce what has happened either off stage or behind the *skene*. There is an "outer" common world of the spectators and an "inner" world between which there are doorways of communication. The words of the drama bring the events of the unseen worlds before the spectators and through the brilliance of the writing they are able to imagine what has happened elsewhere. Very often we see a character leave the acting area and then a messenger picks up what happened when they arrived in the unseen world. Doors swing both ways in Greek drama.

"Theater of the mind"

This is Taplin's (1978: 9) useful phrase to describe the conventions of the Greek stage. Modern audiences are used to the creation of reality in front of them; they expect visual and aural effects that make the dramatic atmosphere "real" and believable. Much is written about the "willing suspension of disbelief" on the part of the spectator, and impressive and realistic effects do much to enable that suspension. We are used to the box theater, where we view the on-stage action through an open fourth wall, although modern thrust theaters, such as that at the Stratford Festival in Ontario, have created a more involved effect for that audience. In the Greek theater the spectators had to do much of the work themselves, to imagine places and settings, import information and relationships from the mythical tradition, visualize in their minds the events occurring off-stage and narrated by others.

There were, for instance, no programs with a list of characters and actors, the settings of the various acts and scenes, and the background information necessary for appreciating the performance even from before its first words. For the Dionysia there was the Proagon ("precontest") just before the Dionysia itself, at which playwrights with their actors and chorus would announce in some fashion the subject of the forthcoming production, but in the case of comedy these probably tantalized and misled more than they informed. The words of the text told the spectators what they needed to know: where they were, who the characters were, and the elements of the plot-line that would develop. Take the opening of Euripides' *Bacchae*, for instance:

> *To this land of Thebes am I come, the son of Zeus, Dionysos, to whom once Semele, the daughter of Kadmos, gave birth with the lightning-bolt for midwife. Having exchanged my divine appearance for mortal form, I stand beside the streams of Dirke and the water of the Ismenos. Over there near the palace I see the tomb of my mother who was struck by thunder and the ruins of her house still smoking with the flame of Zeus' fire, the undying outrage of Hera against my mother.*

Here the speaker tells us that we are before the palace at Thebes, that he is Dionysos disguised as a mortal, that his mother Semele gave him birth after being struck by the bolt of Zeus, and that the play will deal with the story of his return to Thebes.

To take an example from comedy, where the spectators would not know the background to the story, examine the opening lines of Menander's *The Grouch*:

> *Now imagine, people, that the setting lies in Attica, at Phyle, and that the shrine of the Nymphs that I am coming out of is that of the people of Phyle and those who farm the rocky ground here – it's a well-known place. In the farm-house on my right here lives Knemon, a real misanthrope . . . who never speaks to anyone first, except when he passes my shrine (I'm the god Pan) . . .*

Here the spectators learn the setting (Phyle on the rocky outskirts of Attica); the identity of the speaker (Pan); the space behind the central door (a shrine of the Nymphs); and the name, domicile, and personality of the main character (Knemon the *dyskolos*, "grouch").

Very often the text announces the imminent arrival and identity of a character. Thus in *Antigone* Kreon's entry at line 162 is prefaced by a notice by the chorus, "But here comes Kreon, the new ruler of the country . . . ," and later Kreon's son Haimon, Antigone's betrothed, is announced in similar terms, "Here is Haimon, the last-born of your sons" (626). In the same play the entry of Kreon's wife is announced at line 1180, and the return of Kreon himself at line 1260. On these occasions the spectators need to know who this figure is that they see approaching along an *eisodos*. Sometimes a character arrives without introduction, but the audience is rarely kept in doubt. In *Antigone* Teiresias arrives without fanfare at line 988, but in a play set at Thebes the identity of a blind man walking with the aid of a boy would be obvious – just to be sure Kreon calls him "old Teiresias" at line 991. In *Alkestis* Herakles appears completely out of the blue at line 476, but his traditional accoutrements of lion-skin and club will make his identity clear – at line 478 the chorus make it abundantly clear, "Admetos is indeed at home, Herakles."

By the time of fourth-century comedy, the *eisodoi* had acquired distinct identities, the one to the spectators' right leading to a local venue, that to the left a foreign setting. Combined with the entrance via the *skene*, these would allow for some creative staging on the part of the poet, for what has been called "misdirection." The spectators would be expecting an entry from one position and would be surprised either by a character entering via a different entry or by an unexpected development. One of the most interesting such moments occurs at line 924 of *Oedipus Tyrannos*. At the end of the previous scene Oedipus and Jokaste have sent for the herdsman who survived the encounter where three roads meet. A messenger has been dispatched through the "local" *eisodos*, while the chorus perform the second *stasimon* (863–910) and Jokaste reappears through the *skene*-door to make an offering at the statue of Apollo (911–22). Character, and chorus, and spectators will be watching the "local" *eisodos* for the expected herdsman, but from the other *eisodos* without warning or announcement enters the messenger from Corinth to take the plot in an unforeseen direction.

Similarly, the spectators are often prepared for the identity and entry of the chorus. In tragedy they normally enter from one of the *eisodoi* after an introductory scene (or scenes) involving the actor(s), but in two early plays by Aeschylus (*Persians*, *Suppliants*), they are already in the *orchestra* when the action begins. Twice in the extant tragedies they enter through the *skene*-door, in *Eumenides* (perhaps on the *ekkyklema*) and in *Trojan Women*, where the *skene* represents the tents in which the captive women are being held. Choral identities in tragedy are not that unusual, for example elders of the state, handmaidens, townsfolk, and thus their identity is not always specifically announced. But in Old Comedy, where the entire situation is composed *de nouveau*, the spectators are always told something about the chorus before they enter, as at *Acharnians* 178–85:

> I was hurrying here bearing peace treaties for you, when some old Acharnians sniffed them out
> . . . I ran away, but they're following me and shouting

or at *Wasps* 214–16:

> *But they'll be here soon, his fellow-jurors, to summon out my father.*

In the eleven surviving comedies of Aristophanes the chorus invariably enters along the *eisodos*, often rushing violently on-stage – as at *Knights* 247, "get him, get him, get the villain." By the time of Menander (late fourth century) the chorus enters to sing interludes between the acts, and in an early play (*The Grouch*) their identity and arrival are announced to the spectators:

> *I see some worshipers of Pan heading this way, and they've been drinking. I think it's a good time for me to get out of here.* (230–2)

Choros is related to the Greek verb *choreuein* ("to dance"). Again modern usage gets in the way, since for us a "chorus" is a singing group or the refrain of a song. But Greek drama must have been more balletic than our modern theater. We should perhaps look to the Broadway or West End musical for a modern analog to Greek drama. Clearly certain forms of dance will have suited certain dramatic situations – we know of a war dance, an "Athena-dance," the vulgar *kordax*, and at the end of *Wasps* the main character engages in a vigorous contest with three other stage-dancers. It is easy enough for us to envisage dance as part of a romantic or comic musical, but it takes more effort to imagine how the more serious form of tragedy would have incorporated dance. Scenes of mourning and lamentation will have had their own particular physical expression; we can picture the chorus in *Oedipus at Kolonos* miming the off-stage battle with movements of a martial turn, all the more effective if these were older men. In *Eumenides* the chorus of Furies track and surround the fugitive Orestes, encircling him with a binding song of enchantment. We can only imagine the power that the dance of the Angry Goddesses would have evoked. There may not be much "action" in a Greek tragedy, but so much of the effect was created by the emotive spectacle of the dance.

We often regard the chorus as operating on the sidelines of the action, commenting (occasionally with banality) on the exchange between the actors, but they can have a more significant role. Indeed in one or two plays they are a principal character and it is their fate on which the action depends, as in Aeschylus' *Suppliants* and *Eumenides* and Euripides' *Trojan Women*. They take part in the episodes with the actors, sometimes as a major agent, more often commenting on the action, as at *Antigone* 724–5:

> *My lord, if he is saying something to the point, you should pay attention to him, and he to you, since good arguments have been made on both sides.*

Later in *Antigone* (1099–1101) they take the unusual step of advising the main character on what to do:

> Kreon: *What then should I do? Tell me and I will do what you say.*
> Chorus: *Go and let the maiden out of her cave-prison and prepare burial for the dead man lying out there.*

In *Libation-Bearers* the chorus, again unusually, intervene in the action to prevent Aigisthos from bringing his bodyguards with him (770–3). In comedy the chorus is often antagonistic to the main character and especially in *Birds* will be openly hostile. On a couple of occasions the chorus must be converted as a result of the contest (*agon*) and their sympathy and attitude change.

When the chorus take part in an episode, they use the normal Attic (Athenian) dialect and their speech is no different from that of the actors. Also when they process into the *orchestra*, often to the accompaniment of the anapestic meter ($\cup \cup -$), they chant in the usual Attic dialect. But when they perform a standing-song (*stasimon*) or engage in a lyric exchange with a character (*kommos*), their language switches to a quasi-Doric dialect, an artificial construct which would have sounded different to the audience. This has to do in part with the fact that the tradition of choral poetry is Dorian (certainly non-Attic), and thus it was perhaps expected that "song" should sound differently from "speech" (remember that the episodes were in verse, but iambic trimeter, according to Aristotle, is the closest rhythm to normal speech). Similarly the characters, when they engage in song with the chorus, with another actor, or on their own, sing in this artificial dialect. At *Alkestis* 244–6, part of a dialog between the dying Alkestis and her distraught husband in which she sings in Doric lyrics and he responds in less emotive iambics, Alkestis begins: *Halie kai phaos hameras ouraniai te dinai nephalas dromaiou* ("Sun and light of day and sky-swirls of racing cloud"), which in Attic should have run *Helie kai phos hemeras ouraniai te dinai nephales dromaiou*. Not a huge difference, and certainly understandable to the spectators, but carrying the flavor of the Doric dialect and the connotation of "song."

Comic choruses are less prone to singing in this artificial Doric, and when they do (as *Birds* 1058–70), the effect is deliberately to evoke a higher style than the lower norm of comedy. Aristophanes can certainly write in the Doric style. The opening words of the Pindaric poet at *Birds* 904–6 belong to this lyric tradition, but here too the intent is parody of the loftier form. In the entry-songs of the chorus in *Clouds* (276–90, 299–313) the clouds do lapse into Doric on a couple of occasions.

The performers

The choristers were usually Athenian males; at the Lenaia metics could participate for that festival only. Those serving in a chorus were spared military service during the period of rehearsal. We would like to know how large was the body of performers available – a performance at the Dionysia would require ten men's dithyrambic choruses of fifty each, three tragic choruses of twelve or fifteen each, and five comic choruses at twenty-four each. Add to this ten boys' choruses again at fifty each, and we get a total of nearly 1,100 performers, although one might consider the possibility that a dithyrambic performer might also appear in a dramatic chorus. If the pool of performers were small, then the relationship between performer and spectator would be one of "us" and "them," the former doing something that an "average" Athenian did not do. But if performing was something more widespread – just as any Welshman, it seems, can sing – then spectators would be familiar with the experience and technique and perhaps be more drawn into the details of performance.

The chorus of tragedy was originally twelve – this is made clear by a passage in Aeschylus' *Agamemnon* (1348–71) where the chorus disintegrates into twelve distinct individuals – and was increased to fifteen by Sophokles. Choristers would have to perform in the three separate tragedies as well as take the roles of satyrs in the satyr-drama that concluded the production. Acting as a tragic chorister, then, would be a major undertaking and presumably carried more than a little prestige. A chorus of fifteen would allow for three files of five, and there is evidence that the outside file in their entry, that closest to the spectators, was regarded as the most important, with its leader considered the chorus-leader. How the chorus performed in their standing-songs (*stasima*) is a matter of debate. One possibility is that they performed in three ranks facing out into the *theatron*, which would suit production in theaters without the circular *orchestra*. Another is that they danced in a ring around the *orchestra*, much in the manner that Greeks dance in the round today. Supporting this interpretation is the nomenclature of the parts of a choral song: *strophe* and *antistrophe*, "turn" and "counter-turn." Yet another possibility is a triangle of five ranks (5–4–3–2–1), with the chorus-leader at the point. Perhaps an originally circular style of performance was augmented or superseded by other formations, when the number was increased to fifteen.

Comedy had a larger chorus, composed of twenty-four choristers, and would need to operate with twice the space and manpower, probably producing a more crowded and less elegant spectacle. It is possible that a comic chorus might enter from both *eisodoi* – this would make good sense in *Peace* with its Panhellenic chorus and *Birds* with its swarm of winged creatures – but on the three occasions where comedy mentions the *eisodoi* (*Clouds* 326, *Birds* 296, Aristophanes fr. 403) the reference is in the singular ("entrance"). All three passages refer to the entry of the chorus. Either the chorus did enter through one *eisodos* only or attention is drawn to only one entrance, even though both were in use. In at least two comedies, and probably in many more, a pair of opposing half-choruses was employed: old men and old women in *Lysistrate*, rich and poor men in Eupolis' *Marikas*. In the latter we know that the chorus divided and came together again as the play progressed.

Actors were assigned in some way to the productions, perhaps by lot, perhaps by the choice of the *choregos* or the poet. It would be revealing to know how much choice the poet had in his actors. The ancient sources suggest that originally the poet played the lead role in his drama and that Sophokles, having a weak voice, was the first to abandon the acting role. More than one scholar has suggested that Aristophanes himself played the lead role in *Acharnians*, where the comic poet and his chief character merge at least twice – and we would suggest also *Wasps* where Bdelykleon seems to speak for Aristophanes at lines 650–1.

There were three speaking actors in classical tragedy – some of the early plays by Aeschylus can be performed with two – and a case can be made for the same number in comedy, although some scenes would make considerable demands on a third actor, involving rapid changes of costume and movement from one exit to a different entrance. There are a couple of places in Aristophanes where four speaking actors

Figure 1.11 *Tragic performers dressing for their role as maenads, on a red-figure pelike, ca. 430. Reproduced courtesy of the Museum of Fine Arts, Boston, Henry Lillie Pierce Fund. Photo © Museum of Fine Arts, Boston.*

seem certainly to be required, but in one of these (the scene of decision in *Frogs*) the text is confused because of revision. The extant remains of Menander do not require more than three actors at any point.

Actors' dress and costume varied widely among the three dramatic genres. Unlike comedy and satyr-play, we do not have many visual representations of a tragic performer (see figure 1.11), but the tragic actors who appear on the Pronomos Vase (figure 3.1) and the *Choregoi* Vase (figure 4.2) are costumed with grandeur and a more than common splendor. The masks were life-like, the costumes rich and flowing. The effect was to reinforce the "serious" nature of the genre. Many of the vases that are clearly influenced by tragedy do not show masked or costumed actors – they give us a tragic scene with the conventional dress (or lack of it) of Greek art. In the satyr-play, while the satyrs (figure 3.2) wore very little, a mask with an ugly satyric face and a pair of briefs with a small erection, the actors continued to wear the more serious costume of tragedy. Comedy was meant to depict the ridiculous (*geloion*), and its actors wore grotesque masks, padded costumes, and a dangling *phallos*.

Prizes were awarded for the first actor, first in tragedy and later in comedy. By the fourth century lead actors had become international celebrities, "stars" as we understand the term, and at the Dionysia ca. 340 lead actors would be shared by the tragic poets in order presumably to provide a level playing-field. In the fifth century actors would play for one poet only, and it has been suggested that the lead actor might play as many parts as possible in order to increase his visibility. This seems doubtful, as with a few exceptions roles belonged to the same actor throughout the play – the principal exception being *Oedipus at Kolonos*, where all three actors have to play Theseus in order for the drama to work with three actors. In *Libation-Bearers* the same actor plays Elektra, the Nurse, the effeminate Aigisthos, and Klytaimestra, showing that in 458 Aeschylus had an actor who excelled at female roles. Sometimes an actor will take on two significant roles in a play; the most striking are in *Trachinian Women*, where the lead actor will play first the whimpering Deianeira and then her brutal husband, Herakles, and in *Ajax* where the lead actor plays first Ajax and then his brother. In Aeschylus' *Oresteia* an actor's roles between plays can be significant: the actor who plays Pylades, the mouthpiece of Apollo at *Libation-Bearers* 900–2, will play Apollo in the next play, while the actor playing the masculine Klytaimestra will become Athene ("I am always for the male").

Both tragedy and comedy could use other players, *kopha prosopa* ("silent faces"), in all sorts of supporting roles: guards, attendants, kitchen utensils (in *Wasps*), children. There are instances of secondary choruses: of Athenians at the end of *Eumenides*, again twelve to match the twelve Furies; of huntsmen in Hippolytos, who have their own song at 61–71 and then sing with the regular chorus at 1102–50; of boys in Euripides' *Suppliant Women* and also in *Wasps*. Sometimes the extra individual characters might seem actually to speak, but it is more likely that their brief lines were spoken by one of the three canonical actors, who after all were masked and would not be seen to speak – the barbarian god in *Birds*, the Persian envoy in *Acharnians*, the son of Admetos in *Alkestis*. In Aristophanes' *Peace* a large statue of that goddess is hauled out from the *skene*-building. Comedy builds a nice bit of self-reference as Hermes undertakes to speak for the inanimate figure (657–63):

Trygaios: *But tell me, my lady, why are you silent?*
Hermes: *She will not talk to the spectators, since she is very angry at them for what she has suffered.*
Trygaios: *Let her talk a little with you then.*
Hermes: *Tell me, my dear, what you have in mind for them. Go on, you who of all females hate shields the most. I'm listening. That's what you want? Okay.*

In the judgment scene of Kratinos' lost *Dionysalexandros* there could be as many as five speaking characters (Dionysos-Alexandros, Hermes, and three goddesses). We could have had three separate scenes as each goddess appeared to make her appeal to the judge, but all other ancient allusions to the Judgment of Paris shows the three goddesses together. Clearly the easiest way to stage this scene is to have Hermes speak for each goddess in turn.

Figure 1.12 *Aulos-player, fragment of a red-figure skyphoid, attributed to the Palermo Painter, ca. 400. Reproduced courtesy of the Nicholson Museum, Sydney (97.172).*

Accompanying the chorus was an *auletes*, often referred to inaccurately as a "flute-player," as an *aulos* was a reed instrument, played by blowing into it, rather than across the mouthpiece. Visual representations of the *auletes* show him to be playing a double-reed instrument, with pipes of varying lengths. Rather than a flute, imagine a double oboe or double recorder, supported by a mouth- and cheek-piece and fastened by two straps around the head. The *auletes* wore splendid robes with elaborate decoration – witness the figure of Pronomos, who occupies the prime position on the Pronomos-Vase (figure 3.1), more so than the poet himself who sits apart in a less prominent place, or the splendid striding figure on a red-figure *krater* in Sydney (figure 1.12). The *auletes* would accompany the choral sections of tragedy, comedy, and satyr-play and would provide the music for the dithyrambic choruses, leading them into the performance space. At *Birds* 859–61 it appears that the *aulos*-player in that comedy was himself dressed as a bird, at least for the second half of the play:

You, stop playing. By Herakles, what is this? I have seen many strange things in my day, but I've never seen a crow wearing a mouthpiece.

The *aulos* possessed an ambiguous role in classical Athens. An *aulos*-player was a frequent presence in the parties and celebrations throughout the city. In one sense it was something to be officially disapproved of, since a popular myth told of Athene's rejection of the *aulos* which disfigured her face as she blew into it. On the other hand, a splendidly dressed *aulos*-player is portrayed on vases depicting performances of various kinds. Thus the *aulos* was essential to the sense of formal performance in ancient Athens and in fact symbolic of it. It has been suggested that the formal dress of the *aulos*-player indicates that this normally disreputable character is on his best behavior when performing on a civic occasion. The modern equivalent of the *aulos* might be the guitar, since 1950 the universal symbol of popular counter-culture, but also no stranger to a classical music concert.

There are occasions where the spectators themselves become actors in the drama. This would not be at all unusual for comedy in view of its notoriously anti-illusionary approach. In Aristophanes' *Frogs* (274–6) Dionysos wonders where the "murderers and liars" are, whom Herakles said he would encounter in the underworld. We do not have the stage directions, but Xanthias must turn him to face the *theatron*:

Xanthias: *Are you sure you don't see them?*
Dionysos: *By Poseidon, yes I do, I see them now.*

At the conclusion of the *agon* in *Clouds* (1088–1104) the inferior argument wins his case by demonstrating that legal experts, tragic poets, and popular politicians are "assholes":

Inferior Argument: *Look at the spectators and see who are in the majority.*
Superior Argument: *I'm looking. Inf. Arg: And what do you see?*
Sup. Arg.:   *By god, the assholes are everywhere.*

There are places where the spectators are worked more largely into the drama. When Dikaiopolis pleads his case in *Acharnians* (496–556) he is doing far more than appeal to the hostile chorus, he becomes Aristophanes making a point to the larger *theatron*. In fact he begins by altering a line from Euripides to "do not be angry with me, men of the *theatron*."

But there are occasions in tragedy where the spectators are brought into the drama. One of the most striking is the opening scene of *Oedipus Tyrannos*, where a priest appeals to Oedipus on behalf of his plague-struck people. It is sometimes thought that these "children of Kadmos" were either the chorus who had entered with the priest at the start of the play or a subsidiary chorus who departed at the end of the prologue. But suppose that these "pitiful children" were the Athenian spectators who are brought into the drama by the wave of Oedipus' hand. This could be breathtaking not just because the Athenians would be invited to become citizens of what was at the time an enemy city, but also because (if the play is correctly dated to the early 420s) Athenians were recovering from a plague of their own. At the end of Aeschylus' *Eumenides* a jury of twelve Athenians enters the *orchestra* to decide the fate of Orestes.

When the Furies abandon their anger and become Eumenides ("the kindly ones"), they are escorted to their new home beneath the Acropolis by the people of Athens. Aeschylus surely could not have resisted drawing the spectators into this installation. At the end of the National Theatre's production of *Oresteia* in 1981, the audience was urged to "stand and be silent as the Kind Ones pass by." Much of the dramatic impact and success of *Eumenides* lies in the resonance created as the dramatic action approached Athens of the dramatist's own day.

Drama and the *Polis*

While a festival honoring a god might strike us as wholly religious in orientation, participation in religious festivals was an essential part of civic life in every Greek community. Since all religious festivals were at least in part directed toward the protection and prosperity of their participants, when those festivals were community-wide, they all might be said to serve political ends in the broadest sense of that term, that is, to be of benefit to the *polis*. On this most basic of levels, then, the two Dionysiac festivals at Athens at which drama was produced can be said to serve both religious and political purposes. But much recent scholarship assumes an intensely close relationship between drama and the Athenian *polis*, especially the democratic *polis*.

"*Polis*," of course, is the Greek term from which we derive our terms "politics" and "political," but it remains notoriously difficult to convey the depth and complexity of its associations in a single English term. Most frequently translated "city-state," in Greek sources *polis* serves to identify both a town as administrative center of a territory and the territory itself. Thus Athens, an *astu* (town), is also a *polis* in so far as it serves as the administrative center of the territory of Attica, while the territory of Attica, with all its smaller towns and communities, forms the *polis* named for Athens when viewed as a collective entity. But more than this, *polis* also embraced the people resident in its territory, and in the case of Athens/Attica, whether they lived in the city proper or dwelt in an outlying community, these people bore the name Athenians, if they qualified for citizenship. The Greek term for "citizen" was *polites,* and signified one who possessed certain rights in a *polis.* Thus when someone claimed to be an Athenian citizen, he was not making claim to a particular nationality, nor was he necessarily revealing the town of his residence; rather he was identifying himself with a particular collective, a *polis*, in which according to its *politeia* (constitution) he was entitled to certain benefits and obligated to fulfill certain responsibilities in and to the larger community. Different constitutions set different qualifications and restrictions on who could claim citizenship and on what their rights and duties might be, but generally these rights and duties were loosely framed around four activities – defense (military service), policy-making (voting), administration (holding office) and resource management (owning land).

To consider drama in relation to the *polis* of Athens is inevitably to raise the question of drama's relationship to *ta politika* ("the affairs of the *polis*"), its politics, its laws, and its political identity. Was drama "political," that is, "about the *polis*"? Did it contribute to the creation of an Athenian identity, or help to define what it meant to be an Athenian *polites*? Was drama a form of mass education, a vehicle for the instruction of the citizens in matters of "good" and "bad" citizenship? Or was it a vehicle for the airing of concerns that could not be given expression in other public forums? The answers to these questions are not mutually exclusive, for as we will see, drama can speak to its spectators on several levels simultaneously. But to address the issues raised by these questions requires that we view the institutionalization of drama from two perspectives, the context of its performance and the content of the plays, for each may be politicized in different ways.

Drama's political context

Aristotle defined drama as the *mimesis* of "people in action," wherein an actor makes us believe that he is someone other than himself, the desire to represent the words, vocal inflections, posture and gestures, first, of someone known to us, and later, of some imagined or imaginary figure. As a form of behavior, "dramatization" may itself be very old. But as an art-form, it certainly does seem to have its beginning at Athens in the sixth century with the establishment by the tyrants of a new festival in honor of Dionysos (the City Dionysia). Because of its pride-of-place as the first dramatic competition formally acknowledged as such in the city, it is with this festival that our study of drama's contextual relationship to the Athenian *polis* begins.

Whether the festival was in fact established by Peisistratos in the 530s or, as is sometimes maintained, in the aftermath of the Kleisthenic reforms ca. 501, we can say that the City Dionysia came into being as an act of political will, that is, by and through the sanction of Athens' political leader(s). Just as today when a government institutes a new statutory holiday, the establishment of a new festival would serve to increase the ruler's popularity among the citizen population, making it a good political move of benefit to all. The very name of festival was also strongly "political." Whether the Dionysia was referred to as the "Great" or the "City," such a name speaks not only of the grandeur of the event but also of the grandeur of the *polis* capable of sponsoring it.

Drama's "political" connections are further seen in the nature of the figure who would govern its annual production. When the festival was established, the official given the responsibility of its planning and execution was not the *archon basileus*, a man traditionally in charge of the religious celebrations in the city, but rather the *archon eponymous*. He was the magistrate after whom the year was named ("in the archonship of . . .") and was selected from among the eligible Athenian citizens of the upper property classes, who traditionally had charge of *civic* affairs. That the administration of the City Dionysia should have been granted to the chief magistrate in charge of matters dealing with *civic* issues clearly locates the festival in a political context.

It may also seem that the initial timing of the festival was set with the interests of the *polis* in view. By late March the sea lanes had once again opened for the sailing season, permitting the tyrant as well as other prosperous Athenian families to play host to many visiting dignitaries and aristocratic friends from "overseas," showcasing their city, promoting its cultural advances and advantages, and perhaps using the occasion to establish potentially lucrative trading connections and alliances for themselves and the city. As we shall see, the ability to travel by sea at this time of year was used to even greater political effect on the opening day of the festival in the years after the defeat of the Persians with the transfer of the Delian League's treasury from Delos to Athens in the mid-450s.

Unfortunately, we are poorly informed about the way the festival was conducted from the time of its inauguration until the mid-fifth century. However, we do know that toward the end of the sixth century, the City Dionysia was reorganized so that the tragic playwrights were now required to produce three tragedies *and* a satyr play, apparently (according to one source) because by that time the dramas produced at the festival had "nothing to do with Dionysos." This might reflect a political concern based in religious belief: if the god were not being properly honored at his own festival, this could have serious negative repercussions for the well-being of the *polis*. Athens may have been seen as particularly vulnerable at this momentous time in its history when the city had just recently overthrown the tyranny and taken its next tentative steps along the road to a democratic government. At the same time, the introduction of a new dramatic genre to the City Dionysia, and one that self-consciously made humorous the traditional values and stories of old, just as Athens was permitting more of its citizen-male populace to participate actively in its political institutions suggests that the festival's reorganization was also undertaken to reflect the new political freedoms enjoyed by the *polis*. So we have protection of the city from one perspective, and celebration of the city from the other, both serving the interests of the *polis* through its control of the medium of drama.

More clearly reflective of "political things" are the mechanics behind the organization of the festival and the events which are noted as taking place in the opening days of the competition. Here is where the idea of "context" of performance most comes into play, for the figures involved and the type of events enacted have far more in common with the city's public face and political interests than with anything we would recognize as "religious."

The festival as we know it from the fifth century was much akin to one of our modern statutory holidays. As we have seen, all legal and administrative business in the city ceased in accordance to law – at least for the opening day's activities – to permit all citizens to attend the celebration. Later we have evidence indicating that even prisoners were given something like our modern "day-pass" so that they too could attend the festival. By the fourth century a "theoric" fund had been established to pay the cost of attendance for those who could not afford the expense. The "political" context is furthered by the fact that the funding of the festival was jointly undertaken by the city treasury and some of her wealthiest citizens. While the city bore the expenses for the sacrifices on 8th and 9th of Elaphebolion, each playwright "granted a chorus" by the archon was assigned to a *choregos*, a prosperous citizen who was responsible for the expenses involved in bringing the playwright's dramas to public performance. Such an expenditure on the part of the well-to-do citizen was considered an integral part of his duty to the *polis*, as important as funding the construction of a warship or providing for the provisioning of its crew for one year, and equally, if not more, costly. For his expense, but only if his playwright won the contest, he would be permitted to erect a monument to his victory within the city of Athens along the road which led into the theater. But whether this man funded the winning playwright or not, if he was (or had aspirations to become) a political leader, his expenditures on the dramatic competitions could be cited with pride as proof of his commitment to the *polis* and of his standing as a good citizen.

One such position of leadership that a man of wealth might seek to obtain was that of general (*strategos*), a position which in the 480s became an elective office and replaced that of the archons in political power and prestige. Athens maintained ten such figures who were annually elected from a list of such eligible citizens. A story by Plutarch (*Kimon* 8.7–9) records that in the year 468, when these generals entered the theater to pour the ritual libations that opened the competition, it was decided that they should remain in the theater to serve as judges for that year's dramatic contests. Normally the judges were selected by lottery, again from a group of eligible citizens, one for each of the ten tribes into which Kleisthenes had divided the people of Attica/Athens at the time of his reforms. The generals too were elected according to the same distribution, one from each tribe, so this last-minute change in the usual procedures did not adversely affect the equality of representation among the tribal groups.

This account belongs to the late first century AD and to some may seem a romantic anecdote, but if true, two things are telling in regards to the political context of this dramatic competition. The first is the fact that the archon retained the power to change the standard procedure at will and apparently while the festival was in progress. Our source notes that because that year's competitors had generated an especially high level of rivalry "*among the spectators*" (it was Sophokles' first appearance at the Dionysia), the archon determined to make the outcome even more significant by having men of such dignity determine the results. This same passage is our source for the information that the generals regularly poured the opening libations. But why should Athens' foremost military leaders be deemed the appropriate figures to open a dramatic competition by performing this service? The answer would seem to rest in the understanding shared by the Athenians of the relationship between contests of words and contests of war. The generals exemplified (in theory, if not always in practice) the ideal citizen male, a man gifted in the arts of speech and excelling in the arts of war, a ready defender of the city in word and action. Having the generals offer the libation to Dionysos Eleuthereus ("freer") carried two messages simultaneously. For the citizens, it reminded them of their present freedoms as well as their obligations to the *polis* as citizens to rise to its defense to preserve them. It also demonstrated to the visitors that they were in a *polis* that valued its freedoms, one which had sacrificed much to win freedom for others, and one still ready and able to defend itself and others against any who would seek to impose their rule upon it.

In the latter half of the fifth century, three other notable events were played out before the assembled mass of citizens and visitors before any competitions took place. First, the levies that Athens had collected for the support of the Delian League were paraded into the theater, talent by talent. While this accumulated wealth was ostensibly to be held in trust and reserved against the possibility of a renewed Persian attack, it was not long before Athens came to view these funds as tribute (*phoros*) and to use them in building projects for the aggrandizement of the city. This display of the yearly monies newly arrived in the city was intended to remind citizen and visitor alike of Athens' military prowess and glory as the *polis* most responsible for the defeat of the last Persian invasion, a point of pride for the city, and justification for its leadership of the Delian League (also known as the *arche*, "empire"). Following this public display of Athenian glory was the announcement of the names and the special honors granted to citizens (and to foreign "friends" of the city) who had provided exemplary service to the Athenian *polis* over the past year. Then came the parading of the young men in full military panoply (provided by the city), whose fathers had died while on military service and who had subsequently been raised to maturity at civic expense. These war orphans were used to send a strong political message to the spectator: Athens is a *polis* of military might, a people who value service to the city and who are prepared to raise up the next generation of warriors who will, in their turn, fight to protect it. Taken in conjunction with the use of the ten generals to pour the ritual libations, these preliminary displays of wealth, exemplary service, and military prowess would have served to remind all present that Athens, like her festival, was "Great."

According to this overview it would be correct to say that much of what transpired at the pre-play ceremonies of the City Dionysia was designed to display the best of the city to the city and its guests. The *polis* made use of this festival to represent itself in a particular way, as a *polis* with a glorious past and a present equally worthy of renown. So a festival which initially seems to have been instituted partly to celebrate the "freeing" of Eleutherai from Boiotia was first reinterpreted and restructured as a celebration of Athens' own freedom from tyranny. By the time we get a reasonably clear view of the festival's full organization in the second half of the fifth century, the freedom now celebrated has become international in scope, for the Athenian *polis* has styled itself as the liberator of Greece from foreign oppression. Seen from this viewpoint, the context of drama at the City Dionysia is thus highly politicized.

To this point our attention has been focused on City Dionysia, primarily because it was the first and great dramatic competition established by the Athenian *polis*. A second reason for this focus is quite simply the comparative lack of evidence for the companion dramatic festival, the Lenaia. The festival itself is one of great antiquity, organized under the administration of the *archon basileus*, the traditional religious magistrate. But it would seem that its activities were not politicized to the same degree as the Great Dionysia until the 440s when it became a recognized competitive venue, first for comedies, and then for tragedies.

It is quite possible that the presentation of humorous skits and perhaps even longer "scripted" comedies had been a part of this festival from its earliest times. Certainly "jokes from the wagons," insults directed by the performers at the spectators, are recorded as being part of the early celebration of the Lenaia. Being able to laugh at oneself and at others with others is a liberating and unifying experience. If the expectation of the festival was that people were free to "insult" other people, even when some serious issues lay beneath the comments made, they did not need to be taken seriously, because of the context of the festival. Thus, having an event at which the city's residents were permitted to express their dissatisfaction in the form of insults actually worked to ensure the relative stability of the city. During this period of "sacred time" when social niceties could be laid aside and the traditional deference for one's social superiors ignored, tensions among and between the city's residents could be alleviated through their airing in ritualized and controllable ways. This returns us to the idea that community-wide religious festivals contribute to the preservation and prosperity of the *polis*, first by venerating a god who might otherwise withdraw his benefits from the community, and second by bringing the community together in a "sacred time" during which they can reaffirm their collective identity, even if, as at the Lenaia, this meant laughing at themselves. However, it was only when the city granted the Lenaia the status of a competition, awarded prizes, and kept a record of the yearly winners that we can speak of its relationship to the politics of the Athenian *polis* in the same way as we have done for the Dionysia.

Notably, even after it was made a competitive venue, the Lenaia remained a festival closed to outsiders. Things said and done at this contest were apparently only for the eyes and ears of residents of the town of Athens, but this may be due to the season when few visitors would have been able to travel by sea. It differed markedly from the City Dionysia in that metics (resident aliens, i.e., non-citizens with limited rights and obligations in the city) were allowed to participate fully both as performers and as *choregoi*. Granting this right seems to have satisfied two needs of importance to the *polis*. First, it gave a potentially troublesome group of outsiders within the city a sense of belonging denied them in other areas and so reduced the threat that dissatisfaction among them might cause to the city's stability. Aristophanes with magnanimity (and some condescension) pronounces (*Acharnians* 504–8):

> We are here by ourselves, the contest is that at the Lenaia, foreigners are not yet here. The tribute is not coming, nor allies from the cities. Here we are then, clean-hulled (so to speak), for I consider the metics to be the bran of our population.

Second, it served to reinforce the Athenians' view of themselves as an open and inclusive society. So while the Lenaia had already served some important needs of the *polis* before becoming a competitive venue, after the contests for comedy had been granted civic recognition, it became possible for some metics to aspire to win a share in the renown for service to the *polis* that was formerly only available to full citizens. In this context, the Lenaia too was politicized.

In terms of the differences in the context of dramatic productions between these two festivals, we may draw the following conclusions. Both venues were used by the city of Athens as a *polis* to promote Athenian identity, political unity, and shared ideals about citizenship. However, the City Dionysia, early in the fifth century, if not before, was used to showcase its superiority as a *polis* to all, as a center for the arts, as a military might, and as a beneficent world leader. The Lenaia, by contrast, was more inward-focused, more concerned with maintaining the unity and stability of the *polis*, which was then showcased to the world at the City Dionysia.

Drama's political content

This brings us then to a consideration of the relationship of drama's content to the *polis*. The evidence can be assessed along two somewhat different lines: the degree to which the dramas are reflective of the political (and social) institutions of the *polis*; and the degree to which tragedy and comedy engage with current political issues. Again, these matters are not necessarily mutually exclusive.

To begin with the first issue, we can state that many of the structural aspects of tragic and comic drama would seem to owe their form to preexisting institutions of the *polis* – its law courts, assemblies, and councils. In its law courts, prosecution and defense were more akin to competitors in a contest (*agon*), who must convince as many people as possible of the "rightness" or "justice" of their position. Similarly, in both the assembly and the council, where the number of competing voices might be many, men would propose a course of action, entertain counter-proposals, debate their individual merits, and otherwise engage each other in matters of importance to the city, ultimately voting to accept or reject a proposition as "right" or "not right" for the *polis* respectively. In all these institutions, determining the right or "just" course of action, the right outcome in a matter, was their aim and the procedure was akin to a contest.

Contests of words had long been a part of Greek political practice, as evidenced in the epic tales of the *Iliad* and *Odyssey*, while the responsibility for those in positions of power to govern well and choose rightly was divinely mandated by Zeus (as at Hesiod *Works and Days* 225–47). The decision-making process had also long been established as a collective one. In the leaders' council of the *Iliad* (9.9–79), any member was free to put forward a proposal which the council would either endorse or reject as seemed proper. It is not surprising, then, that when the idea of dramatic enactment came into being, it was with one man standing forth from a group and addressing himself to them.

The extant dramatic texts, both tragic and comic, reveal their indebtedness to these political institutions in the way they employ argument and counter-argument, leading to a decision to move their plots forward. The Athenian audience, familiar with this sequence of events through their participation in the city's assembly, council, and courts, would have been encouraged through this familiarity to listen and judge the matter of the drama in the same manner as they would at those other venues. But there was one crucial difference. The dramas that they witnessed revealed the outcome of the decision made, permitting the audience to reevaluate the "rightness" of the course of action taken, turning tragic drama into a type of teaching tool for the hazards of ill-informed, emotional, and short-sighted decision-making and comic drama into a farcical lesson in political incorrectness.

By employing the same form of debate as would be heard in the venerable political institutions of the city, drama puts the city's decision-making processes on display. But there were other institutions that also served as a frame of reference for the content of drama, politicized social institutions governing marriage and inheritance, interstate relationships and treaties, the guest–host obligations of *xenia*, among others, each based on long-established norms of reciprocity and an ethical imperative that demanded that one "help one's friends and harm one's enemies." It is here that the merit of these long-standing socio-political institutions becomes the subject of debate in the dramas and we slide from political institutions in drama to a discussion of political issues in dramatic content.

For comedy there can be little argument that its content is political. Not curtailed by known myths, story-lines, and characters, comic drama was free to present a humorous look at issues of topical interest to the *polis* as well as to shape its characters around well- and lesser-known persons in the Athenian political arena, if it wished to do so. Many did so choose, especially in the latter part of the fifth century. In the extant plays of Aristophanes we encounter the names of politicians, philosophers, businessmen, and other poets. Some are applauded for their contribution to the *polis*, but most become the butt of jokes aimed at various aspects of their personal and public lives and especially at their policies. Kleon, the "demagogue" who succeeded Perikles in the leadership of the Athenians, is a favorite target of Aristophanes. But he is in good company with other famous names such as Euripides, Aeschylus, and Sokrates. At the heart of much of this ridicule is a perceived failure on the part of the named figure to serve the *polis*, to be a good citizen. For instance, a politician named Kleonymos is characterized as a coward, for allegedly throwing his shield away in battle, and thus one who has failed in his duty to defend the city as every good citizen is obliged to do. Euripides and Sokrates are presented as men who encourage the undermining of civic values, and thus as failures in their obligation to the city to set good examples for the youths or to be good teachers. In the 420s the strongest critique is reserved for Kleon whose activities as the "leader of the people" are reinterpreted as vulgar and self-serving. He exploits the jury system to indict his political opponents, using jury-pay to keep the jurors "in his back pocket" (*Wasps*); or, he is a corrupt overseer of the Athenian civic household, bent on personal gain at the people's expense (*Knights*). When Kleon dies in 422/1, other demagogues, like Hyperbolos and Kleophon, become the more frequent targets of Aristophanes' humor. But behind each man so ridiculed in comedy would seem to be a strong critique of the current state of the city's institutions, policies, and citizenry, of the injustices that the system permits and that the people tolerate or even bring on themselves.

From the little that remains of Aristophanes' rivals, Eupolis and Kratinos, it would seem that they too produced plays in a similar vein, although Kratinos is recorded as also producing a comedy on mythological themes, the *Dionysalexandros*, apparently a parody of the "Judgment of Paris" myth, with Dionysos replacing Paris as the figure who must judge the infamous beauty-pageant of the three goddesses. While ostensibly a mythological burlesque, the hypothesis ("plot summary") reveals that "in the drama Perikles was very convincingly made fun of through innuendo for having brought the war on for the Athenians."

To many modern critics the political content of tragedy is equally evident. In both its themes and its language, tragedy can be seen to be an extension of the political debates carried on in the law courts, assemblies, and councils of contemporary Athens, where its citizens were continually redefining themselves and their city through the enactment of new laws or the introduction of new policies that altered to a greater or lesser degree the social institutions that we identified as the subject of debate in drama. Like comedy, tragedy takes the institutions of the city as its point of reference, but these are embedded in a framework of myth, in stories peopled with the great names of tradition, Agamemnon, Odysseus, Oedipus, Theseus, and the like. On the surface, then, it is more difficult for tragedy to be as blatantly topical as comedy, but this does not prevent it from addressing questions of political import for the *polis*.

A few tragic dramas are more transparently topical, or contain sections that make topical allusions, despite the fact that the majority are ostensibly set in the distant past. In the early days of the fifth century, it seems that it was even acceptable to make recent history the subject of tragedy, as in Aeschylus' *Persians* (472), which describes the victory in 480 of Athens and her allies over the Persians from the Persian perspective. We also hear, however, that when Phrynichos (career: 510–470) decided to stage an historical tragedy entitled *Capture of Miletos* (493 or 492), he was assessed a heavy financial fine and this subject was forbidden to be dramatized again. Apparently, the *polis* did not appreciate being reminded of its failure to successfully aid the Milesians in their recent time of need.

Aeschylus' *Oresteia* (458) provides one of the most frequently used examples of a drama which transparently makes allusions to the city's current events, especially in the concluding play of the trilogy, *Eumenides*, while its actions and characters remain located in the mythical past. Produced just three years after the important reforms to the Areopagus council's (462/1) composition and duties, Aeschylus boldly represents the "original" creation of this very council in this play. Athene, the city's patron goddess, selects the "finest of [her] citizens" (line 487) to sit as jurors in the trial of Orestes for murder. The court proceedings themselves closely mirror the actual process as it was conducted at Athens, from the initial "discovery" that Athene undertakes with the disputants, through to the trial's conclusion.

Earlier in this same play (289–91), Orestes is shown offering a pledge that would bind Argos in eternal friendship to Athens, which he later reiterates at greater length in the form of an oath in response to his acquittal on the charge of murder (762–74). Athens and Argos had a few years earlier concluded a treaty that bound them together as allies. On one level, then, historical reality is backdated and justified by a reworking of myth in the context of drama. Argos is presented as a metaphorical "lost sheep" who has finally returned to the fold, its former alliance with Sparta to be excused, since its debt to Athens, because of Orestes' acquittal, has finally been honored. All is now as it was intended to be from ancient times.

Other tragedians have also been seen to bring contemporary issues before the audience in the guise of old myths. Sophokles' *Antigone* and, to a lesser degree, his *Ajax* are both seen to offer comment on a state's right to impose restrictions on funerary ritual, even going so far as to question the justice of the state's ability to deny the right of burial to someone thought to have been a traitor. Euripides' *Trojan Women* has frequently been read as a critique of Athens' inhumane treatment of the citizens of Melos in 416 or alternately as a reaction to the war-fever that was driving the city to launch its massive armada against Sicily. The opening of Sophokles' *Oedipus Tyrannos* with the city of Thebes in the midst of plague has been taken as a reference to the plague that devastated Athens in the opening years of the Peloponnesian war and used to assist in the dating of this play. However, while the playwrights may well have been affected, influenced, or inspired by contemporary events to select a particular myth with which to work, hunting for allusions to these events in every extant tragedy is not a particularly productive task.

Evidence of the relationship between the Athenian *polis* and tragic drama can more fruitfully be found in the study of the plays' engagement with the justness of various decisions and outcomes enacted in the dramas. The general theme of justice (*dike*) is perhaps the most common of themes across all three playwrights. It underlies every surviving play to a greater or lesser degree. For almost every situation upon which a tragedy is constructed, asking "where does justice lie in this situation?" can be an appropriate question. This question is raised by such plays as Euripides' *Medea* and *Andromache,* for instance, or Sophokles' *Ajax,* and Aeschylus' *Agamemnon* in relation to the bonds of marriage and the responsibility of parents to children. Also in *Ajax* and Sophokles' *Philoktetes* and *Antigone* as well as Euripides' *Orestes, Hecuba,* and *Suppliant Women,* to name only three, the justice of the Greek ethical imperative to "help friends and harm enemies" is rendered problematic for it bleeds over into the institution of *xenia* (the guest–host relationship), which has the potential to pit the needs and obligations to friend and family against those of the community-at-large. This in turn leads to the larger political question concerning the demands over which socio-political institutions should take precedence in a given situation. While these problems are presented in the familiar story-line of myth, they can be easily extrapolated to apply to matters of importance to the contemporary audience where these same socio-political institutions give expression to civic values and shape modes of behavior deemed appropriate for a citizen. But the assessment of how well or poorly one treats one's friends is determined by how one's friends are defined. The assessment of whether one is legally married or one's children legal citizens is determined by the laws of the city. For the citizen in any *polis* personal decisions have political implications and consequences, which tragic drama exploits to great effect, providing a basis on which to assess the justness of the contrary demands placed on the individual and so to reassess and make adjustments to the definitions and demands that are the source of problems in the city.

Drama and democracy

Tragedy, then, has a great deal in it that we would identify as political content. But to what degree can this content be called primarily or essentially "democratic" in orientation rather than "about the *polis*" in more general terms? Tragic drama was traditionally instituted in the Athenian *polis* under the tyranny of Peisistratos, and by 486, after the tyrant's overthrow and the first democratic reforms had been established, comedy, too, had its place in dramatic competitions of the City Dionysia. Our textual evidence for drama in terms of its complete texts all comes from a period when Athens was a democracy, and this evidence strongly suggests that drama was deeply engaged in the concerns of a democratic *polis* in which there was great pride. Particularly notable in this regard are the twin principles of *isonomia* ("equality before the law") and *parrhesia* ("freedom to speak") on which democracy was founded, as they are represented in the tragedies.

Despite Hecuba's belief in the culpability of Helen, she insists that Menelaos at least listen to her argument in defense of her actions (*Trojan Women* 906–10). Elektra, in Sophokles' play of that name, on the other hand, suggests that Aigisthos should be denied the right to speak before his execution, for there is nothing he could say that would alter her hatred of him (1484–90). When, in Aeschylus' *Suppliants*, Pelasgos is faced with the difficult decision of deciding whether to accept and thus defend his distant relatives, the Danaids, he insists (365–9) that even though he is king, he must put the matter before the people, an anachronistic projection of democratic practice into the mythical past of Argos. Similarly, Euripides anachronistically has Tyndareos suggest that Orestes could have had his mother prosecuted for the murder of his father rather than dispatching her himself (*Orestes* 492–5), while later in this same play Orestes' guilt is debated in assembly, where even a lowly farmer is permitted to offer his opinion on the matter and propose an appropriate course of action (917–30). The benefits of citizenship in a democratic *polis* are more directly highlighted in a debate between Theseus, Athens' legendary king, with a Theban herald who supports monarchy (*Suppliant Women* 395–510). The examples could be multiplied.

More telling though is the manner is which drama itself is granted the freedom to question and criticize the values and socio-political institutions of the Athenian *polis* in the guise of the mythological reenactments of tragedy and the farcical representations of contemporary civic life in comedy. We do not know whether this challenging of normally unquestioned values and practices was always part of tragic drama at the City Dionysia. But we might suspect it was, given that the City Dionysia, like the Lenaia, was also a period of "sacred time" in which liberties not normally granted to citizens were made available. Part of the reason why tragedy in the fifth century had the liberty to address political issues in the form it did, may be located in the fact that the festival took Dionysos Eleuthereus as its patron.

Under democracy more citizens had been released to participate in the affairs of the city than under any other previous form of administration. But this freedom seems to have generated some perhaps unexpected problems. In Athens in the fifth century, the city's decision-makers and leaders were, in principle if not in fact, the people. Ever since Homer and Hesiod, it had been a taken-for-granted assumption that those in positions of power had an obligation to honor the gods, which by extension meant to honor the law of the *polis*, often presented as divinely inspired. The problem with these divinely inspired laws and the socio-political institutions which they supported was that they were an inheritance from a period of aristocratic rule and in many cases ill-suited to the emerging ideals of a democratic *polis*. Couched in the equally traditional and aristocratic myths of the past in the case of tragedy (and also some comedies), or in the humorous fantasies of comedy, drama became the vehicle through which the city could celebrate its freedoms while it simultaneously challenged and interrogated some of its most cherished ideals.

2

Greek Tragedy

"Tragedy" must be one of the most over-used (and misused) words in modern culture. Open the newspaper, watch the news on television, or listen to reports on the radio, and one hears constantly of "a tragedy," on the roads, in the skies, in a house fire, or in the deserts of Africa. Why not use words with lesser emotive force: "accident" or "misfortune"? Or what does "tragedy" imply that more high-powered terms such as "disaster" and "catastrophe" do not?

In today's terms, "tragedy" involves a loss of life, either immediately or eventually. It is more than just bitter human suffering; it is the death of those involved, usually at the hands of other human beings or the forces of nature. The tragedy is properly that of the victims, and while the perpetrator (if any) may be brought to justice, we do not today speak of the "tragedy of Macbeth," as it was dramatized by Shakespeare. But not all death is "tragic" to us. Most would call a four-year-old, who wanders into a neighbor's yard and drowns in an uncovered pool, a tragic victim, but not an octogenarian, who passes away after a short illness. There needs to be something more than mere loss of life in the modern view of "tragedy." A quick answer is "waste," and coupled with that waste an immense sadness or grief from the point of view of the spectator. A tragedy today is something overwhelming and something unnecessary; it need not have happened, someone or something could have averted it, someone is to blame. This gets us close to a linear plot: if the neighbor had closed the gate or covered the pool, if the parent or child-minder had been watching, then the "tragedy" might not have happened. "Ifs" make for a good plot-line, and for tragedy, as Aristotle maintains, "plot" (*mythos*) is king.

Not all deaths and the stories that go with them need be "tragic." Tragedy today does not deal with the sordid or the everyday, except perhaps in the larger sense where the starvation of a people in Ethiopia can be described as "tragic." Would the death by overdose of a drug addict in a back alley be "tragic"? Perhaps, if the details revealed a fall from a higher station, accompanied by significant "dramatic" events. Tragedy for us, as it did for the Greeks, tends to raise larger issues about humanity and about nature (or the divine), and the place of human beings in that larger scheme. Thus in modern parlance "tragedy" implies death and destruction, in an unexpected and unnecessary fashion, with a perceptible "dramatic" line of events, and an over-whelming accompaniment of grief and sorrow, not just for those involved directly, but anyone who reads or watches the story.

We must prune some of these implications of the modern sense of "tragedy" when we come to the study and appreciation of Greek drama. While many of the plays do end with the deaths or devastation of the characters in the story – and here one thinks quickly of Aeschylus' *Agamemnon*, *Libation-Bearers*, and *Seven*; Sophokles' *Ajax*, *Antigone* or *Trachinian Women*; Euripides' *Medea*, *Bacchae*, *Herakles*, *Hecuba*, *Phoenician Women*, *Iphigeneia at Aulis* – other plays do not end in so destructive a fashion (e.g., Sophokles' *Oedipus Tyrannos* with blindness and exile, and his *Oedipus at Kolonos*, where Oedipus' passing is a relief). In several instances the plays end with catastrophe averted, with what can only be described as a canonical "happy ending" – here see Aeschylus' *Eumenides*; Sophokles' *Philoktetes*; Euripides' *Andromache*, *Ion*, *Helen*, *Orestes*, *Iphigeneia among the Taurians*. Yet the ancients would have called these "tragedies." A Greek tragedy does not have to end in sorrow and destruction, although Aristotle will maintain that this is the best sort of plot-line for a tragedy to possess.

But in Greek tragedies characters are not struck down out of the blue; there is a tragic pattern of events, sometimes that of crime and punishment, sometimes the direct work of the gods, but events happen in a manner that for all the sorrow seems appropriate somehow. Aristotle makes it clear that the stories of tragedy belong to the great families ("those with great reputation and prosperity"), principally so that their fall into misfortune might be more dramatic, but even with Euripides, who treated the traditional myths with considerable realism and a descent to the mundane, we are not dealing with stories of everyday life and characters. Tragedy is about something with grandeur and distance. Aristotle puts it well in *Poetics* (chapter 6), when he asserts that tragedy is "the representation (*mimesis*) of a serious action." The Greek for "serious" is *spoudaios*, something that one must pay attention to and treat with respect. Thus a tragedy may end happily, and disaster may be averted, but the potential for disaster remains, and most importantly serious issues of some magnitude will be part of the story.

"Goat-song"

The Greek for "tragedy" is *tragoidia*, which breaks down etymologically to *tragos* ("goat") and *ode* ("song"). But in the classical period the regular term in use was not the singular noun, *tragoidia* ("tragedy"), but the personal plural *tragoidoi* ("the tragic singers"). In either case we have no problem with the second part ("song"), since the songs ("odes") of the chorus, which in Aeschylus can comprise half the drama, are sung formally in lyric meters and, as we shall see, the genre is traditionally derived from those who sang and danced for Dionysos. But what have goats to do with tragedy? Ancient (and modern) scholars have considered a range of possibilities. One explains the derivation that a goat was the original prize for the tragic competition,

and hence tragedy is "song for the goat" (or *tragoidoi*, "singers for the goat"). Alternatively, the fact that Dionysos is accompanied by goat-men ("satyrs"), combined with
Aristotle's pronouncement that "tragedy originated from something rather satyric"
(*Poetics* 1449a20), led others to conclude that tragedy was so named from these original performers – tragedy is thus "song of the goat(s)" and *tragoidoi* "the goat-singers."
The more recent thesis of Seaford and others has come to dominate the field, that
"tragedy" developed out of a choral performance at the sacrifice of a goat – tragedy
thus becoming "song at the goat." More radically, Winkler proposed that the choruses
in Athenian tragedy were composed of the *epheboi*, young men aged eighteen and
nineteen, going through their formal state-service as part of their rite of passage. Part
of this service, he argues, was to serve as the *choreutai* in the dramatic festivals. He
suggests that *tragos* ("goat") was a colloquial term for boys going through puberty, in
terms of a breaking voice, the smell and lewd behavior of an adolescent male. We
might compare our use of "kids" as the colloquial equivalent of "children." On
Winkler's interpretation the *tragoidia* is again "song of the goat(s)," but in a metaphorical sense.

Winkler's theory is not without its attractions, and certainly young men could
handle the physical effort involved in participating in four dramatic performances in
a single day. Regimen and discipline would apply to ephebic service and choral training alike, again appropriate for these cadets. The problem with this is that these
ephebes would have to have been part of the dramatic choruses from the very origins
of tragedy in order that this nickname be applied to the genre as a whole, and why
name these performers with a colloquial expression? And would a dramatic career in
the chorus last only two years? Would a producer not want talented performers to
continue a lifelong career? The explanation that early tragedians competed for a goat
sounds suspiciously like an ancient commentator trying to explain the etymology of
tragoidoi ("goat-singers"), and it is only later in Greek tradition that satyrs become
"goat-men"; in the archaic and classical age, they are more horse than goat. On
balance the explanation that tragedy is the product of "songs at the goat-sacrifice"
seems the safest at the moment.

The ancient evidence for the early history of tragedy begins with a comment by
Herodotos (5.67.5) that the sufferings of Adrastos, legendary king of Sikyon, were
celebrated there by "tragic choruses," which were transferred by Kleisthenes of Sikyon
to the cult of Dionysos. Kleisthenes was active in the second quarter of the sixth
century, and if these choruses were in fact then called "tragic," they would predate
the introduction of tragedy at Athens by some few decades. We should note two things
about these "tragedies" of Sikyon: (i) that they were songs of sufferings, and (ii) that
they were not at first connected with Dionysos. Herodotos (1.23) also mentions a poet
called Arion (*floruit* ca. 600 and active at Corinth) for his role in turning the primitive
dithyramb (see below) into something more polished and substantial. A much later
source attributes to Solon (Athenian law-giver and poet, active 596–570) the statement
that Arion created "the first tragic drama." Thus the first pieces of evidence reveal
some sort of choral performance that the ancients could, perhaps with the benefit of
hindsight, call "tragedy," that came from outside Athens and was earlier than tragedy
at Athens.

The most influential source for the early history of tragedy is Aristotle in his *Poetics* (chapters 2–5), who makes a number of statements about the development of drama, although with Aristotle there is the ever-present question of whether he knows what he is talking about. Aristotle seems to give conflicting accounts of early tragedy. First is his well-known statement that tragedy arose "from those who led off the dithyramb" (1449a10–1). It is worth quoting in full Aristotle's words here, since it does give us an insight into how he was approaching the subject:

> [tragedy] *coming from an origin in improvisation – and also comedy, the former from those who led off* (exarchonton) *the dithyrambs, and the latter from those* [who led off] *the phallic performances, which still even today remain a custom in many cities – grew little by little as they developed whatever they noticed in it, and after undergoing many changes it stopped [growing] when it had attained its own form.*

Tragedy here is like a growing plant or creature, which reaches its mature form and then stops changing.

The dithyramb was a large-scale choral song and in the fifth century was performed as part of the City Dionysia. Competitions for ten men's and ten boys' choirs of fifty voices each occupied the first day of the festival, and are still recorded as late as the 320s. If tragedy did, as Aristotle suggests, develop out of the dithyramb, then the parent art-form did not pass away or evolve into its child, but remained a living, breathing, developing genre of poetry, whose later practitioners were prominent enough to attract the attention of comedy. The ancient pieces of evidence suggested a neat pattern: the attribution of the dithyramb to Dionysos by Archilochos in the seventh century:

> *For I know how to lead off* [exarxai] *the fair song of Lord Dionysos,*
> *when my wits are thunderblasted with wine,*

the use of the same word *exarchein* ("lead off") in both Archilochos and Aristotle, the association of Arion with both tragedy and dithyramb, and the contests for dithyramb along with tragedy at the City Dionysia.

But immediately after this Aristotle, commenting on the grandeur of tragedy (or perhaps on its length), adds:

> *Then there is grandeur. From slight plot-lines and ridiculous language tragedy was late in becoming dignified, developing as it did from something rather satyric.*

Unless we want to see early dithyramb as something ludicrous performed by men in the guise of satyrs, Aristotle seems to be saying something different here, that tragedy evolved from some sort of primitive performance with men dressed up as satyrs. Finally, just before the passage on tragedy and dithyramb, Aristotle has elaborated upon his earlier distinction of poetic subjects into the serious and the ridiculous by saying:

> *When tragedy and comedy appeared, the poets turned to each sort of poetry according to their own nature, becoming poets of comedy instead of iambic, and creators of tragedy instead of epic.*

In other words the development of tragedy is a literary one, with its ultimate roots in the serious epics of Homer (*Iliad* and *Odyssey*).

It is worth keeping in mind that tragedy was a conscious literary creation, one that may have developed out of some sort of choral performance combined with the themes of epic, but at some point in the mid-sixth century somebody got the idea of enacting the stories of myth before a public audience, rather than just singing about them. The term *exarchon* implies a leader of the chorus, and it may be the case that in the dithyramb or other choral song a dialogue had developed between leaders and full chorus, and from that dialogue drama could have developed as the leader took individual roles in the narration. We see something rather like this in Bacchylides 18, in which a single singer (Aigeus, king of Athens) and a chorus describe the approach of Theseus to Athens. But Bacchylides' poem belongs to the early fifth century, almost two generations after the introduction of tragedy, and we cannot regard his eighteenth ode as a sort of "missing link" in the development of that genre. But it is not impossible that proto-tragedy was something like what we see in Bacchylides.

What sort of choral performance might have given rise to tragedy? The dithyramb, with its possible associations to Dionysos, would be a strong contender, but these performers were not masked. Masks *are* found in religious ritual, and it might have been one of these that gave rise to tragedy – for comedy the worship of Artemis at Sparta involved masked figures behaving in comic fashion. Alternatively the mysteries of Eleusis featured a performance of sorts to a large (indoor) audience, where "things were said, things were done, and things were shown." The search of Demeter for her abducted daughter is drama of a sort, and we might wonder whether tragedy sprang from an enactment of such a cult myth. Perhaps all we can say is that tragedy was the product of an evolution in choral performance: from the group retelling of a myth in song, through a dialogue between leader and chorus, to the point where the leader became an independent performer, doing rather than telling the story, and at that point serious drama was born.

The ancient sources attribute the "invention" of tragedy to a shadowy figure, Thespis, whose first official production is dated to the year 535/4. In particular he is credited with developing dramatic features that belong to the province of the actor: prologues and speeches to the chorus. Whatever the historical truth about Thespis, he marks that point where choral performance gave way to drama, where the actor became a separate entity from the chorus, a process which would lead ultimately to the prominence of the individual and the decline and disappearance of the chorus. A few titles are assigned to Thespis, including a *Pentheus*, the antagonist of Dionysos in Euripides' *Bacchae*; this may or may not be significant for the association of drama with Dionysos at Athens.

Of rather more interest is the date. If the traditional date of 534 is correct, then tragedy becomes the creation of the Athenian tyranny under Peisistratos (546–527) and his son Hippias (527–510). The Athenian tyranny was, apart from its last four years, anything but "tyrannical." In fact the tyrants were responsible for much of the economic, political, and cultural rise of Athens, the latter including the first splendid buildings and sculpture on the Acropolis, the contests for the recitation of Homer, the competitions at the great festival of Athena (the Panathenaia), and the invitations to artists and poets to visit the court at Athens, including the preeminent poets, Lasos, Simonides, and the great Anakreon. A date of 534 for tragedy makes this one of the cultural achievements of the tyrants, one whose effects would be felt for centuries after.

But more recent critics have wanted to downdate the introduction of tragedy to the very late sixth century (502 or 501), when drama first began to be performed on the south-east slopes of the Acropolis, when the ancient records of the dramatic festivals seem to have begun, and when we start to get details about other writers of drama (Phrynichos, Pratinas). Some find an introduction of tragedy in 534 and then twenty-five years of relative inactivity rather too long. Others want tragedy to be the child of the new democracy established in 507, and point to the cult title of Dionysos Eleuthereus ("Freer"). Now this title is related in part to the movement of a cult of Dionysos from Eleutherai on the outskirts of Attica to Athens, and in part to the liberating aspects of the god. But Dionysos Eleuthereus could also be seen as the "patron god" of the new democracy, which was now "free" of tyrants. Those who take this line tend to see a political purpose in tragedy, one that directly relates the genre of drama to the experience of democratic Athens. On this interpretation Thespis becomes a figure of legend from a period before the formal establishment of tragedy. It is possible to consider a combination of these explanations: the introduction of tragedy under the tyrants in 534 (to which we may attach the name of Thespis and which may have had only a minimal association with Dionysos) and then a thorough-going revision of the festival ca. 500, perhaps in the glow of the new democracy. It may have been only at this time, when the theater was physically relocated to the south-east slope, that drama acquired its connection with Dionysos.

On the Nature of Greek Tragedy

We may begin by considering two concise descriptions of tragedy, one ancient, one modern. First, in *Poetics* chapter 6 Aristotle provides his formal definition of tragedy, in terms that do not readily explain themselves and about which there is great debate:

> *Tragedy is the representation* [mimesis] *of a serious and complete set of events* [praxis], *having a certain size, with embellished language used distinctly in the various parts of the play, the representation being accomplished by people performing and not by narration, and through pity and fear achieving the* katharsis *of such emotions.*

By "embellished language" Aristotle means that in the episodes the poet employs spoken verse and presumably the high style, and in the songs sung lyrics. What "the *katharsis* of pity and fear" means is hotly contested: perhaps the ridding ("purging") of these "tragic" emotions by the on-stage spectacle (but this would imply that emotions are something undesirable that need to be purged; Plato might agree but not Aristotle), alternatively the draining of excess emotion (*katharsis* in Greek means more properly "purification") – one's emotional situation is better off after proper exercise and tragedy helps achieve the proper balance. Elsewhere (*Politics* 1341a17) Aristotle uses the same term, *katharsis*, to describe the result of treating emotional excess (pity, fear, *enthousiasmos*) by homeopathic means. Tragedy is the way to restore a balance of pity and fear in the soul. Much of what Aristotle is doing in *Poetics* is to counter Plato's dismissal of poetry in *Republic* (2, 3, 10) and to find a justification for it. For Aristotle then, tragedy is a poetic representation of a serious pattern of events that creates a strong emotional response in its audience.

The noted classical scholar Wilamowitz* provides a modern definition of tragedy:

> An Attic tragedy is a self-contained piece of heroic legend, poetically reworked in elevated style for dramatic presentation by a chorus of Attic citizens and two or three actors as part of public worship in the sanctuary of Dionysus.

We may want to quarrel with the phrase "public worship" and perhaps substitute "popular entertainment," and to wish that Wilamowitz had expanded upon "heroic" to embrace something like Aristotle's "serious" and the emotional power of tragedy. But essentially he has brought to the fore the central aspects of a Greek tragedy. Tragedy is poetical rather than prosaic, performance rather than narration, a self-contained pattern of events, usually concerning the characters and themes from traditional myth, which was intended to arouse an emotional and aesthetic response from a massed audience.

Greek tragedy is not realistic drama. Taplin (1978: 9) has spoken well of its stage conventions as "theater of the mind." For all that the word "drama" implies "doing" or "acting" in Greek, not much happens visibly in a Greek tragedy. The "doings" are done off-stage: murders, suicides (apart from that of Ajax), accidents, debates, rescues. The setting is usually fixed in place and anchored by the chorus. Thus Greek tragedy does not have the mobility of Shakespearian tragedy, where the setting can go from a blasted heath to a castle interior, from streets of Rome to a battlefield at Philippi. What we see are scenes strung along a connecting cord. The action has to come to the central nexus before the spectators. Changes of setting are rare. This is perhaps why *Eumenides* is so breathtaking a tragedy, with three different settings and a theater empty of the chorus at line 234.

Props and stage-effects are also rare. The *ekkyklema* did bring interior scenes to the larger view, such as the tableaux of murderer and victims in *Oresteia*, and the *mechane* allowed for aerial appearances. Sophokles is credited with first employing *skenographia* ("scene-painting"), but this must have been fairly basic and may not even have been changed from play to play. But when an object or a stage property is used, it acquires great significance in both the plot-line and in the larger thematic reading of the tragedy. The purple-red carpet in *Agamemnon* that Klytaimestra persuades her husband to walk

---

*   U. von Wilamowitz-Moellendorff, *Euripides Herakles* (Berlin 1889) 108.

is more than just a sign of her power over him and all males. It is the color of dried blood – Agamemnon walks to his doom on the blood of his victims – and it leads him and the spectators to the open and ominous central door, which will dominate the first two plays. In the third play the Furies, now Eumenides ("Kindly Ones"), will put on new robes of the same purple-red color, no longer sinister but possessing the overtones of majesty. In Sophokles' *Philoktetes* Odysseus and Neoptolemos are intent on retrieving the bow of Herakles, which will be the focus of the attention of all, as it passes back and forth, mirroring the potential movement of the characters from the island to Troy or to Greece. In Euripides we can cite from *Hippolytos* the suicide note attached to Phaidra's wrist, symbolic of the dominant theme of failed communication, or the *thyrsoi* (the wands of power) in *Bacchae*. When tragedy wants to use an object or a "special effect," we should pay attention.

This is verse drama, familiar in the English theater, of course, from the iambic pentameter of Shakespeare, and the dominant iambic trimeter of Greek tragedy is often taken as something equivalent. But there is a choral element in Greek tragedy, which is far greater than the occasional song in Shakespeare. At times the choral songs (*mele*) rival the iambic episodes in both length and importance, and at their best are far more than interludes, especially in Aeschylus (*Prometheus* excepted) and in Euripides' *Trojan Women* and *Bacchae*, where the chorus is integral to the drama. Perhaps we should look to parallels such as grand opera, where the combination of recitative and aria corresponds to some degree to the episodes and songs of tragedy, or the modern musical, where, like tragedy, the grand numbers can be fundamental to the story or essentially digressive. The choral songs were written and performed in an artificial dialect, a form of literary Doric, taken over from the earlier tradition of Greek lyrics. Written in something other than the Attic of the streets and countryside, to the spectator's ear these songs would sound different and detached. They were formal and artificial, just as the language and music of nineteenth-century hymn tunes is something apart from the vocabulary and rhythms of normal speech.

To watch tragedy was similarly to look at something formal and "different." The Pronomos vase of the late fifth century shows us actors in tragic dress, long and ornately decorated robes, far unlike the simplicity of normal Attic dress – the Athenians of the fifth century prided themselves on simplicity; decoration or jewelry was a sign of aristocratic pretension, Ionian luxury, or Eastern decadence. The actors wore a distinctive soft shoe (*kothornos*), able to be worn on either foot, hence a joke at a contemporary politician, Theramenes nicknamed "Kothornos," who had the ability to come down on either side of an issue. The *kothornos* was not, as sometimes assumed in earlier texts, an elevated shoe, designed to increase the actor's height and domination of the scene. It was a stereotypical part of tragedy, and was something different from the usual footwear of an Athenian male. And then there is the mask, which played down the character of the individual personality and played up the role that the actor was portraying. The spectators were not looking at familiar people in the *theatron*, but rather men and men playing women who were visibly different. It was a different world that was unfolding before them. Even in *Persians*, where contemporary people and events form the tragedy, they are assimilated into the world of myth.

The Greek tragic poets did not take their themes and characters from the contemporary society, but from an age of heroes in their long distant past. If we had to date the events at Thebes or the Trojan War or characters such as Agamemnon or Theseus, we would place them historically in the late Bronze Age (roughly 1500–1100), an age of a splendid palace-centered civilization, whose remains can be seen at Pylos or Mycenae on the Greek mainland, at Knossos or Phaistos on Crete, or the site of Troy that commanded the crucial waterway between the Aegean and Black Seas. The art that has survived from this age is sophisticated and breathtaking, be it the grand palaces themselves, the exquisite metalwork and jewelry, or the superb wall-paintings of bull-dancers and imaginative scenes from life and nature. When Hesiod (*Works and Days* 109–201) creates his sequence of the ages of man, tracing the decline from the ideal Golden Race to the current race of iron, he has to insert a fourth race, that of heroes who are called demi-gods, those who fought at Thebes and Troy and who now dwell on the islands of the blest.

The Greeks of the classical age were very much aware that an age of heroes had preceded them, that they lived in the shadow of that age. They had only to look around them at the visible ruins of that civilization or listen to the deeds of these great men and women passed on by the oral tradition of the bards. They created a sophisticated nexus of interconnected myths, which served as the subjects of the visual art and their poetic texts. These stories could be regarded as both actual history, although by the late fifth century historians such as Herodotos and Thucydides could distinguish between the figures and themes of myth and those of "modern" history, and as the subject of art and poetry. Against this background of heroic myth the classical Greeks, especially the Athenians, would explore the issues and raise the great questions of their own age, in much the same way that American novelists, film-makers, and television producers of the last century would create an Old West against which to explore America's expanding manifest destiny and its new role as a major world power.

Perhaps the most distinctive feature of tragedy was the pact assumed between spectators and performers. The former will suspend their disbelief and willingly enter the tragic world that unfolds before them, and the actors and chorus will maintain that fiction. In other words tragedy does not call attention to itself, while comedy, as we shall see, depends on that barrier being broken. Drama calling attention to itself has come to be called "meta-theater," and it works well for comedy, but not for tragedy. In Shakespeare the dramatic illusion is sometimes punctured by a wry comment that for a moment reminds the audience that they are watching a staged performance. One can think of Jacques' lines delivered from a stage, "All the world's a stage and the men and women merely players" (*As You Like It*). Perhaps better is Fabian's comment in *Twelfth Night*:

> If this were played upon a stage now, I could
> condemn it as an improbable fiction,

or from a more serious play (*Julius Caesar*), Casca's words after the assassination:

How many ages hence
Shall this our lofty scene be acted over
In states unborn and accents yet unknown!

It has been suggested that in a number of places Greek tragedy *does* break its allusion and let the audience know that they are watching a play. Critics have long debated whether the chorus in the great second *stasimon* of Sophokles' *Oedipus Tyrannos* is referring to its identity as Theban elders or Athenian choristers, when they assert (895–6) in reaction to Jokaste's rejection of Apollo's oracles, "if these deeds are held honor, why ought I to dance [*choreuein*]?" If the latter, then Sophokles intended the spectators to view the chorus simultaneously as dramatic characters and Athenian performers. But the passage works well within its dramatic context, and these lines are balanced in the antistrophe (909–10) by a similar conclusion that *is* within the dramatic context, "and nowhere is Apollo seen to have honor, and the divine order crumbles." In Sophokles' *Elektra*, when Orestes enters (1098) with the urn supposedly containing his own ashes, this in fact empty urn has been the starting-point for an extended meta-theatrical reading of Sophokles – the spectators *know* that the urn is empty and that Orestes is in more than one sense an actor playing a part.

In the prologue of Euripides' *Medea* the Nurse comments on Medea's frenzied state of mind and fears that she "may be planning something new" (37), and later Medea herself will announce (790) after foretelling the death of Jason's new bride, τόνδ' ἀπαλάσσω λόγον. This is usually taken as meaning "I consider that account (*logos*) closed," or "I close that chapter," but it could also mean "I am changing the plot," Medea then going on to announce "I will kill my children." Here it is argued that Euripides is announcing in advance the major plot-change of his play, the death of the children at Medea's own hand. In *Elektra* a cry is heard in the distance and Elektra fears that this portends bad news, not good, "for where are the messengers?" (759), a wry allusion, it is suggested, to the messenger who arrives just two lines later. Finally, in *Bacchae* we have the dressing-scene of Pentheus (912–76), where his donning of the Bacchic costume is seen as meta-theatrical to the actual drama itself. When Agave, played by the same actor who has just finished his role as Pentheus, enters with the head of her son, what she is carrying is the mask of Pentheus. This (it is argued) allows the spectators to remove themselves from the dramatic illusion and reflect that they are watching a play. But these arguments are speculative at best, and it is a safer conclusion that tragedy guards its illusion very carefully.

The tragic plot-line

In *Poetics* chapters 13–14 Aristotle sets down what he considers the best plot-line for a tragedy, "best" in the sense of arousing pity and fear, which are the characteristic emotions of tragedy:

First of all it is clear that one must not portray admirable men undergoing a change from good fortune to bad, as this is not pitiful or fearful but just dreadful. Nor [should one portray] evil men

*going from bad to good fortune, as this is the most non-tragic of all; it has nothing of what it should,
it is neither pitiful nor fearful nor does it satisfy our human sensibilities. Nor [should one portray]
a thoroughly bad person falling out of good fortune into bad, as such a situation might satisfy our
human sensibilities but would not furnish pity or fear . . . What is left lies in between these: the situation will involve a person who is not outstanding in either virtue or just behavior, who falls into
bad fortune not through vice or wickedness, but through some mistake* [hamartia], *one of those
who enjoys great reputation and prosperity.*

This passage raises quite a number of problems of interpretation: that the word used
for "admirable" [*epieikes*] seems to apply very appropriately to many of the characters
in Greek tragedy, that his first category of rejected plot-lines suits Euripides' surviving version of *Hippolytos*, and that Aristotle does not discuss a fourth possible plot,
a good person going from bad fortune to good, which would nicely describe
Sophokles' *Philoktetes*, and possibly *Oedipus at Kolonos*; Euripides' *Andromache*,
Iphigeneia among the Taurians, Helen; and even Orestes in Aeschylus' *Eumenides*. At the
close of this section Aristotle will complain that tragedies with a happy ending are
the result of poets pandering to the emotional tastes of the spectators and are in fact
more like comedy, "where no one kills anyone."

Based on the thirty extant tragedies, we can find no simple formula for the plot-
line of a Greek tragedy. In some cases the play depicts a tight sequence of events that
end with a result that we would call "tragic." The deaths and devastation that occur
form the climax of the play, and while an epilogue may attempt to redress the matter,
what we are left with is overwhelming loss and sorrow at that loss. This can be seen
particularly well in Aeschylus' *Seven*, Sophokles' *Antigone, Oedipus Tyrannos*, and
Trachinian Women, and in Euripides' *Medea, Hippolytos, Hecuba, Phoenician Women,
Iphigeneia at Aulis*, and *Bacchae*. In these plays we can see operating a sequence of
logical cause and effect, or of action and reaction.

In some plays we are witnessing a tragic aftermath, where nothing "tragic" happens
in the drama itself, but the results of an earlier catastrophe worked out on others
provide the intensity of sorrow and loss that tragedy requires. Such is Aeschylus' *Persians*, in which the "tragedy" is the announcement of the Persian defeat in Greece and
the realization by the characters that Xerxes has offended against the law of the gods,
"nothing in excess." we would include here also *Trojan Women*, for there is no causal
sequence, just the unrelieved series of atrocities committed against the vanquished. In
Aeschylus' *Suppliants* we would suggest that we see the tragic prelude, since the play
sets the stage for the actual tragic action of the next play, where the maidens will
murder their bridegrooms on their wedding-night.

Another variation of the tragic plot-line is that of death followed by redemption to
some degree. In these instances the catastrophe will not come at the climax of the
drama, but at an earlier point, so that events may build upon this disaster. Certainly
this is how *Oresteia* operates, with the earlier extra-dramatic sacrifice of Iphigeneia and
the fall of Troy and within the trilogy the murder of Agamemnon and Kassandra in
the first play, and the mirror-scene in *Libation-Bearers*, the tableau of Orestes with the
bodies of Klytaimestra and Aigisthos. The third play contains no "tragic" moment,
rather the acquittal of Orestes and the reconciliation of the Furies. Sophokles' *Ajax*

also unfolds in this manner, with the suicide of Ajax coming halfway through, to be followed by his "redemption" by his brother and Odysseus, making him the sort of hero worthy to be honored at Athens. A similar thing happens in Euripides' *Herakles*, where Herakles' murder of his family comes not at the end, but in the middle, leaving Amphitryon to bring his son to the awareness of what he has done and Theseus to redeem his friend and give him a new life at Athens.

Then there is the plot-line mentioned above and apparently ignored by Aristotle, where virtue triumphs, disaster is averted, and a resolved and happy ending closes the drama. This was called "tragicomedy" by Kitto, "Romantic Tragedy" by Conacher (1967), and "Catastrophe Survived" by Burnett. To be sure, there is the potential for tragedy, and there is a point where events could take a tragic direction, as in Euripides' *Ion*, where Kreousa's plan to kill her son (unknown as such to her) might succeed, but in these plays the tragedy fails to materialize. Aristotle preferred "complex" tragedy to "simple" tragedy, the former possessing reversals (*peripateia*) and recognitions, and it is such plays as these in particular that characters and situations are recognized and the dramatic direction reversed. Such plays would include Sophokles' *Philoktetes*, Euripides' *Andromache*, *Ion*, *Helen*, *Iphigeneia among the Taurians*, and his dark masterpiece, *Orestes*. One might here also place Sophokles' and Euripides' *Elektra*, on the grounds that Orestes and Elektra begin the drama in distress and end in triumph, having accomplished the revenge ordered by Apollo, and that disjointed events are now restored to their proper heading. But as these plays also contain murder and revenge and as both are permeated with a darkness in the tragic situation and the characters themselves, it is perhaps safer not to group them with the lighter "tragedies" of averted catastrophe.

Finally what does one do with Euripides' pair of suppliant tragedies, *Children of Herakles* and *Suppliant Women*? In each a female character dies, the self-sacrificing Maiden (*CH*) and Euadne (*SW*), who kills herself on her husband's pyre, but these scenes are incidental to the larger plot, and in each Athens intervenes militarily in favor of distressed suppliants. Things seem to be put right by the end: the children of Herakles are now free from the terror of persecution, and the women of Argos may bury their dead. But the endings of both plays are uneasy. In *Children of Herakles*, the aged mother of Herakles goes from pitiful old woman to avenging Fury, proposing to execute the captive Eurystheus with the connivance of an Athenian chorus, and in *Suppliant Women* Athene enters to promise even more war with Thebes. *Oedipus at Kolonos* is likewise not easy to classify. The principal character goes from bad fortune to good, in the sense that he is called by the gods to his mysterious fate in the Grove of the Furies, where he will finally find rest and become something more than human. But it also does end with a death, like so many conventional tragedies.

There are some favored and repeated sorts of plot-line, most notably the suppliant-play and the rescue-play, with considerable overlap between these. In the former a character or group will take refuge at a shrine, often but not always at Athens, and beg for sanctuary and assistance. The drama of the play will develop from whether sanctuary can be given and at what cost and will inevitably feature the debate which Athenian audiences loved, as the issues behind the request are brought into the open.

Sophokles' *Oedipus at Kolonos* is perhaps the most powerful example, where the blind and accursed Oedipus occupies the sacred area before the Grove of the Furies, to remain there seated for over 1,000 lines. Aeschylus' *Suppliants* perhaps set the pattern for this sub-genre, in which the foreign-looking, but Greek-descended daughters of Danaos ask for sanctuary from their cousins who would take them in an unwilling marriage. Euripides was especially fond of combining this theme with the rescue-play, as we find in his *Children of Herakles, Andromache, Suppliant Women*, with individual scenes in his *Herakles, Ion, Medea*, and *Iphigeneia among the Taurians*.

Character in tragedy

The passage quoted above from Aristotle *Poetics* chapter 13 leads into the vexed question of the nature of character in Greek tragedy. When Aristotle asserts that in a good tragedy one falls "into bad fortune, not through vice or wickedness, but through some *hamartia*", this last word has often been mistranslated as "flaw," that is a flaw in personality or character. It is this that prevents the tragic hero from being the "admirable" person of Aristotle's first rejected plot-line. To students brought up on the "tragic flaw" in Shakespeare (Othello: jealousy, Macbeth: ambition) this might seem a promising way to approach Greek tragedy as well. Modern readers and audiences are used to seeking the explanation for action within character and seek to apply this approach to the characters in Greek tragedy, but by distorting what the ancient playwrights have depicted. It is worth observing at the start that Aristotle can write this section with no word for "main character," "protagonist," or "hero." In ancient Greek "protagonist" (*protagonistes*) meant the main actor, and "hero" (*heros*) a human who had become a semi-divine being.

At Aeschylus' *Seven* 181–90, reacting to the terrified utterances of the chorus of maidens, Eteokles dismisses the race of women with contempt, and here the modern reader will seek a window into Eteokles' personal soul and conclude that here is not a nice person. Thus in the scene where he assigns the guardians to the seven gates, one might wonder if he has not been spoiling for a fight with his brother all along, and will get what he deserves from that desire. When Antigone envisions that she will be buried beside Polyneikes and affirms "I shall lie with him, dear one with dear one," is there a hint of her true (incestuous) feelings for that brother? Indeed when Jean Anouilh wrote his *Antigone* in 1941, he made it clear that it is not just a brother whom she is burying, but her favorite brother, the one that was especially dear to her. Consider Hippolytos, the illegitimate son of Theseus and "the Amazon woman," reared far away from his father's house. Does this explain his aversion to Love and his devotion to the goddess of Virginity? Does the young Pentheus in *Bacchae* have an unnatural obsession with the emotional and sexual side of life, and an unhealthy devotion to his mother? All these have been suggested as traits of tragic characters that motivate their actions in their play.

But it is safer to say that in Greek tragedy, especially in Aeschylus and Sophokles, characters are more important for what they represent and how they act than for the personality behind their deeds. Eteokles is at the same time noble defender and cursed child of Oedipus – these are his roles for that play. Orestes and Elektra in *Libation-Bearers* are the "orphaned children of the eagle-father" (247). Aeschylus does not give either child a character with any great depth; it will be left to Euripides to explore what sort of person could obey an oracle that told him to kill his mother. In *Philoktetes* Neoptolemos is the young man who must decide where his priorities lie. Kreon in *Antigone* is the ruler who puts the state before everything else, and all we are told about Antigone's character is that she is as headstrong as her father. Remember also that these characters are masked, that the individual's identity will be subordinate to the role that he or she is playing.

Characters not are not always portrayed in low relief, however; otherwise Greek tragedy would be little more than soap opera. Whole and real personalities are set before the spectators, whose actions are motivated by an underlying character. Oedipus acts as he does because of his desire to know (1170 – "I must hear") and because of his arrogance that he thinks that he knows everything. Winnington-Ingram (1980) writes well that his "flaw" is not one of character, but of intellect. It is not a question of moral good and bad – the opening scene makes it plain that Oedipus is seen by all as father and savior of his city. Aeschylus' Klytaimestra, Euripides' Medea, Elektra, and Kreousa are all extensively and memorably created characters, with vivid personalities that do motivate their actions, but in each case the dramatist is doing something new with the female role and needs to make that character loom large for his audience.

Aristotle comments definitively in *Poetics* chapter 6 that actions and plot (*mythos*), not character (*ethos*), are the essential "end" (*telos*) of tragedy, that tragedy is a representation (*mimesis*) of action (*praxis*), not of people, that without plot there could be no tragedy, but without character there might. Modern readers and audience find this hard to accept, since for us the inner life of the characters explains their behavior. Ibsen, for instance, described his approach to dramatic creation:

> Before I write one word, I have to have the character in mind through and through. I must penetrate to the last wrinkle of his soul. I always proceed from the individual: the stage setting, the dramatic ensemble, all that comes naturally . . . as soon as I am certain of the individual in every aspect of his humanity.

In the "method" school of acting the actor becomes his character down to the innermost detail. But for Greek tragedy we should look at the matter another way, that the playwright decided first upon his plot-line and the actions of his characters and then created the personalities that caused them to behave in that way. Northrop Frye* takes this line in defence of Aristotle:

> In drama characterization depends on function: what a character is depends on what he has to do in the play. Dramatic function in its turn depends on the structure of the play; the character has certain things to do because the play has such and such a shape.

---

* N. Frye, *Anatomy of Criticism* (Princeton 1957) 171.

But not all ancient critics agreed with Aristotle. The author of the *Life of Sophokles* argues:

> *He knows how to arrange the action with such a sense of timing that he creates a character out of a mere half-line or a single expression. This is the essential thing in poetry: to delineate character or feelings.*

There are places where the playwright gives us cause to consider how a character in a particular scene might be played. We are familiar with "version" in modern novels and the cinema, how a character may be played differently in two renderings of the same text. Take the cinematic versions of Shakespeare's *Henry V*, that of Olivier from wartime 1944, full of the martial confidence of the king whose cause is just, and that of Branagh from 1989, where the king himself is uneasy about the justice of his cause and whether he can commit a people to war. With Greek drama it is difficult to play a character in different ways, since the playwright has usually made it clear how this person is behaving, leaving the actor little room to maneuver. With how much sympathy can one play Pentheus, for example, when he has been given every opportunity to realize that he is fighting against a god, or Kreon with his pig-headed determination that the state is all that matters? But in a few scenes the director and actor do have options at their disposal. At *Antigone* 531–81 Antigone rejects her sister and refuses to let her share the blame for burying Polyneikes. Why? Through love and genuine concern that her sister not be hurt, or spite because Ismene had initially refused to help, or through a sense of personal martyrdom that Ismene may intrude into Antigone's spotlight? The text does not specifically favor one or another interpretation, and much would depend on how that scene was acted and directed. In *Philoktetes* and *Oedipus at Kolonos* both protagonists in a crucial scene near the end of the drama angrily reject an appeal from a younger male: Philoktetes to Neoptolemos's request that he come to Troy (1314–1401), Oedipus to his son Polyneikes that he support his claim to the throne (1254–1446). In both cases it has been argued that these characters are too angry, that audience sympathy is inclined toward their acceptance of that request. Again much would depend on how that rejection was staged, the tenor of voice and the body language employed.

Theater of the word

Taplin coined the attractive phrase "theater of the mind" to describe the conventions of Greek drama, that the spectators have very much to do with the impact and effect of the production. It is not theater of illusion, but theater of convention. But for both Greek tragedy and comedy it is also "theater of the word." Of course by its very nature drama depends on its spoken text, but for the Athenian audience much had to do with the words that were spoken and sung. In a large *theatron* holding nearly 15,000 people the visual spectacle would be small, especially for those seated at the back and upper regions. At those distances the performers appear very small indeed, and any subtlety of action or gesture would be lost. What mattered was what was said.

In particular the ancient theater was especially fond of the messenger-speech. In a theater, when the actions are done off-stage and related through the messenger, these speeches must convey not just the gist of what has happened but the dramatic and emotional circumstances that surround them. The messengers themselves are not faceless ciphers, but each has their own place in the story. The man who reports the death of Hippolytos is one of his companions (1153–1267), in *Bacchae* the first messenger has been part of the attempt to capture the women on the mountain (660–774) and the second was Pentheus' lone companion on his fatal journey (1024–1152), in *Trachinian Women* the messenger announcing the death of Deianeira is the Nurse whom we have seen earlier in the play. These speeches provide the context, the opposition, the actual events complete with direct quotation, the conclusion, and often a moralizing comment. They are masterpieces of narration in miniature and must have demanded a high degree of dramatic ability by the actor. Especially memorable are the messenger-scene in *Persians* (290–531), announcing Xerxes' catastrophic defeat, an account preferred by historians to the later "historical" description in Herodotos; the speech of the tutor in Sophokles' *Elektra* (680–763), a brilliant and utterly fictitious report of the chariot-race that "killed" Orestes; and Euripides' *Bacchae* 1043–1120, where the death of Pentheus is narrated in breathtaking fashion. Perhaps the strangest messenger-speech occurs at Euripides' *Orestes* 1395–1502, reporting the attempted murder of Helen by Orestes and Pylades, not spoken but sung in high lyrics by the Phrygian eunuch.

The Greeks loved debate, and just as a courtroom scene in a modern movie or television show makes for successful drama, in Greek tragedy characters often present sides of an issue in what amounts to a formal debate (*agon*). This is especially prominent in the extant comedies of Aristophanes, where the result of the *agon* often connects directly with the development of the great comic idea, but also in Euripides who of the three principal tragedians was especially fond of rhetoric and debate. We have one formal trial-scene, that of Orestes in *Eumenides*, while in *Oedipus at Kolonos* Oedipus and Kreon rehearse the issue of Oedipus' moral and legal innocence and Menelaos presides at a "trial" of Helen in *Trojan Women*. The subject of an *agon* can be law and morality (as in *Antigone*), personal guilt and responsibility (*Hippolytos*, both *Elektra*-plays, *Orestes*), political systems (*Suppliant Women*), heroism (*Herakles*), burial of the dead (*Ajax*), and the justification of a bloody revenge (*Hecuba*). The Athenians maintained a self-stereotype of their fondness for litigious behavior, and this shows in their drama.

Audiences enjoyed also a great speech, a declamation on a particular theme, perhaps on a controversial topic. Just the sound of a character holding forth in argumentative tones and elevated language was something they found appealing. Hippolytos has his great speech (616–68) on the nature of women ("I'll never have enough of hating you women"), Klytaimestra explains the motives for her revenge in terms which approach the blasphemous (*Agamemnon* 1431–47), Kreon pronounces the priority of the *polis* and redefines the familial terms of friend (*philos*) and enemy (*echthros*) solely within the context of the city (*Antigone* 162–210). In a fragment of Euripides' lost *Erechtheus* a mother expounds on why she will let her daughter be sacrificed for the good of the city. In comedy Sokrates will be accused of teaching how to argue the inferior case and win, but it seems that in tragedy also the Athenians enjoyed watching the characters on stage argue and declaim controversial positions.

The parts of tragedy

Contributing to the formalism of the genre is a familiar and repeated pattern of scenes and sub-units. Just as a play by Shakespeare was subdivided into five distinct acts or one's favorite hour-long television show will reach its crisis in the third quarter-hour and its resolution in the last, the Greek tragedians had a repertoire of formal scenes to use in constructing their dramas. Aristotle divides these fundamentally into two: songs and episodes, distinguished partly by meter, partly by accompaniment, and partly by language (the songs being composed in a literary Doric dialect). We may prefer to catalog a series of types of scene: prologue, episode, *kommos*, choral song, and monody.

Prologues are almost always in the iambic trimeter, the closest to ordinary speech in Aristotle's view, and as the name implies, open the drama. They are very much the province of the actor – one of Thespis' achievements was the development of the pro-logue – but two tragedies (*Persians, Suppliants*) begin with a marching-on song of the chorus, not in their artificial Doric and lyric meter, but in the anapestic dimeter, an elevated meter but spoken in the Attic dialect. Prologues may take the form of a soli-loquy (as in *Agamemnon, Libation-Bearers, Hippolytos, Ion,* and *Bacchae*), in which the speaker gives the audience directly the information that they require, or may expound the details in a dialogue, which allows the issues of the drama to surface early (as in Sophokles' *Antigone* and *Elektra,* Euripides' *Iphigeneia at Aulis*). Prologues may consist of more than one scene. In some cases an original speaker will be joined by a second character (*Trojan Women, Alkestis, Medea*) or an entirely new scene will follow the first (*Iphigenia among the Taurians,* Euripides' *Elektra, Eumenides*).

Like the prologue, the episodes are predominantly written in the iambic trimeter, although in early tragedy and again in plays after ca. 415 the trochaic tetrameter catalectic can be found in some scenes. In comedy this meter is used for scenes of excitement and action, and it is fair to consider its use in tragedy as a raising of the emotional level, perhaps like the sinister music at a tense part of a movie or televi-sion show. For the most part actors dominate the episodes, although in plays such as *Suppliants, Eumenides,* and *Bacchae* the chorus may play a larger role. In early tragedy the episodes will have been strictly an encounter between the chorus and the one actor – we see this in *Agamemnon, Suppliants,* and *Persians.* Apart from the prologues, soliloquies are rare in Greek tragedy – one interesting exception is Ajax's great speech at lines 815–65. Here the chorus has left the playing-area, Ajax enters alone and lets the spectators into the plans of his heart. When Jokaste appears at *Oedipus Tyrannos* 911 to ask Apollo's help, she addresses the chorus directly to explain what she is doing. This has something to do with tragedy's desire to maintain the dramatic illusion; an address to the spectators comes dangerously close to acknowledging their presence, too close in fact to comedy, where addresses to the audience are com-monplace. Most episodes involve two actors, especially if they are there to debate the issue on which the play will turn, but as the genre developed, three-actor scenes become more common. In view of the size of the theater, the distance from the actors, and the fact that the actors were masked, it must have been difficult for the spectators to follow who was speaking, even allowing for exaggerated gestures and body language. We can trace the development of the three-actor scene, from the first startling example (Pylades, mute for 900 lines, breaking his silence for three lines at *Libation-Bearers* 900–2 [458]), through an awkward scene in *Antigone* (ca. 440) where Kreon talks first with Antigone and then with Ismene (531–81), to confident and polished scenes in *Orestes* (470–629 [408]) and *Oedipus at Kolonos* (1096–1210 [406]).

By the end of the fifth century the episodes dominate the play, separated by short choral breaks of decreasing relevance. Some of these episodes are of great length: over four hundred lines in *Philoktetes* (219–625) and *Orestes* (356–806), dominated by the actors and leaving the chorus little to do. In these late plays the playwrights insert one episode into another, with the original scene resuming almost as if the interruption had not occurred. In *Orestes* the crucial encounter between Orestes and Menelaos is unexpectedly interrupted by the surprising arrival of Tyndareus – here the intervention changes the expected plot. In Sophokles' *Elektra* the confrontation between mother and daughter suddenly breaks off with the entry of the Tutor with the false tale of Orestes' death, and resumes with a grief-stricken Elektra vowing to accomplish the revenge herself. In *Philoktetes* the deception of Philoktetes by the young Neoptolemos is interrupted by the Merchant with another false tale, a scene that adds nothing to the plot except to increase the urgency and move it along.

The choral odes or songs (*mele*) provide formal breaks between the episodes, and as mentioned above, correspond to some degree with the recitative (or spoken speech) and aria of grand opera. The term *stasimon* ("standing [song]") is used for these songs, as the chorus is now in position in the *orchestra* and not processing into or out of the playing-area. Choral poetry in the Archaic period seems to have been a product of the Dorian cities, and in Athenian tragedy the chorus will sing in an artificial construct set against the traditional lyric meters. Audiences clearly expected choruses to perform in something other than their native Attic speech, which was used for the prologues and episodes. Choral songs tend to be formally structured, divided into corresponding units called *strophe* ("turn") and *antistrophe* ("counterturn"). In each pair the metrical pattern tends to be very close, if not identical – this responsion, as it is called, allows textual scholars to detect corruption in the text and to indicate what sort of restoration or emendation is necessary. The terms "turn" and "counterturn" suggest that the chorus will have danced in one direction around the orchestra in the first part and repeated their movement in the opposite in the next. Choral odes often finish with an "epode," a single stanza in a meter related to but not identical with the preceding *strophes* and *antistrophes*. Sometimes the chorus will process in with a marching-song in an anapestic meter but without the lyrical Doric dialect (as at *Persians* 1–64, *Agamemnon* 40–103) before beginning their initial *stasimon*.

Actors sing in Greek tragedy, both with the chorus and on their own. Aristotle (*Poetics* 1452b24) uses the term *kommos* for a song of lamentation "performed together by the chorus and from the *skene*," the last being his term for "by the actors."

Technically a *kommos* is a formal song between actor and chorus, with the latter responding to the former in metrically responsive stanzas. The classic examples are Antigone's lament at *Antigone* 806–82, and the grand summoning of Agamemnon's spirit to aid Orestes and Elektra in their revenge (*Libation-Bearers* 306–478). But the term can be used conveniently to describe any formal lyric exchange between actor(s) and chorus. In a number of instances these exchanges precede a speech in iambic by the character in distress, who seems to do things twice, once in lyric and again in iambic. Thus Kassandra in her powerful dialogue with the chorus (*Agamemnon* 1072–1330) sings enigmatically in lyric and then speaks more clearly in iambics, and Alkestis appears to die twice, once at the end of her lyric dialogue with her husband (279) and again at the close of her deathbed scene in iambics (392).

Actors also sing alone in what are called "monodies" or solo songs. These preserve the artificial Doric dialogue that was expected for sung lyrics, but the metrical pattern becomes astrophic, that is, not a formal pairing of *strophe* and *antistrophe*. Rather the song is more freely composed and resembles the great arias of an opera by Verdi. The tone is usually sad, uttered by a character in distress, although one important exception is Ion's solo song, where he expresses his joy in being the servant-boy of Apollo (*Ion* 112–83). Kreousa's later monody from the same play (859–922) is a brilliantly emotional display by a character, abandoned by men and by gods, who has reached her breaking-point. In the later fifth century monodies are not sung by Greek adult men, but by women and males on the margin (the young Ion, the Phrygian eunuch). The emotionalism and the deep feelings expressed belonged better in the mouths of women, boys, and foreigners. In *Ion* the boy's monody occurs before the formal entry of the chorus, and it is interesting that the monody is preceded by a marching-on song in anapests (82–111), sung by Ion, however, and not by the chorus.

At the end of the tragedy the chorus would leave the playing-area, but do not seem to have had a formal marching-off song (*exodos*) that corresponded with the *parodos* (the entry of the chorus). Often we get a few lines, in which the chorus announces its departure, as at *Suppliant Women* 1232–4, "Let us leave, Adrastos, and let us make our pledge to this man and this city; it is fitting for us to honor those who have labored for us" or at *Philoktetes* 1469–71, "Let us all go now together, having said a prayer to the Nymphs of the sea to escort us on our journey." Variations of certain "tags" appear at the end of several plays of Euripides:

> *Divine matters take many forms, and the gods bring many things to pass beyond expectation. What was anticipated does not occur, and for the unexpected the god finds a way. Such has happened here*

and

> *O great and awesome Victory, may you rule my life and never cease giving me the crown.*

The first group of lines is found at the end of *Alkestis, Medea, Andromache, Helen, Bacchae,* and the second at the close of *Phoenician Women, Orestes, Iphigeneia among the Taurians.* As the last would seem to be a direct appeal to the judges in the manner of comedy, it is very likely an addition from the fourth century. The chorus, it appears, did not have a formal exit "number," and will have left the *orchestra* presumably with musical accompaniment but not with singing.

Early tragedy (534–472)

THESPIS is little more than a name in a tradition. Late sources assign him some play-titles and one line from his *Pentheus* that resembles a line from Euripides' *Bacchae* (137). As mentioned above, he is associated with the creation and development of the actor. Aristotle will credit Aeschylus with increasing the number to two and in playing down the role of the chorus. This is clearly a stage in the growth of tragedy to its mature form. If Thespis was in any sense an historical figure, his contribution to the development of tragedy lay in giving the actor a formal existence. Early tragedy must have been rather primitive, if the only dramatic interaction lay between actor and chorus, but even in the mature plays of Aeschylus we see how this can operate effectively. *Agamemnon* and *Suppliants* both have extended sections with only actor and chorus, but one can see how the audience might well have tired of entire plays of this form. Presumably the actor would portray one character in one scene, leave, and return as another personality to announce what has happened off-stage in the interim. If *Pentheus* were an early tragedy by Thespis, it might be reconstructed as a one-actor drama with scenes involving Dionysos and the chorus, Pentheus and the chorus (ending with his threat to go to the mountain and crush this new deity), and a messenger announcing the fate of Pentheus, perhaps an epiphany of Dionysos at the end. This might explain why the principal "dramatic action" in Greek tragedy occurs off-stage and why the chorus is continually present on-stage. The chorus, in fact, will have provided both the dramatic continuity and the focus of the drama. News is being brought to them for their information and exegesis. Much of the drama would have consisted of their songs and dances – again Aeschylus' *Suppliants* and *Agamemnon* provide a hint of what that was like. A character in Aristophanes' *Wasps* (1479) refers to "those old dances that Thespis brought on." The introduction of a second actor, attributed to Aeschylus, really does mark the advent of "real" drama, since confrontation and disagreement between principals can now occur before the eyes of the spectators.

Another early name is **CHOIRILOS**, who competed against Pratinas and Aeschylus in 499–6 (the latter's début) and whom the *Suda* credits with employing masks and the *skene*. Pratinas will be discussed in the section on satyr-play, although to compete with Aeschylus and other tragedians he must have written tragedy as well.

The one major name of the early period is **PHRYNICHOS**, whose career (ca. 510–ca. 470) overlaps rather than precedes Aeschylus. No more than two dozen fragments survive, but we know a considerable amount from other sources. He is attributed with inventing the "tetrameter" (probably the trochaic, which Aristotle claims was the original meter of tragedy before the iambic trimeter) and the introduction of female roles. Several sources connect him with beautiful songs and striking dancing, even to the point of Aelian's charming story (*Historical Miscellany* 3.18) that his inclusion of a war-dance in a play led to his election as general. It has been suggested that his tragedies were largely choral in nature.

Two plays, however, connect his drama with events in the outside world. First, Herodotos (2.61.2) recounts how a play of Phrynichos reminded the Athenians of the fall of Miletos in 494, the city which the Athenians had assisted during the Ionian Revolt from Persia. For this he was fined and the play forbidden to be performed again. From Herodotos it appears that the drama was called *Capture of Miletos*, but Snell (*TrGF* I 74) suggests that *Persians* may have been its actual title. It seems that Phrynichos was using contemporary history as subject for tragedy. The likely date for this play is 492, a critical year in Athenian history, when the controversial Themistokles was archon. We are told that Aeschylus' *Persians* (472) was based upon *Phoenician Women* by Phrynichos. The two opening lines are identical except for one word, and both dealt with the ill-fated Persian expedition against Greece in 480/79. Phrynichos' play opened with a eunuch who announces the defeat of Xerxes, while Aeschylus' opens with a chorus, to whom the defeat is announced later in the action. Phrynichos is known to have won in 476, a reasonable date for *Phoenician Women*, and interesting also in that the *choregos* was again Themistokles.

Of the surviving fragments only two are longer than a line or two, both from his *Women of Pleuron*. Fr. 6 in lyrics tells of the death of Meleagros:

> He did not avoid cold death, a rapid flame devoured him, as the fire-log was consumed by his mother's grim malice.

Pausanias, who quotes this fragment, says that the story of Meleagros was not the main plot-line of Phrynichos' play. The lyric meter suggests that this was part of a choral song. Fr. 2 of his *Alkestis*, "he wears down his fearless, limb-twisted body," suggests that his version of the story also featured Herakles wrestling with Death.

Characters in the comedies of Aristophanes (career: 427–385) refer several times to this old tragedian. The aged jurors at *Wasps* 220 enter singing "old honey-sweet Sidonian songs of Phrynichos," the old Philokleon (*Wasps* 269) walks and sings "a song of Phrynichos," and at *Birds* 748–51 the chorus compare Phrynichos to a bee for the beauty of his lyrics. In the dancing-contest at the end of *Wasps* a dancer "crouches like a cock of Phrynichos" (1490) and a high leaping kick is called the Phrynichean (1524). Plutarch (*Ethika* 732f) quotes two lines from Phrynichos:

> all the figures that Dance has given me, as many as the waves that glowering night produces in a storm at sea.

It is the old who seem to have been fond of Phrynichos seventy-five years later, and the comic Euripides at *Frogs* 910 describes Aeschylus' audience as "fools raised on Phrynichos." Thus while the beauty of his songs and vigor of his dances lingered in the memory of later audiences, there was also a suggestion that his was primitive and unsophisticated stuff.

Aeschylus

The chorus at Aristophanes *Frogs* 1004 addresses Aeschylus as "the first to build the towering words of tragedy" and he is the first whose plays we possess and about whom we can say anything definitive. Keeping in mind the uncertainty of any ancient biographical data, we can consider the following details to be reasonably secure:

525 – birth at Eleusis (519 is a less likely date)
499–6 – début in the theater
490 – fought in the battle at Marathon, where his brother Kynageiros died
484 – first tragic victory
480/79 – battles of Salamis and Plataia
472 – victory with four plays, including *Persians*
ca. 470 – first visit to Sicily (restaging of *Persians*)
468 – loss to Sophokles
467 – victory with Theban tetralogy (including *Seven*)
466–59 – victory with Danaid tetralogy (including *Suppliants*)
458 – victory with *Oresteia*
456 – final visit to Sicily and death at Gela

He came, not from Athens city itself, but from the town of Eleusis, one of the last regions to be incorporated into Attica and home of the famous mysteries of Demeter and her daughter. In fact stories in Aristotle and a commentator to Aristotle imply that at some point Aeschylus was accused of revealing the secrets of these Mysteries in his plays. His début as a tragedian is dated to the Olympiad of 499–6, but his first victory did not come until 484, fifteen years into his career. If we assign him twenty or so productions, with thirteen victories in his lifetime (see below), then his first half-dozen entries were unsuccessful, but were followed by an almost unbroken string of victories thereafter, interrupted perhaps only by Sophokles' victory in 468.

The ancient sources attribute from seventy to ninety plays to Aeschylus. A list of known titles slightly exceeds eighty, including the controversial *Prometheus*-plays. Allowing for the possibility of alternate titles and the loss of some satyr-plays, a total in the eighties seems reasonable. This would mean that Aeschylus put on twenty-one or so productions (each of three tragedies and one satyr-play) in a career of roughly forty years. Sophokles staged thirty productions in his sixty-year career and Euripides twenty-three over forty-eight years. A production every other year seems to be the average for a top-rated tragic poet. The only certain instance of productions in back-to-back years is that of Aeschylus in 468 and 467, although Euripides very probably performed in 431 and 430. The ancient *Life of Aeschylus* gives him thirteen victories, the *Suda* twenty-eight. The discrepancy is best explained by the fact that beginning some time before 425 a competitor was allowed to re-stage a production by Aeschylus rather than create his own plays, and that Aeschylus thus won fifteen posthumous victories.

Aeschylus paid at least two visits to the court of Hieron, tyrant of Syracuse in Sicily, the only Greek city which could rival Athens for prosperity and cultural splendor. Hieron attracted the leading poets of the day, Simonides and Bacchylides, Pindar, and included Aeschylus among the notables in his court. Aeschylus made his first visit between 471 and 469, where he reperformed *Persians* and wrote his *People of Etna*, in part to celebrate Hieron's refounding of that city after the devastating volcanic eruption of 476. A later visit is recorded for 457/6 – the *Life* tells a bizarre story of his death at Gela in Sicily. The author of the *Life* has conflated these two visits when he attributes Aeschylus' departure for Sicily to his pique at being defeated by Sophokles [468], concluding that he never returned to Athens.

Aeschylus and the trilogy

When Sophokles and Euripides presented their three tragedies and satyr-plays, these were not usually connected, either in plot or theme, but for Aeschylus and certain other lost poets the plays could be connected, and in this instance we use the terms "trilogy" or "tetralogy." For Aeschylus it was a mainstay of his approach to drama. We have firm evidence for four trilogies (or tetralogies, if we include the satyr-play): one about the cursed house of Laios at Thebes in 467 (*Laios, Oedipus, **Seven**, Sphinx*),* the "Daughters of Danaos" production between 466 and 459 (***Suppliants**, Egyptians, Daughters of Danaos, Amymone*), *Oresteia* in 458 (***Agamemnon**, **Libation-Bearers**, **Eumenides**, Proteus*), and a *Lykourgeia* (*Edonians, Bassarids, Young Men, Lykourgos*). Sommerstein (1996) lists ten other possible trilogies, some more probable than others: on material from the *Iliad* and *Odyssey*, on Ajax and the arms of Achilles, the encounter between Achilles and Memnon, the birth of Dionysos, the aftermath of the attack by the Seven on Thebes, the adventures of Jason, those of Perseus (with *Net-Haulers* as the satyr-play), and the career of Telephos. As his presentation in 472, however, consisted of four separate plays and the three datable trilogies all are later than 472, one's first reaction is to wonder whether the trilogy-form was a later development in his career. But it would be hard to fit eleven trilogies into the period 468–456, if we maintain the rule-of-thumb of productions every other year. Either some of Sommerstein's trilogies did not exist or, more likely, in 472 his choice of *Persians* dictated four separate plays that year.

The trilogy allowed the dramatist to depict events over three plays, to bring characters on-stage in more than one drama, to witness their personal development, to pursue the consequences of actions beyond the action of one drama. In the Theban plays and in *Oresteia* Aeschylus unfolds events over generations, the former showing how curse and individual responsibility operated over three generations in the royal house at Thebes, the latter depicting both father and son in the same dilemma as well as the action and reaction of similar events. But the Iliadic trilogy, as we reconstruct it, covered only about two weeks and maintained a dramatic focus on Achilles, while

---

* Plays in bold are extant.

the hypothetical trilogy about Ajax and the arms of Achilles may have extended over a few months. Both maintained a consistent setting in the Greek camp before Troy. Both *Oresteia* and the *Daughters of Danaos* seem to have employed a dramatic sequence of action–reaction–resolution, but not all trilogies will have operated that way. Certainly the Theban-plays displayed the successive doom of three generations, and the trilogies set at Troy and the trilogy of the aftermath at Thebes seem to end with death, even though there may be a sense of resolution or finality.

The Prometheus-plays

We need to consider one other multiple production, the Prometheus-plays attributed to Aeschylus. We possess a play entitled *Prometheus Desmotes* ("Prometheus Bound") and know of a second play called *Prometheus Lyomenos* ("The Release of Prometheus"), of which some fragments and a Latin translation by Cicero of a speech by Prometheus make it clear that the chorus was composed of Titans freed by Zeus from their imprisonment and that Herakles, Prometheus' eventual liberator, was a character. Two other Prometheus-plays are known: the *Fire-Lighter*, which was the satyr-play in 472, and *The Fire-Bringer*. Two major problems must be considered: (i) whether this was a trilogy, and (ii) the authorship of these plays.

It is clear that *Prometheus Bound* and *The Release of Prometheus* form a sequence of two dramas, but is *The Fire-Bringer* the third of a trilogy, and if so, is it the first or third play? The evidence for its existence is sparse: it is found in a catalog (incomplete) of Aeschylus' plays, one line survives (fr. 351), and an entry by an ancient commentator on *Prometheus Bound* that "in *The Fire-Bringer* . . . Prometheus was bound for three myriads [30,000 years]." It is unlikely to be the first play, since *Prometheus Bound* goes into great detail about what Prometheus has done and the significance of his gift to humanity – granted that the chorus do not know, but the accounts seem rather otiose if the audience had already witnessed the defiance of Prometheus and the theft of fire. If *The Fire-Bringer* is not a first play, is it then the third play? But what need is there of a third play after Prometheus is released? His release marks some sort of reconciliation with Zeus, and there does not seem to be much left over for a play called *The Fire-Bringer*. The most economical explanation is that *The Fire-Bringer* (*Pyrphoros*) is an alternative or a mistake for *Fire-Lighter* (*Pyrkaieus*), the satyr-drama that accompanied *Persians* in 472.

The ancient world assumed that *Prometheus Bound* was by Aeschylus, but in the last century various attacks were made on the Aeschylean authorship, culminating with the thorough discussion by Griffith, who concludes that the play (and with it *The Release of Prometheus*, for the two stand or fall together) was not by Aeschylus, but the work of a later tragedian, writing in the 430s. The arguments against Aeschylean authorship are both stylistic and conceptual. In the other six tragedies the chorus play a crucial role, especially in *Suppliants* (50 percent of the lines) and *Agamemnon* (45 percent), and are vitally involved in their play, either as principals (*Suppliants*) or as setting the moral tone of the drama (*Agamemnon*). Yet in Prometheus they have about 16 percent of the lines and essentially fill the spaces between the episodes, although their scene with Prometheus does give the audience information about past events. This is the sort of chorus we get later in the fifth century. Technical matters of meter (the play's fondness for chanted anapests, rhythms in the choral odes) and language (e.g., the use of enjambment, allowing a sentence to run on into the following line) are also not in the Aeschylean style. At line 266 Prometheus declares, *Hekon, hekon hemarton* ("Knowingly I did wrong, knowingly"), which sounds like a response to Sokrates' dictum *oudeis hekon hamartanei* ("No one does wrong knowingly"), but Sokrates was thirteen years old when Aeschylus died. Finally, the chorus seems to enter in a winged car (128–35), but the first documented use of the *mechane* is in 431 in *Medea*.

The other concern is the presentation of Zeus. In *Odyssey*, Hesiod, and the other plays of Aeschylus, Zeus is a god of Justice and essentially good order. Greek gods do not have to be kind – indeed at *Agamemnon* 182–3 the chorus declare, "grace (*charis*) comes with violence" – but they are not arbitrary and there does exist the powerful will of Zeus, "father of gods and men." In *Prometheus Bound* Zeus is a newly enthroned tyrant (*tyrannis* and *tyrannos* are actually used at lines 10, 305, 756, 942), with all the harshness and arrogance associated with the arbitrary ruler. Defenders of Aeschylus' authorship often assume that Zeus changed during the course of the plays, pointing out that the Titans have been released, and that Zeus will heal Io "with a touch" and father a son by her, whose line will culminate in the hero Herakles. To modern audiences the prequel has become a standard feature of both novel and cinema and it should not present a real problem that we see in this play the early years of Zeus along with the possibility that Zeus may himself be displaced. Alternatively in the second play Zeus may not have changed as much as come to terms with Prometheus, who does know by whom Zeus can be overthrown. On balance the different portrait of Zeus is neither a strong argument for or against the authorship of Aeschylus.

If not by Aeschylus, the extant play certainly has Aeschylean features. There were at least two, if not three plays in the production, and what we can tell of *The Release of Prometheus* suggests a progression with a resolution like that in *Oresteia* and *The Daughters of Danaos*. Io appears in the first play and her future journeys are foretold, while Herakles' future travels are predicted in the second play. This is very much in the manner of the roles and dilemmas of Orestes and Agamemnon in *Oresteia*. Gods appeared on stage in the final play of *The Daughters of Danaos* and they dominate the stage in *Eumenides*; thus a play full of gods such as Prometheus is very much in the Aeschylean style. As much about the play suggests a date in the 430s, critics have suggested that *Prometheus* was part of a posthumous production (in two or three plays) of drama that Aeschylus had left unfinished at his death. We know from the hypothesis to Euripides' *Medea* that Aeschylus' son, Euphorion, won first prize at the Dionysia of 431, and Sommerstein's proposal that Euphorion won with the Prometheus-plays would explain Euphorion's victory, fit a date ca. 430 for *Prometheus*, and perhaps explain the revivals of Aeschylus that certainly began by 425. The Athenian audience after twenty-five years missed Aeschylus.

The dramas of Aeschylus

The six certain plays that we have by Aeschylus all come from the latter part of his career (472–458), and we have no way of assessing what his early plays were like and how his concept and execution of drama changed over his forty years in the theater. We can see a marked distinction between the first three (*Persians, Seven, Suppliants*) and *Oresteia* in a number of ways. None of the first three requires a *skene*-building nor any entries except from the *eisodoi*. The action is taking place in the open with references to a city or a palace, but the *skene* and its central door so crucial to *Oresteia* is noticeably absent. This is strong evidence for the addition of the *skene* about 460 – *Oresteia* may well be the first production with this theatrical device. Similarly there is no hint of an *ekkyklema*, which produces the incredibly dramatic scenes in *Agamemnon* and *Libation-Bearers*, where the murderer stands over the bodies of her/his victims.

The dramatic action of all three earlier plays requires two actors only, but the drama turns largely on the interaction between chorus and character, such as the scene where the Queen asks the chorus about Athens in *Persians* or Danaos and his daughters plan their strategy in *Suppliants*. This is not to say that we do not get confrontations between characters – the messenger in *Seven* describes the enemy leaders and Eteokles dispatches an appropriate adversary – but on the whole the plays are "simple" rather than complicated. But in *Oresteia* we see the theater grow before our eyes, for while Agamemnon is a two-actor tragedy with extensive use of the chorus and minimal interaction of the actors, *Libation-Bearers* uses a third actor with devastating effect (the silent Pylades breaks into speech at line 900, as the mouthpiece of Apollo), and quickens the pace with short brisk scenes, while *Eumenides* employs two changes of scene, a playing-area briefly empty of both chorus and actors, fast-moving scenes (by line 240 we have had a prologue with four separate scenes, while in *Agamemnon* we were still in the first choral song), a chorus that enters through the *skene*-building and two sub-choruses at the end of the play.

A tragedy by Aeschylus was reasonably straightforward in structure, building from the opening dilemma to a climax at the end which brings events to a head. Aristotle praises more complicated plays with "reversals," but there is little of that in Aeschylus' earlier works. *Persians* begins with the chorus worrying over Xerxes and his great army in Greece, builds through the forebodings of the Queen, the disastrous news brought by the messenger, the oracular pronouncements of the dead king, and reaches its climax with the entry in despair of Xerxes – how the mighty have fallen! *Suppliants* opens with the arrival of Danaos and his daughters to their ancestral Argos, builds through the encounters with King Pelasgos and the decision of his people to protect the suppliants, and concludes with the final confrontation between suppliants and their threatening cousins. *Agamemnon* follows this pattern, rising from the misgivings of the watchman on the palace roof to the climax of Agamemnon dead at the hands of his wife. But with the latter two plays of *Oresteia* complications are introduced. Who would expect that the revenge of Orestes would involve Orestes' old nurse and the unexpected intervention of Pylades or predict that the third play would switch from

Delphi to Athens, involve a chorus of Furies, a trial at Athens, and would reach a climax when the order of the cosmos is altered by a human court of justice?

Character in Aeschylus

Characters in Aeschylus are more important for what they do rather than for who they are. The Greeks were not as fascinated by character and psychology as we are, although the plays do show instances of events explained by personality, especially in Euripides. Thus when Orestes at *Libation-Bearers* 247 describes himself and his sister as "the orphan offspring of the eagle-father," we see them in their role as bereaved children rather than as fully delineated characters. In *Suppliants* we do learn the King's name (Pelasgos son of Palaichthon) but he is no real individual, rather the personification of his role as leader of his city. In *Seven* Eteokles must take on the dual role of shepherd of his people and the cursed son of Oedipus, but again we do not glimpse a complex character beneath the role he plays. The hatred that he has for his brother (lines 653–76) is not so much motivated by personal feeling as it is by loathing of his brother's evil nature, "Justice never smiled on him." The chorus do beg him not to "show himself in passion like his brother of ill repute," and we do get hints of personal motivation, but the scene has been so structured that his encounter with Polyneikes is not the result of personal vendetta but of sober calculation of the defenders to be placed at the other gates. The one human to appear in *Prometheus* is Io, and she is more human victim rather than a woman with any individual characteristics. Aristotle and Northrop Frye would approve of Aeschylean characters.

To be sure Klytaimestra makes up for these other characters in low relief, the "man-plotting woman" whose motives are made clear at the end of *Agamemnon* (revenge for her daughter, love for the new man in her life, and spite over Kassandra, and, not directly stated, gender jealousy – this woman has and enjoys "power"). Aeschylus is probably breaking new dramatic ground by making Klytaimestra the chief perpetrator of the murder, and in so doing needs to build up for his audience this incredibly powerful portrait of the "woman-lioness." Some of Aeschylus' minor characters also come alive with a distinctive personality, the watchman who opens *Oresteia* with his mysterious allusions couched in imagery, or the Nurse in *Libation-Bearers*, who reminisces about caring for the infant Orestes, including washing his soiled diapers (734–65).

The chorus in Aeschylus

If characters in Aeschylus are for the most part drawn in low relief, his choruses stand out both for their dramatic personalities and their role within their play. This is especially true of *Suppliants*, where the chorus speaks half the lines in the drama and it is their fate that is on the line. These are no detached observers or "ideal spectators," but vitally involved young women. In the scene with the King (234–523), we might have expected their father Danaos to conduct the negotiations, as one male authority-figure to another. In the previous scene (176–233) he has called attention to the advancing Argives and has marshaled his daughters around the altar. But Danaos is silent for the rest of the scene, leaving the explanation and the formal supplication to the chorus. When Euripides writes his *Children of Herakles* with a similar dramatic setting, only the male figure (Iolaos) will speak for a silent chorus. This chorus pleads its own case, and we can see their motivation as in part due to the influence of their father, who has already arranged their escape from Egypt (11–18), prepares them for their encounter with the Argives, and at the end (996–1013) encourages them not to let their femininity attract men and to value honor over life. We can see here a chorus very much under the influence of their father, so much so that in the following play they will heed his instructions to kill their new husbands on their wedding-night. The mythical tradition tells us that Danaos knows from an oracle that he will die at the hands of his son-in-law. This is not revealed in the play we have, but if it came out in the next, we have a chorus prepared to follow their father in whatever he says.

So opposed are they to this "impious" (*asebe* – line 9) marriage with their cousins that they wish to have no marriage at all. They pray to virgin deities such as Artemis and Athene, and devoutly pray to have nothing to do with Aphrodite ("cowering with hatred for the marriage bed" – 332, "let the fate of death come before marriage" – 804–5). This is in ironic contrast to the very songs they sing of their ancestress Io, the name of whose child by Zeus (Epaphos) means "at a caress," where the sufferings of a human woman come right at the end. Their devotion to their father and their distaste for a forced marriage with their cousins have led them in this play to flee to a foreign land and in the next to murder these new bridegrooms. This is a chorus whose attitudes will have to have been made right. Someone at lines 1034–42 contradicts what the chorus has just sung and observes that Aphrodite is a god with power nearest to Zeus, along with Hera patron of marriage, and that she is honored by "awesome rites" (or "for her awesome deeds"). There has been great debate whether the speaker is part of the chorus disagreeing with the other half, a sub-chorus of servants, or even the male Egyptians, perhaps led distinctively by Lynkeus, the one bridegroom who will be spared on the bloody wedding-night. The chorus in *Suppliants* then is a highly involved character in the play, one with a biased point of view that will have been changed by the end of the trilogy. Aeschylus presumably did not let his trilogy end with an unrepentant chorus guilty of the murder of their husbands.

The other highly involved chorus is that of *Eumenides*, where the Furies are more than observers but active participants in the resolution of the great issues of Justice that the case of Orestes has raised. Furies are children of Night and frightfully described by the priestess of Apollo (lines 48–56):

I do not mean women, but Gorgons, though not like Gorgons either. I once saw a picture of creatures carrying away Phineus' meal [Harpies], but these had no wings and they were black, and completely loathsome. They snore with no gentle breaths and from their eyes drips an awful ooze and their dress is not right to wear to temples of gods or homes of men.

In the first part of the play they are completely unsympathetic, and the audience would side with Apollo in his rejection of them as barely more than animals, whose home is more properly a lion's den. But surprisingly Athene does not reject them outright – "these too have their allotted place, one not to be rejected" (476–7) – and in the ode that follows we (and the ancient audience) realize that there is some Justice on the Furies' side:

> It is good to behave properly through suffering. What man or what city of mortals can ever honor Justice if it has no fear in its heart? (520–5)

In the trial and judgment that follow the Furies have the better of the argument with Apollo and six of the twelve human jurors favor the case of the Furies. This is a brilliant piece of dramatic plotting, first to make these ancient and awful deities the actual chorus, and then to make them partly sympathetic to the audience.

But there is even more in store. In the last third of the drama, after Orestes has left the scene, Athene both threatens and persuades the Furies to abandon their planned vengeance on her city and to become honored residents therein. There were at Athens ancient guardian deities, called the *Semnai* ("the awesome ones"), and what Aeschylus seems to have done is identify these benign spirits with the Furies. In the closing chorus (1033–47) the children of Night are renamed the "*Semnai theai*" ("the awesome goddesses") and are given a home. Characters in *Oresteia* come home: Agamemnon to be murdered, Orestes first to kill his mother and now in *Eumenides* to be restored, and even the Furies can speak of themselves as residents of Athens (916, 1018). The word "Eumenides" never occurs in the play; in fact the term seems not to show up before the 410s, but essentially Aeschylus has turned the angry children of night into the awesome goddesses or the "kind ones," and in so doing has recast the Greek religious concept of these deities.

Other choruses in Aeschylus may not be so directly involved, but they do raise the level of the action from the particular to the general. In the first half of *Agamemnon* (1–781), the chorus sing an entry-song (40–103) and three long odes (104–257, 355–488, 681–781), well more than half the lines, in which they provide both the background to the Trojan War ("so Zeus the god of guests and hosts sends the sons of Atreus against Paris" – 60–2) and Agamemnon's part in it ("he dared to sacrifice his daughter, as the means to wage a war over a woman" – 224–6) and the moral universe against which this story unfolds ("a man said that the gods did not care about punishing a mortal who would trample on things inviolable – that man was wrong" – 369–72, "Justice drives all things to their appointed end" – 780–1). Similarly in *Libation-Bearers* the chorus of captive women of the palace makes it clear that we are in the same moral universe ("what is there that can wash away blood fallen on the ground?" – 48; "let Justice exact blood-stroke for blood-stroke – the doer shall suffer" – 312–13). The chorus also engages with Orestes and Elektra in a lengthy *kommos* (306–478), which widens the scope of the dramatic action and summons up the spirit of the dead Agamemnon. This chorus is not all-knowing, for they believe that Orestes' act will wipe the slate clean ("you did well . . . you freed the entire city of Argos when you so neatly beheaded these two snakes" – 1044–7), but immediately on these lines

Orestes sees the Furies and the cycle begins again. The old men in *Agamemnon* attempt to intervene in the action when they confront Aigisthos at line 1651, but more crucial is their appeal to Orestes at 1646–8 to come and be "the mighty murderer of these two" and again at 1667. Even more significant is the actual intervention by the chorus in *Libation-Bearers*, who at 770–3 advise the Nurse to tell Aigisthos to come alone without his bodyguards.

So too in the earlier plays the chorus will lift the level of the action and display to the audience the moral universe against which the on-stage action is set. The chorus of fugitive maidens in *Suppliants* makes it clear that Zeus is the god operating behind the action of this play, both in his aspect as Zeus *hikesios* ("Zeus of suppliants") and as their ultimate ancestor, who fathered Epaphos upon Io. This is Zeus in control of the moral universe, "from the lofty towers of their hopes he hurls murderous mortals; he wears no armor of violence, for everything for a god is without effort" (97–100), "with impartial scales Zeus examines both sides, dealing out evil to the wicked and good to the righteous" (402–4), "the Argives respect kindred suppliants of sacred Zeus, and so they shall please the gods with pure altars" (652–5). At the same time Zeus is their ancestor and in his healing of Io and his fathering of Epaphos ("at a caress") the chorus seek a parallel for their own plight, ironically missing the point that Zeus and Io were reconciled in the very sexual relationship they are fleeing. The entire ode at 524–99 is devoted to the story of Zeus and Io – "in truth she bore the burden of Zeus and bore a perfect child, blessed through the greatness of time" (580–2).

The style of Aeschylus

Aeschylus the dramatist is probably best known through the caricature in Aristophanes' *Frogs*, and this has had an effect on how we view his work. Aristophanes has "Euripides" describe Aeschylus as using "words the size of a dozen oxen, with eyebrows and crests, terrifying and completely unknown to the spectators" (924–5), while "Aeschylus" himself admits that his words reflect the scope of his dramatic themes and ideas, that "demi-gods should use more inflated language" (1059–60). Yet his iambic scenes, while grand, are not written in dense Greek – they often run smoothly and easily, with touches of the colloquial or commonplace ("an ox stands upon my tongue" – *Agamemnon* 36). But Aeschylus is fond of the unusual word, often one that bears two meanings or that will recur throughout with loaded significance: such as *Agamemnon* 11 of Klytaimestra, "such is the power of her confident man-plotting (*androboulon*) heart," where *androboulon* could mean "plotting like a male" or "plotting against a male" and in fact means both. Or at *Agamemnon* 525 the herald describes Agamemnon as "having brought down Troy with the mattock of justice-bringing (*dikephoros*) Zeus," where *dikephoros* carries the ethos of "the doer must pay, that is law" and will be used pointedly at *Libation-Bearers* 120 in contrast to *dikastes* "judge."

It is in the choral odes and the lyric exchanges that we see the grander and more opaque Greek. Aeschylus can pile up the adjectives, often compound ones, either minted by him or strongly in the tradition of high poetry, and the sequence of thought is often compressed. *Agamemnon* 218–27 shows the state of the king's mind after he has decided to sacrifice his daughter:

> *But when he put on the harness of Necessity, breathing an impious, unholy, unsanctified turning of mind, then he changed to a dare-anything purpose. For delusion, evil-counseling, wretched, source of evils emboldens mortals. So he dared to become a sacrificer of a daughter, an arousal of woman-reprising war, the first offerings for his ships.*

This is powerfully written, with three principal verbs in the past, and the nouns "delusion" and "turning" each qualified by three adjectives, in the case of "turning" all negative compounds, with "delusion" described as "evil-counseling" and "source of evils." Throw in "women-reprising" for "war," "dare-anything" (*pantotolmon*) and "first offering" (*proteleia*), and one sees how Aeschylus' language operates on the level of high poetry. Aristophanes' "Euripides" alleges that as the play unfolded, an Aeschylean chorus "would grind out four whole strings of uninterrupted lyrics" (*Frogs* 914–5). In *Agamemnon* after the parodos we have six pairs of such "uninterrupted" lyric strophes and antistrophes (104–257), in *Suppliants* eight pairs (40–175), and five such pairs in *Persians* (65–159).

One of the most distinctive features of Aeschylus' verbal style is his use of allusive and repeated imagery. It is almost like a leitmotif in an opera by Wagner, where the same musical phrase (evoking a particular theme, e.g., Valhalla, Siegfried, the Valkyries) will suddenly come and go, directing the listener's attention to the theme that the phrase evokes. Image-patterns in Aeschylus are significant and carry much of the verbal meaning of the drama, and are varied with great skill, carrying shades of meaning from one passage to another. In *Oresteia*, the only complete trilogy that we possess, we have a wealth of such image-patterns: light and dark, animals, disease and cure, drops of liquids, hunting and the net. Pick any of these and the reader will find a complex pattern of verbal allusions and meanings. Take the eagle, a king's bird, the creature of Zeus. At *Agamemnon* 48–59 the sons of Atreus are like plaintive eagles robbed of their young, whose cries the gods hear and send "a late-punishing Fury upon the transgressors." Here the image is favorable, but only fifty lines later, the sons of Atreus become a pair of eagles, who attack and devour a pregnant hare (109–20), an image which prefigures the destruction of Troy. Then in *Libation-Bearers* Orestes and Elektra are "the orphaned children of the eagle-father who died in the binding coils of the terrible serpent" (247–9). The snake-image is similarly shifting in its focus. Twice Klytaimestra in her murder of Agamemnon is compared to a female snake (a viper at *Agamemnon* 1233, an *echidna* at *Libation-Bearers* 249), appropriate given the association of snakes with the Mother. But then in her dream, related at *Libation-Bearers* 523–50, she gives birth to a male snake (*drakon, ophis*), who is clearly Orestes (549). If, as for us, snakes carried negative overtones for the Greeks, a comparison of Orestes to a snake is not a happy one. Just to confuse the image further, the chorus will praise Orestes at *Libation-Bearers* 1046–7 for "freeing the whole city of Argos, by lopping off the heads of these two snakes (*drakontion*)," that is, Klytaimestra and Aigsithos. In art Furies either have snakes for hair or hold a snake as they pursue Orestes – if so costumed in *Eumenides*, the spectators will see this image in reality – while at line 181 Apollo threatens them with his arrow, "a flying, biting snake (*ophis*)."

Aristotle (*Poetics* 6) lists *opsis* ("spectacle") as one of the lesser parts of tragedy, more properly the realm of the technician than the poet. Grand visual aspect was a major aspect of Aeschylus' drama. The very term "spectators" implies watching events performed (*drama* = "doing"), but as we have remarked above, there is not all that much pure action in Greek drama. Given the large scope of the ancient theater, physical movements would have to have been grand and theatrical, and Aeschylus is fond of the tableau or the spectacular set scene. Aristophanes in *Frogs* had his Euripides criticize the spectacle of the character silent for much of the play (911–20) – he mentions Niobe and Achilles (in *Phrygians*), but could have added Kassandra in *Agamemnon* – while Dionysos recalls (1028–9) the mourning of the chorus over the tomb of Dareios in *Persians*. We can only imagine the impression left on the spectators by the pageantry of the Persian elders as they opened *Persians*, or the Egyptian-looking women who will claim to be Greek in *Suppliants*, Elektra and the chorus gathered around the tomb of Agamemnon with Orestes and Pylades watching from concealment, or the chorus of Furies who burst through the doors of the *skene* and proceed to track Orestes down by the scent of blood on his hands, finally surrounding him at Athens and enchanting him with their song. Moments with the characters also come to mind: the watchman curled like a dog on the roof of the *skene*, Agamemnon contemplating the purple carpet leading to the door of the *skene*, Klytaimestra standing over her victims with an identical mirror scene from *Libation-Bearers*, the figure of Athene presiding over the first murder trial in history.

Gender-themes in Aeschylus

In *Frogs* Aristophanes' Aeschylus claims never to have put a woman in love on stage (1044), but he makes great dramatic capital out of the theme of gender. One of the great figures in all of Western drama is Klytaimestra, the "man-plotting" woman who dominates all others in *Agamemnon*, who first persuades her husband to walk the carpet of blood and then murders him with a sword, and whose first reaction to danger in *Libation-Bearers* is to demand a "man-killing axe" (889). In her description of the murder of Agamemnon (1384–92) she likens herself to the Earth impregnated by the life-giving rain, in a chilling inversion of the ancient myth of the marriage of Earth and Heaven. It has been argued that in addition to revenge for her daughter, her love for Aigisthos, and jealousy of Kassandra, what really motivates her is gender-jealousy. Hers will be the man's role, and although she bares her breast to Orestes in the great confrontation between mother and son, we know from the Nurse that she never nursed the infant Orestes.

In the third play, *Eumenides*, part of the opposition between Furies and Olympians turns on gender, for the Furies are ancient, dark, and female, while the Olympians are younger, shining, and male. This must have come through dramatically in the confrontation between Apollo and the Furies, especially if Apollo appeared on the roof of the *skene*, clad in light and armed with his bow to drive away these daughters of Night. The Furies deny all but the familial connection, and "treat as nothing the marriage-pledge of Zeus and Hera" (213–14). The trial will be presided over by Athene,

Figure 2.1 *Two scenes influenced by the opening scene of Aeschylus'* Libation-Bearers, *on a red-figure skyphos, attributed to the Penelope Painter, 440–430. Reproduced courtesy of the National Museum, Copenhagen (597).*

a curious blend of female and male; dressed in man's armor, she declares herself "strongly for the father" (738), whether that means males in general, Agamemnon in this case, or as spokesman of her father Zeus. It is she that pronounces (739–40), "And so I will not put first the death of a wife who has killed her husband, the guardian of the house." Yet like Klytaimestra, Athene is a woman of power, with male aspects and attitudes, played incidentally by the same actor, and feminist critics are right to react with unease over the distinction between the "man-plotting" woman and the goddess in male armor.

In *Suppliants* the relationship between male and female formed an important sub-theme of the play, since at times the daughters of Danaos seem to be fleeing not just this marriage, with the arrogant sons of Aigyptos, but all marriage (140–2, 341, 804–7, 1030–3). Indeed someone (a sub-chorus of handmaids, the sons of Aigyptos?) at 1034–42) tells the chorus that Love is a deity not to be rejected, and in a later play of the trilogy (*Daughters of Danaos*) Aphrodite herself proclaimed her role in the cosmos as the mediatrix of the union between the genders:

> The holy sky yearns to pierce the Earth, and desire seizes Earth to join in union; the rain falls from the Sky's fluid abundance and makes Earth conceive, and she brings forth for mortals grazing for their flocks, corn for their sustenance, and the fruit of trees. From this wedlock of the rains come to birth all things that are; of this I am the cause (fr. 44),

the same myth that Klytaimestra blasphemes in her description of her husband's murder. As in *Oresteia*, harmony out of confrontation seems to have been achieved at the end, although the symbol of this union of the sexes is Aphrodite rather than Athene.

Aeschylus' moral and divine universe

While one should not label Aeschylus as either "theologian" or "philosopher," there is no denying that his tragedies operate within a crucial and consistent "religious" dimension. His moral universe is intensely important, as his characters act and are acted upon in accordance with his view of the gods. "Religion" may be the wrong word as gods in Greek drama are not worshipped through faith in a being infinitely better than our own, but as realities in the universe who shape our ends and demand our worship. Gods exist, gods witness human actions, and gods punish wicked humans.

This is especially true of Zeus. As in Homer's *Odyssey* (eighth century) and the poems of Hesiod (ca. 700–675), Zeus is the god in control and he is associated with a divine order of Justice (*Dike*). In the opening stasimon of *Suppliants* the chorus proclaim:

> Destructive mortals he casts from the high tower of their hopes, he dons no armor of force. For the gods everything is without effort. Seated upon his holy throne he accomplishes his will. (96–103)

Aeschylus shows individuals who are responsible for their actions and ultimately for their punishment. In *Persians* the ghost of Dareios asserts what lies at the heart of Aeschylus' moral universe, the famous sequence of *ate–hybris–nemesis*:

> For when hybris *(violent arrogance) blooms, it reaps the fruits of* ate *(folly), from which it gathers a harvest of tears . . . Zeus is present, the punisher of over-boastful minds, a heavy requiter.* (821–2, 827–8)

A man's mental delusion (*ate*) may lead him to perform offensive acts (*hybris*), which lead to a reckoning (*nemesis*) presided over by the gods. In the case of Xerxes he disregarded an oracle not to cross from Asia into Europe and yoked the sea as if it were a slave (739–52), and "when a man himself is eager, the god too lends a hand" (742). Agamemnon dared to sacrifice his daughter to get the winds that would take him to Troy and become a conqueror – at line 221 his mental state has changed to "one that would dare anything" – and the chorus proclaim at line 461–2 that "gods watch for those who kill many." Often in Aeschylus excessive prosperity or worldly success (*olbos*) lies at the heart of a man's ruin: the Persians with all their gold, Agamemnon who reduced a great city, the kings of Thebes, whose prosperity was "too great" (*Seven* 771).

This is the predominant rhythm for *Oresteia*: action → reaction, and in the third play, resolution. Agamemnon is at the same time the agent of Zeus in the punishment of the Trojans for their violation of *xenia* (Paris' theft of another's wife) – "thus Zeus the powerful god of guests and hosts sends the sons of Atreus against Alexander" (60–2) – and the next victim in the cycle of *ate–hybris–nemesis*. His own wife will be his punisher, for motives that she outlines at *Agamemnon* 1431–47 (revenge for her daughter, influence of Aigisthos, jealousy over Kassandra), but she too will be Orestes' victim, when he is commanded by Apollo at *Libation Bearers* 269–305 (and indirectly by Zeus – *Eumenides* 713) to murder his mother to avenge his father. The chorus express this in powerful and metaphoric language, "As Zeus remains on his throne this also remains – 'the one who has acted suffers' – for that is law" (*Agamemnon* 1563–4), "But it is law that blood-drops shed upon the ground call forth new blood, for the deed shouts for a Fury from those who died before, to bring another destruction upon destruction" (*Libation-Bearers* 404–4).

But Aeschylus is not writing morality-plays to justify the gods or to advance a particular ethical line of thought. There are questions in his moral universe: If Apollo is the voice of Zeus, then did Zeus actually instruct Orestes to murder his mother (*Eumenides* 622–4)? Eteokles may be the victim of a curse working itself out in the third generation, but he is also the thoroughly admirable defender of his city, who will assign the appropriate defender to each gate, leaving himself the seventh gate, there fatally to encounter his brother. The chorus at *Agamemnon* 160–83 (the so-called "Hymn to Zeus") has only Zeus to call upon if they are to rid themselves of the burden of worry (165–6), yet admit that Zeus is the product of generational conflict among the gods and that the "grace" (*charis*) of the gods is also "violent" (*biaios*). Sometimes Zeus and the Furies seem to be working together in the pursuit of Justice (*dike*) – as at *Agamemnon* 55–9, 744–9, 1431–3, *Libation-Bearers* 646–51, but in *Eumenides* younger male Olympians and older female Furies collide. But in this cosmic battle the shining young Apollo comes off poorly, while the brilliant stasimon at 490–565 shows that the Furies are not without their place in the universe nor without the sympathy of humans. After all, six of Athene's twelve jurors voted for the Furies.

Gods are no strangers to the stage of Aeschylus. If *Prometheus Bound* is his work (or even his concept completed by his son), all the characters but Io are divine figures, and the theme of the drama is no less than the new tyranny of Zeus in Heaven and how he himself might be overthrown in turn. In the later Prometheus-play(s) it is likely that Earth and a human Herakles appeared, while in the *Daughters of Danaos* Aphrodite presented her role in the cosmos in terms of the archetypal myth of the marriage of Earth and Heaven. No gods appear in *Persians* or *Seven*, although the ghost of Dareios does provide an element of the supernatural and he does proclaim the moral truth about the universe and warn the Athenians and Greeks not to commit the offences that Xerxes has. In *Eumenides* divine beings dominate the stage, and although the trial is about the fate of Orestes, he is acquitted and off the stage by line 777, with nearly 300 lines of the play to run. The trilogy decides not just Orestes' fate but the position of the Furies in the new Olympian order. This was Aeschylus' bold dramatic stroke: the goddesses worshipped as "Eumenides" ("Kind Ones") used to be Furies. If in the Christian universe devils are fallen angels, in Aeschylus the "awesome goddesses" (*Semnai*) are risen demons.

Gods appeared in the lost plays as well. The *Edonians*, part of the tetralogy called the *Lykourgeia*, featured the appearance of Dionysos in Thrace, while three plays may have formed a trilogy on Dionysos at Thebes (*Semele, Wool-Carders, Pentheus*), in which the god will have appeared both in disguise and in his own identity. We know also from fr. 169 that Lyssa, the goddess of madness, was a character in *Wool-Carders*. In the *Weighing of Souls* two goddesses, Eos (Dawn) and Thetis, come before Zeus to plead for their sons Memnon and Achilles in their upcoming combat. Thetis seems also to have appeared in *Daughters of Nereus*, bringing the new armor for her son Achilles. In *Niobe* the title character boasted that her children were fairer than Apollo and Artemis, and will pay the price for her arrogant tongue. A divine presence is very likely at either the start or the end.

Oracles, ghosts, curses all operate in Aeschylean drama. Oracles, of course, underlie so much of Greek drama, and one of the major differences between our world-view and the Greeks is that in the latter oracles come true. Dareios complains at *Persians* 739 that "the fulfillment of the oracle came quickly," and the chorus in *Seven* (742–91) makes it clear that the destruction wrought on three generations at Thebes began with Laios' willful disobedience of a proclamation by Apollo: "three times Apollo spoke in his Pythian oracle at the center of the Earth, that Laios would save his city by dying without offspring" (746–9). In *Libation-Bearers* and *Eumenides* we hear of, then meet the god himself, as Orestes relates his oracle at 269–305, repeated by Pylades (900–2) as mouthpiece of Apollo, and confirmed by Apollo at *Eumenides* 84, 203, 579–80. The oracle to Danaos that he would die at the hands of a son-in-law is not mentioned explicitly in *Suppliants*, but would have made a nice dramatic revelation in a later play, and like all good oracles, would have been realized.

The modern reader or spectator often finds curses a convenient way to explain what happens to characters in Greek drama, especially those who see the predestined workings of gods or "Fate." ("Fate" is a word best avoided in the study of Greek tragedy. The Greek *moira* means really one's lot or portion in life, while Fate has strong overtones of the gods as puppeteers controlling every aspect of one's life and denying any free will.) In Aeschylus we do see curses as part of the moral universe, particularly in *Seven*, where the chorus sum up what has happened over three generations, "heavy are the reckonings of ancient-spoken curses, when they come due" (766–7). In this chorus (720–91) we find all the elements of an Aeschylean moral drama: excessive prosperity, mortal disobedience of a divine proclamation, the curse laid by Oedipus on his sons, which the chorus fear "a swift-footed Fury may fulfill." About Agamemnon one must keep in mind that although his is a house of blood, "a god-hated, guilty, self-murderous place" (1090–1) wherein "dwells a parade of kindred Furies, aroused to even greater rage by drinking mortal blood, difficult to be rid of" (1188–90), and while Aigisthos may speak of the curse of Thyestes (1601–2), Agamemnon is not punished for what his father did to his brother and his nephews – he is not "cursed" by the abominable feast of Thyestes, but for what he himself has done: killing his daughter and destroying a city. It should be remembered that, while we know from lines 60–3 that Agamemnon is Zeus' agent against the Trojans, he does not, and cannot use in his defense of the sacrifice of his daughter that he is merely doing the will of the gods.

Aeschylus and his Age

Aeschylus was part of two events of earth-shaking importance in his lifetime. First there was the conflict with Persia. The Persians under Cyrus the Great first came into contact with the Greeks in the mid-540s, when the kingdom of Lydia in western Asia fell into Persian hands. By the end of the sixth century the Greek states in western Asia and the islands had become subject to Persian control. Certain of these states, led by Miletos, revolted from Persia in 490s, in what we call the "Ionian Revolt." Although Athens as mother-city of the Ionians sent aid to the rebels, the revolt was crushed by the fall of Miletos in 494 – an event which inspired Phrynichos' tragedy *Capture of Miletos* and its reaction at Athens.

The Persians under Cyrus the Great had already spread their influence across the narrow waterways that separate Asia from Europe into the regions to the north of Greece, Dareios reaching the Danube River in the 510s. But the Athenian aid sent to the Ionians gave first Dareios and then his son Xerxes the excuse to launch major military campaigns against Greece, in particular against Athens. A sea-borne invasion in 492 was abandoned after a storm wrecked the Persian fleet at Mount Athos, and in 490 an expedition sent through the islands ended with the glorious Athenian victory over superior numbers at Marathon. Aeschylus' brother is said to have died at Marathon, while Aeschylus' epitaph records his own participation "which the long-haired Persian knew too well." Nine years later Xerxes mounted an immense invasion by land and sea (481–79), crossing the Hellespont and moving down from the

North. This culminated in a decisive sea-victory for the Greeks at Salamis (480) and a land-victory at Plataia (479); these permanently removed the Persian threat to Greece and altered dramatically the course of Western history. Aeschylus is said to have fought in the sea-battle. In any case the description that the messenger in his *Persians* provides is used by historians in preference to that given by Herodotos, a half-century later. First Phrynichos with his *Phoenician Women* (476) and then Aeschylus with his *Persians* (472) made drama out of the victory at Salamis and the repulsion of Persia. Aeschylus' play, however, while glorifying the Greek victory, shows the story from the Persian point of view and places the Persians against the moral background of his tragic universe.

Second was the political sea-change from "tyranny" to democracy. When Aeschylus was born, Athens was ruled by Hippias the "tyrant" (*tyrannos*), a word which for us conjures up overtones of unenlightened despotism, but which for the Greeks at the time meant little more than "one-man rule." Peisistratos had seized power at Athens in the mid-540s and he and his son Hippias, who succeeded him in 527, ruled Athens competently until 510. Indeed in the fourth century the reign of the tyrants would be remembered as a "golden age."

Hippias was ousted from Athens in 510, principally by the agency of the Alkmaionidai, a prominent aristocratic clan who had enlisted the assistance of the oracle at Delphi and the Spartan army. But the result was not the replacement of one-man rule by an Alkmaionid oligarchy, but the establishment in 508/7 of *demokratia* ("democracy"), under the leadership of the Alkmaionid Kleisthenes, who (according to Herodotos) "took the people into his party." Although this was a democracy of sorts, based on the almost sacred principles of *parrhesia* ("freedom of speech") and *isonomia* ("equal laws"), the radical democracy that we associate with Athens did not really develop until the reforms of 462/1. At that time Athens broke off her alliance with Sparta, made a new alliance with Argos, and ostracized Kimon, the partisan of aristocratic and traditional politics. At this point the Areopagos Council lost most of its political influence and returned to being a tribunal for homicide, and it is in 461 that many place the start of "real" democracy at Athens. The names associated with this change to radical democracy are Ephialtes, murdered in 461 by unknown agents, and Perikles.

As one would expect in plays written by and performed by Athenians, the democratic background seeps through. In *Persians* the queen asks about Athens, 'Who is the shepherd of this people and who commands their army?," and is told, "They are called no man's slaves; they are not a subject people" (241–2), and in the account of the battle of Salamis the cry of the Greeks is "freedom" (403). But *Persians* is no eulogy of Athenian superiority, as the ghost of Dareios warns Athenians "not to lose their present good fortune through a craving for greater things" (824–6). In *Suppliants*, produced against the critical backdrop of the late 460s, the king of Argos (Athens' new ally) maintains, "I would not attempt to make any promise until I have shared this matter with my citizens" (368–9) and Danaos describes at 600–24 how the decision was made in good democratic fashion, with the city voting to ally itself with the cause of right. If the traditionally accepted date of 463 for *Suppliants* is right, then this sentiment is being uttered at a time when Athens was redefining her structure of democracy.

But no play is so bound up with current events as *Eumenides*. Whereas the earlier plays were set in the distant mythical past, *Eumenides* seems to move forward in time. Athene inaugurates what will become the Areopagos Council, a court of homicide, the very court whose extensive political powers were curtailed in the reforms of the late 460s. Recent events show through in three places. First the significant change in foreign policy and the alliance with Argos. Aeschylus has changed the traditional setting of the story of Agamemnon from Mycenae to Argos, and in the third play Orestes celebrates his acquittal by promising eternal friendship between Argos and Athens (754–77):

> To this land and to its people for the great length of time to come, I swear this oath as I take my leave: that no leader of my city will ever invade your land with hostile intent. (763–6)

It does seem as if Aeschylus was presenting that treaty, made four years before, in a favorable light.

More awkward is the matter of the Areopagos Council, for the play allows for either a positive or negative spin on the reforms of 462/1. At 704–6 she formally creates her court:

> I establish this council, unaffected by thoughts of profits, a source of respect, quick to anger, a watcher over those who sleep, the protector of the land.

One can argue either way: that Athene established this council as a court of homicide and all that the reformers did was strip its political accretions and return it to its original function, or that Athene established this court and how dare reformers tamper with it in any way. Like all good artists, Aeschylus does not preach one side of an issue, but leaves the matter open. Earlier in her speech we get another of the dramatist's plays on meanings, for when Athene says, "and in this place respect of the citizens and its close kin, fear to do no wrong, shall hold fast day and night" (690–2), does she mean "respect of the citizens for the Council" – remember that the Furies have just maintained that "on occasion what terrifies is good, when one must maintain a watchman on one's thoughts" (517–19). Or does it mean "respect on the part of the Council for the citizens"?

In the early 450s, Athens came perilously close to internal strife (*stasis*), this due to a combination of resentment over the change in foreign policy, the ostracism of Kimon, and the reforms, as well as serious war losses in 459, and the proposals to widen the basis for citizenship. Aeschylus in *Eumenides* displays an Athens where the citizens work together to avoid such faction, where "neither anarchy nor despotism rule" (696), where citizens "do not expel what terrifies from the city" (698), where the reformed Furies pray:

> that civil strife (stasis), which never has its fill of evils, may never echo in this city, that the dust may never drink the black blood of citizens through a passion for retribution and blood-for-blood destruction and prey upon our city. May they exchange good things with common-loving hearts and love with one mind. For that is a cure for many things among mortals. (976–87)

This at a time when Athens was as close as she would get to civil war.

Finally, Aeschylus witnessed and was part of what we term the "Enlightenment," the development of "philosophy," although for a fifth-century Greek there was not the same neat distinction between "religion," "science," "philosophy," and "ethics." In the sixth century thinkers had begun to ponder things *peri physeos* ("about nature"). Xenophanes had written poems in which he questioned the anthropomorphic presentation of gods, that is, gods like men. Parmenides had explored (also in verse) the nature of being, while Anaxagoras (in prose) postulated a universe run by Mind. In *Eumenides*, when Apollo proclaims that only the father is true parent of the child, he is likely uttering the arguments of Anaxagoras. The great age of philosophy lay ahead – Sokrates, Plato, Aristotle come after Aeschylus – but Aeschylus did live in and did know the proponents of intelligent inquiry. Epicharmos, the contemporary comic poet whom Aeschylus must have met on visits to Sicily, also plays with ideas and themes of philosophy. It was an exciting time to have been alive.

Sophokles

The life of Sophokles (496–406), second of the canonical Three, coincides almost exactly with the unfolding of the fifth century at Athens, that high classical period, which witnessed the wars with Persia and Sparta, the splendid building program on the Akropolis, the realization of the human ideal in sculpture, the development of the Athenian Empire, an acceleration in philosophy and science, the democracy for which Athens is famous today, and the high-water mark of Greek drama. Sophokles is seen by many as the tragic representative in this century of perfection and elegance, a worthy companion to the Parthenon or the statues of Pheidias. For Sophokles our "biographical" information has more to do with his life outside the theater, since, unlike Aeschylus and Euripides, the dates of most of his surviving seven dramas remain uncertain. Again allowing for the inaccuracy of our sources and their fondness for manufacturing anecdotes, we can establish the following list of dates with some confidence:

496 – born at Kolonos, near Athens; son of Sophillos
480 – performed in the victory-song celebrating the battle of Salamis
468 – début (with *Triptolemos*?) and first victory (over Aeschylus)
466–59 – finished second (to Aeschylus' *Daughters of Danaos* trilogy)
443/2 – served as *Hellenotamias* (imperial treasurer)
441/0 – served as elected general
438 – first prize (defeated Euripides)
431 – second prize (lost to Euphorion, Euripides third)
420/19 – became guardian of the cult of the god Asklepios
413–411 – served as *proboulos* in the emergency following the defeat at Sicily

Continued

409 – first prize (plays included *Philoktetes*)
406/5 – died at Athens
401 – posthumous production of *Oedipus at Kolonos*

Anecdotes about his personal life are numerous. Ancient sources attest to his good birth – Ion of Chios uses the word *chrestos* ("noble," "decent") of him – his attractiveness as a youth, and pleasant personality, and we can be sure that he received the usual aristocratic education in *mousike* (learning) and *gymastike* (athletics). Unlike Aeschylus and Euripides, he had a public, if not political career. He held the office of *Hellenotamias* in 443/2, a treasurer of the goddess Athene, and two years later was elected as one of the ten generals, the highest elected officials in the state. Perikles is said to have commented that Sophokles was "a good poet, but a poor general," and Ion of Chios describes his public career thus, "he was neither clever nor effective, but behaved like one of the nobles of old." There are various stories about his time on active duty in the East, usually involving *la dolce vita* and sexual conquests. Aristotle (*Rhetoric* 1419a25) tells us that after the disastrous loss of Athenian forces in Sicily in 413, Sophokles was one of the ten old men who held the new post of *proboulos*, created to provide confident leadership in troubled times. Aristotle adds that, when asked if the *probouloi* had consented to turn power over to the oligarchy we know as the "Four Hundred," Sophokles agreed that they had, but could find no better alternative.

He is said also to have been the priest of a healing *heros* (Halon) and for that reason was entrusted with the cult statue (and sacred snake?) of the god Asklepios when his cult was being established at Athens after 420. Less certain is the tradition that following his death Sophokles was worshipped himself as a *heros* under the name Dexion. The stories about the unhappy relationship with his son, Iophon (himself a tragic poet), and the latter's legal action against him for senility are just that, stories, perhaps derived from comedy. So too the various accounts of his death: from joy at winning the prize or by choking on a grape-seed.

His contributions to tragedy form a sub-group of ancient anecdotes. According to tradition he was originally an actor in his own plays, but gave this up because of a weak voice, and thus became the first poet to write rather than perform in his own plays. Aristotle credits him with the introduction of the third actor and of *skenographia* ("*skene*-painting"). As Aeschylus uses the third actor in *Oresteia* (458), if Sophokles did introduce him, he must have done so early in his career. Three-actor scenes remain clumsy until the very end of the fifth century, when they are used with great dramatic effect in Euripides' *Orestes* and Sophokles' *Oedipus at Kolonos*. "*Skene*-painting" does not mean elaborate sets, but more likely that the front of the *skene* was rendered to look like a palace, house, temple or whatever. He is credited with introducing Lydian and Phrygian musical modes into his choral songs, in addition to the basic Dorian and Ionian, and with increasing the number of *choreutai* from twelve to fifteen. The *Suda* claims that he was the first to present four unconnected plays instead of a trilogy or tetralogy, but Aeschylus in fact did this in 472, four years before Sophokles' début. But as far as we know, Sophokles seems not to have used the trilogy form very much, if at all, and it is this that the ancient sources may have seized upon. He is said to have written a prose treatise *On the Chorus*, which might be genuine but could also be the result of a later work, in which Sophokles appeared in the first person (as with Aristophanes and Agathon in Plato's *Symposium*). Finally Plutarch (*Ethika* 79b) quotes Sophokles himself as saying:

> *Having passed through the stages of playing with the inflated language of Aeschylus and then of developing my plots in my own manner, a harsh and artificial style, I am now in my third stage, adopting the best style that also expresses character most fully.*

One has never been sure whether these stages are chronologically sequential, or to which stages the seven plays we possess belong. *Ajax*, in particular, has been assigned by some to "the harsh and artificial style."

Ancient assessments of Sophokles are almost unanimous in their praise of him and his work. We have already mentioned Ion's description, *chrestos* ("noble," "decent"), while Aristophanes describes as him "dipped in honey" at fr. 598 and as *eukolos* ("easy to get along with") at *Frogs* 82. That is why, explains Dionysos, he is going to bring back Euripides from the dead, because Sophokles is at home wherever he is, even in the underworld. At the same festival (405–Lenaia) a character in Phrynichos' comedy *Muses* comments (fr. 32):

> *Fortunate was Sophokles: after a long life he died, a happy and accomplished man. After writing many fine tragedies he came to a happy end, enduring nothing that was evil.*

The establishment of the canonical Three led some to approach Sophokles as a sort of Aristotelian middle as against the "extremes" of Aeschylus and Euripides. This is especially clear in the comparison of the three versions of *Philoktetes* by Dion of Prusa (ca. AD 100):

> *[Sophokles] seems to stand between the two others, since he has neither the ruggedness and simplicity of Aeschylus nor the cleverness and urbanity of Euripides. Yet he produces a poetry which is august and majestic, highly tragic and euphonious in its diction, with the result that there is the fullest pleasure combined with sublimity and stateliness.*

One mysterious joke by Aristophanes at *Peace* 695–9 mars this picture, where Sophokles is said "to have turned into Simonides," who was notorious for hiring out his poetic skill, the point presumably being that Sophokles had written something for financial gain, but the actual details elude us.

The plays of Sophokles

The *Life of Sophokles* attributes to him 130 plays with the *caveat* that seven (or seventeen) are spurious, while the *Suda* gives a total of 123. Assuming that a total of about 120 plays is going to be in the right neighborhood, we may thus attribute to Sophokles about thirty or so productions over a career that lasted about sixty years. As we have seen with Aeschylus, a production about every other year seems the norm for a successful tragedian in the fifth century. The official total for victories at the Dionysia was an enviable eighteen; other sources say twenty or twenty-four. These may be taking into account victories at the Lenaia festival. We are told that he never finished worse than second. We know of victories in 468 (over Aeschylus) and 438 (over Euripides), and second-place finishes in 466–459 (losing to Aeschylus' *Daughters of Danaos*) and 431 (where Aeschylus' son, Euphorion, won, perhaps with a posthumous work of his father). Incomprehensible to modern sensibilities is the statement by Dikaiarchos that the plays which included *Oedipus Tyrannos* finished second to Philokles.

A list of the known play-titles shows that his dramatic subjects ranged all over the canon of Greek myth. Like Aeschylus and Euripides, Sophokles found Troy and the events surrounding the war to be a fertile dramatic subject: (lost plays) *Ajax of Lokris, Ethiopians, Captive Women, Alexandros, Sons of Antenor, Gathering of the Achaeans, Wedding of Helen, Hermione, Eurypylos, Judgment, Lakonian Women, Laokoon, Nauplios, Odysseus Mad, Palamedes, Peleus, Shepherds, Polyxene, Priam, Sinon, Men of Skiros, Teukros, Troilos, Tyndareus, Philoktetes at Troy, Phrygians, Chryses*; (extant plays) *Ajax, Philoktetes, Elektra*. He seems to have avoided use of the trilogy format that Aeschylus found so amenable to his dramatic vision, although a fourth-century inscription does refer to a *Telepheia* ("The Story of Telephos") by Sophokles. Of the lost plays four seem to have portrayed events in the life of Telephos: *Sons of Aleos, Mysians, Telephos*, and *Eurypylos*. This has led some to postulate at least one dramatic trilogy by Sophokles, perhaps an early work.

Of the lost plays, we have several hundred lines of the satyr-drama *Trackers*, dealing with the events related in the *Homeric Hymn to Hermes*, how on his first day of life the infant god Hermes invented the lyre and stole his brother Apollo's cattle. Sophokles' *Andromeda* was an early play (before 450) that made a visual impact, since we have at least half a dozen different representations from the middle of the fifth century of Andromeda being bound on the shore. Few fragments of the play remain, with no hint of how Sophokles treated the story, which Euripides would present memorably in 412. It has even been suggested that Sophokles' *Andromeda* was a satyr-play, but would a satyr-play have had the same impact on the vase-painters? Another disturbing and influential lost play was *Tereus*, which attracted comic attention in *Birds* and Eupolis' *Officers*. Over fifty lines of this play survive, and we know from later sources that the tragedy told the story of Tereus, a Thracian prince, married to an Athenian woman, Prokne. On a journey to fetch his wife's sister (Philomela), Tereus first raped Philomela and then cut out her tongue to prevent her from telling of his deed. But Philomela communicated her plight through weaving and the two sisters killed Tereus' son (Itys) and then served his flesh as food to Tereus. At the end the gods intervene (fr. 589 is clearly spoken by a deity pronouncing judgment), by turning all the participants into birds (Tereus ~ a hoopoe; Prokne ~ nightingale; Philomela ~ swallow). If earlier than Euripides' *Medea* (431), *Tereus* will have been a source of influence on that powerful drama of a woman's revenge.

The seven plays that we possess come from about forty years of Sophokles' career – compare that to Aeschylus where the six certain tragedies come from the last decade and a half of his life. We have no way of knowing why these seven were preserved.

Oedipus Tyrannos was an obvious choice in view of its prominence in Aristotle's *Poetics* – Sophokles' treatment seems quickly to have become the "authorized version" of the story of Oedipus. *Antigone* also had a favorable reception in the ancient world; in fact the end of Aeschylus' *Seven* was rewritten to make it harmonize with Sophokles' play. *Oedipus at Kolonos* would soon have made up a third in an unofficial "Theban trilogy." *Elektra* was chosen, we suspect, to accompany *Libation-Bearers* and Euripides' *Elektra* into the school texts, to provide the three different treatments of "Orestes' Revenge." The little treatise by Dion of Prusa (51) on comparing the three versions of *Philoktetes* may have contributed to the choice of Sophokles' *Philoktetes*. But it is less easy to see why *Ajax*, interestingly enough the most popular play of Sophokles in the Renaissance, and *Trachinian Women*, were chosen, although both are powerful dramas depicting the death of a great physical hero.

With Aeschylus we can be reasonably certain when the extant plays were produced, the doubtful *Prometheus* excepted, and with Euripides we have eight secure dates and for the others we can date the plays to within a year or two. But with Sophokles uncertainty rules. Only two dates are securely attested: *Philoktetes* in 409, and *Oedipus at Kolonos* in 401. As Sophokles died in 406, this last must be a posthumous production. Other dates are argued and supported by varying degrees of evidence.

Dates (conjectural)

early 440s – *Ajax*
443–438 – *Antigone*
late 430s – *Trachinian Women*
early 420s – *Oedipus Tyrannos*
late 410s – *Elektra*
409 – *Philoktetes* (secure)
401 – *Oedipus at Kolonos* (secure)

Antigone is usually placed in the late 440s because of the testimony in the *Life of Sophokles* that Sophokles owed his election as general in 441 to the success of his *Antigone*. As 441 is known to have been the year of one of Euripides' rare victories, critics date *Antigone* to 443 or 442. A more recent interpretation downdates *Antigone* slightly to 438 (when we know that Sophokles competed and won) and sees the mistreatment of the body of Polyneikes as reflecting atrocities that are alleged to have happened to Samian prisoners in the war with Samos (440/39). Sophokles may not have in fact been elected general because of his successful *Antigone*, but the anecdote does show that ancient sources dated that play about the time of the Samian War, ca. 440.

Critics see *Ajax* as a clumsy drama structurally, falling into two parts: the death of Ajax and his redemption and burial, and regard this and certain remnants of the grand style of Aeschylus as evidence for an early date. It is often regarded as the earliest of the seven that we possess, although more recent criticism would put it in the 430s rather than the 440s. *Trachinian Women* has been dated as early as 450, on the argument that Deianeira is something of an anti-Klytaimestra. Both destroy a powerful husband, the latter through her assumption of the male identity and the former by being the almost stereotypically weak female. We prefer a later date in the 430s, close in time to *Oedipus Tyrannos* and the lost *Phaidra*, both of which turn on a dramatic hinge of good intentions gone horribly wrong. The evidence for the date of *Oedipus Tyrannos* is slender, a possible parody of Oedipus' discovery of the truth of the oracle at Aristophanes' *Knights* 1229–52 (424) and the attribution made of the plague at Thebes to the War-God (190–9). In the myth Thebes was not at war at this time, but Athens *was* from 431 onward and had suffered a devastating plague (Thucydides 2.50) from 430 until 426. The mention of the War-God would be a bit of Athens' own background seeping through into the play, which will then have been produced in 429 or 427–425 (we know that Sophokles did not compete at the Dionysia of 428).

Finally, for Sophokles' *Elektra* the question of the priority of the Euripidean or Sophoklean version is a vexed one, but we would favor a sequence: reproduction of *Oresteia* 425–420, Euripides' *Elektra* in 420 or 419, and then Sophokles' play as the latest of the three. The play shows signs of having been written late in Sophokles' career: the monody of Elektra at 85–120, the insertion of one scene within another, and the surprising variations on the normal plot-line (the false recognition-scene, and the actual recognition long delayed, the reversal of the murders). Thus any date from 418–407 is possible, with perhaps 413 as an attractive option.

Sophokles as dramatist

A play by Sophokles seems to fit the assumptions which the student new to Greek Drama tends to make about tragedy. It opens with an appropriate prologue, sometimes a single speech (as in *Trachinian Women*), sometimes a dialogue (as in *Antigone* or *Philoktetes*), sometimes with a two-part scene (as in *Oedipus at Kolonos* or *Trachinian Women*). The action proceeds with a series of strong scenes, usually combative encounters between two characters, until a climactic moment is reached. These episodes are separated distinctly by formal choral songs that have some relevance to the dramatic situation. But unlike Aeschylus, Sophokles' dramas do not always end with the demise or the downfall of the principal character. In *Ajax*, the title character is dead by line 865, leaving his brother and the Greeks to sort out the honors due to him in death. Antigone is gone from our view at line 943, but her sentence of death will have its consequences: the arrival of Teiresias and his stunning denunciation of Kreon, the news of the deaths of Antigone and Haimon, and the final suicide of Kreon's wife in grief for her son. In *Trachinian Women*, the principal character is Deianeira, who rushes off to die at line 812, but the action she has unwittingly perpetrated, the death of Herakles, will dominate the rest of the play. In *Elektra* the formal climax, the death of Aigisthos, does not in fact happen during the action, but is left for the spectators' imagination, while in *Philoktetes* the plot-line takes unexpected twists and turns, with at least three moments at which the drama could reasonably conclude. *Oedipus Tyrannos* is the most straightforward, proceeding from ignorance to the horror of the full truth. It can fairly be considered the "first whodunit," since the action involves the investigation and solution of a murder.

Sophokles' technique becomes more complicated in the later plays that we possess, as the episodes become longer and more complex, with episodes inserted into episodes or new episodes following without a choral break. Compare the straightforward structure of *Antigone*, to be dated around 440, with that of *Philoktetes* (firm date of 409):

Antigone (ca. 440)

1–99: prologue   Antigone & Ismene
100–54: *parodos*
155–331: episode 1   (i) Kreon & chorus [155–222]
                        (ii) Kreon & guard [223–331]
332–75: first stasimon
376–581: episode 2   (i) Kreon & guard [376–445]
                        (ii) Kreon & Antigone [446–530]
                        (iii) Kreon, Ismene & Antigone [531–81]
582–625: second stasimon
626–780: episode 3   Kreon & Haimon
781–800: third stasimon
801–82: *kommos*   Antigone & chorus
883–943: episode 4   Antigone & Kreon
944–87: fourth stasimon
988–1114: episode 5   Kreon & Teiresias
1115–54: fifth stasimon
1155–1353: episode 6   (i) Messenger, Eurydike & chorus [1155–1260]
                        (ii) Messenger, Kreon & chorus [1261–1353]

Philoktetes (409)

1–134: prologue   Odysseus & Neoptolemos
135–218: lyric dialogue   chorus & Neoptolemos
219–675: episode 1   (i) Philoktetes & Neoptolemos [220–541]
                        [chorus at 391–402, 507–518]
                        (ii) Merchant, Philoktetes, Neoptolemos [542–627]
                        (iii) Philoktetes & Neoptolemos [628–75]
676–729: first stasimon
730–1080: episode 2   (i) Philoktetes & Neoptolemos [730–826]
                        (ii) chorus & Neoptolemos [827–64] – stasimon form
                        (iii) Philoktetes & Neoptolemos [865–974]
                        (iv) Odysseus, Philoktetes, Neoptolemos [975–1080]
1081–1217:   *kommos* & lyric dialogue – Philoktetes & chorus
1218–1471: episode 3   (i) Neoptolemos & Odysseus [1218–62]
                        (ii) Philoktetes & Neoptolemos [1263–1408]
                        (iii) Herakles, Philoktetes, Neoptolemos [1409–71]

We note at once the longer and more complicated episodes; the merchant-scene, quite unnecessary for the advancement of the plot (542–627), inserted into the larger encounter between the boy and Philoktetes; and the reduced role of the chorus, given only one formal stasimon in the play. Two places where we might have had a choral song in an earlier play are replaced with lyric dialogue between the chorus and a character (135–219, 1081–1217). *Philoktetes* is certainly a virtuoso piece for the actors, as both protagonist and deuteragonist play one role only – compare *Ajax* where the protagonist plays first Ajax and then his brother Teukros, and the astonishing situation in *Trachinian Women*, in which the lead actor plays both the weak Deianeira and then her monstrous husband Herakles. A glance at the structure of *Elektra* (very probably late) and the posthumously produced *Oedipus at Kolonos* (401) show similar bold departures from the earlier sort of dramatic structure.

We have remarked before on Aristotle's relegation of spectacle (*opsis*) to a place below that of both plot and character as a criterion of good drama. Aeschylus employed a tableau approach, creating dramatically set scenes laden with significance for the watching spectators. Sophokles' use of spectacle is not as easy to detect, apart perhaps from the spectacle of the bound maiden in the lost *Andromeda*. But there are places where a more subtle visual style can be seen. Ajax falls on his sword in plain view of the audience, unusual in an art form where violent acts usually take place off-stage and are reported by messengers. This must take place near an exit (an *eisodos* or the central door), so that the actor playing Ajax may vanish to reappear as Teukros, but a dummy or stage-double will remain, indicative of how this larger-than-life hero still dominates the stage after his death and will remain in full sight until the end of the play. In *Oedipus at Kolonos* Antigone will help an aged and infirm Oedipus into the grove of the Furies where he will take his seat at line 201 (figure 2.2), not to stir until line 1544, when he moves confidently under his own power. This must have been a moving visual moment, for this blind man no longer needs a human guide.

When objects are used in the Greek theater, they are usually significant, perhaps no more so than the bow of Herakles in *Philoktetes*. The Trojan prophet has foretold that possession of this bow will ensure the triumph of the Greeks, and in the play we see it wielded by Philoktetes as the symbol of survival, entrusted to and then stolen by Neoptolemos, its loss lamented by Philoktetes, and finally restored to him. The changing fortunes of the play are symbolized by the movements of this bow. Or consider the empty urn in Sophokles' *Elektra*. At line 1097 Orestes enters carrying what are supposed to be "the small remains of the dead man in this little urn" (1113–14). But we know what Elektra does not, that there is nothing in that urn, that the real Orestes stands before us holding a fiction. More than one critic has seen meta-theater at work here, a symbol of the whole fictive nature of the genre, but even on the dramatic level, it symbolizes the essential lie at the heart of this play, recalling Apollo's injunction "with guile to hide murder done by a righteous hand" (37). In *Trachinian Women* the robe will have a crucial visual role, first as it is brought out and sent off to Herakles (598–632) and then when it returns on the body of Herakles whom its poison is now consuming (1046–1111). Or consider the sword of Ajax, mentioned at line 10, surely in his hand when he enters at line 91, and described by Ajax as "the most hated of weapons" (658) and "the gift from Hektor, the foe I hated the most"

Figure 2.2 *Tableau-scene, influenced by Sophokles'* Oedipus at Kolonos, *on a red-figure kalyx-krater, mid-fourth century. Reproduced courtesy of Mr Graham Geddes, Melbourne.*

(817–18). It is this very visible token that he will plant in the earth and fall upon before the eyes of the theater.

Two other visual moments may be considered. One comes after the prologue in *Antigone*, in which two women have entered from the *skene*, but only one (Ismene) will return to the safety and controlled world of the palace. Antigone will cross the line and leave by the *eisodos* that leads to the world outside the city, in fact eventually to the realm of the dead. The other comes after the crucial scene in *Oedipus Tyrannos* (1110–85), wherein Oedipus learns the truth about his parentage from the Theban herdsman and the messenger from Corinth. Imagine the spectators looking down upon the *orchestra*, as Oedipus walks slowly through the *skene*-door into his palace, as the herdsman leaves by the one *eisodos* and the messenger by the other. The playing-area has, for this scene at least, been a place where three roads meet (Rehm 1992:118).

Sophokles and dramatic character

Aristotle contended that drama is about "doing" not "being," that one can have a tragedy without character, but not without plot. Sophokles was for Aristotle the most perfect of the tragic poets, and ironically he is the one whose dramas depend most upon character. All seven of the surviving plays portray an important central character, not always a strong character (since Deianeira is perhaps the weakest protagonist in extant tragedy), but one around whom the tragedy unfolds. These principal characters are often "lonely" people, certainly set apart from their fellow humans: Philoktetes literally so on his deserted island, Deianeira driven from her home and now abandoned by her husband, Ajax in isolation in his tent on the shore, Antigone and Elektra who operate outside the confined world of the female, and certainly the blind and accursed Oedipus whom all shun in the *Oedipus at Kolonos*. Ironically the one character who is not isolated as the play opens is Oedipus in *Oedipus Tyrannos*, although he does possess the distance that one would expect of a king and savior of his city. But by the end he will become a man apart, unclean and sightless, whom no one will envy.

In Sophokles it seems as if greatness brings disaster, that these larger-than-life "heroes" somehow attract the lightning of tragedy. The chorus sing at *Oedipus Tyrannos* 873 that "being a tyrant breeds arrogance," and this seems to be the underlying theme of a Sophoklean play. Ajax is the great warrior among the Greeks, but his sense of honor and shame lead him to attempt to kill the Greek leaders, when he is not awarded the armor of Achilles, and then to take his own life in shame. He operates in the traditional Greek moral ethos of "do good to your friends [*philoi*] and harm to your enemies [*echthroi*]," and is now out of touch with the realities of a newer world, where the humanism of Odysseus fits better – "his excellence counts more to me than his hatred" (1357). *Oedipus Tyrannos* shows us a great king and savior of his people, whose prime motivations are to rescue his state once again and to learn the truth. The irony of this play is that the truth is discovered (and thus the state saved) by Oedipus' good qualities, and while we do see his hot-headedness and a dash of political paranoia in the scenes with Teiresias and Kreon, these do not lead directly to his downfall in any sort of sequence of cause and effect.

In *Antigone* it seems almost fated that two utterly dissimilar temperaments will clash: Antigone, the woman with her concern for the demands of *philia* ("family"), and Kreon, the male ruler for whom the *polis* ("city," "state") is everything. This is not a play with one protagonist, rather there are two – Kreon, rather like the "hero" of an Aeschylean play who brings his disaster upon himself, and Antigone who goes to her death complaining that she suffers "for respecting what deserved respect," that is, an innocent victim to some extent, certainly on the level of the laws of the gods (see her crucial speech at 450–70).

Even Deianeira, the weakest of the tragic principals, still operates in this way, for her "excellence" is her marriage to Herakles, the strongest hero of Greek myth, and also her beauty, as she herself makes plain in her opening speech, "for I sat there stricken with fear that my beauty might devise some pain for me." This is no Helen, "sent by

Zeus as a Fury for brides," but a mortal woman whose beauty has attracted a god, a human hero, and a monster, and will in fact cause her death and that of Herakles.

These main characters, while "heroic" in the sense that they are larger than ordinary life and given to their own excellence (Ajax: heroism of the hand, Oedipus: intellectual strength, Deianeira: beauty, Philoktetes: survival with honor and dignity, Antigone: devotion to her family, Kreon: devotion to the state), are not always "nice" characters. In fact their excellence often makes them difficult for the "ordinary" spectators to relate to. Modern readers frequently find the secondary figures in the drama more appealing: Odysseus in *Ajax*, Neoptolemos in *Philoktetes* (who can steal the show, if the actor playing Philoktetes is not careful), Theseus in *Oedipus at Kolonos*, Ismene in *Antigone*, and Chrysothemis in *Elektra*. Characters in the plays admire these larger-than-life figures. Odysseus at *Ajax* 1340 calls Ajax "the best of the Achaeans, even though he was my enemy"; the priest regards Oedipus as the "first of men" (*Oedipus Tyrannos* 33), and Hyllos tells his mother that she has killed "the best man on the earth." But they are not entirely comfortable with them either. Modern sentiments regard Antigone sympathetically as a proto-feminist martyr, who takes the cause of the gods against the decrees of men, whose individual conscience prevails over the tyranny of the community. But it is likely that to a fifth-century audience she was not so sympathetic. She was a woman who had invaded the space of the male and challenged Kreon the ruler of the city. Teiresias will say that Kreon was wrong (1064–71), but he never says that Antigone was right, and the chorus will attribute to her "the fierce disposition of the daughter of a fierce father" (471–2).

While Sophokles' dramas focus and turn on these powerful figures, his plays only hint at psychological motivations. It will be left to Euripides to explore the characters' actions in terms of their heredity and personal experiences. A modern reader will want to know what Antigone's relationship with Polyneikes was, why she is so insistent on his burial, whether there is anything incestuous about her desire "to lie beside him, dear one (*philos*) by dear one" (73), whether she has something of a "martyr complex." But for Sophokles it is the issue that matters: that even a traitor to his city is a brother and deserves the rites of burial by his family. Remember that it was the women of the family who prepared the body for burial and gave it the ritual washing and lamentation. Sophokles has given us this issue dramatized in terms of two extreme characters, and some may conclude that it is not a case of right and wrong, but of two characters who are both wrong in their extremes.

Philoktetes might be the example of the great character, who is not destroyed at the end of his drama, but rather saved. But Sophokles goes out of his way to give us a plot that may not achieve the destined happy ending. It is not a case of humans getting in the way of the gods' destined end: that Philoktetes will go Troy, be healed, and do his part in accomplishing the predestined fall of Troy, for Sophokles makes it seem that when Philoktetes refuses to go at 1348–72, this is somehow the morally "right" path, and reinforces this feeling by having Philoktetes promise to protect Neoptolemos' country with the bow of Herakles. At the same time one wonders legitimately if he has gone too far in pursuing his hatred for the Greeks, who stranded him on the island, and in rejecting the attractive prospects held out to him by Neoptolemos (1314–47).

Elektra also ends "happily," in that the revenge commanded by Apollo is success-ful, but Sophokles gives us a title character who is obsessed with her situation, who like Antigone is found "outdoors," who depends on one prop to keep her going: that her brother will come and avenge their father. Then the dramatist knocks that prop out from under her and we observe first her determination to do the deed herself and then her joy in the return of her brother. By a bold dramatic stroke Sophokles has her mime in full view of the spectators the murder of her mother, but one also wonders what sort of life is left for Elektra, who "has been waiting without marriage, without children" (164–5). Klytaimestra declares at 784–6 that Elektra "did the greater harm, for she lived with me drinking the unmixed blood of my life," and we realize that there have been Furies in this play after all – Elektra has taken on herself the venge-ful vindictiveness of the avenging ones.

A comment by the author of the *Life of Sophokles* shows that Aristotle's emphasis on the primacy of plot over character was not shared by all ancient authorities:

> He knows how to arrange the action with such a sense of timing that he creates a character out of a mere half-line or single expression. That is essential in poetry: to delineate character or feelings.

Some of these instant assessments would include Oedipus' definitive declaration just before the truth is revealed, "but I must hear" (*Oedipus Tyrannos* 1170), Antigone's self-declaration at line 523, "I was not born to join in hatred, but in love (*philia*)," and Philoktetes' address to Neoptolemos, whom he has previously called "child" or "son of Achilles," "what have you done to me, *stranger*?" (923).

The chorus in Sophokles

Just in terms of the number of lines, the choral role in Sophokles differs markedly from that in Aeschylus. In the six certain tragedies by Aeschylus, the chorus has between 30 and 50 percent of the lines in the play, and in two plays (*Suppliants, Eumenides*) is intimately involved in the action. But in Sophokles the chorus has barely more than 20 percent of the lines, nor do we get the extended stasima with many pairs of *strophes* and *antistrophes*. In *Antigone*, for instance, the choral pattern is:

parodos:	55 lines	2 strophic pairs
stasimon 1:	44 lines	2 strophic pairs
stasimon 2:	44 lines	2 strophic pairs
stasimon 3:	20 lines	1 strophic pair
stasimon 4:	44 lines	2 strophic pairs
stasimon 5:	38 lines	2 strophic pairs
kommos:	19 lines	2 strophic pairs
(with Antigone)		

Compare this with the three opening choral odes from *Agamemnon*, *Suppliants*, and *Persians*, each over a hundred lines with six, eight, and five strophic pairs respectively.

In the later plays we see the choral role diminish further. In *Elektra* and *Philoktetes* they are virtually invisible and not very necessary to the drama:

Elektra:

kommos	50 lines	3 strophic pairs
stasimon 1:	42 lines	1 strophic pair + epode
stasimon 2:	40 lines	2 strophic pairs
stasimon 3:	14 lines	1 strophic pair

Philoktetes:

kommos	50 lines	2 strophic pairs
interludes	22 lines	1 strophic pair (divided)
stasimon 1:	54 lines	2 strophic pairs
stasimon 2:	34 lines	1 strophic pair + epode
kommos	20 lines	2 strophic pairs
	20 lines	1 strophic pair

In both plays the opening song is replaced by a *kommos* with a character, which in fact becomes the chorus' largest piece in the drama, and the number of *stasima* is reduced significantly. The familiar pattern of episodes separated by choral songs is all but gone.

Sophokles' choruses are not as intimately involved in the dramatic situation as they are in Aeschylus. They are ob6ervers rather than participants, although in *Antigone*, *Oedipus Tyrannos*, and *Ajax* they have more than a passing interest in the situation. In *Antigone* their opening song celebrates the departure of the enemy, in *Oedipus Tyrannos* they are the voice of the plague-ridden city, and in *Ajax* the worried companions of the doomed hero. But it is never *their* situation which is on the line. Particularly in *Elektra* and *Philoktetes* their role is reduced to engaging with the characters in the formal *kommos*. In *Oedipus Tyrannos* Sophokles shows us a meditative chorus reacting to and reflecting upon the events as they unfold:

Oedipus Tyrannos – choruses

151–215: what does the oracle mean?; the plague at Thebes; appeal to the gods.

463–511: what does Teiresias mean?; the public record of Oedipus; "I do not know what to say."

863–910: the power of the gods is great; can Oedipus be behaving as a "tyrant"?; if oracles and Apollo are not honored, what is the point of worship?

1086–1109: Oedipus may turn out to be the child of a god.

1186–1222: "I do not envy mortals at all"; Oedipus destroyed the Sphinx and became "the Great," but now "who is more wretched than he?"

1524–30: "Call no man happy until he is dead."

In each ode they pick up on something that has gone before in the previous episode, and explore two repeated themes: the role of the gods and the responsibility of mortals for their actions. In the crucial fourth stasimon (1186–1222) they lift the situation from the particular to the general ("with your fate, unhappy Oedipus, as an example, I do not envy mortals at all" – 1193–5). They do not immediately sing of the disaster that has personally afflicted Oedipus, but of the fate of humanity in general.

The chorus is thematically strong also in *Trachinian Women*, especially in the choral ode at 497–530. The god beneath the text of this drama is Eros, not so much Love as Lust, and in this tragedy the line between human and the bestial is very blurred – the Greek *theros* ("beast," "monster") is used of both the centaur and the river-god. In this ode the chorus sing of the contest between Herakles and the river-god in the form of a bull, fighting for the beautiful maiden, "like a wandering calf, strayed from its mother." In their first ode (96–140) they compare Deianeira to a "wretched bird" (105), and at the end declare that they have never seen Zeus "without a plan for his children" (139–40), a neat bit of ring composition, since the play ends with the denunciation, "and there is none of these things that is not Zeus" (1278).

Aristotle's definitive statement (*Poetics* 1456a25–30) on the chorus is well-known:

> *The chorus too must be regarded as one of the actors. It must be part of the whole and share in the action, not as in Euripides but as in Sophokles. In the others the choral odes have no more to do with the plot than with any other tragedy. And so they sing interludes, a practice begun by Agathon.*

It is not exactly clear what "as in Euripides" or "as in Sophokles" means, but his following comment implies that choral odes should have some relevance to the tragedy. Some regard the chorus in Sophokles as an "ideal spectator," but they are more than a microcosm of the audience, and perhaps "reflective participants" is better, as they do have a share and a stake in the story, and they do allow the dramatist to express how some people might react to what goes on before them. The chorus is not the dramatist himself "teaching" a "message" to the audience, for choruses can be misled (as in *Trachinian Women* 660–2), puzzled (as at *Oedipus Tyrannos* 463–511), hostile (*Oedipus at Kolonos* 223–26), and supportive of deceit (*Philoktetes* 828–64). Buxton (1984: 24) cites Reinhardt's arresting description of the Sophoklean chorus as

> groups of people standing on the bank and following with their eyes someone who is being snatched away by the current. This is how the chorus stands in safety and watches, participating, but outside,

but at times the choruses of Sophokles have their feet in the water as well.

Irony in Sophokles

At the very heart of Sophokles' dramas lies irony. Not just the well-known dramatically ironic one-liners for which *Oedipus Tyrannos* is so famous, but larger situations permeated with irony. Oedipus, the most gifted of mortals in intelligence, the first syllables (*oidi-*) of whose name mean "know," does not even know who his parents are. The man who saved his city from the Sphinx is himself the pollution of that city. What brings about the revelation of the truth are his good qualities, not his faults. Herakles, the slayer of beasts and monsters, is brought down, not by a warrior male or creature of the wild, but by the weak wife that he despises. The situation in Kreon's Thebes is so out of kilter – cf. Teiresias' words at 1064–90 – that it requires a woman to cross the gender line and put things right in the civic sphere. When Kreon finally realizes the truth, he heeds the chorus' advice at lines 1100–1 to release the maiden and bury the body, but does so in the wrong order. Even when he does the right thing, he gets it wrong. Philoktetes, whom the Greeks rejected, is now found to be the chief cornerstone of their success at Troy.

We get ironies of particular scenes and moments, especially prevalent in *Oedipus Tyrannos*. The blind Teiresias is the only one "who sees what the god Apollo sees," and when Oedipus finally "sees" the truth, his impulse is to blind himself. Jokaste attempts to rid Oedipus of his fear of oracles by telling him of her own experience with oracles, and in so doing leads him to discover the first truth: that he himself is the murderer that he has cursed. Kreon, who has denied any intention of wanting to be king (583–615), will in fact come to power by the end of the play. The Corinthian messenger in his attempt to relieve Oedipus of the fear of committing incest (1016) drives the final nail into Oedipus' coffin. Perhaps the ultimate irony comes when Oedipus asks the herdsman why he did not kill the child and hears "because I pitied it." *Oedipus Tyrannos* is the great play of good intentions gone horribly wrong, and the irony of this situation carries much of the power that the play still possesses.

In *Elektra* we have the irony of deceit, for we know from the prologue that Orestes will send the old man to the palace with an empty urn and a false story that Orestes is dead. Because the irony operates through human deceit rather than the larger workings of the universe, we feel this irony less powerfully, but still with some force when Orestes attempts to take the urn from his sister at 1205–15. Sophokles has so very cleverly structured this play that when Chrysothemis returns at line 871 with the news that someone has left a lock of hair at Agamemnon's tomb, Elektra will have been misled into drawing the wrong conclusion. The recognition-scene in Aeschylus' *Libation-Bearers* was played upon by both Euripides (*Elektra* 487–584), who all but parodies the simplicity of Aeschylus, and here by Sophokles, who accepts the tradition, but ironically has the truth denied.

Oedipus Tyrannos is the play where dramatic irony operates most abundantly. Dramatic irony depends on knowledge, the awareness on the part of the audience of the true state of affairs against which the unknowing statements of the characters will resonate with powerful effect. In a play like *Philoktetes*, where the spectators do not know what happens next, irony cannot work as effectively. But we know the story of Oedipus and so can respond appropriately. Thus Oedipus declares prophetically, "there is not one of you that is as sick as I myself" (60–1), states definitely, "I know of Laios only at second hand, I never laid eyes upon him" (105), swears that "if he [the murderer] lives in my home with my knowledge, I pray that I myself may feel my curse" (249–51), and in words that never fail to elicit a shudder affirms, "I fight

for Laios as if he were my father" (264–5). We feel that we are watching events unfold
against a larger backdrop; there is something appropriate and at the same time terrifying in such ironic statements.

Antigone may not have been as familiar a dramatic theme – Sophokles himself may
be largely responsible for developing this plot-line – but at least twice in his opening
scene Kreon can stir the audience with irony: first at line 220, "there is no one so
foolish as to be in love with death," but we have seen Antigone say precisely that at
lines 69–97; and then at line 248, when informed of the burial of the body, "who was
the man who dared this?," using the gender specific word *aner* ("male"). We know
from the prologue that the perpetrator was not male.

Finally in *Trachinian Women*, we know that Herakles died by his wife's misguided
actions, and we know that monsters bearing gifts cannot be trusted, and can appreciate the subtle ironies of the tragedy. The monster that Herakles killed to claim his
bride will through her connivance finally bring him down. For fifth-century Greeks
the centaur was a metaphor for unbridled male lust, and it is fitting, ironically so, that
what destroys Herakles is a symbol of his own sexuality ("one man, Herkales, has
loved so many women" – 460). Further irony lies in the manner of Deianeira's death
by the sword, a man's method of committing suicide – women usually hang themselves or take poison. Finally at line 576–7 is one of Sophokles' deliciously ironic
lines: the words of the dying centaur instructing Deianeira to dye her robe in his blood
and create a love charm, "so that he will never look at and love another woman again."

Twice in Sophokles' extant plays a woman prays to Apollo for divine assistance in
ironic situations, ironic in that we know that their prayers will not be answered. First
at *Elektra* 634–59 Klytaimestra after her first exchange with her estranged daughter
prays to Apollo for a happy end to her situation:

> *Grant that I may live always with my life safe, ruling the house of Atreus and wielding this scepter,*
> *loving the dear ones with whom I now live, enjoying my life and with those of my children who do*
> *not hate me or afford me bitter pain.*

Ironically her prayer will apparently be answered immediately at line 660, when the
old man arrives to announce the "death" of Orestes, but we know that this is but a
ruse to gain her confidence and admission to the palace. At *Oedipus Tyrannos* 911–23
Jokaste enters and announces that she is making offerings at the temples of the gods
for a happy resolution of the prospect that Oedipus might in fact be the murderer of
Laios. Here the spectators see her approach the altar of Apollo praying that "you may
provide us with a clear solution." This is ironic in three senses, first because in the
previous scene she has denied the power of Apollo's oracles, second because we know
that it will be in vain, and third because the entry of the Corinthian messenger will
for a moment seem as if her prayers have been answered ("prophecies of the gods,
where are you now?" – 946–7).

Buxton (1984: 26) sees irony as not just a dramatic technique, effective as it may
be at rousing a shudder from the spectators, but something "that is at the very heart
of his perception of experience." Human beings think that they know something or
have confidence in some state of affairs, but Sophokles' dramas will demonstrate that

this confidence is built on a foundation of sand. For Winnington-Ingram (1980: 329) irony is essential to Sophokles' view of the universe. Gods know the truth, but are above events, while it is humans who must live and act in this flawed world of disharmony and imperfections.

The moral universe of Sophokles

There has been a strong tendency among students of Sophokles to make the man's universe reflect his own perceived character. Sophokles was *eukolos* ("easy to get along with"), he was *chrestos* ("noble"), he was pious (witness the stories of his devotion to the gods of healing). Phrynichos called him a "truly happy man, who wrote many fine tragedies, and died never having experienced a moment of pain." It is argued, then, that such a "nice" man must have seen the universe as a "nice" place and created his tragedies accordingly against an optimistic background. Gods in Sophokles must represent a morally and ethically better order, and if tragedy occurs, it must be the fault of humans who "sin" and then are punished. This view was especially prevalent when *hamartia* in *Poetics* 13 was mistranslated as "tragic flaw," thus turning these plays into tragedies of character and crime and punishment.

But should we extrapolate from the author to his or her works? We might invoke the "Amadeus principle" here, for in Peter Shaffer's play the character of Mozart admits, "I may be a vulgar man, but my music is not vulgar." Indeed much of that play and film depends on an antithesis between the personality of the artist and his artistic expression. The English composer, Ralph Vaughan Williams, was viewed personally as an attractive and sympathetic person, and his harsh and angular Fourth Symphony (1935) took his listeners and fans by surprise, as it seemed at odds with their expectations of the man himself. We need to be careful of regarding Sophokles as a serene optimist or Euripides as the dramatic rebel.

Critics approach Sophokles in one of four ways generally. First are what Waldock (1954) called the "pietists," who take the line developed above that Sophokles must be presenting an optimistic universe, that he is living up to the title of *didaskalos* ("teacher") which the poets bore, that his tragedies will end with some sort of optimistic closure or resolution. What stand out about the dramas of Sophokles are his larger-than-life heroes, about whom the action revolves and whose greatness somehow attracts disaster. For the "pietists" these heroes are lacking in *sophrosyne* ("moderation"); their behavior crosses the line and incurs a tragic result. Both playwright and spectator are expected to disapprove of this lack of moderation. Thus Ajax is too bound up with his sense of honor and his physical heroism, Oedipus with his intellectual confidence, Philoktetes with his hatred of the Greeks.

The problem with this approach is that it assumes a divine benevolence and human shortcomings which the gods observe and punish. Antigone, a typically Sophoklean isolated hero, suffers for doing what was right – these are her last words in the play – and if Philoktetes goes "too far" at any point in the play, it is at the end where he refuses the persuasive appeal of Neoptolemos. Winnington-Ingram (1980: 325) makes the good point that Aeschylus' solution to the ongoing cycle of action and reaction in the universe was the persuasion of the Furies, but in Sophokles' late plays persuasion fails to work and the result is more disaster. *Philoktetes* in particular is badly served by the pietist view, since on this reading the gods have proposed the return of Philoktetes and the resultant fall of Troy and human interference has halted that course. But Philoktetes is shown to be a true hero, in contrast to the false modern heroism of the tongue, and Sophokles skillfully develops his plot to the point where it seems "right" that Philoktetes leave the Greeks to their dirty war at Troy and that the true heroes (Philoktetes and Neoptolemos) return to Greece.

The second view takes the opposite tack, that the heroes are truly that, heroes, and that the fault lies with the divine background. Antigone suffers for doing what was right, Oedipus does nothing wrong in the play – in fact his good qualities bring about the revelation and the ultimate tragedy, Ajax is driven mad by Athene who invites his mortal enemy (Odysseus) to laugh at him. Hyllos concludes *Trachinian Women* with an indictment of the gods which we might properly associate with Euripides ("and there is none of these things which is not Zeus"). On this view Sophokles has inherited the divine framework from traditional myth, but elevates his main characters to a level of "heroic humanism" (to borrow the phrase from C. H. Whitman [1954]), culminating in the splendid ode from *Antigone*, "there are many wonders in the world, but nothing more wonderful than a human" (332–83).

But Sophokles' heroes are not always comfortable to be with, nor are they wholly admirable, nor do we get the idea that we are to emulate these examples. Antigone is her stubborn father's daughter – a predominantly fifth-century male audience would regard her with some sympathy but with even more distaste. Ajax is just too violent and honor-bound; he may have been a tribal hero of the Athenians, but one who belonged in a Homeric epic rather than contemporary society. Oedipus in *Oedipus at Kolonos* may achieve heroic status at the end, but we witness him becoming more and more angry – and "heroes" in Greek cult are traditionally angry beings. Neither the pathetically weak Deianeira nor the disgustingly unfeeling and violent Herakles is any model of human heroism.

In reaction to these attempts to discern a consistent moral universe a third group of critics has turned its attention to Sophokles' plays as effective and powerful drama, rejecting or playing down a didactic element in his work. Aristotle (*Poetics* chapter 6) maintains that the end of tragedy is the arousal of pity and fear, pity for those who do not deserve their fate and fear for those like ourselves. Critics like Waldock, Heath, Stanford, Griffin stress the emotional and entertaining power of tragedy and Sophokles' ability to create new and exciting plot-lines (especially in *Elektra* and *Philoktetes*). "There is religion in the *Oedipus Tyrannus* but it is not crucial in the drama" (Waldock 1951: 167), "the chief interest of poet and audience in tragedy was in its emotive force, and in the pleasure which accompanies the emotional response which that force can evoke" (Heath 1987: 207). In a landmark article which should be required reading for all students of Sophokles, Dodds (1966) advances and dismisses various interpretations ("heresies") of the *Oedipus Tyrannos*, regarding this last view with some sympathy, but ultimately concludes that there must be some "meaning" in the *Oedipus*.

A more recent trend has been to regard the universe of Sophokles as profoundly disturbing, without committing oneself either to divine providence or to human excellence. While Kreon may be a hero of the sort one finds in Aeschylus, one who collaborates in his own downfall, Antigone is essentially innocent, for she defends the unwritten laws of the gods (as against human decrees) and goes to her death for respecting what deserved respect. Yet she is not a sympathetic martyr; she has the impatience and intransigence of her father, and had she not taken her own life, would have been released from her prison. *Elektra* has provided critics with a wealth of possible interpretations: a return to the values of the Homeric story, a satisfying achievement of a deserved revenge, or a deeply ironic play where the avengers are less than sympathetic. Orestes can be seen as the exemplar of the conscienceless young men who would mount two anti-democratic coups in Athens, Elektra as a Fury personified, who has lived for only one thing: vengeance, and the play will end with Aigisthos foretelling future woes for the house of Atreus. On one reading Oedipus in the *Oedipus at Kolonos* has come to terms with his actions and will find rest at Athens, but his rejection of his son will lead to Antigone's own death as she keeps a promise to her brother.

In Sophokles greatness in human beings seems to attract disaster, and as we have seen, it is the lesser characters whom readers and audiences find more appealing. But it is not a case of a "tragic flaw" or the sequence of *ate–hybris–nemesis* that we find in Aeschylus. The oracles to Laios make this very clear: in *Seven* Apollo attached a definite "if-clause" to his proclamation:

when Apollo three times from his sanctuary in Delphi at the navel of the earth warned Laios, to save his city by dying without children (Seven 745–9),

as opposed to bare statement at *Oedipus Tyrannos* 711–14:

an oracle came to Laios once, I won't say from Apollo himself, but from his ministers, that it would be his fate to die at the hands of a son who would be born to me and him.

Aeschylus' Laios came to grief through disobedience, but in Sophokles it is possible that the oracle comes *after* the birth of Oedipus, in the manner of the blessing or curse pronounced on a newborn child.

Perhaps the most disturbing comment on the world-order in Sophokles comes at the end of *Trachinian Women*, where we have seen a desperate wife, abandoned by her husband, attempt to win him back by resorting to a love-charm that goes fatally awry. Herakles, the greatest of human heroes, is brought down by the woman he has rejected and a monster that he has killed, and is left to die in agony on the pyre that he orders his own son to light. The end of this play is profoundly disturbing, not just in the entry of Herakles in agony, but in his unfeeling request to his son to light the pyre that will kill him and then to take Iole to wife, the young woman who has been the cause of the tragedy, and especially in the words of Hyllos that close the play:

Companions, lift him up, showing your great sympathy to me over this and realizing the great unkindness of the gods over the events that have happened here – these gods who are our parents and are called our fathers watch such sufferings. No one sees the future, but the present is pitiful for

us and shameful for them, and especially hard on him who endures this disaster. Maidens, do not
stay in this house, where you have seen new and recent deaths and many woes beyond precedent.
And of these there is not one that is not Zeus.

Sophokles and the polis

We have seen that Aeschylus' plays, at least the ones that we possess, are very much
involved with the concept of the *polis* and with democratic Athens in particular. *Per-*
sians, *Suppliants*, and *Eumenides* have strong links with the political situation in Athens
of the time. Sophokles is often seen as the expression of Athenian excellence in
the realm of drama, as a product and exemplar of the flourishing democracy that
produced tragedy, but in actual fact his plays are not as overtly "political" as those of
Aeschylus or even Euripides. For example, *Trachinian Women* does contain a theme
of savagery against civilization – Herakles sacking a city to gain his desired "bride"
– but there is little that applies even indirectly to Athens. *Philoktetes* possesses a similar
theme of wilderness against community, and Philoktetes is being pressured to rejoin
his community and to bring down the city of Troy, but unless one wants to see Philoktetes as symbolic of Alkibiades in 410/09, yearning to return to his community, there
is little that is relevant to Athens in this play also. *Elektra* does have more of a political theme, since the dead Agamemnon is as much deposed king as murdered father.
Klytaimestra's dream (417–23) is of Agamemnon and the staff that is emblematic of
his throne, and the recognition is achieved by means of the dead king's signet ring.
The climax of this drama is not the murder of the mother, but that of the usurping
ruler, Aigisthos.

Ajax might have more Athenian relevance, since the title-hero was one of the ten
eponymous heroes of the Athenian tribes and had come from the island of Salamis,
now part of Attica. Under the tyranny (545–510) veneration of Ajax had increased
and his aid was invoked before the critical battle against the Persians at Salamis. It
has been suggested that Sophokles' play shows how this hero, who had turned on his
own leaders at Troy and then committed suicide, could become a *heros*, worth of honor
at Athens. This may be the case, but Sophokles is more concerned with concepts of
honor and heroism than with Ajax' status as an Athenian hero.

This leaves the three Theban plays. Thebes in tragedy is a sort of "anti-Athens," a
city where men might marry their mother, curse their children, and gouge their eyes
out. Thus in tragedy, when Thebes and Athens interact (as in *Oedipus at Kolonos* or
Euripides' *Suppliant Women*), there is a pointed contrast to be made. The *polis* is very
much at the heart of *Antigone*, since that play explores what was a pressing issue in
the early years of the democracy: one's loyalties to one's family as against the *polis*.
But in a drama about the excesses of one man's rule, the word *tyrannos* is not used of
Kreon – he is described as "king," "lord," or "monarch." Kreon is not Perikles, nor
was *Antigone* written against any background of accusations or concern about
"tyranny."

For some, *Oedipus Tyrannos* has definite political overtones for an Athenian audience. Knox (1957) sees in Oedipus an allegorical figure for Athens herself – for

Oedipus the "tyrant" read Athens whose rule over the allies Thucydides (3.37.2) described as a "tyranny." Wiles (2000: 68) takes *Oedipus Tyrannos* as a deliberate counterpoint to Athenian democracy and the spirit of community:

> there is no space in democratic society for such as Oedipus. Athenians, like the chorus of the play, must reject the temptation to believe that one man can calculate the future.

But we assume too readily the political background for tragedy and downplay the extent to which the audience would become engrossed in a powerfully emotive story. After the revelation of the full truth, the chorus at 1186–1222 sing generally of the frailty of humanity and of Oedipus as a paradigm of this. This is the feeling that the spectator is left with, not a commentary on contemporary democracy. Athens is all but invisible in this drama.

Oedipus at Kolonos is another matter, for here the setting is Kolonos, only a mile or so from the city of Athens, and in this tragedy the worlds of Thebes and Athens overlap. We may legitimately compare Theseus of Athens with the representatives from Thebes who appear before us (Oedipus, Polyneikes, and especially Kreon). At 64–7 we get a revealing exchange:

Oedipus: *There are inhabitants then of this place?*
Stranger: *Indeed, taking their name from their god* [Athene].
Oedipus: *Does someone rule them, or do the people have a voice?*
Stranger: *They are ruled by the king in the city.*

In the Athens of *Persians* the people are not subject to one man, in the Argos of *Suppliants* the ruler can not act without the consent of his people, and in Euripides' *Suppliants Women* Theseus must answer to his people (247) and is later described as "general" at 726, the elected office of the Athenian democracy. But this Theseus is king rather than general, and while there is praise of Athens and her conduct, what Athens excels at is not her government, but her respect for the gods (1006–7).

Euripides

With Euripides we come to the third of three great tragedians, whom both ancient and modern critics view as the iconoclastic and unconventional dramatist, a reputation which the evidence does in part support. For Euripides in particular the ancient sources provided all sorts of provocative anecdotes, most based on "deductions" from material in his plays or from the caricature in comedy. We have a *Life of Euripides*, providing the same sort of credibility as for the other ancient *Lives*, a briefer entry in the *Suda*, fragments of an anecdotal dialogue by Satyros (third century), a chapter (15.20) in *Attic Nights* by Aulus Gellius (first century AD), and a summary of his life by Thomas Magister (14th century AD). Allowing for the fictions and exaggerations of the ancient sources, we can provide the following biographical scheme with reasonable security:

480 – born to Mnesarchides and Kleito; from the deme of Phlya
455 – first tragic production (included *Daughters of Pelias*)
447–4 – competed against Sophokles and Achaios
441 – victory at the Dionysia
438 – finished second to Sophokles, with *Cretan Women*, *Alkmaion in Psophis*, *Telephos*, *Alkestis*
431 – finished third to Euphorion and Sophokles, with *Medea*, *Philoktetes*, *Diktys*, *Harvesters*
428 – victory at the Dionysia, with second *Hippolytos*, against Iophon and Ion
415 – finished second to Xenokles, with *Alexandros*, *Palamedes*, *Trojan Women*, *Sisyphos*
412 – production of *Helen* and *Andromeda*
408 – production of *Orestes*
408 – visit to the court of king Archelaos of Macedon
407 – death in Macedon
ca. 405 – posthumous victory through his son, with *Iphigeneia at Aulis*, *Alkmaion*, *Bacchae*

Most of the anecdotes surrounding the life and career of Euripides are the products of comic caricature and scholarly fantasy. That his mother sold green vegetables in the market is a repeated joke in comedy (*Acharnians* 478, *Women at the Thesmophoria* 387, *Frogs* 840), the exact truth of which eludes us still. He is said to have lived in splendid isolation in a cave on Salamis (this too may have come from comedy), and to have kept a good library. The demagogue Kleon supposedly prosecuted him for impiety. His private life was allegedly not a happy one, for he divorced his first wife for an affair with his friend Kephisophon (who also supposedly co-authored his plays). Here we see a classic reading of the poet's work into his own biography:

> They say that when he had married Choirile, the daughter of Mnesilochos and had witnessed her immoral behavior, he wrote his first Hippolytos, in which he trumpets the shamelessness of women, and then divorced her. (*Life of Euripides* 24)

One would like to know if the stories about Euripides' close association with the philosophers have any validity. Vitruvius (first century AD) called him "pupil of Anaxagoras" and "philosopher of the theater." Protagoras is said to have read his treatise *On the Gods* in the house of Euripides – this may just be a collocation of two infamous fifth-century thinkers about the gods. But above all he is connected with Sokrates, as fellow-thinker and even inspiration (Aristophanes fr. 392):

> This [Sokrates] *is the man who writes those clever and chattery plays for Euripides.*

The two would have much in common: an inquiring and critical intelligence, an unwillingness to accept conventional answers, and a rejection of that which was specious and blatantly self-seeking. Some have seen in Euripides' Medea a dramatic character challenging the Socratic dictum, "no one does wrong knowingly," when Medea admits (lines 1078–80) that her *thymos* ("passion") is overpowering her rational deliberations (*bouleumata*):

> *I understand what sort of evil deeds I am contemplating, but my passion is stronger than my reason – passion is responsible for the greatest evils for mortal men.*

Euripides' début is traditionally set in 455, one of the plays being *Daughters of Pelias*. Some have found it a trifle too convenient that Aeschylus died in 456 and that the canonical third begins his career the very next year. If the description in the hypothesis of *Alkestis* (438) of that play as "seventeenth" is chronological – it can certainly not be alphabetical – then allowing for some missing satyr-titles, the production of 438 would have been Euripides' fifth in eighteen years. A début about ten years later ca. 445 might be preferred. But twenty-two or twenty-three productions over the traditional career of forty-eight years (455–407) amounts to an average of every other year, a figure which we have seen fits the careers of Sophokles and Aeschylus. Perhaps Euripides' career was late in developing and he may not have reached his stride until the late 430s. Aristophanes' comedy shows Aeschylus and Sophokles already established in their canonical status and Euripides in the process of becoming a "great" poet. In fact Euripides may have Aristophanes to thank for advancing his status among the Athenians of his day.

Ancient sources tell us that in 408 Euripides went to the court of Archelaos, king of Macedon, a semi-Greek kingdom in the north. Archelaos was attempting to establish a cultured court-life in his kingdom, it seems, and we know that Agathon, a rising young tragic poet, and the painter, Zeuxis, were also present at the court. Why would Euripides, now in his seventies, leave Athens for the wilds of northern Greece? Perhaps a recent bad outing at the Dionysia? One of his plays of 408 was *Orestes*, a devastating retelling of the revenge of the children of Agamemnon, in whose nihilistic ending not even Apollo can restore order. If this play had not fared well, this might have impelled him to move from Athens. Or because he had had enough of war or could see the handwriting on the wall (Athens' ultimate defeat in 405/4)? Perhaps Archelaos had made him an offer he could not refuse. He would not be the only artist to seek out new pastures in his old age. The ancients record bizarre stories of his death in the North (in one version torn apart by the royal hounds of the court) in 407. When the news reached Athens, Sophokles is said to have dressed his chorus at the *proagon* (March 406) in black, Aristophanes wrote his masterpiece, *Frogs* (405–Lenaia), in which Euripides competes with Aeschylus in the underworld for the throne of tragedy, and Euripides' son produced three plays that his father had composed while in Macedon, winning a posthumous victory (Euripides' fifth) with *Bacchae*, *Iphigeneia at Aulis*, and *Alkmaion in Corinth*. The first two are extant, and rank among his most powerful plays. More than one critic has wondered if his experience in less-civilized Macedon contributed at all to *Bacchae*, which turns on an antithesis between urban and wild. Incidentally, the validity of this entire story has been challenged by Scullion (2003), who points out that Aristophanes in *Frogs* (405-L) has not a word to say about Euripides' decease while in Macedon and argues that the whole thing is an ancient fiction, perhaps based on Agathon's known sojourn at the court of Archelaos.

Euripides' plays

We have about ninety titles for Euripides, a figure that suggests about twenty-two productions at the City Dionysia. In the case of the extant *Andromache* a scholiast declares that the play was not produced at Athens, presumably because he could not find it in the official Athenian lists. Thus not all of the plays the ancients knew of may have been performed at Athens, although it seems unlikely that Euripides would write plays for production elsewhere and not submit them for a later performance at Athens. Twenty-two productions mean twenty-two satyr-dramas, although *Alkestis* shows that Euripides could experiment with that position. Including *Alkestis* we can with confidence identify about a dozen satyr-dramas, leaving another ten or so among the known (or perhaps unknown) titles.

With Euripides we have two manuscript traditions: one a collection of ten plays, chosen in antiquity as his "select works" in presumably the same manner that seven plays were chosen each for Aeschylus and Sophokles. These plays tend to be ones with a high profile in the ancient world (e.g., *Medea, Orestes, Phoenician Women*). But a separate manuscript (L) has preserved nine plays roughly in alphabetical sequence, from H through K, and thus has given us a more representative sample that includes the deservedly respected *Herakles* and also *Children of Herakles*, which does not show Euripides at the top of his game. To sum up, we have sixteen tragedies, one satyr-play (*Cyclops*), one quasi-satyr-drama (*Alkestis*), and a play called *Rhesos*. This last is a dramatic rendering of the events of *Iliad* 10, and although Euripides is known to have written a *Rhesos*, this is very likely not it, but rather a fourth-century effort. If it *is* by Euripides, it is probably an early work or just possibly another experiment with a play in the fourth position.

We have nine secure dates, either from the hypotheses that accompany the plays or from comments by ancient scholars, who had access to the official records or to works such as Aristotle's lost *Production Lists*.

438 – *Alkestis*	409 – *Phoenician Women*
431 – *Medea*	408 – *Orestes*
428 – *Hippolytos*	407 – *Bacchae*
415 – *Trojan Women*	407 – *Iphigeneia at Aulis*
412 – *Helen*	

For the remaining nine plays we can be confident of dating these (with the exception of *Cyclops*) to within a year or two. Critics have attempted to find external references within the undated plays: such as the prediction of Eurystheus in *Children of Herakles*, which could not have been spoken after 430, or the issue of the burial of war-dead at Thebes in *Suppliant Women*, which, it is argued, becomes poignantly topical after such an incident with the Thebans following the battle of Delion in 424.

But more reliable is the evidence from Euripides' evolving use of the iambic trimeter, the meter used for most of the episodes in tragedy. Meter in drama, it should be remembered, does not depend on patterns of stressed syllables, as in modern poetry, but on measures of time, such as $\frac{1}{2}$ or $\frac{1}{4}$ notes in music. Behind the spoken, chanted, or sung words of the text lay a rhythm of long and short beats, in a regular pattern and obeying certain rules. The normal iambic trimeter takes the following form, where – is a long syllable, ∪ a short syllable, and x either long or short: x – ∪ – | x – ∪ – | x – ∪ –. Now each of the iambic feet, either x – or ∪ –, can be "resolved" by substituting a three-element foot: a dactyl (– ∪ ∪), an anapest (∪ ∪ –), or a tribrach (∪ ∪ ∪). This creates a less regular pattern for the "music" of the iambs, and when we examine the nine securely dated plays of Euripides in terms of the percentage of iambic lines that are resolved, we find a steady increase in resolutions from less than 10 percent in plays of the 430s to nearly 50 percent in late plays such as *Orestes* (408), with the other datable plays following a steadily increasing line.

Alkestis (438)	------ (6%)
Medea (431)	-------- (7%)
Hippolytos (428)	------ (6%)
TW (415)	-------------------------- (27%)
Helen (412)	---------------------------------- (35%)
PW (409)	---------------------------------- (35%)
Orestes (408)	-- (49%)
Bacchae (407)	-- (44%)
IA (407)	-- (44%)

So when we take the eight undated tragedies and determine the percentage of resolution, we can plot the results against the graph above:

Alkestis (438)	------ (6%)
Medea (431)	-------- (7%)
Children of Herakles	-------- (7%)
Hippolytos (428)	------ (6%)
Andromache	-------------- (16%)
SW	--------------- (17%)
Hecuba	-------------------- (20%)
Elektra	--------------------- (21%)
Herakles	---------------------- (23%)
TW (415)	-------------------------- (27%)
Ion	--------------------------- (28%)

Continued

IT	-------------------------- (29%)
Helen (412)	--------------------------------- (35%)
PW (409)	------------------------------- (35%)
Orestes (408)	--- (49%)
Bacchae (407)	-- (44%)
IA (407)	------------------------------------- (44%)

The following dates will thus not be far off:

438 – *Alkestis*	415 – *Trojan Women*
431 – *Medea*	414 – *Iphigeneia among the Taurians*
430 – *Children of Herakles*	412 – *Helen*
428 – *Hippolytos*	412–410 – *Ion*
427–425 – *Andromache*	409 – *Phoenician Women*
425 – *Hecuba*	408 – *Orestes*
423-420 – *Suppliant Women*	407 – *Bacchae*
420 or 419 – *Elektra*	407 – *Iphigneia at Aulis*
416 – *Herakles*	??? – *Cyclops*

As with Aeschylus, the bulk of these plays lies within the later part of Euripides' life, although I have suggested that his later career was more productive than his early years.

Unlike Sophokles, Euripides was not successful in his own lifetime. The ancient sources credit him with four victories while he was alive, as well as the posthumous success with *Bacchae* and the other plays. One victory was in 441, another in 428 with a production that included the unusual revision of an earlier version of *Hippolytos*. The competition was not strong that year: Sophokles' son Iophon and Ion of Chios, Sophokles himself not competing. It would be in the fourth century that Euripides reached his greatest popularity, apart from the late twentieth century to which his plays have spoken with resonance.

We have been especially fortunate in the fragmentary remains of Euripides and can see what he did with certain versions of particular stories. We possess several hundred lines of a late play, *Hypsipyle*, which featured two of his favorite themes, the rescue of a woman in distress and a recognition scene of mother and long-lost children. A good portion of his *Phaethon* is preserved on papyrus – this told the story of the child of the Sun who begged the use of his father's chariot and came to a disastrous end. We have both traditional and papyrus fragments of a play set at Athens, *Erechtheus*, in which a mother consents to the sacrifice of a daughter to save the state, but whose ending is less than totally happy. A papyrus has given us most of the hypothesis of *Alexandros*, a play produced with *Trojan Women* in 415, which dramatized the discovery of Hecuba's lost son, Alexandros (Paris). As this play had at least two characters in common with *Trojan Women* and as the other tragedy of 415 (*Palamedes*) was also set at Troy, it provides some evidence that Euripides was writing a loosely connected "Trojan war trilogy" in that year.

Euripides the innovator

"Version" is one of the most important terms in the appreciation of Greek tragedy. Greek myths did not exist in any sort of "Authorized Version." There was no standard version of a particular story, and poets and artists were free to retell the myth in any manner they deemed fit. Audiences would be anxious to see how a particular poet treated a particular story, and in the case of Euripides the versions were often free and daring. One of the boldest is Medea's murder of her own children to spite her estranged husband. In earlier versions the children die, but either as the revenge of the Corinthians, whose king and princess Medea has murdered, or in an attempt by Medea to make them immortal. Euripides has made great dramatic capital out of her infanticide, both in her agonizing internal debate and in the audience's gradual realization of what horror she is planning. This is hinted at as early as lines 92–3, "I see her looking at them with strange expression," and when the full revelation comes at line 792, "I will kill my children," the spectators lose all the sympathy which Euripides has built up in the previous scenes. Another equally bold change in plot occurs in *Bacchae*. In the usual version of the story, Pentheus leads his army out against the women of Thebes, and is defeated and killed by the god-possessed maenads. The messenger at 677–774 in fact reports such an encounter by the women with the people living on the plain, and Pentheus at line 809 orders out his troops. The spectators would be puzzled at this point. Would they eventually be getting another messenger-speech, again relating the defeat of men at the hands of women? But at line 810 Euripides with one line subtly changes the entire direction of the play, as Dionysos tempts Pentheus, "Ah . . . would you like to see the women on the mountain?" Pentheus is ensnared and the new plot-line will take him on a lonely track to the mountain, possessed by the god, dressed as a woman, to be torn apart by his own aunts and mother.

Euripides will add new characters and plot twists to the established myths. In *Orestes* Tyndareus, the father of Helen and Klytaimestra, arrives from Sparta to see that Orestes is punished for murdering his mother. In *Suppliant Women* not only are the Seven against Thebes loving family men, rather than the ogres of legend, but Kapaneus' widow, Evadne, appears suddenly to leap to her death on her husband's funeral pyre. Euripides even adds her father, Iphis, in an attempt to dissuade her. In *Hecuba* the title character loses her two last children as two plots come together, the sacrifice of Polyxene and the murder of Polydoros, and in *Phoenician Women* the encounter between Oedipus' sons takes place with Oedipus and Jokaste still alive and in Thebes and a new character added, Kreon's son Menoikeus, who gives his own life in an attempt to save the city.

This innovation in plot was accompanied by a degree of down-to-earth realism. The Aristophanic caricature of Euripides in *Frogs* (951–61) claims that his plays were "democratic" because they contained real people who talked in a way that the spectators could understand. Minor unnamed characters have memorable roles: the nurse who opens *Medea*; the tutor and the nurse in *Hippolytos* (the latter plays a major role in the action); two bloodthirsty old men in *Ion* and *Elektra*, who impel the major characters on their revenge; the Phrygian eunuch in *Orestes* who sings a messenger-speech after scrambling out from under the roof of the palace. The farmer who opens *Elektra* is admittedly from a good family fallen on hard times, but the contrast is deliberately brought out between the traditional aristocrat and "this man of the many" who is proven to be "the best" (*aristos*).

Euripides was especially fond of plots of intrigue, rescue, and supplication. An early group of plays, culminating with *Hippolytos*, presents variations on what is called the "Potiphar's Wife Theme," in which a woman attempts to seduce an attractive younger man, and when rejected, accuses the young man falsely of rape or seduction. In a number of plays a character or characters need to be rescued from a threatening situation (Herakles' family in both *Children of Herakles* and *Herakles*, Iphigeneia in *IT* and *IA*, Andromache and then Hermione in *Andromache*, Kreousa in *Ion*, Helen, Orestes, and Elektra in *Orestes*), and much of the drama deals with effecting that rescue. Characters in distress often beseech others for assistance, as the children of Herakles do in that play and the women of Argos in *Suppliant Women* – in both cases the object of their appeal is Athens. In *Andromache* all three principal characters (Andromache, Hermione, Peleus) have their moment of peril and are rescued after an appeal for help. Orestes in *Orestes* asks Menelaos for help formally and, when rebuffed, puts his murderous plan into operation. Perhaps the greatest supplication in Euripides goes unheeded, the call by the Trojan women (1280–1) to the gods who "did not listen when we called before."

One sub-group of Euripides' late plays (*IT*, *Ion*, *Helen*, and the lost *Andromeda*) shares common characteristics including a rescue, recognition, and a happy ending, sanctioned by the gods. Kitto called these dramas "tragicomedy," Grube "melodrama," but Conacher's (1967) term, "Romantic Tragedy," seems likely to endure. They begin with a divine action, involve a character (usually female) in distress in an exotic setting, employ a theme of mistaken identity, resolved by a recognition and reunion, and finally a clever plot to escape their situation. These tragedies would have an immense influence upon later Greek and Roman comedy, where mistaken identity and recognitions would be a staple of that drama.

Euripides and drama

One of the principal differences between tragedy and comedy is in the maintenance of the dramatic illusion. While comedy (at least that of what we call "Old Comedy") delights in addressing the spectators, calling attention to itself, and engaging with other poets and their works, tragedy faithfully maintains the illusion before the spectators, preserving what we call "the fourth wall of the theater." When a comic character opens a play, he will often consciously address the spectators, as at *Wasps* 56–64 or *Peace* 50–64, but when a tragedy opens with a soliloquy, it is with all the solemnity

Figure 2.3 *Pylades and Iphigeneia, scene influenced by Euripides'* Iphigeneia among the Taurians, *on a red-figure neck-amphora, 350–325. Reproduced courtesy of the Nicholson Museum, Sydney (51.17).*

that we associate with such a speech in Shakespeare. As far as we can determine from the fourteen plays that we have by Aeschylus and Sophokles, this tragic illusion is constantly maintained. It is drama, we know that these are actors playing their roles, and that the action will be consciously structured in a certain way, but we are encouraged to "suspend disbelief" and enter the dramatic world unfolding. Perhaps one exception would be the opening scene of *Oedipus Tyrannos*, where the spectators in the *theatron* might assume the role of the "sick city of Thebes," but this too may be a convention of the theater for the spectators to assume the role of a larger gathering.

But there are times when Euripides appears to be playing with the conventions of drama and demonstrating an awareness that this is a dramatic fiction that he is placing before the spectators. In 438, in place of the usual and expected satyr-drama in the fourth position, he put on *Alkestis*, without satyrs and without Pappasilenos, but at the same time set in the world of European folktale. If we assume that spectators did not know a great deal about the dramatic production they were to see – would the satyr-drama even have had a look-in at the *proagon*? – they would assume that a play called "Alkestis" would be the usual merging of a traditional myth with the requirements of satyr-drama and wait expectantly for the satyrs. But they never arrive and we see here Euripides' playing with the expectations of his audience and exploring the possibilities of a new sort of quasi-tragedy.

In 428 Euripides took the unusual step of rewriting an earlier tragedy in a bold and innovative fashion. Sometime in the late 430s he had staged an *Hippolytos*, to which later scholars added the extra title, *Kalyptomenos* or "covering himself," an allusion to Hippolytos' veiling himself in shame on hearing his stepmother's declaration of love for him. This play, unhappily now lost, but with about forty lines extant and considerable *testimonia*, was an orthodox "Potiphar's Wife" story involving a older woman (Phaidra) in love with a virtuous younger man (Hippolytos), her attempt at seduction and rejection, her false accusation of rape to her husband (Theseus, Hippolytos' father), and the youth's death from a curse by his father. The *Hippolytos* that we possess seems to be an inverted Potiphar's Wife drama, with a less attractive young man – his rejection of Phaidra is due more to a hatred of women – and an older woman in love against her will and motivated by honor, not lust. But especially significant is the absence from our play of the two scenes that one would think crucial to such a story: the declaration of love by the woman to the youth, and her false accusation of rape to her husband. It is not Phaidra who declares her love to Hippolytos, but her Nurse, and Phaidra has already killed herself by the time her husband returns, leaving a suicide note to make her accusation. It seems as if Euripides was consciously giving his audience an inverted Potiphar's Wife drama, without the scenes that they would normally have expected.

At times Euripides comes perilously close to crossing the line of dramatic illusion. In the recognition-scene of his *Elektra* he has the corresponding scene in *Libation-Bearers* firmly in his sights. There the recognition of Orestes by Elektra is effected simply and naturally by a lock of hair identical to Elektra's own, by a footprint that matches Elektra's, and a piece of clothing that Elektra had woven for Orestes. See what Euripides does with the same material – the Old Man is reporting to Elektra what he has seen at the tomb of Agamemnon (514–44):

Old Man: *I saw cut curls of blond hair, and I wondered, child, who on earth had dared come to the tomb. Certainly not one of the Argives. But perhaps your brother has come in secret, and on his arrival has honoured the wretched tomb of your father. Put this lock of hair beside your own and see if the colour of the shorn curl is the same. For it often happens with those of the same father's blood that they have many physical similarities as well.*
Elektra: *Your words, old man, are not worthy of an intelligent man, if you believe that my brave brother has come in secret to this land because he fears Aigisthos. Besides how will there be any similarity in the locks of hair, the one from a man reared in the wrestling-ground of gentlemen, the other brushed with a woman's care? It's impossible. You would find many people with similar hair who are no relation by blood.*

Old Man: *But place your foot in the footprint and see if the mark of the boot fits yours, child.*
Elektra: *But how could there be a footprint on rocky ground? And even if there is, it would not be the same for brother and sister, since the male's will be the larger.*
Old Man: *But if your brother should come, is there not something you once wove, by which you could recognize him, something he was wearing when I stole him away from death?*
Elektra: *Don't you realize that when Orestes fled this land, I was still young? If I had been weaving, how could someone who was a child at that time still be wearing those clothes, unless his garments were growing along with his body?**

Not only is her assertion of Orestes' bravery in direct contradiction to his own words in the prologue, "I have come to the borders of this land, so that I can run for cover, if any of the guards should recognize me" (96–7), but Euripides systematically undoes every detail of the "romantic" Aeschylean scene to fit the prevailing dark realism of this tragedy. The actual recognition is effected when the old man recognizes a scar on Orestes' forehead, perhaps an homage to the most famous recognition-scene in Greek literature, the scar of Odysseus in *Odyssey* 19.

The reader will not have missed an element of humor in the recognition-scene from *Elektra*, and such "comedy" does throw the black and bitter ending of the play into high relief. There are more than a few such comic moments in the extant plays of Euripides. In *Ion* the gruff no-nonsense Xouthos comes out of the temple and embraces the innocent youth, whom he believes to be his son; there is more than a little of "unhand me, sir!" here. In *Children of Herakles* the very old Iolaos attempts to arm himself and join the coming battle, reminding one rather of *Dad's Army*. In *Helen* Menelaos drags himself on stage, tattered and battered from the shipwreck off the coast of Egypt, encounters a fierce old woman at the door to the palace, and when worsted in a humorous exchange, exclaims, "Alas, where are my armies now? (453). When we add the plays called "Romantic Tragedy" with happy endings, recognition-scenes, reunion of lost children and parents, mistaken identities, and complex plots, the sort of stuff on which later comedy would depend, we can see that Euripides seems concerned with redefining tragedy in terms of its sister-genre, comedy, just as Aristophanes is obsessed with tragedy and seeks to define his art as a comic, but serious, complement to tragedy. The comic poet Kratinos, in a fragment very likely from his *Wine-flask* of 423, links both poets together:

> *"Who are you?," some clever spectator might ask, a word-quibbler, coiner of maxims, a Euripidaristophanizer.*[†]

More than one critic has seen Aristophanes' hostility to Euripides as based on the latter's infringement upon the comic poet's territory.

---

*   In some recent texts this passage is deleted as a later interpolation, perhaps by an actor wishing to pad his part. But M. Davies in *Classical Quarterly* 1998 makes a vigorous defense of these lines and they do seem to accord with the spirit of Euripides as we understand him.

[†]   This passage might also be punctuated as "Who are you," some clever spectator might ask, "a word-quibbler, a coiner of maxims, a Euripidaristophanizer?"

Euripides and psychology

Although neither he nor his audience would have understood the modern term "psychology," Euripides was interested in exploring the mental make-up of his characters and how they came to perform the actions that they did. We have seen that in *Oresteia* Aeschylus does not present us with a fully fleshed-out Orestes – he is more important for what he does than for who he is. But Euripides in both *Elektra* and *Orestes* takes us inside the personality of the man whom a god has ordered to kill his mother. In *Elektra* this Orestes crosses the border by night, ready to run for cover, delays the recognition with his sister until it is forced upon him by the old man, and takes no part in the planning of the two murders – Elektra exclaims gleefully at line 647, "Let me be the one to plan mother's death." At the sight of his mother, Orestes (962–87) wonders if he can actually do this deed and if Apollo's oracle was genuine, and in the actual murder Elektra has to guide his hand. Both brother and sister break down with grief and guilt over the murder of their mother. It is not a hero who can obey a god and kill his mother, but rather an anti-hero. In both *IT* and *Orestes* the Furies are phantoms of Orestes' guilty imagination and not the real goddesses of retribution that Aeschylus brings before our eyes.

Also in *Elektra* he explores the very concept of "nobility," for the only truly "noble" character in the play is the farmer, a decent sort who has "married" Elektra but never consummated the marriage, "being unworthy I am ashamed to take and violate the child of prosperous parents" (45–6). When Orestes learns of this man's respect for his sister, he wonders aloud about how one should judge true nobility:

> There is no certain pointer toward nobility . . . for this man here, who is neither important among the Argives nor proud of the reputation of his family, one man among many, has been discovered as truly noble. Will you not stop being foolish, you who wander about full of empty notions, and judge people as noble by their behavior and their character? (367, 380–5)

Ironically Orestes will fail his own test in the play.

In *Ion* he gives us the figure of Kreousa, mistreated by all the men in her life: raped and deserted by Apollo, her baby taken and brought up secretly at Delphi, married to a foreigner for political reasons, and who has not been able to conceive. What would such a woman be like after sixteen years, when she thinks that her husband will be reunited with a long-lost child, while she remains childless? What would such a proud woman do? In the very bitter *Hecuba* Euripides depicts a woman who has lost everything, husband, position, city, children, and who suffers two final catastrophic events: the loss of her last daughter and the discovery that the young son whom she sent away for safety has been murdered. All that is left for her is to wreak a bloody revenge and then madness. Euripides dramatizes the final collapse of a previously heroic woman. In *Medea* we see on stage the heroine torn between a mother's love for her children and her desire to take vengeance. In her great speech at lines 1021–80, we see her tossed back and forth between her options, finally choosing revenge ("I hated you more than I loved them"). In *Elektra* we see a Klytaimestra who did not spend ten years plotting a revenge for her daughter, but a woman who snapped when her husband brought home another woman and acted out of desperate impulse rather than premeditation.

Two young men (Hippolytos and Pentheus in *Bacchae*) can almost be put on the psychiatrist's couch. Hippolytos has rejected Love (Aphrodite) in favor of her rival, Chastity (Artemis), and refuses to allow Love any part in his life, despite the pleadings of an old man, who argues that all deities deserve their respect. His mother was an Amazon, he himself a bastard son of Theseus, brought up, not in Athens, but in Troizen. How much has this sense of apartness contributed to his psychic make-up? His horses will be frightened by a "bull from the sea," a symbol of sexuality, and drag him to his death. Can we read into Euripides' play the notion that a repressed force will destroy one? In *Bacchae* much is made of Pentheus' youth and a youthful obsession with the world of sex. His instant reaction to the rites of Dionysos is that they are an excuse for the women to engage in nocturnal sexual carrying-on. He seems to be intrigued by the indeterminate gender of the disguised Dionysos and to be fixated upon his mother. Here too we can wonder if Euripides is dramatizing the devastating effects of sexuality denied.

Euripides and women

A crusty old man in Aristophanes' *Lysistrate* refers to "these women hated by the gods . . . and by Euripides" (283) and in *Women at the Thesmophoria* the women of Athens assemble to take action against Euripides for slandering them in his plays. Thus in his own lifetime there existed the stereotype of Euripides presenting "bad women" in his plays. In *Frogs* the caricature of Aeschylus adds (1078–82):

> For what evils is he not responsible? Hasn't he shown women acting as go-betweens, giving birth in temples, sleeping with their brothers, and saying "Life is not life"?

Here specific women in specific plays are meant (the nurses in *Stheneboia* and *Hippolytos*; Auge in the lost play named for her; the sister in *Aiolos*; a character in *Polydios*). But Euripides depicted not so much "bad women," but women as characters of importance in the action. He was not doing anything new – witness Aeschylus' Klytaimestra or his daughters of Danaos, or Sophokles' Deianeira or Antigone – but he did show frequently women acting and why they were acting. There *were* plays with "bad women," such as the variations on the Potiphar's Wife theme – his Stheneboia in the lost play of that name seems to have tried it on twice with Bellerophon – or his Auge, when the heroine attempts to explain away her illegitimate children in mock-scientific terms. But the women that we see in the surviving plays are for the most part sympathetic rather than villains: Phaidra in *Hippolytos*, fighting against her role as a "Potiphar's Wife" and obsessed with virtue and her good name, who acts only when she fears that Hippolytos will break his oath and reveal her secret; Kreousa in *Ion*, mentioned above; Andromache, who is the mistress of the man whose father killed her first husband; Iphigeneia in *IT*, who still feels for Greece and for her family; and even Klytaimestra in *Elektra*, who feels sympathy and understanding for her estranged daughter and wonders whether "I pushed my hate against my husband too much." In *IA* Klytaimestra, faced with the imminent sacrifice of her daughter, pleads with her husband not to make her "a bad woman," alluding inter-textually to the earlier portrait of her by Aeschylus.

Perhaps the boldest treatment of women *qua* women lies in his *Trojan Women*, where Euripides chose to present as the principal characters of his play defeated enemy women. One can imagine a modern parallel, such as a sympathetic dramatization of German women in the late 1940s or the women of Iraq after either of the Gulf Wars. Women were expected to be passive entities in Athenian society – compare the fuss made about Antigone and Elektra being outside in Sophokles' dramas – and the Trojan women are just that, passive and completely subject to their male captors. But they are sympathetically portrayed, and every time a male character enters from the Greek camp, something tragic will happen to the women. In his *Medea* Euripides takes a figure of traditional myth with three strikes against her: a foreigner, a woman, and a practitioner of the "dark arts," and makes a living and sympathetic human character out of her, who attracts the sympathy of the chorus of Corinthian women, as well as of most modern audiences, with her proclamation at lines 248–51:

> *They say of us women that we live a life free from danger inside the house, while they fight in battle.*
> *Idiots! I would rather stand three times in battle than bear one child.*

Euripides would gain a reputation as a "woman-hater," because he put "bad women" in his play, but, as we have seen, his tragedies are concerned with women of all sorts. For every Elektra there is an Iphigeneia, for the wanton Phaidra of the earlier *Hippolytos* we can cite the woman of the revision who is truly *sophron* ("virtuous"), and even Helen can go from the egocentric demon of *Trojan Women* to the Penelope-like damsel in distress in *Helen*. That some of his plays (and principally, I suspect, his earlier plays) display women behaving in defiance of accepted custom is not evidence of any misogynism, any more than casting American Indians as the "villains" of Westerns in the 1940s should reflect a personal hatred of aboriginals. This was in accord with the theatrical expectations of the day in both cases. It may tell us something about social standards and expectations on the larger social scale, but Euripides was first and foremost concerned with creating good drama.

Euripides and the gods

For Aeschylus the traditional gods were real, were responsible for maintaining order in the world, and could appear on his stage. On the whole his gods are in control and dispense justice (*dike*), although "their grace comes with violence." Sophokles seems to have been less willing to present the gods on stage in his tragedy, and his view of the world is at times dark and ironic, not to say "tragic." Euripides was the dramatist most prone to bringing gods into the action of his plays, and as with his portrayals of women, a contemporary stereotype had emerged. In Aristophanes' *Women at the Thesmophoria* a woman complains (443–58) that Euripides "has said that there are no gods" and thus ruined her trade in wreaths for religious occasions, and in *Frogs* (888–94) the caricature of Euripides prays to his own new deities: Aither, Tongue, and Mind.

Euripides was especially interested in dramatizing the gap between the reality of gods as they were traditionally portrayed (anthropormophic superhumans with all the failings of mortals) and the ideal as imagined by human beings. Almost always his gods fail the standards imposed upon them by men. In *Elektra* Orestes doubts the wisdom of Apollo's oracle, "I will not say that those oracles were right" (981), and his doubts will be confirmed by Kastor's assertion (1246), "Apollo may be a god of wisdom, but that oracle was not wise." At the end of *Orestes* the gods have lost control of events – Helen, threatened with death by Orestes and Pylades, will be taken to join the gods – and after Apollo has pronounced judgment, Orestes responds, "Thank you, Apollo, for putting all things right, but as you began to speak, I thought I was hearing the voice of a demon" (1669). In *Ion* Apollo has raped and abandoned a mortal woman – Ion's comment is vintage Euripides, "since you have the power, pursue what is right" (439–40)– and at the end Athene appears for Apollo, since he was worried that the human characters "might blame him for what has transpired" (1557–8).

Euripides' dramas do not imply that the traditional gods do not exist. This is abundantly clear in *Hippolytos*, where the play is framed by Aphrodite and Artemis, representing Lust and Chastity respectively. Hippolytos' devotion to Artemis is legitimate and moving in the scene at the start of the play where he lays a wreath in her honor. Likewise both the Nurse and the chorus proclaim Love as a cosmic force:

> *She is in the heaven and in the waves of the sea, everything comes from her; she is the one who sows and grants lust, from which spring all of us, her children on earth.* (447–50)

> *Love over all things you alone command royal power.* (1280–1)

Euripides has created a neat ring composition in this drama: False Love (1–57) + True Chastity (58–87) :: True Love (1268–81) + False Chastity (1282–1439). Love and Chastity may be real and operative forces in the world, but they are not a pair of jealous superhuman beings, playing with humans like chess pawns.

Bacchae is more of a battleground, since Dionysos seems to appear as both traditional unsympathetic deity ("Though a god I was wronged by you – Gods should not be like humans in their passions" – 1347–8) and as a cosmic force that is potentially beneficial and destructive. Are we on Dionysos' side as the play unfolds, and if so, where does our sympathy end and switch to his human antagonist, Pentheus? Or do we with one school of critics see the play from start to finish as a condemnation of a dangerous deity, who is essentially hostile to human culture? There is much to be said for the negative interpretation. The women have abandoned their own infants to run wild on the mountain and suckle the young of beasts. Much is made of the insolence (*hybris*) of Pentheus towards Dionysos – the word used above ("I was wronged"), but the first time the word occurs in the play it is used of divine violence toward a mortal (Hera's against Semele – 9), and at line 113 the chorus hold *thyrsoi*, described as *hybris-*

tai ("assault weapons"). The defenders of Dionysos, Teiresias and Kadmos, appear as a pair of aged would-be revelers, the one mouthing contemporary mock-science and the other just happy to have a god in the family. And what about the chorus? How would an Athenian male audience have reacted to these strangely dressed foreign women, accompanied by incessant drums? And are we actually to believe that their championing of the unquestioned ordinary life at 429–30, "whatever the simple folk believe and practice, that I would accept," could ever represent an actual opinion of the most sophistic of all Greek poets? Pentheus *is* given a choice: accept this new god or suffer the consequences, but on this reading he is toyed with by Dionysos and led to a cruel death, all because he refused to accept that this smooth-talking, cross-dressing charlatan before him was a god.

In the opening scene of *Trojan Women*, we see two gods, Poseidon and Athene, who have supported opposite sides in the war, come together to take vengeance on the victorious Greeks, not because the Greeks have destroyed Troy or will treat their captives cruelly, but because Athene's honor has been compromised. Poseidon comments, "why must you drive your loves and hates so hard?" (67), although his own response to her request to raise a great storm against the Greeks is "This will be done; your request does not require great speeches" (87–8). The prologue has no place in the flow of the play, but it does show us what the Trojan women will realize as the drama develops, not that there are no gods, but that the gods exist and they don't care. *Trojan Women* is thus a bitter drama of tragic knowledge.

There may be the occasional benevolent deity in Euripides. Apollo in *Alkestis* is kindly motivated toward the house of Admetos, although this play is a quasi-satyr-drama and the divine world is that of European folk-tale, rather than Greek Olympos. At the end of *Andromache* Thetis appears to cheer her mortal husband at the loss of his grandson and to promise him an eternal life of bliss with her in her father's house (Nereus the sea-god). But notice that she had left the marriage and is now proposing a reconciliation on her terms. At the end of *Herakles* Theseus attempts to put Herakles' situation in divine perspective by adducing the tales of how the gods mistreat each other. Herakles' reply is blunt and very Euripidean (1345–6):

> *Those tales of chaining I never have and never will believe them. If a god is truly a god, then he needs nothing. The rest is just the lying tales of poets.*

Or from his lost *Bellerophon*, "if gods do wrong, they are not gods" (fr. 292.7). In this lost tragedy Bellerophon was presented as an essentially good man, unfairly treated by life and searching for divine justice.

Euripides and the polis

Unlike Sophokles, who held several offices within the state, we know of no overt political career for Euripides, at least in Athens, for the *Life of Euripides* records (on doubtful authority) that he took over the financial administration at the court of Archelaos. It is possible that he served on an embassy to Syracuse (Aristotle *Rhetoric* 1384b

13–17), although this may well be another "Euripides" – the name is not uncommon. A poem over the dead in Sicily is attributed to him, as well as a victory-ode for Alkibiades in 416.

While his plays lack the direct political connections of Aeschylus' *Persians* or *Eumenides*, there are some places where the contemporary background does influence his drama. The declaration by Eurystheus at the end of *Children of Herakles* that he will protect Athens from the descendants of Herakles (the Spartans) may well reflect the limited Spartan invasion of Attica in 431, and *Suppliant Women* (very likely 423) with its theme of the denial of war burial will have gained much if performed in the aftermath of the battle of Delion (late 424), where the Thebans refused to give up the Athenian dead (Thucydides 4.97–101).

Also in *Suppliant Women*, probably Euripides' most overtly "political" play, a messenger describes the actions of Theseus, king of Athens, as follows (726–30):

> *This is the sort of man to elect as general, who is courageous in time of danger and loathes an insolent people that in their success have tried to climb the top step of the ladder and so lost the prosperity they should have enjoyed.*

The word used for general is *strategos*, not "king," and was the most important elected office in democratic Athens. Theseus is being viewed not as monarch of legend, but as contemporary leader, and the description of an "insolent people that has lost its prosperity" might suit Athens well after seven years of disastrous war. In *Orestes* a speaker proposing the death of Orestes and Elektra is described as a "man with no gates on his tongue, cocky with courage . . . but he was speaking the words of another" has been seen as a specific allusion to a current demagogue, Kleophon, an unlikely reference, but the passage does reflect well the demagogues which currently infested Athenian politics.

But generally speaking, contemporary issues do not find their way into his tragedies, with one exception. Most of his extant plays were written against the background of the Peloponnesian War (431–404) and Euripides uses the circumstances of his own time as a sub-text to his dramatic presentations of the war against Troy. He shows us the sufferings of war, on victors and on victims – in *Andromache* the war at Troy was a "plague that dripped bloody death on both sides alike." In *Trojan Women* he takes the bold step of making the chief characters defeated foreign women and portrays the national gods of Athens (Poseidon and Athene) as caring little for either side. In *Iphigeneia at Aulis* events are out of control. The Greek leaders are "crazed for war," the young Achilles cannot rescue the damsel in distress, and Iphigeneia goes to her death parroting patriotic nonsense about "dying for Greece." Webster's observation (1967: 28–9) remains the classic statement of Euripides' hostility to war, especially unnecessary warfare:

> What is clear is that Euripides hated war and particularly aggressive war. In the *Heraclidae* the Athenians fight to protect suppliants, in the *Supplices* they fight for the Panhellenic law that the dead must be buried, in the *Erechtheus* they fight against a foreign invasion. It is only such occasions that justify war with all its horror and degradation.

It is sometimes thought that Euripides was a critic of his own city, much as American artists and intellectuals attacked the United States for its involvement in Viet Nam, but Athens fares well in his dramas. She is still the protectress of the weak and champion of international law, a democracy as opposed to the monarchies and tyrannies elsewhere. In *Trojan Women* Athens is the first place (218–19) that the captive women would choose, "the holy and sacred land of Theseus." In *Ion* he does show us a woman and a chorus who actually believe that the first Athenian sprang from the earth herself and that the results of a jingoistic patriotism can lead to attempted murder, but at the end gives Athenians a divine pedigree surpassing other Greeks. In *Trojan Women*, however, he does cross the line, for this tragedy (perhaps even trilogy) was produced in 415 against the background of the preparations for the armada that would attack Sicily. Euripides has the two national gods of Athens open the play and foretell the destruction of a Greek fleet returning from an aggressive foreign war – if they appeared on the top of the *skene*-building, could Euripides have resisted having his actors strike their famous pose from the pediments of the Parthenon looming above the theater? Euripides dramatizes the sufferings on both sides in an aggressive foreigner war, at a time when Athens was preparing just such a war in Sicily. Interesting also is the fact that another of the captives' preferred locations is "the land of Etna, belonging to Hephaistos, mother of the mountains of Sicily – I hear it is famous for its crowns of excellence" (220–3).

It would be fairer to say that Euripides used his dramas to question the assumptions and assertions that Athens made in his time. Part of her self-image was the reception of refugees and the protection of the oppressed. But in *Medea* the chorus properly wonders how Athens can be the place of retreat for one who has killed her children. Medea has tricked Aigeus into granting her asylum, but he and his city are now bound by that oath. In *Herakles* Euripides adds the arrival of Theseus to the story of Herakles' murder of his family. Here Theseus will take Herakles with all his blood guilt to Athens, and there cleanse him and provide him with a home and a livelihood. In *Children of Herakles* Euripides takes a myth in which the Athenians took great pride: their championing of Herakles' family against persecution by Eurystheus, and in the course of the drama reminds his audience that the descendants of these children will become the Spartans now at war with Athens. In *Ion* Kreousa and her handmaidens seriously believe the story that her grandfather sprang from the earth itself and was guarded by serpents as an infant (265–72). But three hundred lines later (542) Ion and Xouthos assert, "the earth does not bear children." Kreousa's pride in her Athenian ancestry will lead in the end to the attempted murder of Ion to preserve the purity of the Athenian royal line.

Euripides and the "new music"

The "new music" is a term of modern criticism, which Csapo (in Porter et al. 1999) calls more properly "theater music," that is, developments in the songs of drama and of the dithyramb. At the City Dionysia in the fifth century the first day of the festival was devoted to men's and boys' competitions in the dithyramb, competing by tribes (ten) in choruses of fifty performers. Simonides, Bacchylides, and Pindar all competed at Athens with dithyrambs of the standard pattern: pairs of formal metrically corresponding strophes.

But the dithyrambists of the later fifth century seem to have revolutionized this staid and familiar form of public poetry. The best evidence is a comic fragment (fr. 155) from Pherekrates' *Chiron* (ca. 400), in which Music complains to Justice of her treatment in terms which are more than a little sexually suggestive:

> Music: I'll tell you quite happily, since it will be a pleasure for me to tell and you to hear. My troubles all began with Melanippides, who seized me, pulled me down, and loosened my twelve strings. But still he was all right, compared to now. Then Kinesias, that damned Athenian, just about did me in with his "exharmonic" twists and turns in my strophes, so that in the performance of his dithyrambs you'd confuse left and right, like in a shield-dance. But still I could live with him. Then Phrynis, inserting his own bolt, twisted and turned me, totally ruined me, with his dozen harmonies on five strings. But he was all right, and if he did do something wrong, he made it up to me later. Then Timotheos, my dear, just about buried me and scraped me clean.
> Justice: Who's this Timotheos?
> Music: A red-haired man from Miletos. He's caused me all sorts of trouble, and outdone all those others I mentioned, with his inverted ant-tracks, and when he met me walking by myself, he stripped me naked and undid me with his endless notes.

Phrynis and Kinesias were made fun of in comedy as airy-fairy modern poets, and it is recorded that Timotheos' revolutionary music heavily influenced the later choral songs of Euripides. His poem *Persians* (410–407) told the Greek victory at Salamis from the viewpoint of a defeated Persian. One poet not mentioned above was Philoxenos, whose poem, *Cyclops*, showed that monster in love with a sea-nymph and thus anticipated *Bride of Frankenstein* by 2,300 years. These poets varied the number of strings on the lyre, incorporated informal elements into the strophic structure, introduced lyric solos and musical flourishes, and certainly outraged those whose sensibilities preferred this poetic form in its traditional fashion.

Euripides was part of these innovations in theatrical music, perhaps even in the vanguard of these developments. We may observe a number of things about Euripides' choral technique, especially in his later career. First, the actual role of the chorus decreases both in size and importance. In plays such as *Elektra* and *Orestes* they are limited to *entr'actes*, with little apparent relevance to the plot unfolding in the episodes, although in *Elektra* they do sing of an idyllic age of myth neatly counterpoised to the grim reality of the play. In many plays the chorus seems to be there merely to give the protagonist someone to talk to in the early course of the play. In *Ion*, *Iphigeneia at Aulis*, and *Phoenician Women* they are tourists visiting the scene of the action. To be sure there are dramas such as *Trojan Women* and *Bacchae*, where the chorus is absolutely fundamental and their songs integral to the understanding of the tragedy.

As the choral role decreases, that of the actor becomes more crucial, not just in the episodes, where in late plays episodes can go on for hundreds of lines with multiple scenes (as at *Orestes* 356–806, with four separate scenes). Csapo has shown that the actor's choral part increases dramatically from a minimal role ca. 430 to more than half the choral part by 408. In earlier drama the chorus would sing their songs on the periphery of the circular *orchestra*, but in Euripides the actor brings song to the very heart of the acting area. The innovative rhythms and techniques of the "new music" were well suited to expressing the inner emotional turmoil of the actors, who lay at the center of Euripides' dramas.

Euripides was especially fond of the "monody" ("solo song"), a song performed by an actor on his own. Characters in Sophokles do sing – Antigone, in particular, has a very moving song with the chorus at lines 806–82 – but they do so as part of a formal exchange with the chorus (*kommos*). Monodies are free-standing and unstructured arias performed by a character, usually in great distress and usually by women. In later Euripides three monodies are sung by men: the boy Ion (112–83), the blinded barbarian king in *Hecuba* (1056–82), and the Phrygian eunuch in *Orestes* (1369–1502), that is, by males on the margin. The most powerful of Euripides' monodies is that sung by the childless Kreousa in *Ion*, upon learning that her husband has been given a child by Apollo, the very god who raped her years before:

> *My soul, how do I keep silence, how do I reveal a love long hidden, how do I abandon shame?* (859–61)

> *Before this light of day I proclaim you guilty, son of Leto* [Apollo]. *You came to me, your hair gleaming with gold, as I was gathering saffron-hued flowers into the folds of my gown, flowers that shone back to the sun.* (885–90)

The composition of Kreousa's song is not the familiar strophe + antistrophe of the dithyramb or the choral ode, but a much freer structure: three lines in lyric (859–61), then nineteen lines in anapestic dimeter (862–80), the normal marching-on meter of the chorus, and then over forty lines in free lyric (881–922). Aristophanes would make great comic fun out of Euripidean monodies at *Frogs* 1331–63, where the comic Aeschylus performs a monody in the manner of Euripides, by a woman lamenting the theft of her rooster by a neighbor.

In addition to the free composition of the monody, Euripides would introduce the techniques of repeating words (usually adjectives) and of carrying a single syllable over several metrical beats – nothing strange for the modern ear – but not traditional in Greek lyric. One such example occurs on a papyrus containing the text and notes of a lyric from *Orestes* (lines 322–8), where one syllable is directed over two notes, and Aristophanes twice in *Frogs* has Aeschylus spin out the verb *heilissein* ("wind") over several beats. Csapo points out that Euripides is especially fond of using *heilissein* and *dinein* ("whirl") in his lyrics, which he connects with the wild emotional nature of the Dionysiac dithyramb.

Perhaps the boldest use of song occurs in *Orestes*, when instead of the expected messenger speech announcing what has happened inside the palace we get a Phrygian eunuch climbing out through the *skene*-building and then reporting in song the attempted murder of Helen. Here Euripides has melded monody with the messenger speech and produced a bizarre result. It is often thought that Timotheos' *Persians* is an influence here, since that dithyramb portrayed the battle of Salamis from the viewpoint of the defeated Persians, including direct song by a Phoenician sailor.

Thus a drama by Euripides was something exciting, anticipated perhaps by many – we are told that Sokrates always attended the theater when Euripides was presenting his plays – perhaps dreaded by others of a more traditional inclination. Aeschylus and Sophokles were already "classics," and Euripides in the next century would become the most popular of all the tragic poets. But in his own lifetime he was a figure of controversy, a poet who was *sophos*, a word which carries the connotations of both "wise" and "wise-guy," and *dexios*, "clever" and "too clever by half." Audiences would come to expect a bold and innovative treatment of the traditional myth, with realistic and even unpleasant characters, and above all a sense of discomfort. One is never quite sure where one is in a play by Euripides. In *Ion* Athenian self-pride and her personal myth of autochthony becomes the theme for the play – in the end Athenians are given a superior pedigree over other Greeks, but it has been an uncomfortable trip getting there. In *Bacchae* the exuberant celebration of life in Dionysos gradually yields to the depiction of a typical Euripidean god, who cruelly toys with humans and lacks what we would call morality. In *Medea* Euripides has taken the mysterious and impersonal foreign sorceress of legend, turned her briefly into a sympathetic tragic heroine, before returning her to the status of the inhuman woman of power. Gods do not appear on stage in *Medea*, nor are they active beneath the text, as Apollo in *Oedipus Tyrannos* or Eros in *Trachinian Women*. The play concludes not with a *deus ex machina*, but a *femina ex machina*, for whom passion has triumphed over reason, who disposes future events in the manner traditionally reserved for the gods.

The Other Tragedians

In the third quarter of the fourth century the politician Lykourgos passed a decree that performances of the plays of Aeschylus, Sophokles, and Euripides had to conform to the original texts. This was clearly a measure to counter the rising trend to alter the traditional texts, either to make them compatible with other versions of the story or to increase the prime role of the actor. In doing so he established not only the "official" text of these tragic poets, but effectively created the triad which has dominated both ancient and modern discussions of tragedy. But these three were not the only ones writing tragedy at Athens – in fact some of the "others," even in the fifth century, came from other Greek cities (Ion from Chios, and Achaios from Eretria). Some we can link to specific occasions (Karkinos' victory in 446, Iophon's in 435, Euphorion's victory in 431, Ion and Iophon losing to Euripides in 428, Agathon's victory at the Lenaia in 416, Xenokles winning in 415, and so on). There are over 200 lost tragedians in the first volume of *TrGF*, nearly fifty for the fifth century. The works of the "Big Three" are perhaps a non-representative sample, and we have perhaps been too much influenced by Dionysos' dismissive remarks at *Frogs* 71–95 about the current chatterboxes "who have pissed all over Tragedy." On occasion these "others" defeated the great ones. Euphorion defeated both Sophokles and Euripides in 431

Figure 2.4 *Medea's escape from Corinth, influenced by the closing scene of Euripides'* Medea, *on a Lucanian kalyx-krater, ca. 400. Reproduced courtesy of the Cleveland Museum of Art, Leonard C. Hanna Jr., Fund, 1991.1.*

(perhaps with material left over by his father, Aeschylus), Xenokles in 415 won over Euripides' plays set at Troy (including *Trojan Women*), earning the scornful comment from Aelian (*Historical Miscellany* 2.18), "whoever *he* was," and Philokles defeated Sophokles' *Oedipus Tyrannos* (Aristeides 46.334).

One notices also that writing tragedy ran in families. Both Sophokles and Euripides had sons and grandsons who continued the tragic art, but we know also of the family of Karkinos, like Sophokles a general in the 430s, where three generations of tragedians are documented (Karkinos [21], Xenokles [33], Karkinos [70]),* and especially the family of Aeschylus, spanning five generations and including eight poets (*TrGF* I p. 88). The problem is that in many cases we have a fair amount of *testimonia* about a poet (e.g., Karkinos, Iophon, or Melanthios), but very few actual remains by which to judge them.

---

*   The references in [. . .] are to the entries in Snell *TrGF* I.

PHRYNICHOS [3] has been discussed in the section on "Early Tragedy." He belongs before Aeschylus in the tragic tradition; his career can be dated ca. 510 to ca. 470. He is especially associated with dance and songs – the role of the chorus may have been larger than that in Sophokles or Euripides. At least twice he wrote plays with historically topical subjects, rather than with subjects from myth.

ION OF CHIOS [19] wrote many sorts of poetry and prose and appears in the collections of ancient tragedians, lyric poets, philosophers, and historians. His *Epidemiai* ("Visits") appear to be the first recorded collection of anecdotes, and he moved with and knew the great men of his day (Kimon, Perikles, Sophokles). We can date his career roughly from 450 to 422; a joke at *Peace* 832–7 only works if he is recently dead in 421. The only certain date is 428, when he finished third to Euripides and Iophon. The *Suda* is uncertain whether he wrote twelve, thirty, or forty plays, and over eighty assorted fragments of his work survive. Longinus (33.5) compares him to Sophokles with the dismissive comment that no sane person would trade the *Oedipus* for all of Ion. We know the most about a satyr-play, *Omphale*, which had a journey of Hermes and Herakles (frr. 17a–19), the preparations for Omphale's reception of Herakles:

Well then, you Lydian harpers, and singers of ancient hymns, honor the stranger (fr. 22),

Herakles' typical behavior, "he gulped down the kindling and the coals" (fr. 29), and an interesting comparison of Greek and foreign lifestyles (fr. 24):

It is better to know about perfume and myrrh and Sardian adornment for the skin than about the way of life on Pelops' island.

AGATHON seems to have had only a brief career at Athens. He won with his first tragedy at the Lenaia of 416, and he is certainly gone from Athens by 405. Thus his Athenian career may have lasted only a decade, and only six titles are attested for him. But he has attracted our attention through his appearance in two well-known texts, caricatured as the effete poet in Aristophanes' *Women at the Thesmophoria* (411) and then as a central figure in Plato's seminal work, *Symposium*. Both works combine to produce a picture of Agathon as the beautiful tragedian, both in person and in his works, whose lyrics cause the old man in Aristophanes' comedy to shiver in erotic delight and whose speech in Plato is a brilliant party-piece about Love as Beauty. Aristotle records two distinct contributions to the development of tragedy, that he was the first to write choral lyrics that had no relevance to their plot but were interchangeable between plays (*embolima* "interludes": *Poetics* 1456a29) and that his play *Antheus* contained an invented plot with non-traditional characters and "it pleases no less" (*Poetics* 1451b23).

Only a few dozen fragments remain, only a couple more than two lines in length. Of these fr. 6 (*Telephos*) shows a character unfamiliar with writing explaining the letters of the name "Theseus," "the first character was a circle with a stone in the middle," that is ⊙ "theta." Agathon was renowned for his antithetical expressions, of which fr. 12 is a good instance:

If I tell you the truth, I will not please you; if I am to please you, I will not tell the truth.

He seems to have been something of an experimenter with the form, with a reputation in his own day for charm and beauty.

KRITIAS [43] (born ca. 460, died 403) is best known as the uncle of Plato and leader of the oligarchic government in 404, known as the "Thirty Tyrants." But he was also recognized as a philosopher and as a dramatist. The *Life of Euripides* assigns three plays of Euripides (*Tennes, Rhadamanthos, Pirithous*) to Kritias, and we have fragments of a satyr-drama called *Sisyphos*. An ancient plot summary of *Pirithous* along with the first sixteen lines of the play has survived – the play was set in the underworld and dealt with the rescue of Pirithous and Theseus by Herakles. The lines we have show the arrival of Herakles to the underworld and his meeting with Aiakos, the gatekeeper. The chorus seems to have been made up of deceased initiates of the Mysteries, and one is struck by the parallels to Aristophanes' *Frogs* (405-L), which had a similar setting, a chorus of initiates, and an encounter between "Herakles" and Aiakos. In fact it has been argued that at *Frogs* 111, when Dionysos refers to Herakles' visit to the underworld to fetch Kerberos, he is alluding inter-textually to his recent appearance in *Pirithous*.

The most intriguing bit of Kritias comes from his *Sisyphos*, forty lines on the early history of humanity and the invention of religion as a means for the powerful to control the masses (fr. 19. 12–17, 20–1):

> *Then some clever and intelligent man came up with fear of the gods, so that evil men might be afraid, even if they acted or said or thought something in secret. And so he developed the idea of the divine, that there is a god endowed with immortal life, who hears everything that is said among men and is able to see all that is done.*

Such a skeptical and sophistic attitude fits well with the personality of the man who led the oligarchs in 404, and perhaps also explains how his plays came to be confused with those of Euripides.

In the fourth century tragedy continued to be written and performed, but with considerable change. The theatrical records for 342/1 and 341/0 show that satyr-dramas had been reduced to one performance at the beginning, and that there was a formal production of an "old" tragedy (in those years Euripides' *Iphigeneia at Aulis* and *Orestes* respectively). Tragedy in the fourth century is but a pale reflection of the fifth. Known playwrights from the period abound, including Dionysios the tyrant of Syracuse [76], but the most popular tragic poet of the fourth century was Euripides, who achieved posthumously in that century the popularity that he lacked in his own lifetime.

Among the leading lights of the fourth century we may mention **ASTYDAMAS** the younger [60], who belonged to the Athenian family of Aeschylus, whose career can be dated from the 370s to at least 340. He is credited with 240 plays and fifteen victories, and was honored with a bronze statue in the reconstructed theater. Aristotle (*Poetics* 1453b29–33) cites his *Alkmaion* as an instance of a play wherein a character both commits a dreadful deed and recognizes his relationship to the victim. Over fifty lines on a papyrus *may* come from his *Hektor*. Other tragedians of note would include **THEODEKTAS** [72], not from Athens but from Phaselos, a pupil of Isokrates, who wrote treatises on rhetoric as well as drama. His short career began in the 370s and he was dead by 350. He is credited with fifty plays and eight victories. Aristotle (*Poetics* 1455b29, 1452a27) speaks approvingly of his *Lynkeus*, a reworking of Aeschylus' *Daughters of Danaos*, for the reversal of events in the play. Unfortunately the fragments of any length (frr. 6–18) cannot be assigned to any particular play. Finally there is **CHAIREMON** [71], another tragedian of the mid-fourth century, for whom nine titles are known, including his *Achilles Kills Thersites*. A vase dated ca. 350 shows a scene from this play, as well as a partial list of the characters. Aristotle (*Rhetoric* 1413b8) thought that his plays were better read than watched. The only fragment of any substance comes from his *Oineus*, describing a group of maenads asleep on the hillside.

At the end of the century we encounter the Athenian **MOSCHION** [97], two of whose plays (*Themistokles*, *Men of Pherai*) seem to have revived the historical approach of Phrynichos and of Aeschylus in *Persians*. His longest fragment (fr. 6) describes the early history of humanity, including the gifts of Demeter and Dionysos (bread, wine) in terms that recall Teiresias' discourse in *Bacchae* (266–327). In fragment 4 the speaker praises Athens' vaunted freedom of speech:

> But I shall never pass over in silence what is right and just. For it is good thing nobly to preserve
> the freedom of speech that is ingrained in the citizens of Athene and the city of Theseus.

If this belongs to the period of the Macedonian domination, it has more than a little poignancy about it.

After 300 the center of literary activity passes from mainland Greece to the university city of Alexandria. In the reign of Ptolemy II (285–53) flourished a group of seven scholar poets, known as the "Pleiad" (from the seven stars that make up the stellar group known as the Pleiades). The only author of any note is **LYKOPHRON** [100], for whom twenty titles, but only a few fragments, remain. We can only guess how the artificial and intellectual scholar-poets of Alexandria handled the traditional form of tragedy.

3

The Satyr-Play

The satyr-play is often ignored in the studies of Greek drama. In the fifth century each tragic poet would present three tragedies (connected or unconnected) and then a fourth drama, called in the records "Satyrs." Thus it is often lost in the excitement over the more serious tragedies, and when a satyr-play is considered, it is seen either as a pendant (a nice way to cheer up an emotionally drained audience) or an amusing engagement with a more serious original (usually tragedy or epic), or a lowering of the tragic atmosphere. Rarely is the satyr-play seen as complementing or completing the tragic production, although in Aeschylus the satyr-play could be connected in subject to the tragedies (especially in 467 when the Theban plays, *Laios*, *Oedipus*, **Seven** were followed by a *Sphinx*). On the other hand, satyr-plays made fun out of the serious stories of epic and tragedy, and were intended to arouse laughter. Here one looks more naturally to Old Comedy for humor in drama, and satyr-play becomes an uncomfortable hybrid, being both tragic and comic and neither.

Satyrs are creatures that partake in the realms of the divine, the human, and the animal. In later antiquity and subsequent Western culture they are shown as a cross between men and goats, rather like a lesser Pan-figure – and one vase ca. 460 shows performances of satyrs and Pans, in each case presided over by an *aulos*-player. But in the classical period the animal part is clearly equine, and on vases one sees these man-like creatures with bushy tails, pointed ears, snub noses and high foreheads, beards and often (although not always) massively erect *phalloi*. Technically *satyros* ("satyr") is a creature of the Peloponnese, while the Athenians called these beings *silenoi* ("silens"), but the terms seem to be used interchangeably, with the father of the satyrs in drama called "Silenos" (or "Pappasilenos") and the beasts themselves *satyroi* (as at *Cyclops* 100 – "we see this gathering of satyrs").

Satyrs were creatures of the appetites; their principal desires were for drink, food, sex, and money. Theirs is a certain primitive cunning, and to catch a satyr or a silen was rather like capturing a leprechaun in modern folklore. They were divine beings, yet lower than men in intelligence, and there was a sense of magic about them. In drama they are present when monsters are to be fought, marvelous inventions discovered, heroes or gods born. They are essentially pleasure-loving and cowards – when Odysseus asks their help in blinding the Cyclops, each one finds an excuse to be absent (*Cyclops* 625–55). Singing and dancing, having fun and playing jokes, wining and dining, pursuing women, these are the activities of the satyrs. When the satyrs present themselves as suitors for the daughter of Oineus (or perhaps Schoineus), in a satyr-play that *may* be by Sophokles, their self-description is:

> We are here as suitors, we are children of the nymphs, servants of Dionysos, companions of the gods. We are fit for every suitable trade: combat with the spear; contests of wrestling, riding, running, boxing, biting, testicle twisting. We have songs of music, oracles secret and not false, diagnosis of diseases; we can measure the sky, dance, and make noises down below. (Sophokles fr. 1190)

In both myth and art satyrs appear as the male companions of Dionysos, often shown pursuing the maenads, Dionysos' female followers. The maenads rarely seem to be in any danger, and part of the humor of the satyrs is their inability to achieve their desires.

Essentially they are free spirits, and much of the dramatic force occurs when these free creatures are pent up or forced into a regulated routine, as at *Cyclops* 25–6 "instead of our joyful riots we tend sheep for the evil Cyclops." Kyllene in *Trackers* wonders why the satyrs have given up their service of Dionysos for the craft of a hunter. There was something innately humorous and incongruous about satyrs working, doing the jobs of civilized humanity. When Odysseus enters at *Cyclops* 99 and exclaims "we seem to have entered a city of Dionysos," he is in fact uttering a contradiction, for Dionysos and his satyrs are essentially creatures of the wild and the unregulated life. A community of satyrs is in essence an anti-community.

They were part of Athenian folk culture in the way that witches and goblins appear in modern cultures, especially at Hallowe'en. In fact dressing up as satyrs was part of the festival of Dionysos called the Anthesteria (in mid-February), and it is not surprising that a dramatic form based on satyrs should develop from loosely organized bands of men and boys dressed as satyrs and behaving accordingly. The well-known Pronomos-vase (figure 3.1) shows us what performers in a satyr-play looked like at the end of the fifth century and seems to be the equivalent of the cast-photograph of a modern production. The *aulos*-player (Pronomos) and the poet (Demetrios) are prominently situated and named, while the names beside the satyrs are those of the human performers. Here we see eleven members of a satyr chorus, most holding their masks, one fully dressed and practicing his routine. Their costume was scanty, a full-head mask with beard, snub-nose, high forehead, and pointed ears; a wreath appropriate to the festive occasion; a full horse's tail; and a pair of furry briefs with a small erect phallus (figure 3.2). Even allowing for the wearing of a body stocking, it cannot have been that warm in late March, even by early afternoon when the satyr-play would have been performed, and that may in part account for the short length of the play (*Cyclops* is barely 700 lines).

Figure 3.1 *The Pronomos Vase. Characters in a satyr-play on a red-figure volute-krater, ca. 400. Reproduced courtesy of the Museo Nazionale, Naples (3240). A. Central scene: Dionysos and consort (upper center), Pronomos the aulos-player (lower center), Demetrios the playwright (seated, lower left). B. Herakles and Silenos (upper left).*

Figure 3.2 *Performers in a satyr-play, on an Apulian red-figure bell krater by the Tarpoley Painter, early fourth century. Reproduced courtesy of the Nicholson Museum, Sydney (47.05).*

Aristotle does say (*Poetics* 1449a) that tragedy evolved from "small plots and ridiculous (*geloios*) language, since it developed from a *saytrikon*." This does not mean that tragedy developed from the satyr-play and that satyr-play is thus a relic of an earlier form. Any evidence that we have from the late sixth century is that satyr-play came later and was added to the festival after tragedy, at the time of a reorganization ca. 501. Aristotle in fact says *ek satyrikou* ("from something satyr-like"); if he had meant satyr-play, which he does not mention explicitly in *Poetics*, he would have said *ek ton satyrikon* ("from the satyr-plays"). This does seem to contradict his earlier distinction that tragedy belongs to the serious (*spoudaios*) aspect of poetry and comedy to the ridiculous (*geloios*). But Aristotle may just mean that primitive tragedy was a lesser and disorganized form of drama, rather like satyr-play in his day.

PRATINAS of Phleios (in the Peloponnese) was the man traditionally associated with the development of the satyr-play, but it is uncertain whether he "invented" the genre or (more probably) was involved with the formal introduction of the satyr-play to the dramatic festival at Athens. He is credited with thirty-two satyr-plays out of a total of fifty dramas. If the other eighteen represent six tragic productions of three plays each, then only six of these thirty-two satyr-dramas were part of formal presentations at the Dionysia. Perhaps Pratinas came to Athens in the late sixth century, a time when artists of various kinds were frequenting the court of the tyrants Peisistratos and Hippias, was impressed by the new dramatic genre of tragedy, and turned the irregular and unorganized satyr-performances into a distinct dramatic form. Pratinas appears to have been active at the time when the dramatic festival was reorganized and the satyr-play added to the repertoire, that is, about 501.

We have a fragment of Pratinas, which, if satyric (and there is some debate here), would be the earliest surviving piece of Western drama:

What commotion is this? What are these dance-steps? What outrage has reached the noisy altar of Dionysos? Bromios is mine, mine! I'm the one who should shout and stamp, rushing over the mountain with the Nymphs, singing a song like a swan with dappled wings. The Muse put song in charge – let the pipe dance behind, for it is a servant. The pipe may want to command revels and sparring-matches of drunken young men outside someone's door. Strike the one with the breath of a dappled toad, burn the spit-consuming reed with its garrulous groan, its body shaped by the augur, that goes against the melody and the rhythm. Hey, over here – this is how you thrust out your arms and feet. Lord of the dithyramb, with ivy in your hair, hear my Dorian dance-song.

Athenaios, who quotes the fragment, tells us that the context is a chorus' protest against an *aulos*-player or against the domination of the dance by the accompaniment. Remember that the *aulos* enjoyed an ambiguous reputation in classical Athens, as the appropriate musical accompaniment for "revels and drunken sparring matches" and also for the dramatic and dithyrambic performances. In favor of this fragment as being satyric is the association with the nymphs, the altar of Dionysos, and the self-description as "Dorian chorus," *satyroi* being the Dorian (Peloponnesian) term for these creatures. The principal objection is that the entire context seems meta-theatrical, especially if the "altar" is that in the theater and the *aulos*-player the actual "piper" of the day. Some have seen the "toad" (*phryneou*) as a reference to Pratinas' contemporary Phrynichos, and the "dithyramb" an allusion to Lasos of Hermione, who revolutionized the dithyramb about this time and increased the role and complexity of the *aulos*. But satyr-play, like tragedy, tends to maintain its dramatic fiction and not to refer to itself or anything in the "real" world. That was the province of comedy, but as comedy did not become a formal part of the festival until 486, perhaps early satyr-play was a freer genre. This may be the reaction of a chorus of satyrs who refuse to perform to this "new music" and demonstrate how a dance for Dionysos should be performed.

Why satyr-play? There is no real problem with a mixture of genres at a dramatic performance. In modern culture we are familiar with warm-up acts in music, cartoons and newsreels at the cinema, overtures before the main work at the concert hall. But these tend to precede the *piece de resistance*, not follow. Why put something after tragedy? One ancient source quotes a proverbial saying, "nothing to do with Dionysos," relating this to a debate over the nature of drama. It is argued that tragedy over the first generation after its introduction by Thespis in 534 had moved away from portraying the stories of Dionysos and was turning to other myths that had "nothing to do with Dionysos." Satyr-play was added to retain an essential connection with the god of the festival and the spirit of revel and abandon that Dionysos embodies. But this sounds suspiciously like an explanation made up to explain the proverbial saying, and no other ancient source hints at such a rationale for satyr-play.

More significant, and perhaps unresolvable, is the issue of what satyr-play added to the tragic performances, especially given the fact that they were written by the trage-dians, followed the tragic dramas, and were performed by the same actors, chorus, and *aulos*-player. Obviously there was a relationship, but what was it exactly? The most common explanation is that satyr-play provided a relief after the serious emotional expression of three tragedies, and certainly laughter will have lightened the mass atmosphere appreciably. But why satyr-play and not comedy? And why link satyr-play so strongly with tragedy, if all that was required was laughter? Critics offer a variety of explanations: satyr-play as "attacking" or "subverting" tragedy, satyr-play as rein-forcing the world of tragedy, satyr-play as looking at the same universe as tragedy but from a different point of view, satyr-play as a sort of "dessert" to tragedy, satyr-play as completing tragedy, both tragedy and satyr-play providing a view of the *polis* and its issues, but from different aspects.

Our evidence for the satyr-play in the fifth century consists of one complete play, *Cyclops* by Euripides, over 400 lines on papyrus from Sophokles' *Trackers*, substantial bits of Aeschylus' *Net-Haulers* and his *Spectators or Isthmians*, and various other excerpts and quotations. We can identify about a dozen plays by Aeschylus as satyric, perhaps eighteen to twenty by Sophokles, and again about a dozen for Euripides. The fol-lowing specific dates and titles are known from the hypothesis to an extant play or from an ancient reference:

> 472 – Aeschylus *Prometheus Fire-Lighter*
> 467 – Aeschylus *Sphinx*
>   Pratinas *Wrestlers*
> 466–59 – Aeschyus *Amymone*
> 458 – Aeschylus *Proteus*
> 438 – Euripides *Alkestis* (without a chorus of satyrs)
> 431 – Euripides *Harvesters*
> 415 – Euripides *Sisyphos*
>   Xenokles *Athamas*

In addition, Aeschylus' *Lykourgos* was the satyr-play of a Lykourgos-tetralogy, and arguments have been advanced to place his *Net-Haulers* with two tragedies on the family of Perseus (*Phorkides*, *Polydeuktes*), and his *Kirke* with a supposed trilogy on Odysseus. Some have grouped Sophokles' *Trackers* (with a search scene) with his *Ajax* (where the Greeks search for Ajax), and Euripides' *Cyclops* with *Hecuba* (in each the villainous character is blinded).

From these remains we can make the following observations about the plot and nature of the satyr-play, keeping in mind that the genre will certainly have changed and developed over the fifth century, as indeed did tragedy (or any other living art form). First, it contained satyrs as the chorus and their father Silenos as a character. Silenos may well have begun as the chorus-leader, speaking for his children, but by the time of Aeschylus' *Net-Haulers* (probably between 469 and 456) he is a separate character in his own right. In satyr-drama the satyrs are playful creatures of the appetites (money, sex, food, wine) and they make much of their carryings-on, especially their singing and dancing. They are often out of their element, in captivity (as in the *Cyclops* and *Trackers*) or forced to work (remember that there is something innately funny about satyrs in the human routine). These plays can thus be a rescue and escape, of the sort of which tragedy (especially Euripides) was so fond – at the end of *Cyclops* the satyrs will, with the aid of Odysseus, return to the service of Dionysos. This rescue and escape very often involves a monster or evil human villain – the Cyclops, Bousiris (who killed travelers), the Sphinx, Proteus the shape-shifter – who will be overcome and sometimes killed. Here the theme of hospitality, so familiar from the *Odyssey*, will frequently play a large role.

The overthrow of the villain and the escape of both hero (e.g., Odysseus in *Cyclops*, Oedipus in *Sphinx*) and chorus will often be accomplished by cleverness or deceit (getting the Cyclops drunk or declaring "My name is Nobody," solving the riddle of the Sphinx, penetrating the mystery of the back-facing footprints in *Trackers*). Satyr-plays have also a strong interest in athletics and a contest – solving the Sphinx' riddle is a sort of contest, fr. 282 of Euripides' *Autolykos* is an indictment of athletes (obviously an athletic theme was part of this play), and Aeschylus' *Spectators* shows the satyrs abandoning their wild pursuit of Dionysos for the organized routine of the athletic ground. Sophokles' *Judgment* made satyr-drama out of the famous Judgment of Paris and the enticements of the goddesses.

Magic and the miraculous have their part in the satyr-play. In Euripides' *Autolykos* the arch-thief Autolykos was able to disguise his thefts by substituting an ass for a war-horse or Silenos for a pretty maiden; the witch Kirke was the title character in Aeschylus' satyr-play, and *Proteus* will have featured the shape-shifting prophet, familiar from the fourth book of the *Odyssey*. A character in Sophokles' *Inachos* wears Hades' cap of invisibility. In fact the overall flavor of satyr-play is very much like that of European folk-tale: defeat of evil, a black-and-white universe, cleverness and trickery, the happy ending against all odds. Strange and marvelous items can be found in satyr-play: Aeschlyus' *Prometheus Fire-Lighter* must have had the satyrs present at the invention of fire; in *Trackers* the satyrs are terrified by the sound of the newly invented lyre; and in Euripides' *Eurystheus* someone (Silenos?) is impressed by the statutes of Daidalos which can almost move and talk.

The birth and raising of gods or heroes was another repeated theme for satyr-play. *Trackers* uses the story in *Homeric Hymn to Hermes* of the birth of that god and his theft of Apollo's cattle on the day he was born. Two of Sophokles' satyr-plays were called

Young Dionysos and *Young Herakles* – the divine parentage and miraculous birth of each would make for good drama. In *Net-Haulers* Silenos muses to the baby Perseus about his future life with him and the satyrs.

Romance too has its place, for one of the satyrs' appetites is for sex, witness their questioning of Odysseus about Helen (*Cyclops* 175–87), their appearance as a suitor for Oineus' (or Schoineus') daughter, and Silenos' intention of marrying Danae in the *Net-Haulers*. In Sophokles' *Achilles' Lovers* it seems that the satyrs were offering themselves as the lovers of the youthful Achilles. The Pronomos-vase shows four characters from a satyr-drama by a poet named Demetrios: Silenos, Herakles, an older man, and a younger woman. It has been plausibly suggested that the play involved some sort of romantic plot: the older man, his daughter, and Herakles.

One ancient source describes satyr-play as *tragoidia paizousa* ("tragedy kidding around") and although it was meant to be funny, satyr-play has closer affinities to tragedy than it does to comedy, not just in the fact that it was written by the tragedian and performed by his company. The subject-matter is the same as that of epic and tragedy, that is, "serious" poetry. Aristotle in *Poetics* distinguishes between the "high" style (Homer's *Iliad* and *Odyssey*) in which tragedy shared and the "low" style (burlesque of epic and the poetry of abuse) which the comedians followed. Aristotle does not mention satyr-drama in his *Poetics*, but if pushed, one suspects that Aristotle would have included satyr-play with the former. It unfolds in the same universe as tragedy, with the same plots and heroes. What it adds is the happy ending, the themes of folk-tale, and of course satyrs. Lissarrague (in Winkler and Zeitlin 1990) puts it well: "the recipe is as follows: take one myth, add the satyrs, and observe the result." Satyr-play, unlike comedy, maintains the dramatic illusion, and does not engage the audience directly. While the language and meter of satyr-play are freer than in tragedy, they do not approach the freedom and colloquialism of comedy. The abundant sexual vocabulary of comedy is not found in satyr-play. When the satyrs ask Odysseus about the Greeks' treatment of Helen (*Cyclops* 180), they use a sexual euphemism "did you all knock her?," rather than comedy's blunt *binein* ("fuck"), and nor do we find the direct term *peos* ("prick") at *Net-Haulers* 795, but *posthos* ("the baby is a willy-lover"). The human heroes, as far as we can tell, and it is certainly true of Odysseus in *Cyclops*, come off far better than their counterparts in comic parody. Odysseus must be a worthy champion to counter the Cyclops, and not the butt of the humor. That role is left to Silenos and the satyrs.

This raises again the nature and function of satyr-play and what effect it had (or was intended to have) on an audience after three serious tragic dramas. It may well be the case that satyr-play was included in the competitions to retain something of the enthusiasm of the Dionysiac festival, this assuming of course that tragedy was in fact derived from choruses at the Dionysia. Satyr-play may well have provided a welcome relief after the three engaging and emotional experiences. It may well have been the "dessert" for the tragic banquet. It may have subverted tragedy, as many suggest, or equally well it may have maintained the world of tragedy. Satyrs were like children or irresponsible young men to the audience, and the spectators may have been treated to a tempting world of eternal fun, where responsibilities and daily routine are discarded, where like the Lost Boys in Neverland, the satyrs engage in their endless dreams of irresponsible pleasure, dreams which are nice as dreams but which for the audience will fade before the return of reality.

Aeschylus was said, along with Pratinas and his son Aristias, to have been the best writer of satyr-play. This may surprise those who are accustomed to see Aeschylus through the lens of Aristophanes' caricature in *Frogs*, an august and essentially cold poetic personality. But we have only six (or seven) tragedies with which to assess his work, and we should see in him both a creator of cosmic tragedy and a master of the satyric response. We can say something in detail about two of Aeschylus' lost satyr-plays. First, the two fragments of *Net-Haulers* show a scene where Diktys and Silenos have sighted in the waves the chest that contains Danae and her infant son Perseus and call for assistance in bringing it ashore – this appeal will have been answered by the satyrs. The other fragment comes from the latter part of the play – a numerical note in the margin reveals that we have lines 765–832, where Silenos has proposed marriage to a very unwilling Danae and plays with the baby Perseus, telling him of the life he will lead with Silenos and the satyrs. At 832 lines this play is already one-sixth again as long as *Cyclops*, and unless the play ended with the anapaests of the chorus celebrating the union of Danae and Silenos (hardly a conventional happy ending), there was at least one major scene to go in which Danae and Perseus were rescued from the satyrs. *Cyclops* may be atypically short or perhaps satyr-plays grew shorter with age.

Spectators is interesting for the satyrs' desertion of Dionysos for the pursuit of athletics, for Dionysos' castigation of them for leaving their accustomed life, and especially for their wonder at masks of satyrs, "this craft of Daidalos that lacks only a voice." Meta-theater is an over-worked term, but a chorus of masked satyrs calling attention to masks of satyrs does push at the dramatic allusion.

Some 400 lines of Sophokles' *Trackers* was one of the most important dramatic discoveries of the last century. We have the first half of the play, which was based on the story of the birth of Hermes on Mount Kyllene, his invention of the lyre, and the theft of Apollo's cattle – told charmingly in the *Homeric Hymn to Hermes*. To this familiar story add satyrs, Silenos, and observe the results. We have the opening speech by Apollo where he proclaims a reward for assistance in recovering his lost cattle, a golden wreath and freedom for the satyrs. The satyrs, puzzled by the backward tracks which they sniff out ("lying on the ground like a hedgehog in a bush"), and startled by a new sound, adopt their usual role at the approach of danger (145–51):

> *Why are you so afraid and frightened at a sound . . . you look fearfully at every shadow, terrified of everything, you disordered followers without backbone or resource, just bodies to look at with tongues and phalluses.*

Kyllene, the goddess of the Mountain, explains that this sound emanates from a lyre, an invention of a newborn god, Hermes, now six days old and already a youth, made from the shell of a tortoise and strings of cow hide. This last point convinces the satyrs that this young god must be the cattle thief, but Kyllene refuses to entertain such charges against a son of Zeus. At this point the papyrus breaks down. Presumably the youthful Hermes will have enchanted his brother Apollo with the gift of the lyre, and the satyrs will not have received their desired reward.

In Aeschylus the satyr-play seems to have been more relevant to the trilogies it accompanied: the Theban-production of 467 was completed by *Sphinx*, and *Oresteia* by *Proteus*. In the last instance the disappearance of Menelaos and his ships is mentioned by the messenger at *Agamemnon* 636–80 and we know from *Odyssey* 4 that the encounter between Proteus and Menelaos occurred during his subsequent travels. The plays about Dionysos in Thrace, known as the "Lykourgos-tetralogy," have a satyr-play called *Lykourgos*. From the fragments we have of Aeschylus and the other early dramatists, the satyrs and Silenos seem to have more to do with the plot than in Euripides – it is more than just add satyrs, it is mix them well in. In the portion that we have of *Trackers*, the satyrs do engage directly with Kyllene, but in *Cyclops* they and Silenos are pushed to the edges of the action – the principal engagement is between two of the actors, Odysseus and the Cyclops. While earlier satyr-plays seem to have placed the satyrs in a setting far removed from civilization (the shore on Seriphos, Mount Kyllene, Egypt), in Euripides the *polis*, especially the contemporary *polis*, intrudes considerably on the scene. Euripides' Cyclops seems quite conversant with contemporary sophistry, preaching a doctrine of pragmatic self-interest and rejection of the gods. In *Autolykos* (fr. 282) the speaker criticizes "this custom of the Greeks" to honor athletes, for no athlete "by winning a crown has ever really helped his city," while someone in his *Skiron* mentions Corinthian prostitutes and their fondness for Athenian "maidens" (coins with the head of Athene).

In 438 Euripides made a significant departure from normal dramatic practice. We possess the fourth play of that production, his *Alkestis*, and there are no satyrs or Silenos. Critics have always been at a loss how to classify *Alkestis*: it is certainly not satyr-play, nor is it comedy for the myth and characters are those of tragedy, nor is there any rupture of the dramatic illusion or address to the audience. Did Euripides then just write four tragedies that year and should we then treat Admetos as any other tragic protagonist? But the world of *Alkestis* is not that of normal tragedy. This is not the universe of the Olympians, although Apollo does speak the prologue. Death here is not Hades, brother of Zeus, but Thanatos, the Grim Reaper of popular folk culture. This is a universe where a god may be enjoined to serve a mortal, where that mortal can escape Death by finding a substitute victim, where Herakles can wrestle with Death and rescue the dead woman. It is the world of European folk-tale. It has the happy ending, the presence of Herakles, a favorite figure in the satyr-play, much to do with entertaining and hospitality, a monster (Death) to be overcome, but no satyrs. For whatever reason, Euripides chose not to write a conventional satyr-play that year. Perhaps as early as 438 we can witness a change from the more vital role that satyr-play seems to have had for Aeschylus. It is also worth noting that the next year (437) comic poet Kallias put on a comedy called *Satyrs*, perhaps providing in comedy the chorus that was missing from last year's tragic production.

Other plays without satyrs have also been considered as "pro-satyric" (perhaps the best term that we can come up with to describe *Alkestis*). Sutton argued that the plays of Euripides we call "tragicomedy" or "Romantic tragedy" were further experiments with the fourth position, but this is unlikely, because Euripides produced two of these plays in 412 (*Helen, Andromeda*). One would have to have been a "real" tragedy. Because of the black humor in the final scene and the supposedly "happy" ending, Sophokles' *Elektra* was implausibly suggested to be "pro-satyric," and if *Rhesos* is in fact by Euripides, the best explanation of its strangeness is that it was an early experiment with the fourth play.

We know very little about satyr-play in the first half of the fourth century. An inscription tells us that in 340 the festival opened with a single satyr-play, while the tragedians presented only two new tragedies each. The satyr-play on that occasion was Timokles' *Lykourgos*, Timokles being an intriguing figure in the history of Greek drama in that he may have written tragedy, comedy, and satyr-play. Satyr-play by the 320s was acquiring some of the traditional features of comedy, at a time when comedy was becoming more domestic and much less topical. A fragment of Astydamas the younger, in the eupolidean meter (a meter of Old Comedy), breaks the dramatic illusion by mentioning the poet and his audience. An extraordinary play, *Agen* by Python (called a "little satyr-play" by Athenaios), was performed for Alexander and his army in the East in 324, making fun of real persons, including Harpalos, a powerful figure in Alexander's court, and containing the return from the dead of Pythionike, Harpalos' mistress. Timokles' *Satyrs of Ikaria* contains some vivid passages of personal humor, very much in the spirit of Old Comedy, and this is usually considered as comedy. But some have argued that this too is a satyr-drama, again showing the appropriation of comic elements by satyr-play.

Cyclops

The one complete satyr-drama that we possess is Euripides' *Cyclops*, included in the alphabetical list of plays on the Laurentian manuscript (L). It is a burlesque, not of tragedy, but of the epic story of Odysseus and the Cyclops related in *Odyssey* 9. To the basic plot-line of the encounter between Odysseus and his sailors with the man-eating monster, the abuse of hospitality between guest and host, imprisonment in the cave, the trickery of Odysseus ("my name is Nobody," getting the Cyclops drunk and putting out his eye, escaping on the undersides of the creature's sheep), escape and revealing of his true identity, Euripides adds Silenos and the satyrs for a comic result. Dionysos has been captured by Italian pirates. Silenos and the satyrs have journeyed west to rescue him, but have fallen into the clutches of the Cyclops and forced to tend his flocks. They live a joyless life, no singing and dancing, and above all no wine, for the Cyclops has no knowledge or experience with the greatest gift of Dionysos.

The principal difference with the story as told in *Odyssey* 9, apart from the presence of the satyrs, is that the Cyclops is no savage monster – this creature prepares and cooks his food – and is in fact quite conversant with sophistic techniques of thinking and debating. In his great speech at lines 316–46 he sounds like a comic version of a contemporary materialist and hedonistic philosopher:

I sacrifice to none of the gods, except myself, and to the greatest of deities, this stomach of mine. To eat and drink all day long and never to feel any pain, that is Zeus for intelligent men. Those who have complicated human life by passing laws, I tell them to piss off. And I shall not leave off indulging my soul. How? By eating you. (334–41)

Much is made of the godlessness of the Cyclops' behavior and of his punishment for his actions by Odysseus. The Cyclops in Homer is more beast than conscious human agent, but here we see divine vengeance wrought upon one who has behaved in an "unholy" (*anosios*) fashion.

Also he knows nothing about wine – Homer's Cyclops is acquainted with wine, but is overcome by a surpassingly sweet and strong vintage. At lines 224–8 he mistakes the wine-induced flush on Silenos' cheeks for the result of a physical beating. Satyr-dramas often contain inventions of marvelous items; in this case the "invention" is wine, new to the Cyclops at least. There is no clever escape from the cave, since a drama must be played in the open, nor is the line "Nobody is hurting me" spoken to his fellow Cyclopes, but to a jeering and unsympathetic chorus. The play ends abruptly with Odysseus revealing his name and the Cyclops remembering an ancient prophecy that "I would lose my sight at your hands after you had left Troy" and also that "you will pay for this by wandering on the sea for many years" (697–700). The chorus close this brief drama (709 lines) by declaring that they will join Odysseus' crew and "serve Bacchos forever."

The date of this satyr-drama is in much dispute. The percentage of resolution in the iambic trimeters is reasonably high (35 percent); comparison with the figures for tragedy would suggest a date in the last part of Euripides' career (after 412). But the metrical technique of *Cyclops* is much freer than tragedy in other respects, and we should not put too much trust in this sort of evidence. Two dates in particular have been advanced with some enthusiasm. In the second half of Euripides' *Hecuba*, usually dated in the mid-420s (often to 425), a cruel barbarian ruler (Polymestor) is blinded as an act of vengeance that involves a trick. It is argued that *Cyclops* would have been an appropriate satyr-drama to accompany this tragedy. Seaford has supported a date of 408 on the evidence of an odd expression at the end of the play. The blinded Cyclops proposes to climb to the top of the cliff "through this tunnel." As the only other use of the word for "tunnel" (literally "pierced through") occurs in the prologue of Sophokles' *Philoktetes* of his seaside cave, it might seem reasonable that these two dramas should be close in time and reflect a particular convention of staging. In that case *Cyclops* would have been the satyr-drama that accompanied *Orestes* and would have been produced in the aftermath of the disastrous Sicilian campaign, when Athenian prisoners were brutally treated by their Sicilian captors.

Euripides' play was not the only drama of the fifth century to present a burlesque of the theme of the Cyclops. Aristias, the son of Pratinas (the presumed "founder" of satyr-play), wrote a satyric *Cyclops*, of which one line survives – his career belongs to the 470s and 460s. Epicharmos, the Syracusan comic poet of the early fifth century, also wrote a *Cyclops* – burlesque of myth was an important part of his comedy. Of more interest is Kratinos' lost comedy, *Odysseus and friends*, plausibly dated to 439–7, of which enough remains to confirm that it was also a close parody of *Odyssey* 9, including the use of wine and the trick of Odysseus' name ("come, take this wine and drink it, and ask me my name," fr. 145). Like the Euripidean Cyclops, this creature also takes care over the preparation of his food:

> *And so I will take all you faithful comrades, roast you, boil you, grill you over coals, dip you into salt and vinegar and warm garlic-sauce. Whichever of you soldiers seems to be the best cooked, him I shall devour.* (fr. 150)

Euripides' satyr-drama on the story of Odysseus and the Cyclops very likely belongs to the latter part of his career, and thus later than Kratinos' comedy. In this instance one may entertain seriously the possibility that comedy was influencing a tragic poet.

4

Greek Comedy

With *tragoidia* ("goat-song") the problem lies not with the basic meaning of *tragos* ("goat"), but with the implications thereof ("song of the goats," "song for the goat," "song at the goat"). With *komoidia* ("comedy") the question is which Greek word generated the first part of the term. In antiquity three etymologies were presented: *koma + ode* ("sleep-song"), *kome + ode* ("village-song"), or *komos + ode* ("revel-song"). According to Aristotle (*Poetics* 1448a35), those who believed that comedy was a creation of the Dorian Greeks favored "village-song" on the ground that *kome* ("village") was a Dorian word, the Athenian term being *demos*. But it seems virtually certain that comedy derives its name from *komos + ode* ("revel-song"), a celebration of exuberant release that is inherent in all human civilizations of any time or place. Comedy, like tragedy and satyr-drama then, comes originally from a choral performance. In his *Poetics* (chapter 6) Aristotle defines the particular emotions of tragedy's appeal as pity and fear. He proposes a subsequent discussion of comedy which either was not written or did not survive,* and one wonders what he would have defined as the particular emotions for comedy.

Origins

One is tempted to agree with Aristotle (*Poetics* 1449a38) that "because it was not taken seriously, the origins of comedy have been forgotten" and leave the discussion of the prehistory of comedy at that. Unlike tragedy, with Old Comedy we are confronted with one surviving dramatist, Aristophanes (career: 427 to ca. 385), whose début is nearly sixty years after comedy received official recognition at the Dionysia. To start

---

* Readers of Umberto Eco's novel *The Name of the Rose* will be aware that the last copy of the second book of Aristotle's *Poetics*, that dealing with comedy, perished in an ecpyrosis that consumed an unnamed abbey in northern Italy in 1327.

from Aristophanes and to investigate the origins of comedy or to appreciate the genre
as a whole would be like trying to write a history of classical music based largely on
the works of Mozart or of twentieth-century cinema beginning with the movies of
Alfred Hitchcock. We have no firm evidence for what would develop into Old Comedy
in the early fifth century or for what stages it went through before becoming the highly
political and topical comedy of the 420s.

That said, and because academics, like nature, abhor a vacuum, one must say something about the early history of comedy, especially as there are some tantalizing bits
of evidence that allow the curtain to be even slightly lifted. The evidence comes from
three different sources: (a) the literary evidence of Aristotle and other ancient commentators, (b) the physical evidence from vases and sculpture, (c) the conclusions that
one may draw from the surviving comedies, the play-titles and major fragments,
although these belong later in the history of the genre.

Aristotle (*Poetics* 1448b29–1449b20) makes the following further points about the
early development of comedy: (1) Athenian comedy may have some sort of Dorian
antecedent, in part because of the existence of something called Megarian comedy,
in part because of the known Sicilian poet Epicharmos, and in part because of the
claim that *komoidia* is *kome* + *ode*, *kome* being the Dorian word for "village";* (2) both
comedy and tragedy derive genealogically from Homer, tragedy from the serious epics
(*Iliad*, *Odyssey*) and comedy from the burlesque *Margites* attributed to Homer; (3) while
tragedy comes from those who led the dithyramb, comedy comes from those who led
"the phallic songs," and did so through an evolution from improvisation to formal
performance, the stages of which are unknown; and (4) comedy originally shared
much with *iambos*, the poetry of personal insult, and only later developed what we
would call plots.

Aristotle's text does not give us great cause for optimism, since he seems to be providing at least two independent traditions about comedy: something which evolved
from primitive "phallic-songs," and also an art form that developed as a literary genre.
That comedy is "revel-song" may be nothing more than an intelligent observation based
on the festive parades (*komoi*) that marked many Greek festivals, and the statement
about "phallic-songs" as the ancestor of comedy could just be Aristotle's extrapolation
from his conclusion that tragedy arose from those who led the dithyramb. If Aristotle
did have reasonable evidence for the latter, he may have sought a similar ancestor for
comedy and found it in the "phallic-songs," without any real evidence to support this
conclusion. Handley's (1985: 111) summary takes us as far as we can go:

> Aristotle's derivation of comedy is a hypothesis which is interesting and possibly correct,
> but he does not offer, and we cannot adequately supply, the means by which it might be
> verified.

The later writers on comedy provide little of any value. They are singularly un-
original and uncritical, and present as fact certain tales and stereotypes about comedy:

---

* There were two cities called Megara, one next to Athens and the other in Sicily – both were Dorian.
Epicharmos was active in Syracuse, also a Dorian community.

that comedy was the creation of certain farmers wronged by townspeople, that the quintessence of Old Comedy is personal humor (*to onomasti komodein*), that comedy has three firm and distinct divisions (Old, Middle, and New), and that these changes in comedy were due to outside political forces. Their etymology of *komoidia* is usually *kome* + *ode* ("village-song"), although the derivation from *komos* + *ode* ("revel-song") does occur as well.

The visual evidence consists principally of some sixth-century vases containing scenes and characters that have been viewed as the ancestors of Old Comedy. There are some twenty vases dating from 560–480 that show men dressed up as beasts, often in groups, clearly celebrating some occasion. Are these animal-choruses the sort of "volunteer performance" that Aristotle describes as the precursor of formal comedy? These vases often feature a piper with these costumed men, a clear sign that a performance is being depicted, and include men dressed as cocks, men in armor mounted on other men disguised as horses – here Aristophanes' *Knights* is invariably cited with the intriguing possibility that in Aristophanes' comedy the chorus appeared as twelve pairs of rider-and-mount – men riding dolphins or ostriches. Some Old comedies do have theriomorphic choruses – *Birds*, Krates' *Beasts*, Kratinos' *Cheirons*, Archippos' *Fishes*, Eupolis' *Goats* – and it is argued that this element stems from such animal choruses as depicted on these vases. But such choruses do not form a large part of Old Comedy, and we need more than these disguised humans to explain the whole of the genre. While these vases do show a musical performance of men in animal form, there is no guarantee that these performances must be causally connected with a proto-comedy of the sixth century. It may explain part of the ancestry of Old Comedy, but more is needed.

Certain Corinthian and Athenian vases of the late seventh and early sixth centuries depict dancers ("komasts") who seem to be performing in a choral fashion (figure 4.1). Some of these are grotesquely padded, others (later ones) are definitely phallic, and remind one of the grotesque costuming of later comedy, as viewed on the South Italian vases of the fourth century. It is argued that these padded dancers from Corinth are the ancestors of Athenian comic actors. Again we have a reasonable and mildly compelling hypothesis, but it is still a jump from Corinthian choral dancers of the early sixth century to Athenian actors of the fifth century. Nor is there any overt connection with the worship of Dionysos, although these komasts are certainly celebrating with wine and with abandon. Also these scenes disappear after the middle of the sixth century, after which we see either ordinary komasts or scenes with satyrs, who do have a definite association both with Dionysos and with drama. Csapo and Slater conclude that:

> it seems certain that both satyrs and padded komasts performed dances in either a private or festival context from the late 6th c. BC. Their costumes suggest they were professionals.

But it is still a long step from these exuberant dancers to the organized comedy of the fifth-century festivals.

The extant comedies themselves provide only hints of the past history of their genre, apart from exuberant choruses and characters engaged in interacting humor-

Figure 4.1 *Padded dancers on a Corinthian aryballos, sixth century, in the Department of Ancient History & Classics, Trent University. Photo by Mike Cullen, Trent Photographics.*

ously with the chorus, each other and the spectators. Attention has been drawn to certain songs in iambics (e.g., *Acharnians* 836–59, *Frogs* 416–39, Eupolis fr. 99.1–22), where the chorus formally (ritually?) pokes fun at certain individuals. This, it is argued, is a relic of the primitive iambic verse-form that marked Athenian festivals. But not all iambic passages contain abuse, nor is it likely that Aristophanes and the other comedians of the 420s would slavishly resurrect an old-fashioned form in the midst of their "sophisticated" comedies. Similarly the *parabasis* with its distinct substructure and direct address to the audience is viewed as a relic of an earlier primitive comedy, where the chorus interacted directly with the audience with less concern for dramatic illusion. But the variation in both use and structure among the comic poets has shown that the *parabasis*, as used by the poets of the 420s, is a lively and sophisticated device rather than a primitive relic. The *agon* likewise with its formal and repeated structure could be a traditional feature of comedy – competition and argument were something that the ancient Greeks loved – but it is a long way from a vulgar Punch-and-Judy routine to the *agon* of *Clouds* or of *Frogs*, where the issues are far from vulgar and the humor elevated and sophisticated in the extreme.

From whatever its origins, comedy achieved official status at the Dionysia of 486, considerably later than both tragedy and its off-shoot, satyr-play. More than one critic has pointed out that to the early 480s also belong the first use of ostracism (against aristocrats with alleged Persian sympathies) and the institution of the election of political leaders. Comedy could thus be viewed as originally a weapon against prominent men, especially those with a right-wing bias, but which two generations later was subverted by the right-wing as a weapon against the popular democracy. This seems to impute to comedy far too much of a political sense from the start. Granted the evidence before 440 is very sparse, but we prefer to see the political element entering comedy in the late 440s along with the influence of the literary iambus; we shall argue below that the important figure here is Kratinos. Comedy is very probably the product of animal choruses, padded dancers, prancing satyrs, *komastai* abusing spectators and one another at festivals. By the early fifth century it had attained a language and style of its own, and in 486 was accorded official dramatic status in the competitions at the festivals of Dionysos.

Old Comedy (486–ca. 385)

Our principal problem in studying Old Comedy is that we are dependent on one author only (Aristophanes, career: 427–ca. 385), rather than on the three (or perhaps more) for tragedy, over a period of less than forty years. Questions immediately arise. Is Aristophanes "typical" of Old Comedy as a whole, or is he the brilliant exception, who wrote comedy that outshone the rest of the genre? Can we detect the other sorts of comedy that won prizes and attracted popular approval? Comedy will change immensely in the fourth century. Can we detect the seeds of that change in the fifth century?

We may conclude that Aristophanes was not necessarily typical of the genre, that other sorts of comedy were being produced with success, but also that Aristophanes did win the acclaim of posterity and, when compared with what we know of the lost poets, does seem to have written comedy at a superior level. Aristophanes, Kratinos (career: 454–423), and Eupolis (career: 429–411) were seen as the canonical triad of Old Comedy, perhaps selected to match the tragic triad of Aeschylus, Sophokles, and Euripides. They are usually linked together for the political nature of their comedy, their powerful and indecent language, and their indulgence in personal humor. But Aristotle says of Krates, an older contemporary of Aristophanes, that he "was the first to begin to abandon the iambic [abusive] form and to write continuous plots and stories," while an anonymous commentator says of Pherekrates (career: 440–400) that "he began as an actor and protégé of Krates; he refrained from personal abuse and was especially successful in introducing new themes and inventing plot-lines." The plots of Krates and Pherekrates may well have been more linear and more like what we understand by a dramatic comedy. Another comic poet, Platon (career: 424–ca.

370), seems from an analysis of his play-titles and the surviving fragments to have written two distinct sorts of comedy: political and topical comedy like that of Aristophanes, and burlesque of myths. These may well be two chronological stages in his career.

Comedy of the great idea

Again we have to use Aristophanes as the principal source of our evidence, but enough of the other comic poets survives to show that they did write something similar. "Plot" is not a useful term in dealing with much of Old Comedy; of the eleven extant comedies of Aristophanes, only *Women at the Thesmophoria* has anything like the linear plot-line of a modern comedy. "Farce" or "fantasy" might be more appropriate descriptions of what Aristophanes created. Old Comedy depends not on a complicated plot of intrigue or a subtle interaction between characters, but on the working out of a great idea, the more bizarre the better. Imagine a fantastic idea, wind it up and let it run, watch the splendidly "logical" conclusions unfold, and let the whole thing end in a riotous final scene. A typical comedy might run: formulation and presentation of the great idea, debate (*agon*) to put the idea in action, the comic consequences of the idea, culminating in a resolution. For Aristophanes the background is always topical and immediate, the city of Athens in the present; this can be detected for several comedies by the other poets as well.

Acharnians – Dikaiopolis ("Just City") makes a personal peace treaty with the enemy and enjoys the results of peace.

Knights – the city of Athens becomes a household, its politicians domestic slaves including the dominant Paphlagon (Kleon), who is overthrown by a an even viler figure, a Sausage-Seller.

Clouds – in order to avoid paying his debts Strepsiades ("Twister-son") enrols in the "reflectory" of Sokrates.

Wasps – an old man ("Love Kleon"), in love with jury service, is persuaded by his son ("Hate Kleon") to become a juror at home and to adopt a brand new lifestyle.

Peace – an old farmer flies to Olympos on a gigantic dung-beetle to rescue Peace from a cave.

Birds – two old Athenians, sick of the problems of Athens, flee to the birds and there found the city of Cloudcuckooland.

Lysistrate – Lysistrate ("She who breaks up armies") persuades the wives of Greece to engage in a sex-strike to end the war.

Women at the Thesmophoria – the women of Athens discuss putting Euripides on trial for abusing them in his tragedies; Euripides dresses a relative up as a woman and sends him to plead his case before the women.

Continued

Frogs – Dionysos, the god of drama, descends to the Underworld, dressed as Herakles. There he judges a contest between the dead tragic poets, Aeschylus and Euripides.

Assembly-Women – Praxagora ("She who acts in public") has the women of Athens dress up as their husbands, attend the assembly, and vote to turn power over to the women.

Wealth – Wealth (Ploutos) is blind, but what would happen if Wealth regained his sight?

Lost comedies:

Kratinos' *Wealth-Gods* – the Titans (or Ploutoi – gods of wealth) have been freed by Zeus and have come to visit Athens.

Kratinos' *Odysseus and friends* – a comic rendering of the encounter between Odysseus and the Cyclops in *Odyssey* 9.

Kratinos' *Wine-flask* – Kratinos the comic poet has left his true wife, Comedy, for an affair with Methe ("Drunkenness"). Comedy and Kratinos' friends (the chorus) must recall him to his true love.

Kratinos' *Dionysalexandros* – Paris cannot be found to judge the famous beauty-contest of the goddesses, and Dionysos must take his place.

Eupolis' *Demes* – Pyronides ("son of fire") recalls four deceased politicians to put things right at Athens.

Eupolis' *Officers* – Dionysos joins the navy.

Archippos' *Fishes* – fishes attempt to turn the tables on humans who have been eating them for centuries.

These comedies often feature a strong central character – avoid the word "hero," since classical Greek does not have a word for our concept of the term – who is responsible for the formulation and execution of the great idea. The late fifth century sees the rise of the individual personality set against the mentality of the group, and perhaps even more so than in tragedy Old Comedy depicts an individual standing apart from the larger community. More than a little roguery (*poneria*) goes into their personalities, but all are not cut from the same cloth. Some are old men (Dikaiopolis, Strepsiades, Trygaios, Peithetairos, Chremylos); two are mature women (Lysistrate, Praxagora); and in *Frogs* the main character is the gender-challenged god Dionysos. In *Wasps* we have a pair of principal characters, cleverly juxtaposed with one another. The great idea (jury service at home) is devised by a younger man, Bdelykleon, for the benefit of his elderly father, Philokleon, who shares much of the characteristics of the usual "comic hero." Comic protagonists stand up as individuals against a situation that they find intolerable, find a brilliant and fantastic solution, and keep the comedy bubbling to the end of the drama. The characters are not totally sympathetic. Dionysos plays the role of the comic buffoon in *Frogs*, Strepsiades in *Clouds* can be intensely tiresome in the teaching-scenes with Sokrates, and more than one critic has seen in Peithetairos (*Birds*) a comic portrait of an incipient tyrant.

The chorus in Old Comedy

Comedy, as we have seen, originated with some sort of group performance which involved both singing and dancing. Comedy shares with tragedy and satyr-drama the use of the non-lyric meters, most notably the iambic trimeter (which Aristotle insisted was the closest meter to normal speech), but also the trochaic tetrameter (a meter of excited movement), the iambic tetrameter (rather more elevated than the corresponding trimeter), and the anapaestic tetrameter (a noble meter, to which the ancients gave the name "aristophanean"). Comedy likewise has its episodes, scenes primarily involving the actors (with more participation, however, by the chorus than in tragedy), and its lyric sections, both dialogue in song between actor and chorus and purely choral songs and recitations. When monodies occur in comedy, they are usually parodies of tragedy or deliberately pitched at a comically high style.

The chorus was larger than in tragedy, twenty-four as opposed to twelve or fifteen in the earlier genre, and could participate more largely in the action of the play. In some Aristophanic comedies the chorus provides the primary opposition to the main character and the great idea – as in *Acharnians*, *Wasps*, *Birds*, *Women at the Thesmophoria* – and on other occasions supports that great idea (as in *Knights*, *Clouds*, *Peace*, *Assembly-Women*, and *Wealth*). In *Lysistrate* we get a pair of opposing half-choruses (old men and women), while in *Frogs* the chorus is largely neutral, appropriately so since they provide an audience for the debate between the tragic poets.

In tragedy choruses are almost always human – the chorus of Furies in *Eumenides* is an obvious exception – and in satyr-drama invariably made up of satyrs, but Old Comedy has considerably more freedom. One subset of comic choruses, as we have seen, is that in animal form, which some have seen as indicative of the origins of comedy. But these choruses are not that numerous – perhaps about 20 percent of the total number of comedies where we can identify the chorus. Other comic choruses are formed of entities of concepts, such as *Clouds*, Eupolis' *Cities* and *Demes*, Kratinos' *Seasons* – here the comic poet must blend the concept with a human personality – while still others are composed of figures from myth, such as in Kratinos' *Men of Seriphos*, *Wealth-Gods*, and *Dionysalexandros* (satyrs). But the vast majority of the choruses of Old Comedy are made up of humans of all sorts and conditions – farmers, old men and women, members of various communities (demes, cities) and classes (knights) and occupations (officers). Of the sixty or so comedies of the "Big Three" (Aristophanes, Kratinos, Eupolis), where we can ascertain the chorus' identity, more than half have human choruses, including here *Wasps*, where the old men are only metaphorical wasps.

As with tragedy, the role and importance of the chorus in comedy declines rapidly. In *Frogs* (405) the chorus is a vital and integral part of the drama, dominating the *parodos* and in the *parabasis* speaking directly for the comic poet on matters political. But less than twenty years later, in *Assembly-Women* and in *Wealth*, the chorus is all but invisible. They do have a major role in the first half of *Assembly-Women*, being as intimately involved as the women in *Lysistrate*, but in both late comedies the formal and familiar *parabasis* is lacking, and on several occasions the expected choral song between the episodes is missing, the manuscript having only ⟨chorou⟩, "of the chorus."

The language of comedy

In his *Poetics* Aristotle distinguishes tragedy from comedy in that the latter concerns itself with "inferior people" (1448a17) and achieves its aim by depicting what is ridiculous (*geloion* – 1449a33). Thus the language of comedy will assist in producing what is ridiculous and will descend to a cruder and more colloquial level than tragedy and satyr-drama. Comedy shares much in its language with the earlier iambic poets (most notably Archilochos [career: 680–640] and Hipponax [career: 550–520]), especially in its attacks on personal targets, striking creations of words, and colloquial and obscene vocabulary. The bizarre and the incongruous naturally provoke a humorous reaction, and Old comedians were fond of assembling marvelous verbal combinations, such as those describing the devotees of the new learning at *Clouds* 332–3:

> *Thouriomanteis, iatrotechnas, sphragidonuchargokometas,*
> *kuklion te choron asmatokamptas, andras meteorophenekas*

Thourian-prophets, medical-experts, long-haired layabouts with onyx signet-rings, song-twisters for the dithyrambic chorus, meteorological quacks.

Names were especially prone to comic innovation, as at *Acharnians* 603: Teisamenophainippoi ("Teisamenos + Phainippos"), Panourghipparchidai ("nasty sons of Hipparchos"), or at Eupolis fr. 424: Amphiptolemopedesistratos ("Double-battle-leap-istratos").

Old Comedy is a deceptive genre in that at one pole it can be highly literate and sophisticated, requiring an intellectual response from its watchers, and at the other can wallow in the gutter of the ancient equivalent of four-letter words and explicit sexual allusions. This serves to distinguish comedy sharply from satyr-play, in that the latter preserves the language and level of tragedy, while Old Comedy at its crudest is blunt. In tragedy sexual intercourse is described by innuendos and circumlocutions:

one of my friends says that she lay with Apollo (*Ion* 338),

Zeus is inflamed by the arrow of desire and wishes to join in love with you (*Prometheus* 649–51).

But comedy is far more direct and would use the basic word *binein* ("fuck"):

Praxagora: *Do I smell of perfume?*
Blepyros: *What? A woman can't get fucked without perfume?* (*Assembly-Women* 524–5),
Chorus: *What are we suffering from? Don't keep it from me.*
Lysistrate: *Fuck-itis, to put it as succinctly as possible.* (*Lysistrate* 714–15)

Another source of humor created by language lies in comedy's fondness for characters speaking in something other than Attic Greek. One can easily identify modern comic stereotypes, in which characters speak in deliberately over-stated Scots or Italian or German or the English of the Indian subcontinent. The purpose does not have to be hostile; in fact the caricature is just as often wrapped in a smile as a sneer. In Old Comedy we get barbarians speaking either virtual gibberish or barely passable Greek (the Persian ambassador in *Acharnians* or the Scythian policeman at the end of *Women at the Thesmophoria*), and comedies with titles such as *Thracian Women* (Kratinos) and *Lydians* (Magnes) suggest that foreign characters appeared in these. We would very much like to know to what extent the chorus in Aristophanes' controversial *Babylonians* (426-D) acted and talked like Babylonians. Eupolis' *Marikas* is known to have had a Persian theme and perhaps had its title character (a thinly disguised demagogue, Hyperbolos) speak with something of a Persian accent.

Greeks from other states, and thus speaking something other than Attic Greek, appear also in the comedies of Aristophanes. A Megarian in dire straits appears in *Acharnians*, followed by a Boiotian, both speaking in the dialect appropriate to them. More considerable is the role of the Spartans in *Lysistrate*, first an envoy and then a chorus who sing local Spartan songs along with their Athenian hosts. As the great rival, Spartans (and their Doric manner of speech) would be well known to Athenians, occupying the role that Germans did to British and Americans in the 1940s. We do observe that comedy does not make fun of non-Attic Greeks by their dialect, which is usually well presented by the comic poets. The humor lies elsewhere, in their difference from Athenians and their customs, in their poor circumstances because of the war, and in their treatment by more clever Athenians.

The iambic trimeter in Old Comedy is used with considerably more freedom than in tragedy. Resolutions, which are tightly controlled in the tragic poets, occur more often and with greater abandon. Some comic lines pile on the short syllables to the point where the metrical scheme is all but lost. When the line switches speakers, awkward breaks in the meter can be observed. But when comedy parodies tragedy, the metrical form switches back into the much more restricted style of tragedy.

With the comedy of Menander (325–290) the language of comedy becomes less "classical" and more in the style of what would be called *koine* ("common") Greek, less rigorous in its forms, vocabulary, and syntax. This may in part account for Menander's lack of survival in later antiquity, when authors writing the pure or classical Attic were diligently sought as models. Aristophanes was celebrated for the purity of his language, language that accorded well with the canons of classical taste. Quintilian (10.1.65) comments that "Old Comedy is almost the only form to retain that pure grace of Attic language." An anonymous writer contrasts the clarity of New Comedy with the "power and grandeur" of the Old, while Phrynichos (AD third century) ranks Aristophanes with Plato and Demosthenes as the pillars of classical Attic Greek. Ancient writers may have shrunk from the personal humor and political themes, but they were also quick to see that Old Comedy possessed *charis* ("grace") and charm in its speech. It should be noted, however, that Aristophanes himself displays signs of a comic style in transition, as his latest extant comedy (*Wealth* – 388) shows distinct

Figure 4.2 *The* Choregoi-*vase, showing a scene from an unknown Old Comedy (Aristophanes'* Precontest?*), on a terracotta Apulian red-figure bell-krater, early fourth century. Reproduced courtesy of the J. Paul Getty Museum, Malibu, California.*

signs of a more "demotic" form of Greek. In the fourth century more than the themes of comedy changed.

The costume of Old Comedy

Aristotle stresses that comedy represents what was "ridiculous" or "laughable" (*geloion*, from *gelan*, "to laugh"). Its visual aspect reflects this emphasis on the ridiculous. Whereas tragedy concerns itself with what is serious and more elevated than "normal" life, comedy lowers its level to what the spectators will laugh at. We do not have that many visual representations of tragic performances, but two vases do illustrate very neatly the difference in costume and aspect between the dramatic genres. First, the Pronomos-vase (ca. 400) shows the cast preparing for the performance of a satyr-play (figure 3.1), on which we see two actors in splendid high costume – granted that this is satyr-drama, but it does belong to the same realm as tragedy and we may

Figure 4.3 *The Würzburg Telephos, showing a scene from Aristophanes'* Women at the Thesmophoria, *on an Apulian bell-krater, ca. 370. Reproduced courtesy of Martin von Wagner Museum der Universität Würzburg, Photo: K. Oehrlein.*

fairly deduce that tragedy did dress its actors in splendid fashion. This gives all the more force to Aristophanes' pointed jokes about Euripides' characters as dressed in rags, or the comments of 'Aeschylus' at *Frogs* 1060–1:

> *Similarly it is reasonable for demi-gods to use grander words and to dress far more elegantly than us.*

The other vase is the *Choregoi*-Vase (figure 4.2), which shows a character from tragedy (Aigisthos) in company with and in pointed contrast to a set of characters from comedy.

Characters in Old Comedy were grotesquely presented in large masks with distorted features, large mouths and eyes, unlike the realistic features of the tragic mask. Bodies were padded, especially in the shoulders, giving a stooped appearance, in the belly, and in the buttocks. Male characters wore a dangling phallus, unlike the small erections in the briefs worn by satyrs – Aristophanes makes a wry comment at *Clouds* 537–9 about the delicacy of his new comedy:

> *Just look at how decent she is. First of all she doesn't come on stage wearing a stitched ⟨phallus⟩ of red leather, thick from the tip on down, to make the little boys laugh.*

An erect phallus would imply sexuality and suggest that the origins of comedy lie in fertility ritual, but the red dangling phallus is intentionally ridiculous (*geloion*) and implies that it was worn to be funny and the object of laughter. In one hilarious scene from *Women at the Thesmophoria* (463–8) a female impersonator is unmasked and proved definitely to be male by the discovery of his phallus, which moves back and forth as his inquisitors press on him from front and rear:

Kleisthenes: *Stand up straight. Why are you pushing your prick down?*
Woman: *It's popped out here. And what a nice color!*
Kleisthenes: *Where is it?*
Woman: *It's gone back to the front again.*
Kleisthenes: *No it's not.*
Woman: *It's back here again.*
Kleisthenes: *You've got an isthmus here, man! You're shuttling your prick back and forth more often than the Corinthians.*

The business about the color and the movement suggests that Aristophanes has outfitted Euripides' kinsman with a particularly red-colored and versatile appendage. Characters in comedy were meant to be ridiculous and laughed at.

The structure of Old Comedy

As far as we can gather from the eleven comedies of Aristophanes and the fragments of the other comic poets, Old Comedy was a loosely structured thing, lacking the linear plot of later situation or romantic comedy. Other comic poets may have written plots more like those of later comedy – we have seen that Krates and Pherekrates are credited with success in putting plots together. Aristophanes' comedies display a series of recurring and formally constructed sub-units that can be found also in the fragments of the other poets. It is a fair conclusion that the comedies of Aristophanes' rivals will not have been unlike his own, although they may have used these structural features in different ways. Even Aristophanes himself varies his material from play to play. Not every comedy has a formal contest (*agon*); in three plays an exposition by the main character replaces the formal debate. Both the actual form and the subject of the *parabasis* (see below) vary within the comedies of Aristophanes. The other comic poets seem to have been much freer in their use of meter in the *parabasis* proper.

Prologue: Unlike tragedy, comedy has to create its own plots and characters, and also must warm the audience up to ensure that they will respond well to the unfolding comedy. Prologues in comedy usually run from 200–300 lines, and consist of several scenes – tragedy tends to be much more economical and to use one or two scenes – often in rapid-fire succession. The meter is usually the "prosaic" iambic trimeter, although actors can resort to song. In the first 315 lines of *Frogs* we have a comic dialogue between Xanthias and Dionysos (1–34), a door-scene with Herakles (35–163), a brief scene with a corpse (164–80), an encounter with Charon the ferry-man of the dead (180–208), Dionysos rowing across the lake and engaging in a singing contest with a group of unseen frogs (209–67), and a final bit of banter between Xanthias and Dionysos (268–315). Comedy depends upon constant reaction from the spectators and the pace and humor of the play must not be allowed to flag. Sequences of personal jokes are especially prevalent in the prologue.

Parodos: As in tragedy, this is the entry of the chorus, whose identity is usually revealed in the prologue so that the spectators will know whom to expect:

> Herakles: *Then a breath of flutes will envelop you and you will behold a very beautiful light,*
> *like that of the sun up here, myrtle-groves, and happy bands of men and women, and much clap-*
> *ping of hands.*
> Dionysos: *Who are they?*
> Herakles: *These are the initiated.* (*Frogs* 154–8)

The chorus may enter to support the main character (as in *Knights*, *Peace*, *Assembly-Women*, *Wealth*), or to oppose him (as in *Acharnians*, *Wasps*, *Birds*), or just to observe (*Frogs*). In *Lysistrate* there are two opposing half-courses; the old women have entered during the prologue, while the formal entry belongs to the old men. The *parodos* must have been one of the most spectacular parts of the comedy. The chorus can rush violently on stage, prepared to do battle (*Acharnians*, *Knights*), while in *Wasps* and *Lysistrate* the old men can do little more than shuffle onto the scene, accompanied by a sub-chorus of boys. In *Clouds* Aristophanes brings the spectators into the game, since everyone except the main character can see the chorus of clouds as they drift into the *orchestra* – "there they are, over by the *eisodos*" (326). The *parodos*, like the prologue, can consist of a sequence of scenes, especially in *Frogs*. The chorus will either sing in lyric meter or employ a grander meter, such as the trochaic tetrameter (used for vigorous rushes on stage) or the anapestic tetrameter (with solemn and declaratory overtones). When the actors intervene in the *parodos*, they continue to use the iambic trimeter.

Agon: Drama thrives on competition and conflict, witness the great popularity and success of the courtroom drama in modern entertainments. Often the action in comedy will turn on the result of a formal debate (*agon*) between two characters. In its purest form the *agon* develops in a symmetrical pattern with formal and repeated sub-units, as formal as an aria in opera or a lyric number in a Broadway or West End musical. Again using *Frogs* as a model we have:

song by the chorus: 895–904
   introduction of speaker 1 (Euripides): 904–5
   speaker 1: 907–70
   pnigos ("choking-song"): 971–91
song by the chorus: 992–1003
   introduction of speaker 2 (Aeschylus): 1004–5
   speaker 2: 1006–76
   pnigos ("choking-song"): 1077–98
final song by the chorus: 1099–1118

The two songs of the chorus correspond closely in length and meter, while the speeches of the combatants are in an elevated meter, usually the anapestic tetrameter or the iambic tetrameter. The former is the more solemn, and it is worth noting that in two *agons* (those in *Clouds* and *Frogs*) the more traditional and dignified speaker uses anapests, while the more avant-garde and modern opponent employs iambics. The speeches are frequently interrupted by the antagonist, by a third character, and by the chorus, all using the same meter as the main speaker. Each formal speech will end in a *pnigos* ("choking-song"), in which the tetrameter is cut in half to become dimeter and the whole thing sung in one breath, hence "choking-song."

Some comedies have two formal *agons* (*Knights*, *Clouds*). In *Knights* the first *agon* is a warm-up to the more decisive second, while in *Clouds* the second is but an echo of the first. In *Frogs* the order of events is reversed, with the episodes coming in the first half of the comedy and the *agon* reserved for the second half. In a "normal" comedy the episodes would show the working out of the great idea, whose fate is decided in the *agon*. In *Birds* and *Assembly-Women* the formal structure is retained, but both halves are spoken by the protagonist who outlines his or her great idea to the chorus. This is not an *agon*, but an exposition. Three plays (*Acharnians*, *Peace*, *Women at the Thesmophoria*) lack a formally structured *agon*; they do, however, have an important and dramatic speech by the main character. Usually the second speaker wins the debate, but in *Wealth* the second speaker (Poverty) seems to have the better of the debate, but loses, leading many scholars to impute an ironic tone to the rest of the comedy: Universal wealth is not in the long run good for humanity. In the lost comedies there are only hints of the *agon*, but in Eupolis' *Marikas* (421-L) we can detect at least two *agons*, between the demagogue Hyperbolos, portrayed as "Marikas," and an unknown opponent.*

Challenges and competitions in comedy are by no means restricted to the formal *agon*, although this feature is worked formally into so many of the extant plays. At the end of *Acharnians* Dikaiopolis returns triumphant from a drinking-contest; at the end of *Wasps* Philokleon challenges Karkinos and his sons (performers in tragedy) to a dancing contest. Dionysos takes on the chorus of frogs in some sort of bizarre

---

* At *Clouds* 551–8 Aristophanes accuses Eupolis of plagiarizing his *Knights* to create his *Marikas*. Two *agons* involving a disguised demagogue and an opponent are very much what we find in *Knights*.

musical contest; later in the same comedy he and his slave Xanthais will be subjected to trial by beating in order to determine who is the real god.

Parabases: Perhaps the most curious and formal feature of Old Comedy, the *parabasis* comes at a natural break in the action and is performed by the chorus with the actors off-stage and is aimed at the spectators, who are often addressed directly. It thus makes no attempt at preserving the dramatic illusion. A *parabasis* breaks down into certain formal and repeated sub-sections. Not every *parabasis* possesses all these features, but in its full form, found in *Wasps*, *Knights*, and *Birds*, it looks as follows:

> [a] song by the chorus: *Birds* 676–84
>
> [b] parabasis proper: *Birds* 685–722
>
> [c] *pnigos* ("choking-song"): *Birds* 723–36
>
> [d] lyric song ("ode"): *Birds* 737–52
>
> [e] *epirrhema* ("declaration"): *Birds* 753–68
>
> [f] lyric song ("antode"): *Birds* 769–84
>
> [g] *antepirrhema* ("counter-declaration"): *Birds* 785–800

The *parabasis* proper is chanted in a fifteen-syllable meter, usually the anapestic tetrameter catalectic; in fact on more than one occasion the chorus announce that they are about sing their "anapests" (*Acharnians* 627, *Birds* 684). In *Clouds*, however, Aristophanes "borrows" the eupolidean meter, named for his rival Eupolis (explicitly accused of plagiarizing Aristophanes at *Clouds* 551–8), and thus reinforces his point about the originality of his comedy and the failings of his rivals. Fragments of the other comic poets suggest that a variety of fifteen-syllable meters could be used in this section. The *pnigos* employs the anapestic meter of the *parabasis* proper, but in dimeter rather than tetrameter. As the eupolidean is a more complicated metrical form and does not divide neatly in half, there is no *pnigos* in *Clouds*.

In Aristophanes' comedy of the 420s, the chorus in the *parabasis* proper speak directly for the comic poet himself, often employing the first person singular (*Acharnians* 659–64, *Clouds* 518–62, *Peace* 754, 765), where "I" and "me" are not the chorus but Aristophanes himself. In these five comedies the poet speaks directly to the spectators through his chorus, discoursing about the superiority of his own comedy, the inferiority of his rivals, and the inability of the spectators and judges to distinguish true comic quality. In *Birds* the chorus stays in character throughout and says nothing on the comic poet's behalf.

The last four subdivisions (song + *epirrhema*, song + *antepirrhema*) form a single integrated unit, often given the name of "epirrhematic syzygy"). The two halves correspond exactly in both the number of lines and the meter. The songs are sung in lyric meters – unlike tragedy they remain within the Attic dialect – and the *epirrhema* / *antepirrhema* usually in trochaic tetrameter catalectic or on occasion the rare paeonic tetrameter. *Epirrhemata* in trochaics invariably consist of units of lines of multiples of four.

Not all comedies have a *parabasis* with a full and perfect format. In *Acharnians* the opening song [a] is reduced to two anapests at the start of the *parabasis* proper. In *Peace* we get only [b] + [c] and the ode/antode [d] + [f]. In *Lysistrate* we have two opposing half-choruses, who sing combative syzygies, with no *parabasis* proper or *pnigos*. *Women at the Thesmophoria* has a very stripped-down *parabasis*, consisting only of [b] + [c] and one *epirrhema* [e]. The formal *parabasis* of *Frogs* (674–737) consists solely of the epirrhematic syzygy, although the anapests of the *parabasis* proper are found much earlier at lines 354–71. In *Assembly-Women* and *Wealth* there is no formal *parabasis* at all. Many comedies have a second (or even a third, as in *Acharnians*) *parabasis*, which consists only of the epirrhematic syzygy. In these the chorus usually stays within its dramatic character, although at *Wasps* 1284–91 Aristophanes himself tells of his latest encounter with Kleon and his revenge in this particular comedy.

The chorus will do a number of things in a *parabasis*: speak for the poet and his comedy in the *parabasis* proper and *pnigos*, explain the appropriateness of their dramatic role and costume, sing hymns to the gods, indulge in sustained personal invective (usually, but not always, in the ode and antode), give advice to the citizens, and appeal to the judges, but always within its dramatic persona – as at *Birds* 1102–17: why it is advantageous to have a grateful chorus of birds and dangerous if they are disappointed.

It is sometimes assumed that the *parabasis* with its formal and repeated features was a relic of a traditional element in the development of comedy, that it was something expected by the audience. But recent studies have shown that, far from being a venerable appendage to the comic action, the *parabasis* is very skillfully integrated into the themes of the comedy, both in terms of the subject-matter of the play and the repeated patterns of imagery. Notice must be taken of one particular *parabasis*, that of *Frogs*, which according to the ancient scholar, Dikaiarchos, was responsible for that comedy's unprecedented honor of a second formal performance.

Episodes: These are scenes dominated by the actors, although the chorus may certainly participate and both chorus and actor may shift briefly into lyric meters from the usual iambic trimeter. In a typical comedy the episodes follow the adoption of the great idea and demonstrate the logical working-out of its consequences. Perhaps the single best scene in extant Aristophanes is the trial of the dogs at *Wasps* 891–1008, which proceeds from the son's victory in the *agon* and his insistence that his father can still act as a juror, but at home. In *Birds*, *Acharnians*, *Peace*, *Assembly-Women*, and *Wealth* we see series of "intruders" arrive to share in the benefits of the great idea – most will be driven off with suitably comic violence. *Frogs* is an interesting exception in that the episodes occupy the first half of the comedy and precede the contest between the dead poets. In Eupolis' lost comedy, *Demes* (417?) we can surmise that each of the four politicians raised from the dead had an episode in which he tackled an appropriate denizen of modern and decadent Athens. A South Italian vase (ca. 350) shows a scene from this comedy in which the main character, Pyronides ("son of the fiery one"), encounters Phrynis, a contemporary and somewhat *avant-garde* poet. With Aristophanes we observe how he varies these scenes with great finesse and imagination. In *Birds* we have three distinct sets of "intruder-scenes," which might stretch this longest of extant comedies, but they succeed admirably in maintaining the interest and response of the spectators.

Songs (*kommatia*): The episodes are separated by choral interludes, in which the chorus may respond to the unfolding action, sing songs of personal abuse, or engage in lyric dialogue with an actor. Some of these interludes are in fact second or third *parabases*. One sequence deserves more than a passing mention: the songs in trochaics at *Birds* 1470–93, 1553–64, 1694–1705, where the birds, remaining within their dramatic character, reflect on certain strange sights which turn out to be certain notorious creatures of contemporary Athens, most notably the Kleonymos-tree (1470–81), which in the winter sheds, not leaves, but shields.

Exodos: Aristophanes' comedies end in a number of ways: reconciliation of the combatants (*Lysistrate, Women at the Thesmophoria*), a marriage of a man and a deity (*Peace, Birds*), a great party and celebration (*Acharnians, Assembly-Women*), a sense of victory and rejoicing (*Knights, Frogs*). Two finales are worth specific mention: that of *Wasps* where the old man dances all contenders into oblivion, including the real figures of Karkinos and sons – Aristophanes claims that he is the first to send a chorus off dancing – and that of *Clouds*, where the old man undergoes a complete change of mind and the entire action of the comedy is reversed with the burning down of Sokrates' "reflectory."

The theme of the Golden age

We should not expect all comedies from a period of nearly a hundred years to be the same sort of thing, any more than we would expect situation comedies on modern television to be all the same. Comedies will vary in their subject, theme, approach, humor, and what the comedians can "get away with." Chronology plays a major role, since today we look back at the "sit-coms" of the 1950s and 1960s with a mixture of nostalgic affection and supercilious superiority. What amused the spectators in the time of Magnes (470s) may have seemed very passé by the time of the 420s; in fact if we can trust what Aristophanes says at *Knights* 507–50, comedy had become much more "sophisticated" by the mid-420s. Aristophanes has the advantage of having survived and having become the exemplar for all subsequent critics, but he may have preferred to raise his comedy to an intensely topical and personal level and thus to eschew certain other themes, for example the mythological burlesque or the theme of the Golden Age – when he did write burlesque, he preferred to write parodies of tragedies, usually those of Euripides.

The theme of the Golden Age, the ideal place with an ideal life, goes back to the islands of the Blest in Homer and Hesiod where the heroes of myth live (*Odyssey* 4.561–9, *Works and Days* 156–73), or to the first of Hesiod's ages of man (*WD* 109–20). Comedy found much in the traditional account of the de-evolution of humanity that it could exploit – there is always good entertainment to be had from the comparison of modern reality with an ideal past utopia.

Utopias can be located in the past (paradise lost), in the future (paradise attained), or somewhere "out there" (paradise found); all three of these can be found in Old Comedy. In Kratinos' *Wealth-Gods* the utopia is plainly in the past: when Kronos ruled, men played dice with bread-loaves, and cakes fell out of the trees (fr. 176). In Krates' *Beasts* two speakers seem to be debating (frr. 16–17) the details or the realization of a future utopia. In this ideal age (or place), meals, including tables and food, will prepare themselves automatically. Telekleides' *Amphiktyons* (fr. 1) has an unknown speaker outline the blessings of a utopia past, where "all necessities came automatically," when "men were fat and like giants." Pherekrates' *Miners* (frr. 113–14) intriguingly locates utopia, not "out there," but "down there," in the underworld, again in terms of the gastronomic delights to be found there, while his *Persians* (frr. 137–9) presents an ideal existence either "out there" (presumably in Persia) or in the future (note the future tenses at fr. 137.5, 6, 10, although these may be future in the sense of "when you get there").

Aristophanes did not write entire comedies on this sort of theme, although a "great idea" permeates many of his comedies, whose realization will create or restore a happier environment. The end of *Knights* returns Demos to better days, the wish of the son in *Wasps* is to make his father happy and comfortable, while *Birds* does to some degree create a utopia "out there," that is, among the birds, and the two last plays (*Assembly-Women*, *Wealth*) are certainly utopias to be created in the future. But what is missing is the *automatos bios* ("the automatic life"), the rivers of drink and compliant food and furniture. Also these Aristophanic comedies create not a distant ideal, but a very concrete Athens. Aristophanic comedy is full of the pleasures of food and drink, but he does not indulge in this aspect of life in the Golden Age.

Artistic parody

Humor is a natural human reaction to what others take seriously or set upon a pedestal. In Lucian's *Twice Accused* (33) Dialogue complains of his treatment by Lucian, who has created a comic hybrid including "Eupolis and Aristophanes, men who are very skilled at mocking what is serious." The ancients attributed to Homer not only the deeply serious epics (*Iliad*, *Odyssey*), but also the burlesque epic, *Margites*, and the delightful *Battle of the Frogs and Mice*. Tragedy was accompanied at an early date by satyr-play, *tragodia paizousa* ("tragedy kidding around"), which made dramatic fun of the serious themes of tragedy and epic. Even in the *Odyssey* and the *Homeric Hymns* a serious theme will be tempered by moments of humor. Athenians could at the same festival weep over the fortunes of tragic heroes and laugh at the juxtaposition of mythical themes with modern reality, the high level tempered by the language of reality.

Aristophanes avoided the mythological burlesque, preferring to parody specific tragedies, mainly those of Euripides, and the high style of the lyric poets, rather than the subjects of their songs. Even in *Wealth*, when he parodies the story of the Cyclops (290–321), his model is a specific one, the *Cyclops* of Philoxenos. As Eupolis also did not write burlesques of myth, we have tended to play down these as a major theme in Old Comedy. Too often in the critics we see the mythological burlesque identified as a major theme of Middle Comedy, without sufficient attention to the fact that parodies of myth can be found in comedy of the 430s. The political-topical comedy that became the vogue of the 420s and 410s, perhaps coupled with a decrease in the number of productions, appears to have so dominated the genre for a generation that it is not until the early fourth century that this earlier theme reemerges.

As many as one-third of the comedies of Kratinos (career: 454–423) seem to have been burlesques of myth: *Dionysalexandros* (Dionysos replaces Paris for the famous judgment), *Runaways* (fr. 53 was spoken by Theseus and parodied his wrestling-bout with Kerkyon), *Nemesis* (the birth of Helen), *Odysseus and friends* (Odysseus and the Cyclops), *Wealth-Gods* (the return of the Titans), *Men of Seriphos* (the adventures of Perseus), *Cheirons* (fr. 253 shows that these were the chorus). Some may depend on a particular source text, for example *Odysseus and friends* on *Odyssey* 9, *Wealth-Gods* in part on the Prometheus-plays, but the one we know best, *Dionysalexandros*, does not seem to be playing against any one version of the story of the Judgment of Paris. Hermippos (career: ca. 435–410s) is similarly known to have written burlesques of myth. We have at least five titles (*Agamemnon, Europe, Kerkopes, Fates, Birth of Athene*) that seem to belong to this sort of comedy, the last, *Birth of Athene*, being the earliest instance of a sub-genre, the birth of a deity, which would become more common in the early fourth century, the heyday of the mythological burlesque. The humorous story of a god's birth occurs also in the *Homeric Hymn to Hermes* and in the satyr-play. Of the other pre-Aristophanic comedians, Kallias wrote *The Cyclopes*, Myrtilos a *Titan-Pans*, and Phrynichos an early play which featured a burlesque of the Andromeda-myth with a drunken old woman replacing the damsel in distress.

Three gods in particular lent themselves to comic treatment: Herakles, the familiar glutton of satyr-play and comedy; Hermes, a god who crosses boundaries and runs errands for Zeus, is especially good for comedy – we see him in *Peace, Wealth,* and in fr. 61 of Phrynichos, as well as in the amusing *Homeric Hymn* and Sophokles' satyric *Trackers* and *Inachos*; and, of course, Dionysos, whose misadventures are a familiar and favored theme. Kratinos' comedy shows that myth can overlap with politics, although it is debatable whether plays such as *Nemesis* and *Dionysalexandros* were fully political and topical comedies.

Comedy of ideas

Old Comedy is an interesting mix of low-level humor (bodily functions, slapstick, beating a joke to death) and a much more sophisticated comedy of ideas, which involves the spectators being able to appreciate an elaborate and sustained parody of Euripidean tragedy, the poems of Homer and Pindar, and the theories and teachings of Sokrates and the sophists. It will not do to say that the latter appealed to a minority audience of "intelligentsia," since in a competitive genre a comedian is unlikely to alienate or mystify the bulk of his spectators. We should rather suppose that the Athenian audience as a whole could and did appreciate this sort of sophisticated humor, that Aristophanes' claims at *Frogs* 1109–18 of the cultural abilities of Athenian spectators are not exaggerated:

> Now if you both fear that the spectators are in the grip of stupidity, that they would not appreciate it when you say something clever, don't be afraid on that account. Things aren't like that any more. They're seasoned campaigners; each one has his own book and knows what's clever.

Perhaps Aristophanes was unusual in this regard, perhaps one of the features that marked his comedy out was this sort of elevated comedy that appealed to more than the groundlings of fifth-century Athens. He certainly claimed this for himself. Obviously, since all we have are fragments of other poets, we cannot immediately assess how typical Aristophanes may have been, but we can say something about how other comic poets used parody or the comedy of ideas.

A passage from Kratinos takes us from the realm of poetry to that of philosophy, the statement of Σ *Clouds* 95, that the analogy of the sky as a giant chafing-dish (*Clouds* 95–7):

> In there dwell men who make a compelling argument that the sky is a giant chafing-dish which surrounds us, and that we are the coals

had already been used by Kratinos in his *All-seers* (fr. 167).* That this arresting analogy should find its way into popular comedy is no more surprising than that Anaxagoras' ideas about parenthood are put in the mouth of Apollo at *Eumenides* 657–61. The so-called "Enlightenment" of the fifth century was not restricted to the intellectuals but could become the stuff of popular comedy. We are, of course, obsessed with Sokrates and the caricature of him in *Clouds*, but Aristophanes was not breaking new ground in 423 with his first *Clouds*. Telekleides fr. 41, two iambic tetrameters from an unknown play, connects Sokrates and Euripides, the former laying the "kindling" for the latter's play. Everything we know of Telekleides suggests a career before the début of Aristophanes, and thus comic jokes at both Euripides and Sokrates were not new with Aristophanes.

The 420s saw a spate of comedies with philosophers and ideas as major or minor themes. Aristophanes' first comedy (427), *Banqueters*, featured an old man with two very different sons ("the good son and the asshole") – it does not require much of an effort to see a theme of comparative education and behavior here. Eupolis' comedy, *Goats* (424-D?), had a teacher called "Prodamos" teaching an old farmer to dance and adopting the supercilious manner of the intellectual. Ameipsias' *Konnos*, named after a famous musician and produced with *Clouds* at 423-D, possessed a chorus of "thinkers," fr. 9 of which shows that Sokrates was a character in that play also. Eupolis' *Spongers* (421-D) featured the sophist Protagoras as a character, perhaps also Sokrates. Σ *Clouds* 96 in fact asserts that Eupolis attacked Sokrates more vehemently than Aristophanes "in the whole of *Clouds*." Comedy fastened not only on the distinctive physical traits of Sokrates and other philosophers and on their *adoleschia* – more than anything else they "talk nonsense" – but also on what they taught: "making the inferior argument appear superior" (*Clouds* 112–15), the finer points of "physics" (*Clouds* 143–216, Kratinos fr. 167, Eupolis fr. 157), grammar and *mousike* generally.

---

* The analogy depends in part on a pun: "men" (*andres*) and "coals" (*anthrakes*).

Domestic comedy

Old Comedy is essentially comedy of the *polis* ("city"), while the comedy of Menander is comedy of the *oikos* ("home"). For Aristophanes the contemporary city, its individual personalities and issues are never far away, while in New Comedy we may be conscious of an urban setting, but it is rarely more than a backdrop. Old Comedy does have its domestic settings – in *Knights* the city has become the household of Demos ("People"), in *Wasps* the basic issue is preventing Philokleon from leaving his house for the jury-courts, in *Lysistrate* the women have essentially turned the acropolis into their own household – but here the house and the city are inextricably merged. Even in *Wealth* where the house of Chremylos is the setting, the issue of Ploutos regaining his sight is a larger one for all of Greece. When we get to Menander, the house is everything. Relationships are all-important, be they father-and-son, boy–girl, brother–sister, and the plots on which these depend have to deal with the adventures within relationships. There is very little of this in Aristophanes, at least in the eleven plays that we possess. The *Life of Aristophanes* records that in his very late play, *Kokalos*, "he brought on stage seductions and recognitions, in which Menander followed him." But in his high period, there is not much that will prefigure Menander, apart from some cheeky and cunning slaves and a love duet in *Assembly-Women*.

We have only hints of the settings of the lost plays, but there are several where a house and its domestic life may be discerned. Kratinos' *Wine-flask* featured the poet's wife and a chorus of friends; the implication is very strong that the setting was Kratinos' house to which the drunken poet at one point returns – compare the closing scene of *Wasps* (produced eight months later). Eupolis' *Spongers* was set at the house of Kallias, where a major party is planned and narrated; this comedy was probably more personal than political, although the main players were real individuals rather than fictional characters. It is very likely the case that Aristophanes was more given to the politicization of the setting; both Eupolis and Kratinos, not to mention Pherekrates (for whose *Korianno* see below), could write plays with a more domestic background.

Many have seen the appearance of Lysistrate in that comedy of 411 as a watershed in the comic depiction of women:

> there are no earlier examples of a female protagonist like Lysistrata . . . female speaking parts in earlier plays are personifications . . . figures from mythology . . . or relatives of prominent men. (Henderson 1987: xxviii)

Henderson's thesis *is* somewhat borne out by looking at the comedies that we can date before 411. There is no obvious ancestor for Lysistrate; we do find women of myth in Kratinos' *Dionysalexandros* (Helen) and *Nemesis* (Leda), Phrynichos' old woman, perhaps Atalante in Kallias' *Atalantai*, as well as personifications (Kratinos' *Wine-flask* with Comedy, Pherekrates' *Tyranny*), and women connected with famous people, Hyperbolos' mother in *Marikas* and *Bread-sellers* by Hermippos. As far as female characters in Eupolis and Aristophanes are concerned, Henderson's thesis certainly holds.

But one wonders about his dismissal of certain female characters as "mythological." We assume that he means that they are not "real-life" women in domestic settings, but surely there was stereotypical comedy to be had from the portrayals of Helen and Leda by Kratinos, who must have had more than incidental roles. Euripides was producing his "Potiphar's Wife" plays by the 430s, and comedy could well have picked up on this theme of "bad" women in a domestic situation. Surely the comic depiction of women as wine-loving, sex-crazed gossips did not begin with Aristophanes' plays of 411. *Wine-flask*, we know, had a domestic setting involving Comedy, the wife of Kratinos, and his mistress, Drunkenness, both of whom must have had substantial roles. There are also early plays with female choruses, such as Kratinos' *Thracian Women* and Hermippos' *Bread-sellers*, both of which would have allowed for the comic depiction of women.

Two comedies of Pherekrates do show that there was a role for women apart from the strictures laid down by Henderson, very likely before 411. His *Korianno*, of which several fragments remain (73–82), reveal a scene of entertainment, including drinking (the ever-present vice of women), with one character named "Glyke" ("Sweetie"). Athenaios (567c) says that Korianno was a *hetaira* ("prostitute") – the verb *eran* ("love") occurs at fr. 77, and we may suspect that his *Thalatta*, *Petale*, perhaps *Tyranny* and *Pannychis*, were also plays of this sort, the titles being names of courtesans. Pherekrates is for the most part a comedian of the 430s, and unless we want to postulate for him a renaissance ca. 400 with these *hetaira*-plays, it seems that he was writing the domestic comedy of the *hetaira* well before 411. Like the mythological burlesque, the *hetaira*-play will become a staple of early fourth-century comedy, but its origins can, we believe, be traced back into the classical period of Old Comedy. Pherekrates is attested by one anonymous writer as having refrained from personal humor and introducing new themes, and it makes more sense if this was a description of his whole career, and not just a later phase. We do not have enough to allow us to conclude whether these sorts of comedies had the linear plot that would characterize New Comedy, with the recognitions and reunions that populate the comedies of Menander and Roman Comedy. This is very likely to have been the result of Euripidean Romantic tragedy. There is very little hint of any sort of "romance" in the fifth-century remains of comedy; the earliest would seem to be the "love-scene" at *Assembly-Women* 877–1111. There may be one exception here. In the *Life of Isokrates* we read that "the comedians were in the habit of making fun of important people, as they bring Sokrates on stage in love with young men." Perhaps it was not comedy of "boy meets girl," but of "boy meets man."

Political and topical comedy

As we have seen, some modern critics find the date of the institution of Comedy (486) as part of the political life of the 480s, the reaction to the aristocrats who allegedly supported the Persians. But there is no real evidence for any sustained personal humor or topical theme before the comedy of Kratinos and his contemporaries of the 440s and 430s. The 440s were a crucial time for Athens (the peace with Persia, hostilities and truce with Sparta in 446, the ostracism of Thoukydides, the revolt of Samos). Attested by Platonios as "an emulator of Archilochos," the author of an *Archilochoi* with parodies of that iambic poet, and described by Aristophanes (*Knights* 528) as "sweeping all his enemies before him," Kratinos was the poet who made major comic capital out of topical personalities and issues and developed the aggressive and vigorous stance of the comic poet. But there is no conclusive evidence that his comedies were politically saturated from start to finish; certainly his mythological burlesques seem to have been parodies of myth first and political tracts second. The last sentence of the hypothesis to Kratinos' mythical burlesque, *Dionysalexandros*, asserts that "in the play Perikles is very convincingly made fun of by innuendo for bringing the war on the Athenians," but this does not have to mean that Dionysos is meant to represent Perikles throughout the comedy or that the Trojan War is meant to cover the Peloponnesian War as a whole. All that the hypothesis may mean is that at some point in the comedy "Perikles was very convincingly made fun of because of the war."

Political and topical comedy reaches its high point in the last three decades of the century, and it was probably Aristophanes who raised it to its height. He makes whole plays out of political imagery, such as wine in *Acharnians*,* or the house and the wasps in *Wasps*, or the metaphor of weaving in *Lysistrate*. With his caricature of Kleon as Paphlagon in *Knights* he also pioneered the demagogue-comedy. Here an entire comedy is dedicated to an attack of a single politician; whether the comic poet is actually indulging in outright political propaganda or catering to a popular taste must remain an unsettled matter. Much has been written of the seemingly conservative stance adopted by the comic poets, and caution should be exercised here. In this he was followed by Eupolis with *Marikas* (Hyperbolos), by Platon with three comedies of this sort (*Kleophon, Peisandros, Hyperbolos*), and perhaps by Theopompos (*Teisamenos*) and Archippos (*Rhinon*). Given the topical nature of Archippos' *Fishes* (frr. 14, 23, 27–8) and the fact that he is attested as the author of four plays by Aristophanes, we may wish to include him in the political style practiced by the canonical Three.

It is worth distinguishing between the presence of personal jokes and a deliberate larger topical theme in a comedy. Eupolis' *Spongers*, for instance, was centered around the figure of Kallias. Protagoras and possibly Sokrates and Alkibiades appeared in the comedy and there are jokes at various "spongers" of the day (frr. 172, 177–80), but it is hard to see any political theme here – these *komodoumenoi* are made fun of for their personal lives, not their politics. In the fourth century personal jokes can be found as late as the plays of Menander, but what does disappear early on is the political joke *per se* at a prominent figure.

Thus when we find jokes even at political figures throughout the fragments, there is no guarantee that these came from intensely political plays of the sort that Aristophanes reveled in. It is clear that Eupolis' *Cities, Marikas,* and *Demes* (and perhaps his *Golden Age*, modern Athens being an ironic antithesis of the good old days) were politi-

---

*   The point is that the word for "truce" in Greek (*spondai*) also means "drink offering."

cal comedies, and we might wish to include some plays by Platon here (his *Greece or Islands*, *Envoys*, *Alliance* suggest themselves). But these plays by Platon seem to be early in his career, and we would make the argument that the intensely political comedy that we take as typical of Old Comedy is really only a vogue, a very successful one, of the last third of the century. Begun with Kratinos and his caricature of Perikles as Zeus, it was perfected by Aristophanes, Eupolis, and Platon, and reached its apogee with the demagogue-comedy where the comic poet took on one particular target. It is a tempting and entirely natural conclusion that this implies personal conviction on the poets' part and has allowed many modern critics to talk of the Old Comic poets having a "Cimonian bias" or as operating as a sort of unofficial political opposition.[†] But care must be exercised here. To make fun of someone or something is not necessarily to attack it. Comedy often follows the popular lead and it is difficult to detect instances where comedy had any definite effect on popular opinion or political policy.

"To make fun of by name"

Aristotle attributes the humor of Old Comedy (*Ethics* 1128a21–4) to what he calls *aischrologia* ("shameful language"), by which we would include not just the obscene language with which the text of Old Comedy is peppered, but also the abuse of persons outside the drama – for which we have a convenient one-word term, *komodoumenoi*, "those made fun of in comedy." Anyone coming to Old Comedy for the first time is struck immediately by the constant stream of jokes at real persons of the time, very probably sitting among the spectators. These jokes can be just a quick cut-and-thrust, barely disturbing the flow of the action, as at *Assembly-Women* 166–8:

Praxagora: *You fool, you did it again, refer to men as women.*
Woman: *It's all because of that Epigonos. I caught sight of him over there and immediately thought I was speaking among women.*

Sometimes a series of one-liners is strung together to form variations on a malicious theme, such as at *Birds* 1290–9, where the messenger plays the game: If X were a bird, what bird would he be? In places whole songs are devoted to extended attack on a particular target, as at Kleophon at *Frogs* 674–85 or Kleon at *Knights* 973–96. (This is the only place in *Knights* where the Kleon-character (Paphlagon) is actually called "Kleon." We suspect that Aristophanes intended this to be a stand-alone song that would become a popular favorite.) Finally, a character in the comedy may be a real Athenian, sometimes with name disguised (Kleon as Paphlagon, Lysimache the

---

[†] Kimon (Cimon) was a major political figure at Athens from 480 to 450. He favored rapprochement with Sparta, pursuing open hostilities with Persia, and an easy hand on the allies. His ouster in the late 460s marked the sea-change in external and internal policies at Athens that lie behind Aeschylus' *Eumenides*. When he is mentioned in comedy, it tends to be with respect and the comic poets seem to be advocating policies in line with those that he favored.

priestess of Athene as Lysistrate), but more often with identity perfectly clear. The best known instances here are the appearance of Sokrates in *Clouds* and that of Euripides in at least five comedies. In *Acharnians* as many as five (or even six) of the *dramatis personae* represent real Athenians.

The ancients were obsessed with this distinctive feature of Old Comedy, principally because it was conspicuously absent from later drama. When an ancient writer attempts to explain the origins of Old Comedy, he tends to explain the presence and rationale for personal jokes. When another writer attempts to explain the change in comedy in the fourth century, he concentrates on the loss of personal humor and the influence of outside political forces. The very pragmatic Romans were quick to find a "redeeming social value" in the personal humor of Old Comedy, in that it attacked men who deserved to be singled out. The *locus classicus* here is the opening to Horace's fourth satire (late first century):

> *Eupolis, Kratinos, and Aristophanes and indeed all the poets of Old Comedy, would single out with great freedom anyone who deserved to be pointed out, for being a wicked person or a thief, an adulterer, a pickpocket, or in any way notorious.*

The notion that a comic poet might be making fun of a target unfairly or just for the fun of it was not one that the ancient critics found comfortable, nor for that matter do some modern critics.

The ancient commentator, Platonios, writing at some point between AD 100 and 500, perceptively connects personal abuse in Old Comedy with the vigorous and flourishing democracy at Athens in the classical period. One of the hallmarks of that democracy was *parrhesia* ("free speech"), and the comic poets of the last third of the fifth century indulged themselves in that privilege in the public atmosphere that was the theater. Ancient commentators were often on the hunt for laws and controls on comedy by the state and frequently attributed the change in comedy in the fourth century to interference by the political authorities. In his *Art of Poetry* Horace gives what became the standard view of Old Comedy and personal abuse (281–4):

> *Then there came Old Comedy, which enjoyed considerable acclaim, but its freedom descended into abuse and a violence that had to be regulated by law. A law was passed and the chorus fell silent, having lost its right of shameful abuse.*

But this "law" is a later fiction, and only one stricture on comedy is actually documented, passed in 440/39 and repealed in 437/6. The ancient source reads *me komodein* ("not to produce comedy"), but as we know that comedies were produced in 437, *komodein* must mean, as it often does in ancient sources, "to make fun of by name." The early 430s were a critical time for Athens, both externally with the revolt of Samos, one of her major allies, and certain internal infighting around Perikles. The decree also suggests that personal humor was something new in the development of Old Comedy and that this legal measure was Athens' attempt to come to terms with the arrival of personal and political invective on the comic stage.

The Generations of Old Comedy

The early years

We know very little about the first generation of Old Comedians. The earliest attested writer of comedy is the very shadowy **SOUSARION**, while the *Suda* names **CHION-IDES** as the first official producer of Old Comedy and provides us with the canonical date for the start of Old Comedy (487/6), "they say . . . that he produced eight years before the Persian Wars." Aristotle (*Poetics* 1448a33) links Chionides with Magnes as early creators of Attic Comedy.

MAGNES does allow us some scope for discussion. He is named by the *Suda* as being young when Epicharmos, the Sicilian comic poet, was old, intimating perhaps a master–pupil relationship. Diomedes links him with Sousarion and Myllos in creating a comedy that was "less polished and charming." One anonymous writer on comedy gives him eleven victories, the highest total of any Old Comedian. If *IG* ii^2 2325.44 (. . . . c) refers to him, six of these were at the Dionysia, and his career must therefore have lasted until the competitions at the Lenaia began (late 440s). Aristophanes (*Knights* 518–25) implies that Magnes as an old man failed as a comic poet; this presumably was an event of recent memory. He won at the Dionysia of 472 (*IG* ii^2 2318.7). If this was his first victory, we can deduce for him a career from 472 to the 430s.

Aristophanes describes him as having "set up the most victories over rival choruses" and as "having spoken in every kind of voice for you, strumming the lyre, flapping wings, playing the Lydian, humming like a gall-fly, and dyeing himself frog-green" (*Knights* 521–4). This last is explained by the scholiast as referring to actual play-titles (*Lyre-Players*, *Birds*, *Lydians*, *Gall-Flies*, *Frogs*). Of these only *Lydians* is attested by other sources, and we must remain skeptical whether the scholiast had any real evidence for these titles beyond the comic text. Aristophanes' comments suggest that Magnes' comedy was something more crudely humorous and less sophisticated.

Epicharmos

It was at Athens that drama made its greatest impression, and it was Athens that sprang first to the minds of ancient students of drama. But in the fifth century Athens was not the only home of original theater. In particular we should look to Syracuse in Sicily, whose tyrant Hieron (rule: 478–466) had by the early fifth century established his city as one of the leading Greek states, not just in political and military influence, but in culture as well. All the great poets of the day, including Aeschylus, paid visits and plied their poetic trade at the court of Syracuse. A formal theater may have existed there as early as the late sixth century, while the remains of the great theater of the fifth century, heavily altered in the Hellenistic and Roman periods, reveal a structure of impressive size and sophistication.

Aristotle knows of a separate and earlier comic tradition for the West. At *Poetics* 1449b5–6 he attributes the creation of comic plots originally to Sicilian poets, with the implication that these inspired Athenian comic poets. Earlier (1448a32–3) he has placed in Sicily a comic poet, **EPICHARMOS**, "much earlier than Chionides and Magnes" (two of the earliest comic poets at Athens). Ancient writers placed Epicharmos' birthplace in various cities of the Greek world, but all agreed that he was active principally in the city of Syracuse. One source assigns him to the 73rd Olympiad (488–485), another to "seven years before the Persian Wars" (ca. 486). The Marmor Parium dates him specifically to the year 472/1 and the reign of Hieron, rather too late to be "much earlier than Chionides and Magnes," but a career spanning the late sixth and early fifth centuries would explain all the dates. He is credited variously with thirty-five, forty, and fifty-two plays. One ancient writer sums him up as "the first to embellish comedy considerably and to make a scattered art-form into something substantial."

A persistent tradition identifies a pupil of Pythagoras, one Epicharmos of Cos, with the comic poet, who would later move to Syracuse and turn his hand to comedy. But one suspects that two men with the same name may have been confused or that quotations from his comedy could have been manipulated to yield a philosophic theme. Certainly ancient critics saw Epicharmos as both comic poet and philosopher – remember that early Greek philosophy was written in verse, usually the epic hexameter. Much of Norwood's (1931) chapter on Epicharmos is given over to exploring possible philosophic themes in his comic fragments. But it is more likely that these are either the result of confusion with another Epicharmos or the products of later attempts to link the comic poet with later philosophers. His comedies probably contained expressions of clever thoughts and witty ideas, which were magnified into "philosophy." Frr. 172–3, for example, shows Odysseus, the epitome of cleverness, explaining to the swine-herd Eumaios the universal aspects of wisdom. Several of the fragments show an awareness of Platonic philosophy (e.g., fr. 171) and are probably fourth-century inventions.

His play-titles suggest rather a fondness for the burlesque of myth, especially the stories of Herakles (*Bousiris, Marriage of Hebe, Herakles and the Girdle*) and Odysseus (*Cyclops, Sirens, Odysseus the Deserter, Odysseus Shipwrecked*). We have mentioned already Odysseus' address to Eumaios, perhaps from *Odysseus Shipwrecked*. Fr. 83 of his *Cyclops*, "here, pour (this) into the cup," suggests that this comedy, like Euripides' later satyric *Cyclops* and Kratinos' comic *Odysseus and friends*, treated humorously the encounter between Odysseus and the Cyclops in *Odyssey* 9. Epicharmos adds an inventive and witty touch in fr. 99 of *Odysseus the Deserter*, with Odysseus rehearsing a fictitious account of his success on a dangerous away-mission. One of the strengths of Epicharmos' comedy may have been to present these mythical figures as more realistic and down-to-earth individuals.

Like the later comedy at Athens, especially that of Middle Comedy, the fragments of Epicharmos have much to do with the pleasures of food. We have over twenty fragments of his *Marriage of Hebe*, almost all of which concern the marriage banquet of Hebe and Herakles, the latter now a god but still possessing his mortal appetite. A fragment of Epicharmos' *Wealth* (35) provides an early look at a figure to become a staple of later comedy, the sponger (*kolax*). Eupolis' *Spongers* (421) will feature a chorus of these experts at cadging a free meal, fr. 172 consisting of sixteen lines chanted by the chorus about their style of life, and in both Menander and Roman comedy a clever sponger or parasite will be instrumental in resolving the plot-line. The life of Epicharmos' sponger, however, is not a happy one, and this character trudges home to a cold and uncomfortable rest.

Old Comedy at Athens was intrinsically bound up with the life of the democracy, and in the last three decades of the fifth century produced a comic drama that was overtly and intrinsically "political." On the surface it might seem understandable if the comic drama of Syracuse produced under one-man rule at Syracuse lacked the freedom and topicality that flourished under a democracy. But drama at Syracuse might have been used to glorify that city and its rule by the tyrant – notice that Aeschylus wrote his *People of Etna* to celebrate Hieron's re-founding of that city and reproduced his *Persians*, in which Greece triumphs over a barbarian enemy. Syracuse saw herself as an outpost of Greek culture against a background of Sicilian barbarians and hostile Carthaginians. Epicharmos' comedies do contain much "modern" material: coins, weights, institutions, festivals, local settings, contemporary writers (including Aeschylus [fr. 214] and Aristoxenos of Selinous [fr. 88]). His comedy, then, may not have been as politically based or as personally humorous as later Attic Comedy, but it was anchored in the Sicily of his day.

Epicharmos' comedy contains some intriguing anticipations of later comedy. We have already mentioned the presence of the figure of the sponger, and the possible overlap in the themes of the Cyclops and Busiris. From his *Philoktetes* (fr. 132) comes an idea that Kratinos will explore in his *Wine-flask* (423-D), "there is no poem when you drink water." Fr. 125 (*Skiron*) contains a question-and-answer exchange, which an ancient scholiast saw as the original of *Peace* 185–7. In his *Odysseus and the Girdle* the hero is confronted with "an army of Pygmies on rather large dung-beetles, which they say live on Etna" (fr. 76). Aristophanes' hero in *Peace* rides to Olympos on "a gigantic dung-beetle from Etna"; the immediate reference is to Euripides' Bellerophon and Pegasos, but a further intertextual allusion to Epicharmos' comedy is not impossible and would show that dramatic ideas traveled both to and from mainland Greece in the ancient world.

One of the mysterious aspects of Sicilian drama is that we know of original drama only in the first half of the fifth century, and then only of comedy. Of other comic poets, along with Epicharmos are attested a contemporary, Phormis, and Deinolochos, described as both rival and "son or pupil" of Epicharmos, "who wrote fourteen plays in the Doric dialect." Aeschylus produced tragedies there, and we have the poignant story (Plutarch *Nikias* 29.2–3) of how Athenian prisoners after the Sicilian disaster of 413 enchanted their captors by reciting songs from Euripides and thereby won their freedom – clearly his plays were known to a Syracusan audience. But we can name no Sicilian tragic poet in the fifth century. What sort of serious plays were performed in the great theater? Was there a local tragic tradition, or did they depend principally on restagings of tragedies originally produced elsewhere?

Kratinos and the second generation

For **KRATINOS** we have twenty-four reasonably secure titles, some substantial fragments (including ninety lines of the *parodos* of *Wealth-Gods* – fr. 171), most of the hypothesis to *Dionysalexandros*, and a fair idea of the theme of his brilliantly meta-theatrical *Wine-flask*. We also possess a variety of ancient assessments, which must be used with care, but which provide for the first time an individual personality. Two important things happen to comedy at this time: (i) the institution of dramatic competitions at the Lenaia in the late 440s which would double the number of comedies produced, and (ii) the development of political and personal themes in comedy.

One anonymous writer says that "he won after the 85th Olympiad" (440/39–437/6), but this results in an improbably short career (twenty-four plays in about sixteen years), and more significantly his name is also restored on the victor-list for the Dionysia, two places after Euphronios, victor in 458. On the victor-list for the Lenaia, Kratinos is fourth in chronological order. Since these productions began in the late 440s, this might explain the date in the early 430s. At the lower end we know of productions for 425-L (*Storm-Tossed*) and 424-L (*Satyrs*) and *Wine-flask* at 423-D, and then a joke from *Peace* (700–3: 421-D):

> Hermes (speaking for Peace who has been absent since 431):   *Well then, is Kratinos the great ⟨poet⟩ still alive?*
> Trygaios: *He died, when the Spartans invaded.*
> Hermes: *What happened?*
> Trygaios: *He fainted, he couldn't bear to see a jar full of wine smashed.*

As the Spartans had not invaded since 425 and Kratinos was alive and well in 423, he could not literally have died during a Spartan invasion, and the joke may just be a crude backdating of his actual demise in 423 or 422 or possibly a total fiction. But as no fragment or play requires a date after 423, it is fair to set his career as roughly 454–423.

Aristophanes' descriptions of Kratinos are a blend of respect and abuse. We must always be careful with compliments from a comic poet, since he is ever ready to run down a rival (especially one competing at the same festival), and if Aristophanes builds Kratinos up in one passage, it is only to bring him down in the next. From *Knights* 526–36:

> Then with Kratinos in mind, who flowing with a wave of praise coursed through the open plains, and sweeping headlong from their roots oaks and plane-trees and enemies. Singing at a party had to include "Goddess of Bribes with fig-wood shoes," and "Makers of clever hymns." He was great then. But now you look on and have no pity for him in his dotage – his frets have fallen out, he's lost his tuning, and his harmonies are full of holes. An old man, he stumbles about like Konnas, with withered crown and dying of thirst. Because of his previous victories he ought to have a lifetime of free drinks in the Council House, and instead of spouting nonsense should be sitting splendidly beside Dionysos

we notice the following: the previous success of Kratinos, the image of a torrent sweeping all before it, the existence of "enemies," and his reputation as a writer of songs. Also the clever put-down: "he was great then, but now . . . ," he should have retired long ago instead of "spouting nonsense" – remember that Kratinos was competing against Aristophanes at 424-L. Elsewhere Aristophanes plays on Kratinos' alleged drunkenness (*Knights* 400, *Peace* 700–3), makes a series of enigmatic allusions at *Acharnians* 848–53 ("his hair always cut in the adulterer's style"), wishes at *Acharnians* 1168–73 that Kratinos be hit in the face with a fresh turd, and equates familiarity with comedy as "being initiated into the rites of bull-eating Kratinos" (*Frogs* 357). As so often with comedy, allusions to a comic target become complimentary some time after that person's death.

One anonymous writer calls him the comic Aeschylus, while another attributes to him the establishment of formal comedy. He is very often seen as a "blame poet," who "would attack more bitterly and shamefully than was necessary" (*Life of Aristophanes*). It would be useful to know if any of these writers had ever read Kratinos. Similarly, Platonios creates a spectrum between the rough and graceless directness of Kratinos and the charming elegance of Eupolis, with Aristophanes as a very Aristotelian middle. His position as the earliest of the canonical Three and his equation with Aeschylus have combined to create this picture of the rough genius, the grand old man, the immediate predecessor of the master, Aristophanes.

Of the twenty-four or so titles that we know of (about 500 fragments) four comedies deserve particular mention. First, there is *Odysseus and friends*, a parody of the story of Odysseus and the Cyclops in *Odyssey* 9. Platonios (I. 29) says that this comedy had neither "choral parts nor parabases" and that there was no personal humor, only the parody of the *Odyssey*. The latter may well be true; none of the fragments contains any personal jokes, and the play has been plausibly dated in the period of the decree *me komodein*, "not to make fun of by name," (439–436). But the plurals in frr. 148–151, the firm mention of "you trusty companions" at fr. 150.1 and statement of fr. 151 in a lyric meter ("our homeland is Ithaca and we sail with god-like Odysseus") make it clear that there *was* a chorus in this play. It would be interesting to know how closely this comedy resembled Euripides' *Cyclops*, the satyr-drama based on the same material, and which dramatic treatment was the earlier.

Wealth-Gods has provided us with the only extended piece of Kratinos, fr. 171, some ninety lines of a second century AD papyrus, only a few of which afford any connected sense. The lines, in anapestic dimeter, are clearly from the parodos of the comedy and explain to an interlocutor that "we are Titans by race, and were called 'Ploutoi' ('Wealth-Gods') when . . ." (11–12.). Some lines later we learn "now that the rule of tyranny is over and the *demos* rules, we have rushed here seeking our ancient brother, even if he be old and decrepit" (22–26). The "ancient brother" might be Kronos, Ploutos, the Athenian *demos*, or (most attractively) Prometheus. Many have taken the description of the end of tyranny and the rule of the *demos* as referring specifically to the brief removal from office of Perikles in 430/29 (Thucydides 2.65) and thus date the play to 430 or 429. But it is not necessary to read such a serious or consistent political level into Kratinos. The humor of the passage may just be that the political experience on Olympos parallels that at Athens in the late sixth century (tyranny replaced by democracy). Frr. 172 and 176 (along with fr. 171) show that *Wealth-Gods* employed the theme of the Golden Age, familiar from Hesiod, and given the prevalence of utopian themes in Old Comedy, we may conclude that the bulk of the humor lay in the juxtaposition of that ancient ideal era with modern Athens. It remains doubtful whether there are any serious politics in *Wealth-Gods*. The latter part of fr. 171, in trochaic tetrameters, rather resembles the *epirrhema* of a *parabasis*, and attacks a contemporary politician named Hagnon.

We have already mentioned the clever burlesque *Dionysalexandros*. Here the fragments (frr. 39–52) are not very revealing, and we must depend upon the papyrus remains of the hypothesis (*POxy.* 663). The plot-line is clear: a burlesque of the story of the Judgment of Paris, set on Mount Ida, in which Dionysos replaces Paris (also known as "Alexandros") for both the actual judgment and the consequences. Paris himself eventually appears and the story of Helen and Paris (and the Trojan War) continues in its traditional form. The chorus was composed of satyrs, more appropriate perhaps for a satyr-play, but attested elsewhere for comedy. Dionysos appeared in his familiar comic role as anti-hero, being the object of the satyrs' laughter, running for cover at the advent of the angry Greeks, and being handed over to them for humiliation and punishment at the end.

The hypothesis ends with the intriguing statement, "in the play Perikles is very convincingly made fun by innuendo for bringing the war on the Athenians." Most regard "the war" as the Peloponnesian War (431–404) and thus date the play to 430 or 429, since Perikles died in late 429. But an equally good candidate for "the war" is the Samian War (440/39), which popular opinion blamed on Perikles and his foreign mistress Aspasia. Thus the Trojan War, a "war for a woman," would become a mythological allegory for the Samian War, and the comedy could be dated to the early 430s. This is the period of the decree *me komodein* ("not to make fun of by name"), and thus the need for "innuendo" could be explained. Some see the comedy as one large political allegory, with Dionysos/Paris intended to refer throughout to Perikles, but there is no guarantee that the allusion to Perikles was an extended one, that "in the play" means "throughout the play," or that Dionysos/Paris would have been recognized as Perikles. The comedy may just have been an amusing mythological burlesque, with one song or a *parabasis* that applied to Perikles.

Finally there is *Wine-flask*, the comedy of 423-D which defeated *Clouds* and aroused Aristophanes' comic ire. This was a meta-theatrical piece which took its inspiration from Aristophanes' dismissal of him at *Knights* 526–36 ("his lyre has lost its strings" and "perishing of thirst"). Kratinos made himself the main character in his own comedy, as having abandoned his wife (Comedy) for a mistress (*Methe*, "Drunkenness"). A chorus of friends tries to recall the poet to his senses, but from there the ultimate direction of the comedy is unclear. Fr. 199 shows someone contemplating how to "stop him from drink" and fr. 203 contains the famous defense "you cannot create anything great by drinking water." It is entirely possible that the attempt of Kratinos' friends did not succeed and that the poet made his case that drink, the vice that Aristophanes makes so much of, was necessary for his craft, indeed for a productive "marriage" with Comedy. Certain of the fragments suggest a scene where a comedy was being composed.

This clearly was a masterpiece of intertextuality, depending for its inspiration on Aristophanes' caricature in *Knights*. What is bold is the merging of author and plot, and the willingness of Kratinos to present himself in an unflattering light, something that Aristophanes could do only with difficulty and not without blaming someone else. It was a brilliant stroke and earned its author a well-deserved first prize at 423-D, a particularly satisfying one since Aristophanes' play finished third.

Kratinos' comedy acquired a political dimension, in part with frequent jokes at prominent leaders (Kimon, Perikles, Lampon, Hagnon, Lykourgos, Androkles, Kleon, Hyperbolos), and in part with the use of themes that included Athens of the time. Several of the ancient sources fasten on the abusive aspect of his comedy, and we should regard this as one of his major contributions to comedy. But was his comedy as obviously political as that of the next generation, especially the demagogue-comedies of Aristophanes, Eupolis, and Platon? Was every mention of Zeus a veiled (or not so veiled) allusion to Perikles? Were his mythological burlesques always meant to hide an Athenian situation? Too many critics have built complicated allegories based on one or two fragments, and have detected in Kratinos a serious sort of political satire, where there may only have been simply comedy.

At least one-third of his comedies were burlesques of myth. We have already mentioned *Dionysalexandros* (the Judgment of Paris), *Odysseus and friends* (Odysseus and the Cyclops), *Wealth-Gods* (the Titans released), and from the titles and fragments can add the following burlesques of myth: *Bousiris*, *Runaways* (about Theseus), *Eumenides*, *Nemesis* (the birth of Helen), *Men of Seriphos* (Perseus), and *Cheirons*. If Kratinos did bring a topical and political theme into these burlesques of myth, we suspect that these themes were subordinate to the parody of myth, and that it was Aristophanes who developed the overtly political comedy.

The older generation (Kratinos, Kallias, Telekleides, Hermippos) dominated Old Comedy in the middle third of the fifth century, and it is clear from the victory-lists at the Dionysia that no new poet won at that festival after Hermippos' victory (435 at the latest) until Aristophanes with *Babylonians* in 426. We shall turn to the "next generation" in a moment, but we need to comment briefly on these other poets who preceded Aristophanes and Eupolis, the younger contemporaries of Kratinos. They do not vanish with the advent of the new comedians of the 420s; indeed Hermippos, Pherekrates, and very likely Kallias continued to produce into the 410s and in the case of Hermippos we can perhaps detect a change in comic style. If comedy was reduced from five productions per festival to three during the War, then these older comedians may have found it harder to get a look-in, given the immense early popularity of Aristophanes and Eupolis. That they can be glimpsed again in the 410s, when presumably the reduction was reversed (at least from 420–416), seems entirely reasonable.

Norwood (1931: 145–77) spoke rather too confidently of "the school of **KRATES**," and saw in this poet as well as in the works of Pherekrates, Phrynichos, and (quite improbably) Platon a "school" which produced a different sort of comedy from that of the abusive topical and political style of Aristophanes and Eupolis. It may be safer to see them as individuals operating within the larger framework of comedy rather than creating "schools." Krates' career belongs to the 440s and 430s; the reference at

Knights 537, "he endured your anger and abuse," seems to point to an event of recent memory. The *Suda* mentions seven plays and gives six titles; one anonymous writer also assigns him seven plays, another eight.

The ancient descriptions of Krates' comedy are: (i) Aristotle's *Poetics* (1449b5–9), "of the Athenians Krates was the first to abandon the iambic form and to write whole plots and stories"; (ii) the statements of an anonymous writer that "he succeeded Kratinos, was a very funny and humorous poet and the first to bring drunken people on stage in comedy," and that "Pherekrates was an actor for and emulator of Krates and also refrained from abusive language"; and (iii) the description of Krates at *Knights* 537–40, "kneading very refined ideas from his very dry lips." These produce the picture of a poet creating a different form of comedy, one that in the eyes of Aristotle was the ancestor of comedy in his day. To some extent the meager fragments bear out this assessment. No title suggests an obvious political theme, nor are there any examples of personal humor. But it is hard to see where the "whole plots" would come in. The only substantial remains are fragments 16–17 from *Beasts*, where two figures debate the nature and realization of the Golden Age, passages which do not seem radically different from other such descriptions in Old Comedy. Perhaps the comedy, which sparked the "anger and abuse" of the audience, was a late play in Krates' career, competing with the newer sort of political comedy pioneered by Kratinos.

PHEREKRATES is a more substantial figure, whose career (ca. 440–400) seems to have been as long as that of Aristophanes and who deserves a more prominent place in the history of Greek comedy. The anonymous writer links him with Krates, both as his mentor and in his avoidance of personal abuse, and goes on to say that "he did well by introducing new material and becoming an inventor of plots." In one very late source he replaces Kratinos as one of the canonical Three of Old Comedy.

The fragments tend to bear out the ancients' assessment. There are not many *komodoumenoi* among the nearly 300 fragments, and apart from a jibe at the dubious gender of Alkibiades (fr. 164), none is aimed at a political figure. In fact most of the *komodoumenoi* in Pherekrates are poets or musicians. There is no hint in any of the titles of a political comedy or anything like a demagogue-comedy. His *Korianno* seems to have been a domestic comedy with a woman in the main role, while his *Chimney or Pannychis*, *Thalassa*, *Petale*, and *Graes* appear also to have been plays about women, especially *hetairai*. *Miners* and *Persians* seem to have turned on the Golden Age or Utopian theme. Fr. 113 (*Miners*) is a familiar catalog, narrated by a woman, of the delights of a utopia located in the land of the dead, including the best of foods and deep red wine served by alluring maidens. Fr. 137 (*Persians*) gives us part of a debate in anapaestic tetrameters (a meter often used in the *agon*) about the ideal life. Someone has said that wealth or the good life will eliminate those practicing the *technai*, to which our speaker replies that there will be no need of *technai*, since all things will be provided "automatically" (line 3) – is a standard theme of utopia.

Krapataloi provides fascinating echoes of Aristophanes' *Frogs*, all the more interesting since Pherekrates' is almost certainly the earlier play. Pollux 9.83 tells us that *krapatalos* was a unit of coinage in the underworld (confirmed by fr. 86), while fr. 85 instructs someone how to get to Hades (cf. *Frogs* 117–64). Thus this comedy may well have been a literary play in the style of *Frogs*, set perhaps all or in part in Hades, especially as fr. 100 ("I who built up and handed on to them a great art") is known to have been spoken by Aeschylus. The plural title should refer to the chorus, but one does wonder about a chorus of coins, not impossible for an Old Comedy; Kaibel speculated that the members of the chorus were people called "*krapataloi*" for whatever reason – compare our idiom "small fry."

Wild Men, dated to 420, seems to have been part of comic theme of the 410s of escape to the wilds (cf. *Birds*, *Hermit* in 414). Plato (*Protagoras* 327cd) tells us that the chorus of the comedy were *misanthropoi*, "who possessed neither education nor law-courts nor laws nor any necessity to practice virtue." If *Birds* is any guide, the comedy featured one or two men from civilization (very probably Athens) who go to the wilds looking for a better life (see fr. 10) and discover that the "wild men" are hardly congenial neighbors (fr. 14). Some of his titles and fragments suggest plays of mythological burlesque: *Human-Herakles*, *Deserters* (see fr. 28, gods complaining about men), *Ant-Men* (fr. 125 is addressed to Deukalion, the survivor of the Flood), and perhaps *Tyranny* (fr. 150 concerns the gods and sacrifices). If the bulk of his career belongs in the 430s and early 420s, these comedies with the utopian theme and those that burlesque myth fit very well with the sort of comedy that was common in that period.

But the longest fragment (fr. 155 – *Cheiron*) is certainly the most revealing.* It is quoted by pseudo-Plutarch (1141c) who records that "Pherekrates the comic poet brought Music on stage in female attire, her whole body mistreated, and he had Justice ask the cause of her condition." There then follows a denunciation of four dithyrambic poets (Melanippides, Kinesias, Phrynis, Timotheos) in a clever series of *double entendres*, mixing physical and sexual assault with the terms of music. This fragment has been the subject of recent discussions, which focus on the issue of gender, whether Music is to be seen as a virtuous wife or as a *hetaira* and how this fragment typifies an almost pornographic view of women by men. It is a very clever piece of comic writing and gives us a glimpse of a poet whom we are sorry to have lost, one who perhaps gave a different spin to comedy of the late fifth century and deserves a place of higher recognition.

Old Comedy: the next generation

In the early 420s four major comic poets burst on the scene with a vengeance. Between 429 and 424, the comic stage witnessed the débuts of Phrynichos and Eupolis (429), Aristophanes (427), and Platon (by 424), who would be responsible for the high period of Old Comedy, for perfecting the intensely personal and political style for which it would become famous. If we are correct to see comedy of the 440s and 430s as for the most part depending on the mythological burlesque and the themes of utopia and the Golden Age, with any political theme muted and indirect or limited to choral songs of abuse, then what happened in the 420s was the development of more explic-

---

* This fragment is given in full in the section, 'Euripides and the New Music'.

itly topical and political comedy, especially the demagogue-comedy that began with *Knights* in 424. In view of the tensions of the War, the factionalism of Athenian politics, the arrival of the sophists, and the prominence of challenging artists such as Euripides and the "new musicians," this may be seen as a natural reaction to life in interesting times.

EUPOLIS, the third of the canonical Three, was often seen as both friend and rival of Aristophanes. Much of this depends on how we take Aristophanes' accusation (*Clouds* 551–8) of Eupolis' plagiarism of his *Knights* to create *Marikas* and Eupolis' reply in a *parabasis* (fr. 89):

> *As for those* Knights, *I helped you write them, and gave them to you as a gift.*

His career was short: début in 429 and death in 411, most probably at the sea-battle of Kynos Sema. Ancient accounts assigned him fourteen or seventeen plays; we have fifteen secure titles, including a second version of *Autolykos*. In this short career he enjoyed considerable success, with three Dionysia-victories and four at the Lenaia.

We have been fortunate in the last hundred years in recovering more than just the odd fragment – the longest before the papyrus discoveries were fr. 172 (*Spongers*), a sixteen-line *epirrhema* in which the chorus of spongers describe their *modus operandi*, and fr. 16 (*Goats*) where the chorus of goats list their various foods. In 1911 a papyrus gave us three leaves (120 lines) from a book containing material from Eupolis' best-known comedy (*Demes* – fr. 99), the same papyrus (Cairo) that produced parts of three comedies of Menander; three papyri from Oxyrhynchus have given us parts of commentaries to *Marikas*, *Men of Prospalta*, and *Officers*, while fr. 260 provides about thirty lines of a scene from Eupolis' earliest comedy, *Men of Prospalta* (429).

Four comedies deserve special attention. First, *Marikas* (421-L) did for Hyperbolos what *Knights* had done for Kleon. In this comedy Hyperbolos, who had become the leading demagogue after the death of Kleon in late 422, appears under the Persian name, "Marikas," which denoted foreign origins, servile status, youth and roguery, with a hint of passive homosexuality. Aristophanes would claim (*Clouds* 551–8, possibly also fr. 58) that Eupolis had plundered his *Knights* to create his *Marikas*, and examination of the fragments and commentary reveals an extensive reuse by Eupolis of material from *Knights*, even to the statement in fr. 201 (very likely from the prologue) "that we are not doing *Knights* this time." But Eupolis did not just serve a reheated *Knights*. The antagonist of Hyperbolos-Marikas is not a worse demagogue as in *Knights*, but one of the "rich and famous," and the most striking change is the use of a double chorus, of rich men and poor men, each supporting one antagonist in the struggle (frr. 190, 192). Hyperbolos' mother had a role in the comedy, probably in the final scene, where she appears to mourn her son and perform a vulgar dance, a scene which Aristophanes alleges Eupolis has stolen from the comic poet Phrynichos.

In the same year (421-D) Eupolis won first prize with *Spongers*, in which he made fun of the extravagant lifestyle of Kallias son of Hipponikos, recently come into his inheritance as the richest man in Greece, whose house is beset with philosophers and expensive parties – the opening scene of Plato's *Protagoras* gives a similarly comic look at Kallias' ménage of tame philosophers. The fragments reveal that Kallias is the polar opposite of his thrifty father (fr. 156), that Protagoras had a role as the pretentious expert (fr. 157), and that a feast of massive proportions is being planned. The chorus was composed of professional "spongers," who are not, as some have supposed, philosophers themselves. There is some evidence that Sokrates and Alkibiades appeared in episodes in this comedy and one wonders if Plato got ideas for his dialogues *Protagoras* and *Symposium* from Eupolis' comedy. It is an attractive supposition that the feckless Kallias was despoiled of his fortune and came to financial ruin at the end.

Baptai had quite the reputation in antiquity, and several ancient sources combine to produce the long-running story that this comedy was directed against Alkibiades, who not only produced a witty couplet in response to his treatment by Eupolis but also wreaked vengeance on him during the voyage to Sicily, either drowning him or just dunking him, at the same time bringing the freedom of Old Comedy to an end. The play seems to have featured the arrival at Athens of a wild goddess from the north, Kotyto, and her reception by the chorus of Baptai, whom the scholiast to Juvenal (II.92) describes as "Athenian males dressed as women dancing in honor of Kotyto." The title remains a mystery as "Baptai" occurs only in connection with this comedy – the verb *baptein* means either "to dip" or "to dye." The most prevalent suggestion is that these devotees were "baptized" into the rites of Kotyto, but the title "Baptai" surely suggests agents, "dippers" rather than "dipped ones." Perhaps these effeminate males dyed their hair, but the most common force of *baptein* in classical Greek is "to dye ⟨clothes⟩," and more preferable is a chorus of active dyers, perhaps preparing robes for the new goddess. It is not at all clear whether Alkibiades was the subject of the entire comedy, or just made fun of in one memorable and visual scene. Most critics assume the former, but we must be careful not to assume too much.

Finally there is *Demes*, very likely produced in 417, although the traditional consensus prefers 412 in the aftermath of the disaster in Sicily. In this play four former leaders of Athens (Solon, Miltiades, Aristeides, and Perikles – the last dead for only twelve years) were raised from the dead and returned to Athens, where they interacted with modern denizens of the city, and presumably in good Old Comic style put things right with their city. Fr. 99.78–120 gives part of a scene between Aristeides and a *sykophantes*. (*Sykophantes* is a difficult term to translate. This was a person who zealously initiated legal prosecutions and appears in comedy as a blend of "blackmailer" and "informer.") The play turned on the familiar comic opposition of old (good)/modern (inferior) – see frr. 102–4, 106, 111, 129–30 – and fr. 131 makes it clear that the Four were honored by the chorus at the end.

The main character was named Pyronides, the "son of fire," an appropriate name for an Old Comic protagonist. If *Demes* was anything like an Aristophanic comedy – the two most likely parallels are *Peace* and *Birds* – Pyronides will have been distressed by the state of Athens of his day and sought the aid of deceased leaders, whom he raises through a necromancy. The *agon* should belong after the return to Athens and would resemble that of *Lysistrate*, the issue being in this case turning the state over to the Four. The episodes represent the working out of the grand idea, as each of the Four encounter an appropriate foil and put things right in their field. The South Italian vase by Assteas shows a comic scene, where a character named "Pyronides" drags a reluctant musician named "Phrynis," known from several comic passages as a contemporary musical innovator. Phrynis, it seems, was a typical intruder on the comic scene, manhandled in good comic fashion by the protagonist.

It is not immediately clear what a chorus of "demes" should be. Were they an individuated chorus, consisting of particular Kleisthenic demes – here compare Eupolis' *Cities* where the chorus was comprised of twenty-four cities of the empire (frr. 245–7)? Or should "deme" be taken in its most natural force, as "country-town" as opposed to the city? Here one may wonder why Eupolis did not just create a chorus of country-folk. At fr. 99.11–15 the chorus complains about "those in the Long Walls, for they eat better than we do." The obvious inference is that the chorus is less well off than even the temporary residents of the city.

Eupolis' comedy seems to have closely resembled that of Aristophanes. Topical and political themes are prevalent, although only three or four comedies appear to have been overtly political (*Demes, Marikas, Cities*, and perhaps *Golden Race*). Eupolis created his comedy out of prominent personalities; *Spongers* (Kallias and his household), *Autolykos* (the boy-athlete known from Xenophon's *Symposium*), *Baptai* (Alkibiades), *Demes* (Perikles), *Officers* (the general Phormion). We get also the familiar comic figure of Dionysos in *Officers* ("Dionysos joins the navy"), but what we fail to find is large-scale literary parody, like that of Euripides by Aristophanes. For all his reputation and considerable success, the fragments do not show a comedy of the same depth and verbal brilliance as that of Aristophanes. We can agree with Platonios that "Eupolis comes up with great ideas for his plots," but also with Silk that there is "nothing to suggest that Aristophanes learnt anything about writing poetry from him."

With **PLATON** (K.-A. VII 431–548) we meet the last figure of the 420s, one who, like Aristophanes, wrote well into the next century and who spans the transition to Middle Comedy, if that term is at all meaningful. More than one ancient source makes him the chief exponent of Middle Comedy. The *Suda* assigns him twenty-eight plays and lists thirty titles, to which we must add *Theater Police*, unknown before the publication of *POxy*. 2737. Since the figures for Aristophanes and Eupolis indicate an average of one production per year, on a début of 424 Platon will have been producing well into the 390s. Secure dates are 405 (*Kleophon*) and 391 (*Phaon*); likely dates are *Feasts* (410s – see frr. 29–30), *Victories* (410s – see frr. 85–6), *Peisandros* (mid-410s), *The man in great pain* (410s – frr. 114–6), *Envoys* (390s – fr. 127), *Sophists* (late 400s – fr. 150), *Hyperbolos* (early 410s). The Dionysia victor-list (*IG* ii² 2325.63) lists him after Kantharos (won in 422), Phrynichos, and Ameipsias, suggesting that his first victory came in the 410s.

The thirty or so titles reveal a variety of subjects and treatments. There are three instances of the demagogue-comedy, pioneered by Aristophanes in *Knights*, against Peisandros, Hyperbolos, and Kleophon, where we see that familiar elements of the comic depiction of the demagogue: foreign birth and accent, low social status, arrogant and threatening behavior, personal and selfish motives, tactics of intimidation, lack of proper education. Whereas Aristophanes and Eupolis disguised their demagogues under suggestive names (Kleon~Paphlagon, Hyperbolos~Marikas), Platon seems to have attacked his demagogues openly and directly. Certain other titles could imply topical themes: *Greece or Islands, Feasts, Ambassadors, Alliance*. Four plays suggest literary, meta-theatrical, or intellectual comedies: *Laconians or Poets, Theater Police, Sophists, Properties*. So far we have a poet very much in the style of Aristophanes. But perhaps one-third of his total output is mythological burlesques: *Adonis, Europe, Zeus Mistreated, Io, Laios, Menelaos, Long Night, Phaon*. It is tempting to conclude that these two styles are chronological and the mythological burlesques reveal a poet leading the way into the fourth century and into Middle Comedy. The problem is that the mythological comedies by their apolitical nature do not yield datable references, and Platon may well have written plays like *Europe* or *Laios* from the start of his career. That there are so many mythological plays implies that, unless Platon was especially prolific in the 390s, he began to write this sort of comedy well before the end of the fifth century, at a time when Aristophanes was still creating his intensely topical comedies such as *Lysistrate* and *Frogs*.

Old Comedy: the final generation

The later poets of Old Comedy pale beside the great names of the 420s. Many are but names, others have only a few titles attested. Perhaps the comments of Dionysos on the state of tragedy in 405 apply equally well to comedy, apart from Aristophanes and Platon: (*Frogs* 92–5):

> These are just small fry, chatterboxes, "halls of swallows," degraders of their art, who get their one chorus and then are gone, after pissing on Tragedy.

But we can usefully call attention to three comic poets, who do give us an idea of Old Comedy during its last generation.

First there is **ARCHIPPOS**, to whom the *Suda* attributes one victory in the 91st Olympiad (415/2). The *Life of Aristophanes* records that four of the forty-four comedies attributed to Aristophanes were assigned by some to Archippos. Do we detect here another possible instance of collaboration between Old Comic poets? Was Archippos, like Philonides, producer for Aristophanes as well as a comic poet in his own right? The similarities between his *Fishes* and *Birds* are worth considering in such a light. His comedy, *Rhinon*, probably has to do with Rhinon of Paiania, a major figure in the democratic restoration after the fall of the Thirty (403), and his best-known comedy, *Fishes*, mentions "Eukleides, who has served as archon" (fr. 27), yielding a date after that man's archonship (403/2). We have here then a comedian of the late fifth century and very early fourth.

Of his six known titles two or three suggest mythological burlesques (*Amphitryon, Marriage of Herakles*, and perhaps *Ploutos*). But it is *Fishes* that attracts the most interest. It seems to have done for fishes what *Birds* had done for creatures of the air, including a formal treaty between men and the fishes and the handing over to the fishes of those epicures who had enjoyed a diet of fish. A papyrus published in the 1980s very probably belongs to *Fishes*, and contains over forty lines of connected text – a not very inspiring dialogue between a pair of characters expatiating on the superiority among fish of the *silouros* ("sheatfish"), where one finally declares that "Isokrates has never made such a praise of Helen as you have delivered over the *silouros.*" This would give us more than sixty lines of Archippos' comedy, and make *Fishes* one of the few lost Old Comedies of which we have any connected remains.

For **STRATTIS** the *Suda* lists fifteen titles, while one of the anonymous writers on comedy gives a total of seventeen plays. If his name is correctly restored on *IG* ii² 2325.138 (the Lenaia list), then he won one victory at that competition. His *Atalante* (or *Atalantos*) mentions Lagiske (fr. 3), the mistress of Isokrates, and according to Σ *Frogs* 146 is "much later than *Frogs.*" A date as late as the 370s has been assumed for that comedy, thus suggesting a career from the late 400s to the 370s. From the titles and ninety fragments, he appears to have shared Aristophanes' fondness for literary parody, especially that of Euripides. His *Anthroporestes* contains (fr. 1) one of the several allusions to the actor Hegelochos' verbal gaffe in Euripides' *Orestes*. His *Lemnomeda* seems to have been a combined parody of Euripides' *Andromeda* and perhaps his *Hypsipyle*, and the titles of *Medea, Philoktetes, Chrysippos, Phoenician Women*, and *Myrmidons* all strongly suggest tragic origins. His *Kinesias*, which may owe much to the portrait of that dithyrambic poet in *Birds*, contains the fine line from the prologue (fr. 16), "these are the tents of chorus-killing Kinesias." Like Aristophanes, he made jokes against his fellow-comedians, Sannyrion (frr. 21, 57), Philyllios (fr. 38). Very few of the personal jokes in Strattis have a political flavor.

Another important lesser light from the same period is **THEOPOMPOS**, who appears on the victory-lists along with other late minor poets such as Nikophon and Polyzelos. The *Suda* gives a total of twenty-four plays, an anonymous writer seventeen; we have reasonably secure evidence for nineteen or twenty titles. References in the fragments suggest a career from ca. 415 into the 380s. We find examples of the burlesque of myth in titles such as *Admetos, Althaia, Aphrodite, Theseus* (fr. 18 suggests a journey for Theseus to Persia), *Odysseus, Penelope, Sirens, Phineus*. There are hints of the *hetaira*-comedy in his *Nemea* and *Pamphile*, perhaps also *Althaia* and *Aphrodite* (fr. 5 makes fun of Philonides, the object of Aristophanes' joke at his relationship with Lais at *Wealth* 304). Of the 100 or so fragments, about a dozen contain personal jokes, and two titles might refer to contemporary political figures (*Kallaischros, Teisamenos*), although neither reference is secure, and *Teisamenos* could also be a mythological comedy based on the son of Orestes. *She-soldiers* sounds as if it could be a comedy of the same sort as *Lysistrate* or *Assembly-Women* – fr. 58 refers to Anytos the democratic leader and accuser of Sokrates, and if *Teisamenos* refers to the law-giver of the late 400s, this might be a political comedy like *Knights* or *Marikas*. I suspect that we have here another comedian in transition, as the political and topical comedy of the earlier generation yields to something different in the fourth century.

Aristophanes

Old Comedy deliberately and often broke the dramatic illusion and allowed its choruses to speak directly to the spectators on behalf of their poets. Thus the ancient biographers had much more to work with than for the tragic poets, and much of what

Aristophanes says his prologues or *parabases* is lifted straight into the ancient lives and the entries in the scholia. We do possess a *Life of Aristophanes*, rife with expressions such as "some say" or "according to others," and as such is hardly serious biography. Aristophanes was creating a public persona for himself in his comedies: the young and sophisticated, groundbreaking, politically beneficial, but unfortunately unappreciated, comic poet. Aristophanes deliberately cultivates this image, but the biographical truth need not be the same.

That said, we can make the following reasonably confident assertions about the life and career of Aristophanes, son of Philippos, of the deme Kydathenaion. He was born about 450, although some have interpreted a reference at *Clouds* 528–31 as suggesting that he was not yet eighteen when he produced his first comedy in 427. He would have been an almost exact contemporary of the notorious Alkibiades, the unprincipled and charismatic Athenian leader of the late fifth century, and would have grown up in the "golden years" of Perikles, reaching his age of majority at the same time as war broke out with Sparta. His deme, Kydathenaion, one of the five demes in the city of Athens, was a well-off neighborhood, but we should remember that a man's deme was determined by where his paternal ancestor was living in 507.

ca. 450 – born, probably at Athens
427 – début with *Banqueters* (not extant)
426-D – *Babylonians* (not extant) and subsequent row with Kleon
425-L – *Acharnians* (first prize)
424-L – *Knights* (first prize)
423-L – production (comedy unknown)
423-D – first version of *Clouds* (not extant – third place)
422-L – *Wasps* (second prize)
421-D – *Peace* (second prize)
ca. 418 – revised version of *Clouds* (not performed)
414-L – *Amphiaraos* (not extant)
414-D – *Birds* (second prize)
411-L(?) – *Lysistrate* (result unknown)
411-D(?) – *Women at the Thesmophoria* (result unknown)
408 – *Wealth* (first version, not extant)
405-L – *Frogs* (first prize)
393–391 – *Assembly-Women* (result unknown)
388 – *Wealth* (result unknown)
387-D – victory through his son, Araros
ca. 385 – death

Aristophanes began his dramatic career with his *Banqueters* in 427 – a passage from *Clouds* reveals that this initial comedy fared well. For his first three or four plays he employed others as *didaskaloi* ("directors") – a practice which he continued later in his career. Initially this may have been due to his youth and inexperience with the theater, but he may just have preferred to leave the physical direction to others. At the Lenaia of 422, it appears that he was responsible for two of the three plays performed: *Wasps* in his own name and *Precontest* through Philonides. There may well have been some subterfuge at work here. The first comedy produced in his own name was *Knights* at 424-L. His early career has been the subject of some recent speculation, and depends on the interpretation of two passages from the *parabases* of *Knights* and *Wasps*. On one reading his early years as a comic poet had three stages: (i) aiding other comic poets (who?) before 427, (ii) his début with *Banqueters* in 427 and subsequent productions of *Babylonians* (426) and *Acharnians* (425) through other men, and (iii) the production of *Knights* in 424 in his own name.

Aristophanes burst on the scene with a vengeance. Of the fourteen festivals at which comedians could produce between 427 and 421, we can find at least ten plays by Aristophanes, perhaps as many as twelve. It seems that one could not go to the theater and not see a comedy by Aristophanes. Another similar burst of activity can be detected from 411 to 405. But one of the great mysteries surrounding Aristophanes is why we are never given a victory-total for him. We know of so many victories by this poet, and so many for that, but for Aristophanes, silence. He won victories at the Lenaia of 425, 424, 422, and 405, and victories at the Dionysia of 426 and again in 387, but perhaps that was all he won out of his forty productions. Perhaps, like Euripides, he had to wait for posterity for his greatest popularity.

Some more personal details would include a connection with the island of Aigina – see *Acharnians* 652–4:

> That's why the Spartans are asking for peace and demanding Aigina back. They don't care about the island, they just want to take this poet from you.

The easiest explanation is that he or his father were settled on Aigina after Athens expelled the inhabitants of the island in 431. At *Peace* 1183 the chorus describes a man from the tribe of Pandion complaining about seeing his name appear on the posted list for military service. The vehemence of the passage and the fact that Aristophanes' deme, Kydathenaion, belonged to this tribe makes one think that a personal experience lies behind this reference. By age thirty he seems to have become prematurely bald; at *Peace* 765–74 the chorus imagines that the triumph of their poet will be a boon to bald men everywhere. An inscription from the early fourth century records an Aristophanes of Kydathenaion as a *bouleutes* ("councillor"). If this is our Aristophanes, it would be the only indication of a public career for a comic poet whose dramas were political in all senses of the word. His comedy *Frogs* (405-L) was accorded the unprecedented honor of a second production, "because of its *parabasis*" according to an ancient source, although the occasion of that second production is not certain. He had three sons, two of whom, Araros and Philetairos, followed their father as writers of comedy.

Old Comedy is largely defined by Aristophanes, and it requires careful use of the remains of the other poets to get a fairer and larger picture of the genre. In fact there were certain types of Old Comedy being written and performed in which

Aristophanes seems not to have indulged, specifically the burlesque of myth, and purely domestic comedy. He had the advantage of arriving in a developed tradition of comedy, and if we look at his early play, *Acharnians* (425), we observe that his distinctive style of comedy is already formed. Either he inherited an established comic tradition from Kratinos and others or (more likely) his own particular genius for comedy was with him from the start of his career. As his own chorus puts it a few years later (*Peace* 749–50):

> he has created a mighty art for us and built it up to towering proportions with great words and concepts and language above the norm.

Aristophanic comedy is intensely political and topical, fueled liberally with doses of personal humor. His comic themes are drawn from Athens of his day: peace with Sparta, political leadership at Athens, the Athenian legal system, ideas and intellectuals of the day, Euripides and other dramatic poets, the position of women in a male-dominated society. Even when characters from myth intervene, the setting is still contemporary Athens, Dionysos seeking a tragic poet "to save the city" (*Frogs*) or arriving at Athens and encountering a demagogue (*Babylonians*), or a chorus of divine entities appearing at the "reflectory" of Sokrates (*Clouds*). Whereas later comedy will be concerned with personal relationships and centered on the *oikos* ("house"), the focus of a comedy by Aristophanes will be the *polis* ("city"). Even when households are the center of a comedy, as in *Knights* and *Wasps*, the political is never far away. In *Knights* the house is the city in allegorical guise, with the people (*demos*) becoming Demos:

> our master has a farmer's temper, he's a bean-muncher, with a short fuse, Demos of Pnyx Hill, a bad-tempered, almost deaf old man. (40–3)

In *Wasps* the old man is encouraged to continue his jury duty at home, trying domestic cases; the political space has moved indoors.

One of the basic questions in interpreting Aristophanes is whether he is writing comedy or satire. In short, is there a "message" being conveyed along with the humor of the piece? Did Aristophanes intend his audience to act upon the advice that his characters or choruses were giving? Is this propaganda? His comedy is aggressive, with jokes launched at individuals and issues within the state. In *Acharnians* (515–18) the war with Sparta is blamed on

> not the city, I do not mean the city, but certain worthless guys, counterfeit types, valueless, mis-struck, foreign currency.

In *Wasps* the demagogues are allegedly employing the jury-system for their own political ends. In *Peace* the true supporters of peace are Athenian farmers and the Spartans – others are getting in the way or actively working against peace. In the *parabasis* of *Frogs* the chorus (or the poet?) makes specific proposals within the *polis*: amnesty for those implicated in the coup of 411, and the removal of the current crop of political leaders. It is frequently assumed that to make fun of something or someone is to display a serious hostility toward that target. That a comic poet could merely exploit for the sake of humor or even make up a joke out of whole cloth is seen as unworthy and unfair. Pseudo-Plutarch comments:

> *Aristophanes seems not to have created his poetry for the reasonable sort of man at all, but wrote his unseemly and indecent stuff for the ignorant, and his bitter insults for the malicious. (Comparison of Aristophanes and Menander 854D)*

Satire, on the other hand, is understandable – one may not agree with the direction of the attack, but one can understand the impulse.

As mentioned above, the ancients regarded personal humor as essential to Old Comedy, and here Aristophanes, along with Kratinos and Eupolis, was a master of this sort of humor. Comedy shares with earlier iambic poetry both its vulgar and colloquial language and the technique of making fun of people. Archilochos (7th century) and Hipponax (6th century) both created literary targets for their poetry, targets that could be built up from poem to poem. One may wish to read the caricatures of Euripides and Kleon as literary constructs, without necessarily implying a serious attack. The modern analogy of the editorial cartoonist is aptly brought out here, and we must distinguish between the humorist who exploits his target for humor and the one whose purpose is satirical attack.

There are three principal developed caricatures in Aristophanic comedy: those of Kleon, Euripides, and Sokrates. In the case of the first we do seem to have hostile satire. It could be argued that demagogues were something new on the political scene in the 420s and that what is new is automatically the stuff of good comedy. But there is too much sustained and impassioned attack, the evidence of at least two public confrontations between Kleon and Aristophanes (*Acharnians* 377–82, 503–5; *Wasps* 1284–91), the fact that both came from the same deme hints at a personal hostility. Kleon has suffered from a bad press in antiquity, especially since two contemporaries (Aristophanes and Thucydides) had little use for him, a view that Aristotle (*Constitution of Athens* 283) has reinforced. It may well be that Kleon was not the self-motivated, corrupt, and ignorant political leader that comedy describes, but an honest and useful player – in that case Aristophanes has performed a "hatchet-job" on Kleon, one that was funny and did create a successful comedy (*Knights* won in 424), and at the same time a vicious attack.

With the other two figures satire is less likely. What comes through again and again is Aristophanes' appreciation for and fascination with Euripides. He is well steeped in the works of this tragedian, alludes to and parodies him repeatedly, and as we shall see, has redefined his art of comedy in terms of tragedy, "comedy too knows what is right" (*Acharnians* 500). Those who would see Aristophanes as a hidebound traditionalist through and through will have no problem with regarding him as hostile to Euripides and will point to Aeschylus' ultimate victory in *Frogs*. But the terms often applied to Euripides in comedy, *sophos* and *dexios*, are also used by the comic poet of himself. Aristophanes is not one of "us" making fun of Euripides, one of "them"; he himself is a *sophos poietes*, who asks "us" to admire and applaud him. Kratinos (fr. 342) joins Aristophanes together with Euripides:

"Who are you?," some clever spectator might ask, a word-quibbler, a coiner of maxims, a Euripidaristophanizer (see p. 141).

Apart from the little song after the victory of Aeschylus is confirmed (*Frogs* 1482–99), there is little in Aristophanes' caricature of Euripides that is hostile and much that laughs with him.

Sokrates is a much more controversial *komodoumenos*. The picture that Aristophanes gives in *Clouds* is blatantly unfair and, apart from physical details (*Clouds* 362–3), turns him into an archetypal sophist, which is something that Sokrates certainly was not. A sophist would teach all sorts of subjects (including science, rhetoric, grammar), receive pay for that teaching, teach his students in a school, and very often question the traditional portrait of the gods and accepted ethical norms. The real Sokrates indulged in none of this, but Aristophanes gives us the physical Sokrates of Athens in the guise of a sophist, and one must wonder why he presented such an unfair comic depiction. Again the traditionalist view of Aristophanes sees Sokrates as one more modern innovator, of whom Aristophanes disapproves, and the portrait in *Clouds* as intentional and hostile satire. But Plato in his *Symposium* (written ca. 380) places Aristophanes and Sokrates at the same dinner-party, with no hint that the comedian's presence is at all incongruous, and Alkibiades in that dialogue can allude to *Clouds* with no hint of rancor. Thus a second view is that the caricature of Sokrates is more well intentioned than hostile, that it may have been a joke that got away from its creator, that the popular prejudice against Sokrates, which Plato mentions with some indignation at *Apology* 19c, was not Aristophanes' intention with this comedy. A final view would see Aristophanes as one of "us" making fun of "them," a sophistic Sokrates being one of "them." Neither Aristophanes nor his audience understood the difference between Sokrates and a sophist, and would not have cared. It will be clear that we prefer the second view.

Aristophanes' comedy is full of parody, of the epics of Homer and earlier poets, of contemporary poetry (both the grand style of Pindar and the more *avant garde* new composers of the dithyramb), but especially of tragedy, and the plays of Euripides in particular. We have argued above that Aristophanes is not attacking Euripides as much as he is parodying him or making comic capital of such a prominent figure in the cultural life of Athens. Euripides appears in three comedies (*Acharnians*, *Women at the Thesmophoria*, *Frogs*) and very probably was a character also in the other *Women at the Thesmophoria* and in *Precontest* and *Plays*. The other poets of the time (Eupolis, Kratinos, Hermippos, Pherekrates) do not seem to have fastened onto Euripides or indeed onto tragic parody to the same extent, and it is interesting that Aristophanes' fascination with Euripides begins with his very first plays. The titles and fragments of certain lost plays (*Phoenician Women*, *Lemnian Women*) suggest that these were play-length parodies of Euripidean tragedies – in *Women at the Thesmophoria* (411) we get scenes that parody four different plays of Euripides, and in *Acharnians* Euripides' lost *Telephos* (438) acts as a sub-text for the first half of the comedy, but in these plays the entire comedy seems to have been devoted to making fun of one Euripidean play.*

But Aristophanes goes farther and defines his comedy in terms of tragedy. In his early *Acharnians* he coins a new term for comedy, usually *komoidia* but here *trygoidia*, "song of the wine lees," clearly intended to recall *tragoidia* ("tragedy"). Here the context is significant, spoken by Dikaiopolis disguised as a character from tragedy (Telephos), pleading a controversial case with contemporary political associations. Dikaiopolis is pleading to be heard, not only as a beggar among princes, but as a comic poet among his fellow-citizens. His culminating point is "comedy (*trygoidia*) too knows what is right" (line 500). It is assumed that tragedy is serious drama, with serious moral and cultural points to be made in the course of a tragedy. What Aristophanes is doing is claiming the same serious and moral high ground for comedy and seeing his art as fulfilling the same function as tragedy.

Domestic comedy is noticeably absent from Aristophanes' extant plays. While houses and families can be the scene and subjects of his comedies, most notably in *Wasps* and *Acharnians*, the dynamics of familial and personal relationships are ignored as a source of comic humor. Wives and husbands, slaves and children do appear in the comedies, but Aristophanes is not interested in making comic capital out of them. In *Clouds*, for instance, we hear of Strepsiades' marriage to a wealthy and shrewish wife (42–74), and we might well expect her to appear at some point to berate or harass her harried husband, but Aristophanes passes all this up in favor of scenes between father and son. We meet Chremylos' wife in *Wealth*, but again the domestic comedy is incidental and dominated by the narration of the healing of Wealth. We have some evidence of domestic humor in both Kratinos and Pherekrates, but Aristophanes explored another aspect of the relationship between the genders.

This we get in his three so-called "women's plays," where women invade the larger public space, usually restricted to men. This, of course, has been a principal theme in tragedy, most notably in *Oresteia*, *Antigone*, and *Medea*, but in comedy the transgression is successful. In *Lysistrate* the women occupy the Acropolis to take possession of the treasury and thus impede the prosecution of the war, and use their normally passive role as sex objects to their advantage, bringing the husbands of Greece literally to their knees. It takes a woman at the end to instruct both Athenians and Spartans in their proper relationship – "I may be a woman, but I have a mind, and no small amount of intelligence" (1124–5). In *Women at the Thesmophoria* the women of Athens take Euripides to task for his derogatory treatment of women in his tragedies, and they do succeed in fighting the clever Euripides to a draw. But beneath the literary theme lurks the Athenian political process. The meeting of the women is a closely worked parody of the assembly, at a time when the democracy was under threat and in fact would be suspended only weeks later. Similarly in *Assembly-Women* the main character Praxagora ("she who acts in public") persuades the women to take on their husbands' role and take control of the state and to establish a new order, which bears a striking resemblance to the fifth book of Plato's *Republic*.

---

*   Useful cinematic parallels would be *Robin Hood, Men in Tights* (~ *Robin Hood, Prince of Thieves*), *Spaceballs* (~*Star Wars*), and *2001: A Space Travesty* (~ *2001: A Space Odyssey*).

At the same time Aristophanes does exploit the stereotypical male-oriented view of women for comic value: women as addicted to wine, food, sex, and gossip. Lysistrate herself admits that this stereotype will be the saving grace of their cause, "But that's exactly what I think will save us, the saffron dresses, our perfume, sandals, rouge, and see-through robes" (46–8). A little later her plan, the sex-strike, is revealed:

Lysistrate:	*We must abstain from . . .*	Myrrhine:	*From what? Tell us.*
Lysistrate:	*So you'll do it?*	Myrrhine:	*We will, even if we must die.*
Lysistrate:	*Well then, we must abstain from . . . sex.*		
Myrrhine:	*I can't do that. Let the war continue.* (122–4, 129)		

In *Women at the Thesmophoria* Euripides' kinsman must prove he is a woman by reciting what the women did at last year's celebrations (628–32):

Woman:	*Tell me, what was the first thing we did in the ceremony?*		
Relative:	*What was the first thing? We had a drink.*		
Woman:	*And what was the second thing?*	Relative:	*We had another drink.*
Woman:	*Somebody told you!*		

But to this stereotype he adds a public role for women, and in one passage at least puts words in Lysistrate's mouth that must have struck uncomfortably on the ears of a largely male audience (587–97). One could look at these women's plays as strictly absurd humor and as a way of making fun of the male citizenry, by showing that women can accomplish what men cannot, but Aristophanes does expect his main characters and choruses to be "onside," and there is more than a little empathy in his depiction of women.

One feature that particularly strikes the student approaching Aristophanes for the first time is the wide range of humors that he employs. From complicated metrical and lyric parodies and allusions based on a good knowledge of tragedy or contemporary ideas, he descends to physical slapstick, bowel humor, colloquial and obscene language. Much of the latter is typical comic stuff, part of what the audience would expect in certain scenes. Intruders come on stage and are driven off with comic violence, opponents in the *agon* exchange insults and abuse before the actual contest (especially at *Knights* 335–81 or *Clouds* 889–948). Characters are humiliated physically in embarrassing situations – the *sykophantes* packaged up like a pot at *Acharnians* 910–58, the beating-scene of Dionysos and Xanthias at *Frogs* 605–74, the unmasking of Euripides' relative in *Women at the Thesmophoria*. *Lysistrate*, in particular, operates largely at what we might call a "low level." The prologue seethes with sexual innuendo, with Lysistrate examining Lampito as if she were a prize heifer. The chorus of old men can barely climb the steep slopes of the Acropolis, only to be doused with pitchers of water from the women. The *proboulos* enters backed by his Scythian archers (the Athenian police force), who are summarily dismissed by the women. Myrrhine ("Myrtle bush," a slang term for the female genitalia) seduces her husband (Kinesias – "Mover") and takes him to the brink of sexual satisfaction, only to leave him at the crucial moment. The Spartan herald arrives in a state of sexual excitement, prompting the first known version of a famous line attributed to Mae West (983–5):

> Kinesias: *Who are you, a man or a fertility god?*
> Herald: *Young man, I am a herald from Sparta, come about the peace.*
> Kinesias: *Then why have you got a spear under your cloak?*

Finally the negotiations are conducted over and around the naked figure of Diallage ("Reconciliation"), complete with some bawdy *double entendres*.

Aristophanes, like many of the poets of Old Comedy, engages in the great game that involves poets, rivals, and spectators. Lacking so much of Old Comedy, we can only suspect places where an illusion to another comedian may lurk. Old Comedy never lets the spectator forget that they are watching a play, and Aristophanes will address them directly in the prologue, the *parabasis*, choral interludes, and at the end of the play. The spectators, and through them the judges, are constantly cajoled, encouraged, taken to task, and brought back onside again. To listen to Aristophanes, we would believe that he was the unappreciated genius of the comic stage, who gave the citizens good advice about the state, who pioneered a brilliantly new and original sort of comedy, and who had to contend with vulgar rivals and unappreciative audiences. But all this must be taken with a grain of salt. The rivalry and bitterness that Aristophanes displays could be as much poses as they are serious biographical facts.

Above all, Aristophanes is a poet of brilliant wit and imagination. A play by him depends on a fantastic idea, rooted in the reality of the times, but allowed to proceed in the most imaginative and unexpected manner. Plays move rapidly from scene to scene, pausing for the set pieces of the *agon* and the *parabasis*, and he is always careful not to let a serious section go on too long. Much of the dramatic force depends on who may show up in the episodes. *Birds* is especially good in this regard. Who would have foreseen from the outset that these two old men fleeing Athens and all its problems would meet Tereus, a human of myth transformed into a bird, create a city in the clouds, starve the gods into submission, encounter a bevy of deities (Iris, Prometheus, Poseidon, Herakles), and that one of these Athenian refugees, Peithetairos ("Persuasive Companion"), will enter in splendor at the close, married to "Princess" and now ruler of creation?

Aristophanes is an aggressive comic poet. His plays tackle great issues of the day: peace and war, women and men, universal poverty, the Athenian democratic system and its leaders. Personal humor, along with his penchant for fantasy, remains the single most noticeable feature of his comic style. Modern readers and audiences, steeped in political correctness, may find him uncomfortable, some preferring the blander, but certainly less offensive, comedy of Menander. In a penetrating observation Norwood (1931: 304) defined three aspects of comedy:

> Wit, fun, and humor are each the amusing self-expression of one who envisages the incongruous. When the intellect is the function employed, wit results; when it is the imagination, fun results; when it is the emotions, humor results.

The first two Aristophanes possesses in great abundance, but Norwood (1931: 298) denies him and his comedy humor, "for he is without pity or reverence . . . he is almost everywhere metallic." He may be fond of the characters whom he has created, but cannot resist the temptation to laugh at them. Many have seen Philokleon in *Wasps* as the most sympathetic character in Aristophanes, but he loses the debate over the role of a juror to his son and at the end of the play must be guided by his son on proper social behavior – in the teaching-scene (1122–1264) he is the buffoon and the butt of the humor. Incidentally, lines 650–1 and 1462–73 make it clear that Aristophanes identified himself with the son, rather than with the father.

Perhaps we may sum up this brilliant, vibrant creator of sublime fantasy again by looking to tragedy, the eldest of the dramatic sisters, with which Aristophanes appears to have been obsessed and which seems to have defined his view of comedy. In *Frogs* the debate between Aeschylus and Euripides is between a poet who is morally and socially beneficial and one who creates real and appealing dramatic characters and situations. At the start of his half of the *agon* (1008–10) , "Aeschylus" asks his opponent for a definition of what makes a poet "good":

Aeschylus: *Answer me this, why should one praise a poet?*
Euripides: *For cleverness and for his counsel, that's how we make people in the cities better.*

One suspects that Euripides, who spoke first, would have stood out for "cleverness" (*dexiotes*), and Aeschylus for "counsel" (*nouthesia*), but Aristophanes would have contended that for a poet who exemplified both dramatic excellence and good advice one need look no farther than the comic stage and Aristophanes himself.

Middle Comedy

The earliest subdivision of comedy is in fact a twofold one, by Aristotle in his *Nichomachean Ethics* (1128a23–5, probably from the 330s), where he describes "former comedy" as operating through *aischrologia* ("saying disgraceful things" – here he probably means a combination of "obscenity" and personally directed humor) – while "modern comedy" achieves humor through *hyponoia* ("subtle suggestion"). Aristotle, writing before the début of Menander (325 or 321), the great exponent of what we call "New" Comedy, is calling attention to a fundamental change in comedy, from the vigorous topical comedy of the late fifth century to the more polished and less offensive comedy of his time.

But later ancient scholarship regarded comedy as tripartite, identifying its three periods as "old" (the Greek here is usually *palaia* or *archaia*), "middle" (*mese*), and "new" (*nea*). This was probably a development of the third century, either by the scholars at Alexandria or by pupils of Aristotle, following what we call the Peripatetic tradition. The three subdivisions do not always agree, since the ancients in fact had four periods to deal with: (i) the very early period of comedy (486–ca. 455), (ii) the high period of Old Comedy (late fifth century), (iii) comedy between Aristophanes and

Menander (ca. 380–ca. 320), (iv) the later comedy of Menander and his contemporaries. Most ancient writers ignore (i) and identify the three phases as:

Old Comedy: roughly 440–385
Middle Comedy: 385–320
New Comedy: 325–290 or so

But occasionally (iii) is ignored in favor of (i), and a case has been made that the original subdivision into three was (i) + (ii) + (iii), made before the advent of Menander, which had to be revised to take New Comedy (iv) into consideration.

We may most usefully understand "Middle Comedy" as a chronological term, "between Aristophanes and Menander," rather than as a generic term. If the sands of Egypt were to yield a significant portion of a comedy, would we be able to assign it confidently to Middle Comedy on anything other than chronological grounds? Is there anything distinctive or idiosyncratic about Middle Comedy, or is it just comedy in transition? Some have tried to assign it distinctive characteristics. Norwood (1931: 41) writes, "The main topics of Middle Comedy are eating, sex, riddles, philosophy, literature, and life." The student will be forgiven if he or she wonders what this excludes. But a quick glance at the titles and fragments will show that the political intensity of Old Comedy has all but disappeared. The demagogue-comedy ceases to be found, principally because in the fourth century a demagogue was nothing new and (one suspects) because after the right-wing coups at the end of the fifth century, it was no longer funny (or safe) to make comedy out of the *demos* and its leaders.

Personal humor, however, does not die out immediately in the fourth century; in fact Menander in his *Samian Woman* (very late fourth century) can still launch a pair of "one-liners" at targets of the day. But the force of the jokes is tempered – there is not the same vitriol as Kratinos employed against Perikles or Aristophanes against Kleon or Platon against Hyperbolos. Often we laugh with the target as well as at him. When a political figure is made fun of in Middle Comedy, it is hardly ever for his politics, but for a personal detail: his appearance, his appetite, his sex-life. Kallimedon of Aphidna belonged to an important political family in the fourth century and was a rival of Demosthenes in the 330s and 320s. Comedy makes fun of him often, but for his appetite, nicknaming him "the Crab":

> If I like any other strangers [guests] more than you, may I be turned into an eel so that Kallimedon the Crab may purchase me. (Alexis fr. 149)

In fact the man most frequently caricatured in Middle Comedy is Plato, whose Academy and philosophical teachings were the stuff of public gossip. One particularly clever fragment shows Plato and his pupils playing "Animal, Vegetable, or Mineral" with a pumpkin (Epikrates fr. 10). Comedy had always found humorous potential in striking ideas and the personalities of those who advanced them. Sokrates was caricatured in *Clouds* as a "new thinker," with interests in teaching science, grammar, music, and "making the worse case seem the better." The sophist Protagoras appeared in Eupolis' *Spongers*, and we know that Ameipsias' *Konnos* (423-D) featured a chorus of named thinkers. In Middle Comedy we get titles such as Alexis' *The Female Pythagorean* or Aristophon's *Plato* or his *Pythagorean*. Alexis has a nice joke from his *Meropis*:

> Woman: You've come just in time. I'm totally at a loss, walking back and forth like Plato, and have come up with nothing except tired legs.

In the last years of Old Comedy and on into "Middle" Comedy, the mythological burlesque achieves its greatest popularity. In the hypothesis to *Wealth* (388), of the four competing plays three (*Admetos, Adonis, Pasiphae*) are clearly plays of this sort. A quick glance through the titles of those poets whom we can reasonably date to the years 410–380 reveals how prevalent plays were that made fun of myths and characters from myth. Aristophanes himself in his last comedies (*Aiolosikon, Kokalos*) turned to this form, and it is interesting to note that Araros, the most successful of his sons, wrote an *Adonis* and a *Birth of Pan*. In particular, the comedies of such lesser lights as Philyllios, Alkaios, Theopompos, and Nikochares are dominated by the burlesque of myth. In the titles of Antiphanes and Anaxandrides, two of the leading lights of Middle Comedy, one finds many examples of the burlesque of myth, somewhat fewer in the titles of Alexis, who belongs later in the century, confirming the conclusion that parody of myth was a mainstay of comedy in the first half of the fourth century.

With the rise of domestic themes and settings comes what we would call "romantic comedy." In particular, the figure of the prostitute (*hetaira*) becomes a familiar character in the fourth century – we get a hint of her in Aristophanes at *Wealth* 179 when the *hetaira* Nais is mentioned. Indeed some of the titles which one might take as suggesting a burlesque of myth could just as easily apply to courtesans. Were the Danae-plays by Apollophanes and Sannyrion comedies about that mythical heroine or about current *hetairai* named Danae? The comedian Alexis, in particular, wrote plays with female titles that hint strongly at the romantic themes that would dominate later comedy (*Flute-Girl, Woman at the Well, The Lovesick Woman*).

We may glimpse the development of the comic stereotypes that will populate later comedy: the braggart soldier, the cunning slave, the expert cook or doctor, the young man in love, the object of his desire, the sponger (*parasitos*). Not that these are characters new to comedy – most can be found in Old Comedy – but comedy seems to be moving toward an ensemble of such personalities. We can observe titles such as: *Heiress, Banker, Seers, Pimp, Doctor, Hunters, Wild-Men, Ephebes, Vine-Cutter, Soldier*, that reveal the sort of type characters that this later comedy was fond of portraying.

The poets continue their interest in their profession and, like the poets of Old Comedy, indulge in both intertextuality and meta-theater. In his *Sponger* Alexis makes a joke quite in the style of Old Comedy against Aristophanes' son, the comedian Araros:

> *I'd like you to taste this water. I have quite the deep well inside, with water more frigid than Araros*

and in his *Epidaurian* (fr. 77) alludes specifically to one of the plays by Timokles. We can cite titles such as *Poets*, *Third-Actor*, *Lyre-Player*, and the very suggestive *Lover of Euripides*. From Antiphanes' *Poetry* (fr. 189) comes a well-known and informative commentary on the relationship between comedy and tragedy:

> *Tragedy is a fortunate art-form in all respects, since first of all the plots are familiar to the specta-tors before anyone opens their mouth. The poet just has to make one allusion. If I say "Oedipus,"all is known: father Laios, mother Jokaste, daughters, sons, what he has done, what he will suffer. Again if someone says "Alkamion," even the children can recite it all: in a fit of madness he killed his mother, an upset Adrastos will enter and then leave. Then when they can't think of anything more to say and have completely screwed up their tragedies, they just lift the* mechane *like a finger, and the spectators are happy. But this isn't our situation – we must invent everything, new names, what's gone on before, what's happening in the present, the prologue, the resolution. If a Chremes or a Pheidon slips up on anything, he gets hissed off the stage. But a Peleus or a Teukros can get away with anything.*

The ancients regarded the principal poets of Middle Comedy as **PLATON**, whom we have seen falls uncomfortably between Old and later comedy, with two distinct dra-matic styles, perhaps in chronological sequence, and **ANTIPHANES**. The latter illus-trates a growing trend in Greek Comedy, in that he was a foreigner come to Athens to practice his dramatic career – the ancient sources describe him variously as coming from Smyrna, Rhodes, Kios, and Larissa and as acquiring Athenian citizenship through Demosthenes. His birth is given as 408–404 and his début between 388 and 384, suspiciously just after the production of Aristophanes' last extant comedy (*Wealth* – 388). He typifies another trend in comedy, in that he is attributed with 260 or 280 or 365 plays, far more than the forty of Aristophanes or the twenty-five of Kratinos. He must have written comedies for production other than at Athens, and the size and scope of a fourth-century comedy must have been less than an intricately crafted comedy of Aristophanes. For Antiphanes, we know of over 130 titles and just over 300 fragments. He won thirteen victories at Athens, eight of these at the Lenaia.

His play-titles reveals a considerable number of mythological burlesques (*Adonis*, *Andromeda*, *Ganymede*), plays named after characters in professions (*Farmer*, *Chariot-eer*, *Doctor*), women in intriguing roles (*She-Trainer*, *Javelin-Throweress*, *Fisherwoman*), plays with ethnic titles (*Egyptian*, *Man from Epidauros*, *Lemnian Women*), and comedies that sound like they could be romantic intrigues (*Adulterers* [fr. 159], *Woman from Corinth* [fr. 124], *Chrysis* [fr. 223]).

A comic poet of considerable interest is the Athenian **TIMOKLES**, active in 340s and 330s. The fragments of his comedy remind one considerably of Old Comedy. Plural titles as *The Women Celebrating the Dionysia*, *Heroes*, *Men of Marathon* are very much in the spirit of earlier comedy, as are *Philodikastes* ("The Juror-Lover," with echoes of *Wasps*?), and *Orestautokleides* (Autokleides, a contemporary politician in the role of the mythical Orestes). Of the forty or so fragments of Timokles' work, twenty contain jokes at real persons, some quite developed caricatures, such as those in frr. 15–16 aimed at the *hetaira* Pythionike, the metaphorical rendering in fr. 19 of Autok-

les as Marsyas and Aristomedes as Tereus, and the comparison of the orator
Hypereides to a river (fr. 17):

> Then you will cross the River Hypereides, flowing with fish, murmuring gently with sensible speech
> and then boiling over with compressed waves of purple prose . . . when well-paid, it waters the fields
> of its donor.

Timokles exploits a sexual presence and a use of vulgar language reminiscent of Old
Comedy. One comedy was called *Konisalos*, after a minor Priapic deity, another
Kentauros – for the aggressive sexual overtones of the centaur here see *Clouds* 350. In
fr. 5 (*Demosatyroi*) Ktesippos shaves so often that he belongs among women, not men.
Pythionike in fr. 16 is "insatiable" in a context of a sexual *double entendre*, and the
jokes describing bodily functions in fr. 18 are as crude as anything in Old Comedy.

Timokles also engages with tragedy in the manner of Aristophanes: fr. 6, giving
examples of how comparison with tragic *exempla* "helps each man bear his own problems more easily"; fr. 17.1, a parody of *Prometheus* 717–8; and fr. 27 (*Orestautokleides*),
where "around the wretched man sleep old women, Nannion, Plangon, etc." Here
the Furies of *Eumenides* are replaced with aging *hetairai*, all the more appropriate in
light of Autokleides' homosexual appetites. In good Aristophanic fashion Timokles
breaks the dramatic illusion and addresses the audience directly at fr. 19.6–7, "*B*. Bad
joke! *A*. But by the gods, stop [plural] and don't hiss."

Timokles' overall *vis comica,* in the same league (if not the same division) as Aristophanes and Kratinos, makes one suspect that he may well have been trying to revive
Old Comedy, in an age where drama looked to the past. It cannot be an accident that
Timokles was an Athenian, at a time when comedy was becoming more and more
international. Perhaps he might have succeeded if the world had not changed in the
late 320s with the imposition of Macedonian rule and the advent of Menander.

Menander and New Comedy

The student who finishes reading *Wasps* or *Frogs* by Aristophanes and then opens a
translation of Menander's *Samian Woman* or *The Grouch* is in for a shock. Both comic
poets were Athenians, competing in the same dramatic festivals, winning prizes and
delighting their audiences, but the two could not be more different. Aristophanes'
comedy is intensely topical, passing in and out of interest very swiftly, very much
bound up with the life of the *polis* of his time. His characters are often oversized
figures, tending to the bizarre, with significant names ("Just City," "Love Kleon").
Menander writes a more universal comedy, with no defined background and characters whose names and personalities are drawn from real life. Above all, Menander's
plays focus on the family, the *oikos*, and the relationships within it, be they father and
son, husband and wife, brother and sister, boy and the girl next door. This is comedy
of the neighborhood.

In an age when many of the comic poets came from abroad to ply their trade at
Athens, Menander was an Athenian. We know his parents' names, Diopeithes and

Hegesistrate, and one tradition makes him the nephew or pupil of Alexis, a leading poet of "Middle Comedy." This is not impossible, since a young man of good family could have had a prominent teacher, but it is more likely an example of the teacher–pupil tradition that is so common in ancient literary criticism. Another more trustworthy source makes him a pupil of Theophrastos, successor of Aristotle at the Lykeion, but again this could be a deduction based on Theophrastos' charming set of sketches, called "Characters," whose types share a great deal with the personalities of New Comedy. Dates and biographical information are rare, but the following can be advanced with reasonable confidence:

342/1 – birth at Athens
325 or 322 or 320 – debut with *Anger*
316 – *The Grouch* (first prize)
315 – victory at the City Dionysia
312 – *Charioteer* (fifth place)
301 – *Imbrians*
292/1 – death, while swimming off the Peiraieus

A much later writer, Alkiphron, created an exchange of letters between Menander and an alleged mistress, Glykera ("Sweetie"), while the *Suda* describes him as "with keen mind, but crazy over women." These need be nothing more than "deductions" based on the romantic themes of his comedy. The *Suda* says also that he had a squint, and at least two later artistic representations of Menander do show him with a definite squint.

His career then was relatively short, thirty years or so. The ancient sources credit him with just over 100 comedies; we know of ninety-seven reasonably secure titles. An average, then, of three comedies per year suggests that, like Antiphanes and other poets of the fourth century, he wrote for production at Athens and elsewhere. As with Aristophanes, no victory-total is given, and we are faced with the intriguing observation that for neither of the two great figures of Greek comedy do we know how many victories they won. Menander had an immense reputation in the ancient world. His plays were staged again soon after his death, adapted into Latin by the Roman playwrights, and nearly fifty visual portraits of him are known. In addition, scenes from his comedies show up in mosaics and frescoes from various locations around the ancient world, including the so-called "House of Menander" at Pompeii and a third century AD villa on Lesbos, whose dining room was decorated with mosaics showing scenes from Menander, several of which can be matched with the existing texts.

The writers of antiquity regarded him as one of the greatest writers of the Greek world, put on the same plane as Demosthenes, Euripides, and Homer. Quintilian, writing a handbook for the would-be *rhetor*, praises the clarity of Menander's comedy and also the speeches put in the mouth of his characters as eminently suitable models for the student of oratory. Ausonius in the fourth century AD advised his grandson to "read all that is worth reading – you should explore first the author of the *Iliad* and the romantic works of Menander." Plutarch's essay comparing Aristophanes and Menander, to the favor of the latter, has done much to establish these two as the leading lights (and polar opposites) of Greek Comedy. Perhaps the most extravagant description of Menander is that attributed to the Alexandrian scholar, Aristophanes of Byzantion (3rd century), "O Life, o Menander, which of you is the original, and which the copy?"

Menander and the other creators of New Comedy perhaps enjoyed their greatest success in their influence upon the Roman comic poets, Plautus and Terence, (ca. 220–ca. 160) and through them upon most Western comedy down to the twentieth century. We have twenty-one plays by Plautus and six by Terence, which are self-confessed adaptations into Latin of Greek New Comic originals. Both Roman poets quite freely admitted their literary debts, announcing in their prologues the author and source of their own comedy. Although written in Latin for a Roman audience, the comedies of Plautus and Terence had Greek settings and characters with Greek names – they were called *fabulae palliatae* ("plays in Greek dress"). Perhaps to the less cultured Romans a Greek source and setting carried a cachet of elegance and sophistication. Thus we know that three of Plautus' comedies were adapted from originals by Menander (*Bacchides* from *Double Deceiver*, *Casket* from *Women Dining Together*, and *Stichus* from *Brothers*), while Terence claims to have melded Menander's *Girl from Andros* and *Girl from Perinthos* to produce his own *Girl from Andros* and Menander's *Eunuch* and *Sponger* for his own *Eunuch*.

Ovid claimed that "as long as the cunning slave, the hard-hearted father, the wicked pimp, and the sweet young thing survive, there will be Menander." But posterity did not bear out this claim. Menander's immense reputation continued through the late classical age, but his plays were not included in Byzantine schoolbooks and thus did not enter the medieval manuscript tradition. By the late nineteenth century Menander was known by his great reputation and almost a thousand scraps and quotations, often chosen as "familiar quotations" for their wit and brevity, for example "the character of a man is known by his speaking" (fr. 72). Why should the works of this celebrated creator of witty and human comedy have been lost? Some think it was because his Greek did not conform to the rigorous standards of classical Greek – only the pure would survive – but another possibility is that he was too well known, considered an "easy" or "elementary" author and not to be included among "serious" writers.

At the turn of the twentieth century critics lamented the loss of Menander and a complete play by him would have been on any classical scholar's wish-list. Wishes are sometimes granted, and in little more than a century Menander has gone from being an author known only in bits and pieces to one with scenes, acts, and entire comedies extant. The curtain began to lift in 1898, when eighty-seven lines of his *Farmer* provided us with the final scene to one act of that comedy. We now had a whole living scene with which to work. A more important discovery was that of the Cairo papyrus in 1905, a collection of plays that included about half of the *Arbitrants*, and two acts each of *Samian Woman* and *The Woman with her Hair Cut Off*. We had thus moved to entire acts and could see a comedy and its characters develop. Figure 4.4 shows a page from the Cairo Papyrus, the opening of the fourth act of *Samian Woman*, lines 616–51. Note the entry Χόρου (*chorou* – "of the chorus") at the top, the unusual insertion of the speaker's name in the second line (MOS[CHION), and the trace of the *paragraphos* at the left above the eleventh-last line, the usual manner of indicating a change of speaker. In 1957 the Bodmer Papyrus yielded a virtually complete comedy, *The Grouch*, although with each successive discovery Menander was becoming less of an icon and more of a "normal" author, warts and all. *The Grouch*, in particular, turned out to be a juvenile work, with far too many characters, some nice moments in the first and fourth acts, but an unfunny and gratuitous ending. The same book that produced *The Grouch* in its entirety also produced more of the *Samian Woman*, now giving us four of the five acts, and the opening two acts of *The Shield*, both of which display a more polished and mature comedian at work. A most intriguing discovery in 1968 gave us about a hundred lines of *The Double Deceiver*, the play adapted by Plautus in his Roman comedy, *Bacchides*. For the first time we could compare a Greek original with its Roman adaptation and observe (what we should have expected) that Plautus was no slavish translator of his Greek original, but an innovative comedian in his own right.

We have mentioned before that Menander's comedy is that of the *oikos*, that comedy has essentially moved from the wider community of the *polis* to the domestic realm of the neighborhood. Plots involve young men in love, the course of true romance, mistaken identities, long-lost children, conflicts between parent and child. Above all, this is comedy of errors, where characters think that they know the truth, and produce scenes of humor based on partial knowledge and mistaken assumptions. The third and fourth acts of *Samian Woman* features three characters, each of whom thinks that he knows who has been sleeping with whom and who the parents of the infant are. In *The Shield* a young Athenian named Kleostratos is presumed dead in battle and a greedy uncle has designs on his sister and her inheritance. This comic "error" is cleverly handled by Menander, who opens the play with the return of the "dead man's" slave, followed by the actual "prologue" spoken by the goddess of Chance, who puts the spectators right. *The Grouch* does not turn on any major comic "errors," apart from Sostratos pretending to be a hardworking farmer in order to impress his girl's father.

By the time of *The Grouch* (316) the structure of comedy had altered greatly. Old Comedy was more unstructured farce or fantasy than tightly organized drama, with loosely connected episodes that follow more or less logically from what goes before. But the plays that we possess to any great degree show a tight five-act structure, distinctly divided, with the playing-space empty of the actors. The plot-line is outlined in the first act, elaborated in the second, complicated and resolved in the third and fourth acts, with the fifth act (at least in *The Grouch* and *Samian Woman*) providing something of a coda to the action.

One of the most striking differences between New Comedy and earlier comedy lies in the role of the chorus. One cannot imagine an Aristophanic comedy without the chorus of metaphorical wasps or the insistent Acharnians or the exuberant women in *Lysistrate* and *Women at the Thesmophoria*, not to mention their intense *parabases* on behalf of their poet, their songs of personal abuse, or their exploration of their dramatic identity. But by the time of Aristophanes' last plays the text merely has <*chorou*> ("of the chorus") in several places, and in Menander this has become the rule. There

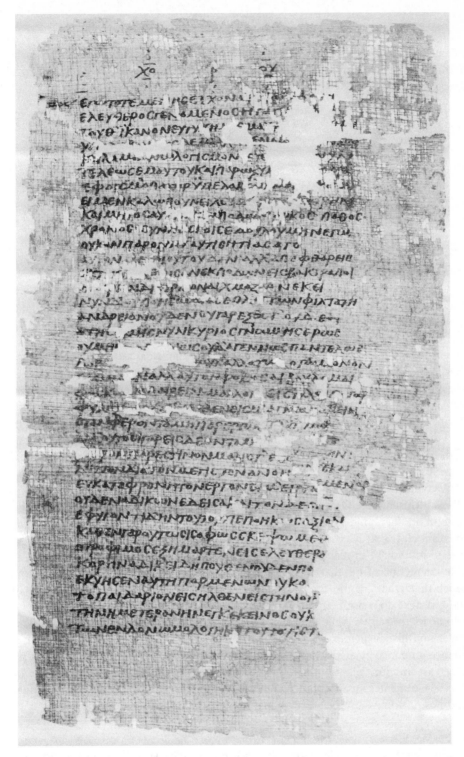

Figure 4.4 *P. Cair. J. 43327, Plate XLV, Menander* Samian Woman *616–51. Reproduced by kind permission of the Institute of Classical Studies, School of Advanced Studies, University of London, from* The Cairo Codex of Menander (P. Cair. J. 43327): A Photographic Edition, *prepared under the supervision of H. Riad and L. Koenen (London: University of London, Institute of Classical Studies, 1979).*

is a chorus to be sure, but they enter to perform what is essentially an intermission, a song and dance between the acts with no dramatic identity or relevance to the comedy. At the end of the first act of *The Grouch* Daos exclaims (230–2):

> *I see some Pan-worshippers heading this way, to this very place, and they're quite drunk as well. I don't think it would be a good time to run into them.*

In almost identical words Chairestratos in *The Arbitrants* says (169–71):

> *Let's be gone, since a crowd of young drunks is heading towards this place. I don't think it would be a good time to run into them.*

New Comedy is almost exclusively the province of the actors and the character types that they portray.

Characters no longer bear significant names. We will find no "Just City" or "Love Kleon" in Menander, but names from the average Athenian street: Sostratos, Nikeratos, Kleostratos, Smikrines. Settings are usually, but not always, a street in the city: *The Ghost, The Lyre-Player, Samian Woman, The Shield* ~ Athens, *The Woman with her Hair Cut Off* ~ Corinth. Three comedies have more unusual settings: *The Grouch*, set before the shrine of Pan in very rural Phyle; *The Arbitrants*, in a village on the east coast of Attica; and *The Girl from Leukas*, on a rocky point on the island of Leukas.

An Aristophanic comedy proceeds less on logic than on fantasy. Bizarre events occur with ridiculous and illogical ease (a city in the sky, a successful sex-strike, a ride on a dung-beetle to Olympos), but in Menander the plot proceeds in realistic sequence, with twists and turns, contrived suspense, and skillfully delayed recognitions. Unlike Aristophanic comedy, "plot" is a word that does belong in the vocabulary of the critic of Menander. The spectators are partly in on the plot – in the prologue to *Samian Woman* Moschion tells all about his fathering of a child on the girl next door and the birth of another child by his father's Samian "wife," in *The Shield* the goddess Chance makes it clear that Kleostratos is not dead. What Menander will do is bring the plot-line to fulfillment in realistic fashion, with unexpected turns of the plot, the believable interaction of his characters, and the tricks he plays on the audience. It is not so much the "what" as the "how." In the second act of *Samian Woman* Moschion and the girl next door are betrothed, precisely what everyone wants, and the spectators will be forgiven for asking what the problem will be. But Moschion seems a little too eager and his suspicious father wonders what his real motive is, a suspicion that a chance utterance by an old nurse arouses in the next act and sets off the chain of mistaken assumptions that dominate the next two acts. Plutarch (*On the Glory of the Athenians* 347e) relates an anecdote, which, if true, speaks volumes about his technique of composing comedy:

> *The story goes that one of Menander's friends said to him, "Menander, the Dionysia is getting close, and you haven't written your comedy." Menander replied, "I have indeed written my comedy. The plot is all worked out; all I have to do is add the lines."*

His first priority, it seems, will have been to work out the complexities of the plot-line and the interrelation between the characters, and then to put the words in their mouths.

When Aristophanes of Byzantion commented, "O Life, o Menander, which of you is the original, and which the copy?," he is not likely to have been talking about Menander's plot-lines or dramatic situations, unless Athens were populated with long-lost children miraculously discovering their parentage (and a well-off one at that), soldiers mistakenly presumed dead, boys seducing the girls next door, and an accompanying retinue of clever slaves, cooks, and spongers. Real life is not a series of happy coincidences, of recognitions and reversals, of rings and baby clothes appearing just when needed. Menander's comedies do depend on certain tried and true conventions in the comedy of errors, but these are but the surface workings of the plot-line. What Aristophanes of Byzantion was talking about was how Menander's characters come alive as truly breathing and whole people, how he constantly surprises his spectators and readers with a variation on type, how small scenes and descriptions imply much more about their personalities.

A few examples will suffice. *Samian Woman* opens with Moschion, Demeas' adopted son, giving us the details that we need to know. An adopted son might well be portrayed as a hellion, the ancient equivalent of the modern "preacher's kid," chafing at the bit and given to unruly behavior. But listen to his words:

Through my father's doing I became a man, and I repaid what I owed him in full – I behaved myself.

Of the two old men in *Samian Woman* Demeas is the deeper-minded of the two; he quotes tragedy, gets angry quickly, and then cools down just as rapidly. Nikeratos, on the other hand, is more abrupt, not too bright, but when he does put two and two together, takes a lot of calming down – "he's a tough old bird, shit-eater, completely set in his ways" (550). In *The Arbitrants* the "other woman," Habrotonon, has one eye on her future, "Do you think I want children? I just want to be free" (545–7), but earlier we have seen her doting over the baby and genuinely interested in the fate of its mother. Sostratos in *The Grouch* is a rather spoiled young man from the city, who has fallen in love with Knemon's daughter at first sight ("did you get up this morning and plan to fall in love with someone?" [54]), but who acquits himself well in an interview with the girl's step-brother (306–13):

I'm a free-born man, with a considerable fortune; I'm eager to marry her without a dowry, and ready to take an oath always to love her. Young man, if I have come here planning to do anything untoward against you, may Pan himself and the Nymphs strike me dead right here by Pan's house.

Later he will describe in an amusing and self-deprecating fashion how he did next to nothing while Gorgias rescued Knemon from the well and will subsequently persuade his wealthy father that wealth is not the sole thing in life:

And so, father, I say that as long as you have money, you should use it generously, help people, do
all the good that you can . . . Far better than a wealth which you keep hidden is a friend that all
can see. (805–8)

Unlike Aristophanes, Menander is intimately involved in his characters. He may laugh
at them but always with good humor. Even the great misanthrope Knemon (*The
Grouch*) is given a chance to redeem himself by his *apologia pro vita sua* and his subsequent recantation. If Norwood was correct to deny "humor" to Aristophanes
because of his lack of human empathy, then we can certainly attribute it to Menander, as one intensely interested in and sympathetic to the human condition.

Menandrian comedy also provides a useful window into the social norms of the
late fourth century. The plots and situations may be dramatically contrived, but
the characters and equally importantly the backdrop provide a context of reality for
the spectators. From Menander we learn about the dependence of sons on fathers
(*Samian Woman*), of the position of the mistress in society (*Samian Woman, The Arbitrants*), the laws of inheritance (*The Shield*), the role of the *kyrios*, a woman's "protec-
tor" (*The Grouch, The Shield*), the proper behavior of women (*The Grouch, The Woman
with her Hair Cut Off*). Young men were dependent on their fathers for their livelihood;
Moschion's only option for independence in *Samian Woman* is to join the ancient
equivalent of the Foreign Legion. Chrysis (*Samian Woman*) may be a foreigner and
thus unable to be Demeas' legal wife in Athenian law, but she is his *de facto* wife and
mistress in his house. We witness the negotiations for a dowry (*The Grouch*), preparations for a wedding (*Samian Woman*), and the results of personal indiscretions at
various festivals (Adonia ~ *Samian Woman*, Tauropolia ~ *The Arbitrants*). In this last
play we watch an informal arbitration as a contested issue of ownership takes place
with Smikrines deciding who owns the articles found with the child.

At least two ancient writers attempted to establish a triad of New Comedy, presumably to match that of Old Comedy: Menander, Diphilos, and Philemon. Sometimes this triad is increased to five with the addition of Apollodoros and Philippides.
Both Diphilos and Philemon wrote comedies that we know also to have been adapted
by Plautus, and this may account in part for their inclusion in this later triad. **DIPHI-
LOS** came originally from Sinope in the Black Sea region, but moved at an early age
to Athens, where he became a fixture on the comic stage. He follows Menander on
the victors' list at the Lenaia, and we may reasonably assign him a career of ca. 320
into the third century, although the bulk of evidence places Diphilos in the late fourth
century. Of the sixty or so titles, some suggest burlesques of myth (*Herakles, Daughters of Danaos, Theseus, Daughters of Peleus*), others situations appropriate to the comedy
of intrigue (*Ignorance, The Heiress, Parasite*), others the type characters of comedy
(*Soldier, Merchant, Painter*). The 133 fragments are especially rich in themes of food
and the characters of the cook and the sponger. One of the two longer fragments, fr.
31 (*Merchant*) describes the competition in Corinth for food and drink, while in fr. 41
(*Painter*) one character describes to another (Drakon) the delights that await him in
terms of food, drink, and sex.

PHILEMON of Syracuse seems to have been a larger player on the comic stage.
His career began around 330, a little before that of Menander, with his first victory

at the Dionysia in 327, and carried on well into the third century. By 307 he had acquired Athenian citizenship. The ancient sources attribute nearly a hundred comedies to him and a reputation almost equal to Menander's. There is little evidence of the burlesque of myth so common in Middle Comedy. Many of the titles are ethnics, suggestive of the principal character of the drama: *Babylonian, Thebans, Corinthian Woman, Rhodian Woman*. Several suggest a stereotyped character: *The Property Disputer, The Youth, The Adulterer, The Soldier*. Fr. 3 (*Brothers*) is an intriguing invocation of Solon, the sixth-century Athenian law-giver, by a pimp, praising him for alleged sexual reforms making women available to all. Solon, it will be remembered, was a character in Kratinos' *Cheirons* and also in Eupolis' *Demes*. *The Soldier* provides the longest extant fragment (fr. 82), a declaration in almost tragic style by a cook about to prepare a succulent fish. Quite a few unassigned fragments of Philemon exist, several more than a few lines long, of which fr. 118 reveals well the fourth-century fascination for Euripides:

> If in truth the dead have consciousness, as some maintain, then, gentlemen, I would gladly hang myself so that I might meet Euripides.

In the third century drama moves elsewhere, although it continued to be written, performed, and appreciated at Athens. The great names of Greek tragedy in the third century are those of the scholar-poets of Alexandria, and we may wonder whether they were writing for a general public or the elite of the Greek court of the Ptolemies. We have now realized that the so-called *phlyax*-vases of Southern Italy are reflecting Athenian Old Comedy, which clearly crossed the Ionian Sea to Italy in the fourth century. In the late third century Greek Comedy again went west to Italy, as the Roman comic poets, notably Plautus and Terence, adapted these Greek originals into Latin for Roman audiences. Tragedy followed comedy to Rome as well, where Euripides continued the posthumous popularity that he enjoyed in fourth-century Greece. The earliest Roman tragedians (Livius Andronicus, Naevius, Ennius) found him as the principal source for their own tragic dramas. In Plautus' comedy *Curculio*, the title character enters muttering:

> I have heard that an old poet once wrote in his tragedy that two women are worse than one,

an allusion to the sentiments of the chorus in Euripides' *Andromache* 465–70. In Plautus' *Rope* Sceparnio enters the morning after a violent storm and exclaims:

> My God, that was some storm out at sea last night! The wind just about took the roof off. Wind? That was no wind, but something straight out of Euripides' Alkmene.

Unless Plautus was just slavishly passing along the words in his Greek original, he expected his Roman audience of the early second century to have more than a passing acquaintance with Euripides.

5

Approaching Greek Drama

As the preceding discussion of the tragedies and comedies of fifth-century Athens has made clear, this is a literature rich in imagination and cultural history. As literary documents, each genre of Greek drama offers literary critic and student alike a treasure-house of information to be analyzed and interpreted. Because language is the basis of literature, the first approaches to appear were those that focused first and foremost on that language. The Greek plays first appeared in the modern world as written texts emerging from the manuscript tradition of the Middle Ages. They were read before they were acted.

Textual Criticism and Commentary

For the reader with knowledge of ancient Greek, textual criticism and commentary, the hallmark of classical philology, remains a valid and valuable way to study these ancient texts. Established by German scholars of the nineteenth century, this approach begins by solving textual problems that have entered the manuscripts through the vagaries of the transmission process, where grammatical, metrical, or problems of meaning signal errors in the transcribing process. Its aim, as far as possible, is to get back to the "original" text, to what the playwright actually (or most probably) wrote, or at least to the "official text" established by Lykourgos ca. 330. It is therefore not concerned with the play as a literary whole, but focuses on specific sections in a text that appear to require emendation and elucidation.

In commenting on an ancient text, explanations of the problem with the received word or phrase are provided, previous emendations reviewed, and new suggestions recommended and supported by parallel uses of the recommended term in other texts. These decisions are based on more than what is possible metrically and grammatically, however, for word choice is also informed by assumptions made about what the playwright wanted to say. The emendation must make sense both in the context of the sentence and in relation to the larger content of the play's general themes and plot. Commentaries proceed line by line, often word by word, and more than occasionally lose the forest for the trees. Parallel expressions for a word or phrase are sought out, literary indebtedness explored, allusions in the text explained, metrical subtleties elucidated. For those of us who approach Greek drama in translation, we are deeply indebted to the work of textual critics and commentators, who through their labors have given us more accurate editions of the Greek manuscripts on which to base our translations. Nevertheless, this approach does not really say much about how literature works to engage us as literature, nor is its concern to consider the "meaning" of the drama.

In this chapter we shall use Sophokles' *Oedipus Tyrannos* as a template for our discussion. A textual point of some magnitude occurs at line 873, where the received text gives *hybris phyteuei tyrannon* ("arrogance breeds a tyrant"). Neither the grammar nor the meter is problematic, but Sophokles does not use *tyrannos* or *tyrannis* in a negative sense. Several times in the play Oedipus can be called "tyrant" merely in the sense of "king" or "ruler." Thus Blaydes suggested reversing subject and object: *hybrin phyteuei tyrannis* ("tyranny [being a king] breeds arrogance"). The point would be that those in power (*tyrannis*) often behave with arrogance (*hybris*). Is this what has happened to Oedipus, as evidenced by his rejection of Apollo and his oracles in the previous scene? The debate has been fierce and is not yet resolved.

New Criticism

An approach developed to redress this perceived shortcoming in traditional philology, but one still firmly located in the language of the text, was New Criticism which, though now decidedly no longer "new," remains the most commonly applied approach to literary texts at the secondary and first-year undergraduate levels. In New Criticism a literary text is a self-contained, discreet object for study. Between its first word and its last is contained all that is required to appreciate it as a living, breathing work of art. Indeed, the project of New Criticism is to understand how literature is generated through a study of its form and content. This approach is deeply interested in identifying the structure, or component parts of a literary text, such as its plot, episodes, climax, and denouement and to demonstrate the way language is employed to carry its themes within those structures. So identifying the motifs, imagery, ironies, and tensions in a text, as well as how other uses of language (e.g., metaphors, similes) contribute to the whole, becomes an important element in analysis. Through what is termed a close reading of these elements and their interrelationship within a text, this approach traces how the tensions which build as the story progresses are finally resolved by its end. Exemplary of a New Criticism approach to Greek drama is the statement by R. P. Winnington-Ingram that "the main function of criticism is the interpretation of individual works of art . . . each in its own unique form, quality and theme (1980: vii).

New Criticism is not solely interested in how a particular text accomplishes the telling of its own story, however. It is also concerned with matters of interpretation.

So for instance in a play such as Sophokles' *Oedipus Tyrannos*, which has two plot lines, (1) the discovery of King Laios' murderer and (2) the discovery of Oedipus' parentage, a close reading of this text will reveal the way in which the poet develops his theme by exploiting the tensions in a set of polarized terms carried in the play's imagery (light/dark, sight/blindness, knowledge/ignorance), a tension also embodied in the play's characters (especially Oedipus and Teiresias) in order to turn plot-line 1 into plot-line 2 and bring the action to its exciting climax where Oedipus realizes that he is the murderer of his own father, King Laios. It then falls to the critical reader to interpret the play, to provide a commentary on what the play "means," based in the way the language has been employed within its structure to lead one to a particular conclusion. Thus any interpretation of a drama must be supported by things said in the play itself. New Criticism tends to treat the plays as written texts, designed to be read, and its principal techniques are those of the literary critic at work in his or her library.

Structuralism

As informative and insightful as New Criticism can be, many theories initially developed in the disciplines of anthropology, sociology, and psychology have been found to be applicable to the study of literary texts. Under these approaches the text is no longer seen to be a timeless work of art, but rather a cultural artifact and thus a bearer of information about the society that produced it. These approaches share in a desire to understand more about the producers of the literary artifact by revealing the ways in which the taken-for-granted assumptions about the way the world is are embedded in the language of the text.

The approach known as structuralism is rooted in a branch of anthropology which deals with language systems, that of structural linguistics pioneered by Ferdinand Saussere. But its theory was also informed by the ideas of thesis, antithesis, and synthesis expounded in Marxist and Hegalian philosophy. It is based on the premise that beneath a society's kinship systems, social and political institutions, myths, and, especially, its language lie particular conceptual patterns and structures of thought based on interrelated sets of binary oppositions. Thus the three sets of bipolar terms that New Criticism would read as part of the play's imagery, in an approach based on structuralism's principles, would be indicative of conceptual patterns that extend far beyond their literary usage. The space or state between light and dark is the space or state in which humanity must confine itself, for to live wholly in the light is to possess immortality, while to be wholly in the dark is not to live at all. The terms in each bipolar pair serve to define the boundaries of human existence. But Teiresias becomes the mediating figure between these two extremes, a man who actually lives in darkness, being blind, but who is internally illuminated, having full knowledge of the ways things are because he is the prophet of Apollo, the god of illumination.

In its simplest application, structuralism will set about identifying all the terms within a given drama that mark one pole or the other in a binary set of oppositions. It will then attempt to read beneath these sets to discover the "codes" that are governing the language and the action(s) of the play. For as has been demonstrated by scholars working with this form of analysis, the codes informing one institution in society will be conceptually related to those governing others. Thus alimentary codes will be consonant with kinship codes, which are consonant with gender codes, which are expressed in legal codes, civic and domestic architecture, the use of space, etc. In both tragedy and comedy, these codes are made particularly visible when they are transgressed, for the transgression often poses a challenge to the status quo, drawing attention to the arbitrary and thus artificial rather than "natural" distinctions upon which the society operates. The best studies employing this approach will do more than merely identify the binary pairs and the codes they reveal; they will also critically assess how drama generally, or a single play in particular, participates in the representation of society's codes and whether that participation serves to critique or endorse a particular aspect of the system or the entire system.

Oedipus Tyrannos begins with a city afflicted by a death-bringing plague and ends with the familiar dictum of the ancient world, "call no one happy until he is dead." Thus one obvious set of opposites is life and death, an antithesis which is commonly expressed metaphorically as "light" and "dark" ("to look upon the light" is an ancient Greek way of saying "to be alive"). But Sophokles cleverly turns the opposition of light and dark into that of knowledge and ignorance, and creates two mediating figures in the play: Teiresias, blind but "illuminated," and at the end Oedipus, also blind but in full knowledge of the truth ("I know clearly, though in the dark" – 1325–6). Other plays that respond well to structuralist interpretation would include *Antigone* (life/death, male/female, house/city), *Trachinian Women* (male/female, human/god, human/animal), and *Hippolytos* (city/wilderness, love/chastity mediated by the institution of marriage).

Myth and "Version"

On occasion, comedy did take myth as its starting point, most notably in the subgenre of the burlesque of myth, but in the extant comedies myth is more generally used to inform individual scenes in a play. In *Birds* Prometheus appears hiding from Zeus under a parasol and reveals the situation among the gods to humans. Clearly the spectators (and modern readers) are expected to begin from the familiar myth of Prometheus as enemy of Zeus and benefactor of humanity. In Aristophanes' *Wealth* Hermes' arguments for a place in the new world order are predicated on the honors he is traditionally granted in myth. Familiarizing oneself with Greek mythology can thus provide a fuller insight into the humor generated in some Aristophanic scenes.

Myth's relationship to tragedy is much stronger, for as we have seen, the plots for these dramas are taken from the mythological treasury of Greece. The important term in assessing what a playwright does with a given myth is "version," and to make that assessment, one must have some knowledge of the other versions of the myth with which the playwright might have worked. For this approach, one would first seek to determine if there was a version of the story that predominated, that is, that would seem to have been more frequently told than others. Then one would compare the story as it appears in the play with that version, taking particular note of any differences between the two. A further comparison of these differences with other known versions of the myth would help to determine the degree to which the playwright was selecting and blending elements from two or more versions. It would also permit one to discuss the ramifications of these changes on the interpretation of the play. The same would apply if it could be shown that the playwright introduced elements to the story that were not in evidence in any previously known version of the myth. This is one useful way of assessing authorial intent, since the playwright will have chosen or altered a myth for a dramatic purpose.

In the case of *Oedipus Tyrannos*, earlier versions of the story were considerably different from that of Sophokles, which has become the canonical version. In Homer (*Odyssey* 11.271–80) Oedipus marries his mother, Epikaste (not Jokaste), but the gods soon contrive that the truth come out. She commits suicide, leaving a curse and future woes on Oedipus. In the lost early epic *The Story of Oedipus* he marries again and fathers the four children familiar to us. Thus traditionally Oedipus' children are not his brothers and sisters, as they are in Sophokles. Homer says nothing of Oedipus' self-blindness, and one early version has him blinded as an act of revenge by servants of Laios. In Aeschylus, although only the third play in his Theban trilogy of 467 survives, we know that he was chronicling the curse on the family as it came to fall first on Laios in the first play, then on Oedipus in the second, and in the third play, *Seven*, the curse will come to rest on Oedipus' two sons. Aeschylus was much concerned with an operative curse, but this is all but invisible in *Oedipus Tyrannos*. Sophokles prefers to concentrate on the magnificent figure of Oedipus, his essential innocence of the most horrible of offences, and his own responsibility for the tragedy (1329–33):

> It was Apollo, my friends, Apollo, who brought these wretched sufferings of mine to fulfillment, but I did the deed, no one else.

Sophokles' changes made it not only a more intriguing story for dramatic reenactment, but also served to invite the audience to see a character familiar to them from myth in a new light. And so we can ask what might the reasons have been for these innovations in the context of the drama? Do they effect a change in the myth's focus, toward or away from an action or character, and if so, what is gained dramatically by the change(s)? And in terms of drama's relationship to the *polis*, is a playwright manipulating a myth in a particular way to make it more relevant to contemporary political concerns?

Version is an especially important approach in what have come to be called the "Elektra plays," more properly the story of Orestes' revenge, of which we fortunately possess a version by all three playwrights (*Libation-Bearers* and the two *Elektras*), as well as the closely related drama, *Orestes*. Both Euripides and Sophokles engage with the seminal version of Aeschylus, and past him with the whole earlier tradition of Greek myth. The student can usefully compare the settings (both general and local), the identity and role of the chorus, the dramatic personality of the principal characters, the recognition-scenes, the order of the murders, the role of Apollo, and the nature of the aftermath. Euripides, in particular, responds well to the examination of dramatic version. In his *Medea* he horrifies audiences and readers by having Medea murder her own children, and in *Bacchae* has Pentheus conducted alone to the mountain and there torn apart by his mother and her sisters. The extant *Hippolytos* is a particularly significant use of version, since Euripides took the unusual step of rewriting an earlier drama, most likely because he felt he could do something dramatically different with this new version.

Ritual and Drama

From anthropology also comes a type of study which considers the relationship of myth and ritual to drama. In its early development as a perspective through which to interpret dramatic literature, theorists working in this area believed that drama originated in the reenactment of myths associated with the god Dionysos and, more specifically, that the reenactment of these tragic myths was the actual ritual which honored the god. This particular formulation of the relationship between myth, ritual, and drama has long since been abandoned. However, there is no question that both myth and ritual are important aspects of tragic drama, and in some of our surviving tragedies the establishment of a cult at the end, usually for one of the key figures, permits these plays to be read as a reenactment of the etiological myth that underlies a contemporary practice (e.g., *Hippolytus, Iphigenia Among the Taurians*). Nevertheless, such plays are in the minority, and it may be more productive to consider a particular play's reworking of myth or its use of ritual as two separate approaches to its interpretation.

In terms of drama's use of ritual, it is first necessary to familiarize oneself with the types of ritual and uses that were made of them in their more usual contexts. Here we are interested in both "religious" ritual and ritualized forms of civic behavior that have the force of religious belief behind them. These include petitions for protection (supplication), the reception of strangers (hospitality) and the swearing of oaths as well as the more overtly religious practices of blood and bloodless sacrifices, rites of passage (e.g., initiation, marriage, and funerary rituals), and hymns and prayers addressed to the gods.

In almost every tragedy and many comedies, at least one ritual or ritualized activity is used within the drama to frame or to carry forward the action. For the original audience who were intimately familiar with these rituals and their significance for the proper maintenance of order within the *polis* the appropriateness or inappropriateness of its use in the play would have been immediately clear. And so, for example, when the priest in the opening of the *Oedipus Tyrannos* appeals to the King to help the people as the best of men alive (46), the audience would immediately recognize that there was trouble ahead for Oedipus, for their understanding of the way the world worked indicated that men who rose too high, or thought too highly of themselves, would be brought low by the gods. Later when Oedipus has received the word from Delphi to find Laios' murderer, he makes his pronouncements in the form of an oath (216–75), which in practice always included a curse upon the swearer if he failed to fulfill what he had sworn. While this passage entails one of the great ironies in the play (because Oedipus is the man he seeks), its power resides in its ritual form.

Another ritual form that is deeply ironic in its use in this play, is Jocasta's prayer accompanied by an incense offering to Apollo (911–23). There is nothing amiss in its form but it is being performed by one who is polluted by incest as well as by one who had recently denied the accuracy of the god's prophets. The audience would realize the folly of the piety shown here (cf. Sophokles' *Elektra* 634–59). Other examples from Sophokles' plays alone would include the corrupted sacrifice (*Elektra*), the exploitation of hospitality ritual (*Elektra, Philoktetes*), and the manipulation of funerary ritual (*Antigone*). By studying the way that rituals and ritualized behavior are built into the tragedies and comedies of the dramatists, we gain a fuller understanding of the multiple levels on which these plays communicated with their audiences.

Psychoanalytic Approaches

At roughly the same time as anthropology and sociology were forging fresh understandings of human culture and societies, Sigmund Freud was generating theories for an understanding of the human *psyche* ("mind," "soul"). In myth he saw early man's attempt to articulate what he would later style as "complexes," problems in the psychic development of the child as he or she matured to adulthood. Freud was particularly concerned with identifying what he believed to be universal subconscious desires experienced by every child but successfully repressed and controlled through the processes of maturation. Deviant behavior, behavior which was not in accord with societal norms, from phobias to madness and everything in between, was to be understood as the "return of the repressed," which, according to Freud, was usually sexual in nature. In the myths of Oedipus and those of Elektra in particular Freud found models for his complexes and confirmation of his insights. It is not surprising then that the use of psychoanalytical theory has become a popular approach in the study and interpretation of Greek drama.

Some very successful studies have been produced using this method. Certain characters such as Pentheus and Hippolytos have proven to be particularly good subjects. Even the much over-played Oedipus Complex does have its roots in a significant comment by Jokaste (980–2):

> *Do not be afraid about marrying with your mother. Many men have slept with their mothers in their dreams.*

However, there is a danger. The characters that populate Greek drama are not living, breathing human beings with pasts and childhood experiences to analyze in order to determine where the processes of psychic maturation went wrong. Additionally, we do not get in Greek drama the sort of character development that we find in the dramas of later periods. The characters of Greek drama tend to be one-dimensional, each scene in which they appear designed to reveal their dominant mind-set and temperament, not to "develop" a fully human personality. To apply psychoanalytic theory to the majority of these figures is to create a hypothetical past based on what the theory would require in order to produce the mental and/or emotional problems evidenced in the drama and to perform the analysis. This creates a rather circular argument.

Nevertheless, there is no question that we do respond to certain character-types positively and negatively and this, in itself, becomes an area worthy of study. A more productive application of the insights gained from psychological inquiry would be to ask how and why these one-sided characters of Greek drama can affect us so deeply. What is it in the construction of an Antigone or an Oedipus that moves us to respond to them as we do? Freudian theory would suggest that it is because we can take vicarious pleasure in seeing another act out the desires which we ourselves have so carefully repressed. Seeing it done, even as "make-believe," reduces the internal need to do it ourselves. Moreover, when the outcome of such behavior produces negative consequences for the agent, we are further discouraged from undertaking the action ourselves. Drama, in this view of its relationship to psychic responses, would seem to provide us with an "eat your cake and have it too" experience. We have the pleasure of consumption without having to personally undergo the losses. But this does not answer the question posed, for it postulates that it is not the character, *per se*, that we respond to but the acts they perform.

Perhaps then we need to apply psychological insights in a different direction. We might ask what is it about the situations in which these characters are placed that makes their responses understandable and believable? On what level or levels do we identify with them? Here, theories of mind and emotion may serve to give insight not so much into the characters of drama but rather into our own cultural values. Such an approach may not lead us into an interpretation of the drama, but it provides valuable information dealing with the reception of these dramas in a modern context. And that too is a worthwhile reason for engaging with these texts.

Gender Studies

One interpretative approach to Greek drama that has grown in importance lies in the area of gender studies. Critical readings of the literary texts draw on the theories and insights from a number of disciplines, including those that we have already considered. Until recently the field has been dominated by an interest in the representation of women in drama, the manner in which their dramatic characters are constructed, how their actions and attitudes are critiqued, and how the dramatists use women both to reinforce the status quo and to explore issues surrounding the identity of the citizen males who made up the majority (if not all) of the spectators.

From the surviving texts of Greek drama the student may glean details about the lives of real women within the *polis*, their place in society, and the sort of activities in which they engaged. For comedy the women's plays of Aristophanes (especially *Lysistrate* and *Women at the Thesmophoria*) are especially useful in this regard. For tragedy one may look at *Antigone* or *Medea* or *Ion* for useful sociological and cultural information on fifth-century women. The texts can also be read as an exploration of male anxieties, about women and about themselves, for these plays reveal the ways in which both masculine and feminine identities are constructed, gender roles defined, and behaviors stereotyped.

We have seen that gender-themes loom large in Aeschylus, not just in his creation of Klytaimestra, the woman with the "man-plotting heart," but also in his depiction of Aigisthos as a weak and effeminate male (*Agamemnon* 1625–7). His *Suppliants* turns on the relationship between the genders, in this case women who fear marriage with their aggressive male cousins. Over all this presides Love herself, who appeared in the third play and enunciated a great statement of the marriage between Earth and Heaven (fr. 44). Euripides likewise created women such as Phaidra, Medea, and Kreousa, whose dramatic personalities depend on their role as "the other." Sophokles' *Oedipus Tyrannos* does not depend greatly on gender themes, but in his *Antigone* the title-character stands up to the male-dominated *polis*, whose new leader Kreon has usurped authority over burial, properly the province of female members of the family. His *Trachinian Women* turns on violent relationships between male and female, as the well-meaning but weak Deianeira brings about the death of her abusive husband.

Since these dramas were all written by men, performed by men, and watched by an audience that was notionally male, Greek drama gives us a particularly good insight into the ways in which men viewed the social identities of women and of themselves in both domestic and public settings. In tragedy, in particular, we frequently see females forced by circumstances to involve themselves in activities normally restricted to males, often because some male has failed to take the appropriate action himself. This inevitably creates disorder in both the public and domestic sphere, suggesting that the proper maintenance of social roles is essential for the health and stability of both. Aristophanes' *Lysistrate* and *Assembly-Women* operate in this way as well. The term "female intruder" is sometimes used in this study of Greek drama, a misleading one, perhaps, since women as well as men have a stake in the life of a healthy *polis*. Greek drama was particularly effective at exploiting the imbalance that undermined a *polis*.

Other studies in the area of women's themes or gender studies focus on the issues associated with a male taking on the dramatic role of a female, the reasons behind this convention, and the problems it creates for any simple equation being made between "real" women and the women of Greek drama. This leads us to consider one further approach to Greek drama.

Performance Criticism

Related to the idea of reception is a field of study dealing with the text as dramatic script and with the text in performance. Work in this area can proceed along several lines. One may attempt to reconstruct the staging of the play in the ancient theater of Dionysos. Another may consider the challenges faced in modern stagings of these ancient plays. But each will have to consider on a more theoretical level the ways in which meaning is produced and conveyed in performance.

Although there has been much work done on the ancient theaters in Greece, many questions remain unanswered concerning the form and features of the theater where our extant plays would have been performed. All attempts to provide a reconstruction of an ancient play in this space must therefore, of necessity, remain hypothetical. With that caveat made, there is still a sufficient amount of evidence about certain features of the competition to permit us to undertake a discussion of the stagecraft involved in ancient drama and to apply that information to a particular play.

Here familiarity with the conventions of the competition is crucial; things such as the "three actor rule," the use of masks, and the number of entry-ways into the *orchestra* will affect any reconstruction of the play. In the division of parts, one will have to consider how much time entrances and exits take, how much time would be required to make a costume change, how would an actor get from exit A to entry-way B in time. The answer to the first of these questions would be determined by where the character is in the *orchestra* when his exit occurs and whether the dialogue indicates a slow or a hasty withdrawal through a particular *eisodos* or through the *skene*. Decisions made concerning the positioning of actors in the *orchestra* may thus be affected by the needs of their next exit. But also affecting blocking (the positions of the actors relative to each other in the space) would be the presence of large objects such as the altar thought to have been located in the center of the *orchestra* and whether the text demands that a person be at or near this object. A reconstruction of a play will likewise have to take into account the positioning and movement of the chorus as well as how many extras (non-speaking parts) are required by the text and where they will be positioned. Additionally, costumes must be considered, the use of small and large stage-properties taken into account, and a decision made as to whether there was a stage, and if so how high it was and how far it projected into the *orchestra*. There may have been a colonnade on the far side of the *orchestra* in the classical theater at Athens. If high enough, it will have cast a shadow into the crucial playing-area before the *skene*.

This may all sound rather mechanical; however, such reconstructions are not devoid of interpretative decision-making. In order to make decisions about staging that are not embedded in the text, and even when dealing with the execution of those that are, one's sense of the relationship of part to whole is invaluable, as is some theoretical understanding of how meaning is produced and conveyed. Things such as power dynamics in spatial relationships must be considered. The symbolism of colors and different types of materials will also be a factor, as will the relationship between gesture, emotion, and vocal inflection. One will have to decide if certain lines were delivered in earnest or with ironic inflection. The aim of all of this is to attempt to come to an understanding of the stagecraft available to the ancient dramatist and how he employed it in conjunction with the spoken word to limit and direct the reception of his play by the audience. As examples of some of the symbolism at work in this ancient space, for *Oedipus Tyrannos* we can consider the possible identification of the spectators with the afflicted citizens of Thebes; the tableau of the three characters, each taking their own road at 1185; and the use of the *eisodoi* at 923, where all expect the summoned herdsman to enter from the "local" *eisodos* and a totally unexpected character enters by the other. The whole point of this drama is that humans must not make confident assumptions; here a visual symbol reinforces that point.

Many of the same decisions involved in reconstructing the performance of play in the ancient theater will still be important when reproducing an ancient play in a modern context. But the decisions are complicated by the issue of authenticity. Given that we have neither the same type of performance space nor the same cultural norms and language as the ancient playwrights and their audience, how much liberty can we take with the "script" before it is no longer ancient drama that we are producing? Has the very fact of the script's translation turned it into a different play? How many ancient conventions can we import into a modern theatrical space without confusing or alienating our audience? For instance, will a modern audience go along with the convention of the three-actor rule and all that it implies? Will they accept an all-male cast or be alienated by the masking convention and male voices for female characters? If it is impossible to re-create the ancient theater experience, should we attempt to get as close as possible or abandon the enterprise in favor of making the power of these ancient dramas come alive in a wholly modern context, perhaps even updating the plays to reflect modern concerns? Once we have adopted a position on these questions, we can begin the process of bringing our production to performance. And these questions are equally valid when assessing a performance of an ancient drama as a spectator.

Although each of these approaches has been presented as a separate and distinct way of engaging critically with the literary texts of Greek drama, in practice there is a great deal of overlap, especially among those approaches with their roots in anthropology. Each is in some way dependent upon or employs insights gleaned from alternate methods, but these are then shaped to serve the interpretative frame of the present interpreter. All contribute something, small or great, to the appreciation of Greek drama, of ancient Greek culture, and of our own. However, the most important approach to Greek drama, regardless of the methodology chosen, is the self-aware and self-critical approach. If the reader begins from the premise that his or her own responses to the dramas are inevitably shaped by his or her own preexisting belief systems and understandings of how the world works, and that the questions that are brought to the text are, in part, shaped by those understandings and beliefs, he or she will be less likely to universalize or to project anachronistically modern concerns and attitudes into the texts. The project is always partial, as we can never wholly disengage ourselves from the experiences that shaped us. We cannot get back to that original performance, cannot experience the play as a member of that first audience, cannot say with absolute certainty what any particular play "meant." But we can explore possibilities. And we can learn both to appreciate and to critique the insights that these various approaches to Greek drama and the culture that produced it afford us as modern readers.

6

Play Synopses

Aeschylus' *Persians* (*Persae*, *Persai*)

DATE: 472

COMPETITION: Aeschylus won with *Phineus*, *Persians*, *Glaukos of Potniai*, and *Prometheus Fire-Lighter* (satyr-play)

CHARACTERS: *Queen Mother of Persia, Messenger, ghost of Dareios, Xerxes*

CHORUS: *Persian elders*

SETTING: the tomb of Dareios before the Persian royal palace at Susa

SYNOPSIS: The chorus enter and describe the glory of the great army that the Persian king Xerxes, son of Dareios the Great, has led against the Greeks and wonder with some concern how it has fared. The queen mother enters, distressed by a dream and by a waking vision, and asks about this city of Athens which her son is attacking. A messenger arrives to report that Xerxes was tricked into fighting by a deceitful message from the Athenian side, that the Persian fleet has been decisively defeated in a sea-battle at Salamis, and that Xerxes with the remnants of his forces is making his way back to Susa. In grief the chorus and the queen call upon the ghost of the late king Dareios. The specter appears and asks what has befallen Persia. The queen tells Dareios how Xerxes crossed over to Europe from Asia, bridging the waters and casting chains into the sea to subjugate the waves. Dareios reveals that Xerxes "has cast his thoughts too high" and has offended the gods with his pride and by destroying their temples. Finally Xerxes enters lamenting the loss of the flower of his army.

ANALYSIS: This is the earliest extant play that we possess, and certainly its structure and style are less developed than Aeschylus' later plays. It needs only two actors and no scene-building and the chorus takes a particularly prominent role. Three things will interest the student of this play. First, its subject is not taken from traditional myth but from recent history. Aeschylus' predecessor Phrynichus wrote such drama on two occasions, his *Phoenician Women* (476) covering the same ground as *Persians*. Second, history is treated as myth. Xerxes is the familiar tragic hero of Aeschylus who goes too far and offends the gods, and indeed the moral universe of the Persians is identical to that of the Greeks – "Zeus is the chastener of overboastful minds . . . cease sinning against the gods." Finally the play has much to do with Athens and her pride in the crucial battle of Salamis in 480. Athens is a city "subject to no individual," the critical battle is precipitated by a message from the Athenians (from Themistokles who was in a political crisis in 472), and the great victory is told from the point of view of the vanquished. In the play's crucial scene, the ghost of Dareios, in fact, warns Greece and Athens to remember the fate of the Persians and not to "lust after more, squandering your present prosperity."

Aeschylus' *Seven* (*Seven against Thebes*)

DATE: 467, part of a Theban tetralogy: *Laios, Oedipus, Seven, Sphinx* [satyr-play]

COMPETITION: won first prize

CHARACTERS: *Eteokles, Messenger, Antigone, Ismene, Herald*

CHORUS: *women of Thebes*

SETTING: the palace at Thebes

SYNOPSIS: The Argive army, led by Polyneikes, is at the gates of Thebes. Eteokles rallies the spirits of his terrified people and leads them in a prayer to the gods. A messenger reports that seven leaders command the Argive force, and in the central scene names and describes each to the king. Eteokles assigns an appropriate defender to each gate, finding that he has left for himself the seventh gate and his own brother, Polyneikes. He realizes that the curse of their father has in fact come to pass, confirmed by the chorus in a major ode, revealing that this trilogy has depicted the operation of a family curse over three generations. The messenger brings news that both brothers have killed one another. The bodies are brought back, escorted by the mourning sisters (Ismene, Antigone). The text concludes with a herald forbidding the burial of Polyneikes, but this is almost certainly a later addition influenced by Sophokles' *Antigone*.

ANALYSIS: It is obviously difficult to appreciate the entire trilogy from the basis of the last play only. Aeschylus was showing the destructive effects of a family curse and in this play we see it worked out on the third generation. Whereas the *Oresteia* trilogy operates with the sequence: action → reaction → resolution, this trilogy has no resolution at the end, but only the final working out of an inherited curse on a doomed family. A major difference from the story as told in Sophokles' *Oedipus* is that Laios is given a conditional oracle in Aeschylus, "if he would save his city, have no children," thus turning the story into one of disobedience and punishment. The play is slow-moving, almost archaic in its language and pace, and does not immediately appeal to modern audiences. The chorus of women, almost stereotypically frightened, provides a strong contrast to the male world of arms and violence that engulfs the city. We are made aware that forces larger than humans are at work here: Furies, curses, the justice of the gods, the inevitability that the two brothers will meet at the same gate, and the realization of this by Eteokles and the chorus. The play is dominated by Eteokles, who is both noble king and cursed son; in good Aeschylean fashion he works his fate out on himself, tragically and ironically as defender of his people.

Aeschylus' *Suppliants* (*Suppliant Women, Hiketides*)

DATE: between 466 and 459, with 463 being the favored date; part of the "Daughters of Danaos tetralogy," the other tragedies being *Egyptians* and *Daughters of Danaos*, with *Amymone* as the satyr-play

COMPETITION: won first prize

CHARACTERS: *Danaos, King of Argos (Pelasgos), Herald of the Egyptians*

CHORUS(ES): *the daughters of Danaos, their cousins the sons of Aegyptus*

SETTING: Argos

SYNOPSIS: Danaos and his daughters live in Egypt but are Greeks by descent. He has refused to allow the marriage between his daughters and their cousins, sons of his brother Aegyptus. Fleeing their home in Egypt, they arrive at Argos, from which their ancestress Io had come, and claim sanctuary, both as Greeks in descent and as suppliant refugees. King Pelasgos is faced with a difficult decision: to reject the suppliants, who are protected by Zeus, or accept them and risk conflict with the Egyptians. He will not make this decision without consulting and gaining the approval of his people. Danaos reports that Pelasgos has in fact persuaded his people to protect these suppliants and refugees. A threatening herald from the Egyptians arrives and attempts to coerce the maidens into leaving with him, but King Pelasgos intervenes to repulse this threat and take the Danaids into the protection of the city of Argos. Danaos commands his daughters to resist any attractions of desire or love, and the chorus (or part thereof) agrees to avoid marriage. A dissenting voice argues that Love is a powerful deity and one that must be respected.

ANALYSIS: We are again dealing with only one play of a trilogy, and here we are not certain whether our play is the first or second of that trilogy. Subsequent events are known: the defeat or death of Pelasgos, the forced marriage of the Danaids, the murder of all the Egyptians (save one) by their brides, and the trial of the one Danaid, who spared her husband, her acquittal and the establishment of a new royal dynasty in Argos. The god beneath this play is Zeus *Hikesios* (Zeus the god of suppliants), and the theme turns on the rights of refugees and the danger that accepting them will entail. If the date of 463 is correct, the play was written at a crucial time for Athens, the events that would lead to the reform of the Areopagos council and the full flowering of Athenian democracy. Thus when Pelasgos insists that a ruler cannot decide for the people (*demos*), the play may well be striking a responsive note in contemporary politics. A final theme is that of gender, since it becomes clear that the chorus is not just fleeing this marriage (with their cousins), but marriage in general. They are told that Love is not a god to be avoided, but by whom? A sub-chorus of handmaidens, the other half of a divided chorus, the sons of Aegyptus? In the later *Daughters of Danaos* Aphrodite herself will defend marriage by citing the most ancient of human myths, the marriage of Earth and Heaven. Danaos, we know from other sources, is refusing marriage for his daughters because of an oracle that he will be killed by his son-in-law. This will have been revealed in a later (or earlier) play.

Aeschylus' *Oresteia*

Agamemnon, Libation-Bearers, Eumenides; Proteus (satyr-play)

DATE: 458

COMPETITION: won first prize

CHARACTERS, CHORUS(ES), SETTING, AND SYNOPSIS: see the discussions of the individual plays.

ANALYSIS: The trilogy takes the form: action → reaction → resolution, and depends on a definition of *dike* ("Justice"), by which the "doer shall suffer, that is law." We see in the first play Agamemnon come home from Troy to be murdered by his wife, but the chorus have presented the previous events in this moral universe in such a way that we recognize that Agamemnon was both the gods' agent in bringing *dike* on the Trojans for their violation of the moral order and his own actor who willingly sacrificed his daughter and killed many on both sides in the war. At the end of *Agamemnon*, we realize the same about Klytaimestra, that she has punished her husband for her own motives and will be so in turn.

The second play keeps us in the same universe, as Orestes is directed by Apollo to bring justice (*dike*) for his father's death by killing his mother. Orestes admits that he too has his personal motives to carry out this act. The chorus sing how he was aided in her murder by "Dike, daughter of Zeus we call her, breathing destruction on her enemies." In both plays it seems that an end has been put to events, but almost immediately Orestes sees the Furies, "the bloodhounds of my mother's hate." But in the third play we run into problems, for the gods (at least the male-dominated Olympians) try to stop the wheel from turning one more time. Apollo purifies Orestes from his guilt, but that does not stop the Furies, ancient goddesses of vengeance, from pursuing him. Family vendetta, which will never end, is to be replaced by civic justice, the court of law whose word will be final and bring matters to an end (*telos*, an important word in this trilogy).

Here another major theme of *Oresteia* emerges, the gender-conflict between males and females of power. We see this early in *Agamemnon*, where Klytaimestra ("a man-plotting woman") dominates every character in the play and where women strike back for the violence done to them by men. This conflict seems to be resolved in the ambiguous figure of Athene, the goddess who dresses as a male, is a patron of violence, and "is always for the male." The Furies are persuaded by her not to devastate Athens with their curses, but to find a home here, where they will become the Eumenides ("the Kindly Ones"), dispensing fertility and blessing on the people.

Not all would concur in an optimistic reading of the trilogy, for the Furies are persuaded (with the threat of violence in the background) to become part of a new order which is profoundly patriarchal. The gender conflict is resolved at the expense of the female by Athena, a female of power like Klytaimestra and played by the same actor. Gods actually come on stage in *Eumenides*, and Apollo comes off poorly – he has told a man to kill his mother, his purification of Orestes has not rid him of the Furies, and his arguments in the trial are not compelling. *Dike* ("Justice") in the trilogy is rather more complicated than an opposition of blood-for-blood vendetta and trial by jury.

All would agree that this is one of the great works of Western literature. Cosmic in scope and brilliant in execution, *Oresteia* raises great issues, presents fascinating characters, and is resolved with great splendor, as the Furies don robes of purple and prepare to be escorted by men and women from Athens to their new home.

Aeschylus' *Agamemnon*

CHARACTERS: *Watchman, Klytaimestra, Messenger, Agamemnon, Kassandra, Aigisthos*

CHORUS: *elders of Argos*

SETTING: the palace at Argos

SYNOPSIS: A watchman on the roof of the palace at Argos sees the beacon announcing that Troy has fallen to the Greeks. The chorus in flashback narrate the fateful omen that attended the departure of the army, the dilemma of Agamemnon (sacrifice his daughter or abandon the expedition), and her awful murder at Aulis. Klytaimestra describes how the news of Troy has reached Greece. The chorus sing of the wrath of the gods against Troy in language that shifts to suggest their anger at Agamemnon over the war with Troy. A messenger announces that Agamemnon will shortly be home, but that Menelaos and his ships have vanished in a storm. As the chorus proclaim that Justice "brings all things to fulfillment," Agamemnon enters with his captive mistress, Kassandra. Klytaimestra persuades him to enter the house walking on a purple carpet, a symbol of the blood that he has shed. Kassandra laments her fate, formerly virgin servant of Apollo and now a king's concubine. She tells of the murder of Thyestes' children by Agamemnon's father, Atreus, and predicts the death of Agamemnon at Klytaimestra's hands. She goes inside and we hear the death cry of Agamemnon. The doors open to reveal Klytaimestra standing over the bodies of her victims, claiming vengeance for the murder of her daughter. Her lover, Aigisthos, Thyestes' only surviving son, enters to join in the triumph, but the chorus insist that this matter is not over.

ANALYSIS: Aeschylus' Klytaimestra dominates this drama. This is a magnificent portrait of a woman with power, a figure that must have terrified the audience and yet earns our grudging respect. The chorus, who have half of the lines, create the moral universe in which "the doer must pay; that is law": this is *Dike* or Justice. Agamemnon is essentially a minor character, and when he enters his doom must already be sealed; the chorus show that he too is guilty of moral offences and must pay. Much of the power of the play is carried by the patterns of imagery, of which dark/light, hunting and animals (especially the lion, the eagle, the dog, and the snake), and the dripping of liquids (tears, blood) recur in various fashions, flickering in and out with subtle shades of meaning. Kassandra stands at the intersection of past, present, and future, looking back to past horrors, and ahead to more. The play turns greatly on gender themes, for we see the harsh treatment of women by men (Iphigeneia, the women of Troy, Kassandra) and the reaction by the female. Klytaimestra dominates all the men in the play, and only Kassandra does not move at her beck and call.

Aeschylus' *Libation-Bearers* (*Choephoroe*)

CHARACTERS: *Orestes, Elektra, Klytaimestra, Nurse, Aigisthos, Attendant, Pylades*

CHORUS: *servant women*

SETTING: the tomb of Agamemnon; the palace at Argos

SYNOPSIS: Orestes has come home to Argos from exile with his friend Pylades. He makes an offering at the tomb of his father, Agamemnon, and withdraws as a group of women approach. Klytaimestra has had a disturbing dream, and Elektra has been sent by her mother to appease her murdered husband's wrath. Orestes reveals himself and is recognized by his sister. He tells her that Apollo has commanded him to avenge his father by killing his mother. In a grand *kommos*, brother and sister with the chorus re-create the moral universe of *Agamemnon* ("blood stroke for the stroke of blood") and summon the spirit of their dead father. In the second half of the play the scene moves to the palace, where Orestes and Pylades gain access by announcing the "death" of Orestes. Klytaimestra sends a nurse to fetch Aigisthos; the chorus intervene to have the nurse tell Aigisthos to come alone. He arrives and is promptly killed by Orestes. In a great confrontation Klytaimestra bares her breast and asks Orestes if he can kill his mother. Pylades unexpectedly speaks and reminds Orestes of the words of Apollo. After the off-stage murder of Klytaimestra, we see a tableau, reminiscent of the first play, Orestes standing over the bodies of his victims. He sees in his mind the Furies ("the bloodhounds of my mother's hate") and in madness rushes off the scene.

ANALYSIS: If *Agamemnon* was the "action," this play is "reaction," "blood stroke for the stroke of blood." Agamemnon and Orestes, played incidentally by the same actor, each finds himself in a dilemma imposed by the gods, each commanded to murder a female member of his family. One is in serious doubt about the moral universe, where a god commands murder, and the blood-for-blood vengeance seems to be sanctioned by Zeus. All of this, the chorus sing, was steered by Justice (*Dike*), the daughter of Zeus. The same powerful imagery pulses through this play (Orestes and Elektra as the "orphaned children of the eagle-father," the dripping blood from the Furies' eyes, the breath of Justice as "fury and death"), and one wonders where this will all end. A crucial opposition is found at v. 120, where Elektra wonders if she seeks a revenge-bringer (*dikephoros*) or a judge (*dikastes*), for in the next play revenge will yield to the order of civil justice. If the first part of the play preserves the same expansive pace of *Agamemnon*, the second half moves swiftly from scene to scene, until the action culminates with the confrontation of mother and son, "Stop, my son, respect this breast on which you nursed," "Pylades, what do I do, kill my mother?," and the surprising intervention of Pylades (speaking as the voice of Apollo) which turns this into a three-actor play.

Aeschylus' *Eumenides* (*Furies*)

CHARACTERS: *The Pythia (priestess of Apollo), Apollo, Orestes, Athena*

CHORUS(ES): *Furies (ancient goddesses of vengeance); Athenian men and women*

SETTING: the temple of Apollo at Delphi; the Acropolis at Athens; the Hill of War (Areopagos) at Athens

SYNOPSIS: The Pythia arrives at Apollo's temple to find a man with bloody hands (Orestes) inside surrounded by horrible sleeping creatures (Furies). Apollo sends Orestes to Athens to seek judgment there and then drives the Furies out of his shrine, regarding them as no better than animals. Orestes reaches Athens and takes refuge at the statue of Athena, followed by the Furies who surround him with a song of binding. His appeal to Athena is answered by her arrival, but surprisingly she does not reject the Furies outright and submits Orestes' case to a jury of twelve Athenian men. In the subsequent choral ode we begin to realize that the Furies have some justice on their side ("there are times when fear is good"). Apollo appears to defend Orestes and answer the charges of the Furies, who have the better of the arguments. The vote is evenly split, and Athena breaks the tie in Orestes' favor, because, although female, she is always "for the male." Orestes leaves swearing eternal friendship between Argos and Athens, while Athena and her citizens must deal with a chorus of angry Furies, who feel that these younger gods are robbing them of their rights. Athena persuades them to make their home in Athens, as guardians of order and bestowers of fertility. The Furies become Eumenides ("the Kindly Ones") and a court of law (the Areopagos Council) replaces the vendetta of blood justice.

ANALYSIS: Whereas *Agamemnon* has a slow pace and an archaic feel, this play positively races. By line 240 we are already in Athens, with much behind us and more to come. The structure is bold, two scene-changes and at one point the stage is completely bare. With the twelve jurors and another sub-chorus of women, the scene must have been crowded at the end. Where *Agamemnon* was set deep in the past world of myth, *Eumenides* bridges past and present and stops just short of present-day Athens. It was a brilliant coup by Aeschylus to make the Furies real and have them appear as the chorus, even more brilliant to identify them with the Eumenides ("the Kindly Ones") and thus alter the structure of the moral universe. The trilogy is also about coming home: Agamemnon comes home to die, Orestes to kill his mother, but in this play Orestes can now go home and the Furies finally find a home, in Athens. Topical Athenian issues are close to the surface: a controversial treaty with Argos in 462, the reform of the Areopagos Council (founded in this play by a god) which many regard as the beginning of true democracy, and the prayer of the Furies ("civil war shall not thunder in *our* city"), at a time when Athens was on the brink of internal conflict. Aeschylus does not take sides; this is not propaganda, but brilliant drama, made more compelling by the contemporary issues.

Aeschylus' *Prometheus Bound* (*Prometheus Vinctus, Prometheus Desmotes*)

DATE: unknown, if by Aeschylus late in his career (460–456)

COMPETITION: unknown

CHARACTERS: *Power, Hephaistos, Prometheus, Okeanos, Io, Hermes; Force* (silent)

CHORUS: *daughters of Okeanos*

SETTING: a crag in the Caucasus mountains, at the eastern end of the earth

SYNOPSIS: In the recent war between the older Titans and the younger Olympian gods, Prometheus (a Titan) had sided with Zeus and been largely responsible for the victory of the Olympians. When he learned that Zeus was intending to destroy the human race, he gave men fire, in this play a symbol of all human civilization and technology, and saved them from extinction. As punishment Zeus has Prometheus chained to and impaled upon a rock in the Caucasus Mountains. He is visited by the daughters of Okeanos (the god of the sea that surrounds the world) and then by Okeanos himself, to whom he justifies what he has done and foretells (his name means "fore thought") that even Zeus is subject to Necessity. Io arrives, the play's only human character, with whom Zeus has fallen in love, whom Hera has changed into a heifer and is cruelly driving around the world with fits of madness and pain. Io recounts her past and Prometheus predicts her future: she will end up in Egypt, be healed by Zeus, and bear him a son; her descendant (Herakles) will release Prometheus from his rock. He then tells the chorus his secret: by whom Zeus can be overthrown. Hermes, official emissary of the Olympians, arrives to wring this secret from Prometheus, but Prometheus refuses, and is catapulted into Tartaros by a violent tempest.

ANALYSIS: For the past generation the authorship of this play has been seriously questioned. In many ways it is more like a play by Sophokles in the 430s than a mature work by Aeschylus. Features of style and meter, the reduced role of the chorus, matters of staging, and the radically different concept of Zeus have led some scholars to conclude that this might be an unfinished work, perhaps completed by Aeschylus' son Euphorion, who won the prize in 431. Another play, *Prometheus Unbound*, certainly followed, and a *Prometheus Pyrphoros* ("Fire-Bringer") has been seen as the first or third play of a trilogy. The most significant feature of the play, apart from the controversy over author and date, is the concept of Zeus, who elsewhere in Aeschylus is the patron and dispenser of *Dike* (Justice) but here is a rough young ruler, with all the stereotypical arrogance of a tyrant. Did Zeus "evolve" in the later play(s), or was he simply forced into a deal to release Prometheus in return for the secret? Prometheus and his gift of fire represent great symbols in human existence: practical knowledge, "blind hope," the desire to progress and succeed against all odds, community and civilization": "all arts (*technai*) that humans have are owed to Prometheus."

Sophokles' *Ajax* (*Aias*)

DATE: probably the early 440s

COMPETITION: unknown

CHARACTERS: *Athene, Odysseus, Ajax, Tekmessa, Soldier, Teukros, Menelaos, Agamemnon; Ajax' son* (silent)

CHORUS: *sailors from the ships of Ajax*

SETTING: the tent of Ajax, in the Greek camp before Troy

SYNOPSIS: Ajax, a hero of the traditional sort, a man of action and honor, was second only to Achilles among the Greeks at Troy. When Achilles died, Ajax and Odysseus contended for his armor, which was won by Odysseus. In a fit of mad anger Ajax attacks the leaders of the Greeks, but Athene tricks him by substituting cattle and sheep, which he slaughters thinking they are his enemies. The chorus and Tekmessa (his wife) bring him to his senses. When he realizes the truth, he is greatly ashamed and debates his future. He appears to accept his wife's pleas to live with his grief and shame, to submit himself to the gods and the leaders of the Greeks, but after a moving soliloquy falls on his sword. His body is found by Tekmessa and the chorus, who communicate the bad news to Ajax' brother (Teukros). The second half of the play deals with the burial of the hero, since Menelaos and Agamemnon, the leaders of the Greeks and Ajax' great foes, forbid the burial of one who took arms against his own side. In a pair of debates Teukros reminds the Greeks of Ajax' great exploits, and finally Odysseus takes his enemy's side and insists that Ajax be buried with proper honors.

ANALYSIS: Some see the structure of the play as a pair of disjointed halves, with title character dead by the mid-point. But the theme is also the death and burial of a hero, and the first actor will play the brothers Ajax and Teukros, thus providing a unity in production. As in *Philoktetes*, two sorts of heroism are seen: the traditional hero of strength and honor and a more modern sort, given to thought and expression, but in *Ajax* the old is found wanting and the new more enlightened. Ajax (as well as Teukros and the sons of Atreus) operates on the traditional ethical distinction of helping friends (*philoi*) and harming enemies (*echthroi*) – even at the end Teukros will not allow Odysseus, Ajax' great rival, to participate in the burial – while Odysseus expresses both respect and pity for Ajax ("though he is my enemy, I pity him") and sees that he could just as easily be in the position of Ajax. There is also an Athenian connection, since Ajax' home, Salamis, was now part of Attica and Ajax himself one of the ten tribal heroes of Athens. Sophokles had to give Athens a hero whose greatness they could recall with pride, but as so often in Sophokles, greatness attracts disaster. Ajax is a hero out of touch with modern reality, and therein lies his tragedy.

Sophokles' *Antigone*

DATE: probably 443 or 442, although a case can be made for 438

COMPETITION: won first prize

CHARACTERS: *Antigone, Ismene, Kreon, Guard, Haimon, Teiresias, First Messenger, Eurydike, Second Messenger*

CHORUS: *elders of Thebes*

SETTING: the palace at Thebes

SYNOPSIS: It is the morning after the Argive army has attacked Thebes and been defeated. Oedipus' two sons, Eteokles and Polyneikes, have killed each other, and the new king, Kreon, their uncle, has decreed that Eteokles, who died defending his city, shall be buried with full honors, while the traitor Polyneikes is to be left for the dogs and birds to devour. Antigone fails to persuade her sister Ismene to defy the edict, and leaves to bury her brother's body herself. After Kreon enters and gives the chorus his views on the priority of the state, a guard announces the mysterious burial of the body. The guard will return later with Antigone, having caught her giving funeral rites to the body. Antigone defies her uncle, claiming the priority of the gods' unwritten laws (as opposed to his "edicts") and the rights of one's *philoi*. Haimon, Kreon's son, enters to plead for Antigone, to whom he is betrothed, but Kreon pronounces her death sentence: to be walled up in a cave. In a very moving *kommos* with the chorus, a much subdued Antigone laments her fate "for doing what was right" and is led away to die. The blind prophet, Teiresias, enters to proclaim that Kreon has confused the worlds of the living and the dead, and that all Thebes is polluted by the unburied corpse. Kreon departs to bury the body and to release Antigone, but arrives at the cave to find Antigone dead by hanging in the arms of Haimon, who attacks his father and then kills himself. On hearing the news, Kreon's wife Eurydike hangs herself, leaving a distraught Kreon to realize that he has got it all wrong.

ANALYSIS: One of the greatest of Greek dramas, and not easy to appreciate fully. Is this a play about Antigone, or Kreon? Is there a "tragic hero" in this play? In Kreon we seem to have a typical tragic hero, who collaborates in his own downfall, but in Antigone an innocent who also perishes. Hegel saw the play as dramatizing two "rights," the claim of family and the claim of the state; others see her as right and Kreon as obviously wrong – but Teiresias never says she was right. Is this then a play of two unsympathetic characters who are fated to collide? What would an ancient audience have made of Antigone? We see her as the sympathetic and lonely martyr, but to the fifth-century male audience she was a dangerous woman meddling in men's affairs and upsetting the order of the *polis*. The play responds well to a structuralist approach, as the sides can be divided neatly into male/female, state/family, logical order/emotion, light/dark, life/death, with even the physical staging playing a role here, the visible palace representing order and civilization and unseen off-stage the world of the dead, where all the characters come and go.

Sophokles' *Trachinian Women* (*Trachiniai, Women of Trachis*)

DATE: unknown – placed as early as 450 or as late as 410; probably late 430s

COMPETITION: unknown

CHARACTERS: *Deianeira, Nurse, Hyllos, Messenger, Lichas, Old Man, Herakles; Iole* (silent)

CHORUS: *women of the city of Trachis*

SETTING: the city of Trachis (in central Greece)

SYNOPSIS: Because of her beauty, Deianeira, the wife of Herakles, had been sought by many suitors. One of these, the centaur Nessos, was killed by Herakles, who then claimed her as his bride. Years later she and her children are exiles in Trachis because of an act of violence by Herakles. Alone now for over a year, she wonders what has become of Herakles and sends her son Hyllos to find out. News arrives that he has conquered the city of King Eurytas in Euboia, and captives arrive from that sack, including Iole the king's daughter. Deianeira learns from Lichas that Herakles has sacked that city, not because he had been insulted, but because he wanted the king's daughter. In jealous despair, she sends Herakles a robe anointed with blood from the centaur's wound, which turns out not be the love charm she thought but an incurable poison. Hyllos brings news of what the robe has done to Herakles, and Deianeira kills herself with a sword. Herakles is brought on stage in great pain, cursing his wife and asking Hyllos to marry Iole and then to light the funeral pyre that will put him out of his agony.

ANALYSIS: Perhaps the most Euripidean of the surviving plays of Sophokles, full of the monstrous and with a cruel god (Eros – Love) beneath the action. Beauty and love are seen as irrational forces affecting the lives of men. At the end Hyllos blames the gods for what has happened to Herakles ("There is nothing here that is not Zeus"), and even the prospect of Herakles' apotheosis is left uncertain. There is no guarantee in the drama that the pyre on Mount Oita is Herakles' gateway to godhood. It is more than a little ironic that what destroys Herakles is no monster or armed opponent, but the weak woman he despises – all the more striking since the same actor played both Herakles and Deianeira. This may be Herakles' first appearance in tragedy – he was a frequent character in comedy and satyr-play; if so, it is the presentation of a bestial and unattractive hero, in perfect company with the monsters he conquers. This play responds well to structuralist criticism, balanced as the setting is between the civilized world and that of the wild and the monstrous, and its characters between order and disorder. Trachis is "a city on the edge of forever," poised between civilized Greece and the wilderness. Gender themes loom large in this play. Deianeira is the polar opposite of Klytaimestra, but achieves the same effect, the destruction of her husband, and her own death-weapon is a sword, not a woman's usual means of suicide.

Sophokles' *Oedipus Tyrannos* (*King Oedipus,* *Oedipus Rex, Oedipus the King*)

DATE: before 424 – the plague at the start of the play *may* reflect the plague that struck Athens early in the War (430–425); most scholars argue for 429 or 427–5.

COMPETITION: Sophokles' presentations finished second to Philokles.

CHARACTERS: *Oedipus, Priest, Kreon, Teiresias, Jokasta, messenger from Corinth, Theban herdsman, Messenger; Antigone, Ismene* (silent)

CHORUS: *elders of the city of Thebes*

SETTING: before the royal palace at Thebes

SYNOPSIS: Oedipus, the great and prosperous king of Thebes, has in all ignorance committed the horrible crimes of killing his father (Laios) and marrying his mother (Jokasta). The play opens many years after Oedipus, by solving the riddle of the Sphinx, had saved Thebes and become its king. A plague on fertility has struck Thebes, and Kreon (Jokasta's brother) brings from the oracle of Apollo at Delphi the proclamation that the murderer of Laios must be discovered and driven out. Oedipus pronounces a formal curse on that man. Teiresias enters reluctantly and after an angry exchange declares that Oedipus himself is the guilty party. Oedipus concludes that Kreon and Teiresias are conspiring against him, and Jokasta intervenes as the two quarrel. Her comments about the unreliability of oracles and the history of Laios lead Oedipus to suspect that he may indeed have killed Laios, in self-defence, at a place where three roads meet. They send for a herdsman who survived the encounter, but in the meantime a messenger from Corinth arrives to announce the death of Oedipus' "father" and in trying to remove his fear concerning his mother reveals that Oedipus was not the son of Polybos and Merope of Corinth. The messenger in fact had received the infant Oedipus from a Theban herdsman, the very same man whom they have summoned concerning the murder of Laios. This herdsman reluctantly reveals that Oedipus was the son of Laios and Jokasta. Jokasta hangs herself and Oedipus blinds himself now that he sees the horrible truth.

ANALYSIS: Aristotle regarded this as one of the greatest of classical tragedies. In no other play does the theme of knowledge, carried by the imagery of light and dark, operate so strongly, and with it the powerful dramatic irony ("I will fight for Laios as if he were my father") that underpins this tragedy. Sophokles creates a moral universe not of crime and punishment, but where an essentially innocent man suffers dreadfully. Oedipus' "guilt" is not one of character – he is essentially a great man – but intellectual – he thinks he knows when he does not. The first syllables of his name relate to the Greek verb *oida* ("I know"). The very economy of the plot adds to the horror: the same man who took Oedipus as a child will reveal the dreadful truth in the end. More than one scholar has seen an Athenian dimension: Knox that Oedipus represents Athens, Ewans that he recalls Perikles, and Wiles that "there is no room in a democratic society for such as Oedipus." The god beneath this play is Apollo, god of light and knowledge, whose oracles provide the motivating action for the plot.

Sophokles' *Elektra* (*Electra*)

DATE: a matter of great uncertainty, but 418–410 seem most likely.

COMPETITION: unknown

CHARACTERS: *Orestes, Paidagogos, Elektra, Chrysothemis, Klytaimestra, Aigisthos; Pylades* (silent)

CHORUS: *women of the palace*

SETTING: the palace of Agamemnon at Mycenae

SYNOPSIS: Orestes returns home to Mycenae with the faithful tutor (*paidagogos*), to whom his sister Elektra entrusted him after their father's murder. Elektra appears and laments with the chorus her own state, the murder of her father, her relationship with her mother and Aigisthos, and especially Orestes' long absence. Her sister Chrysothemis can live with this situation, but she cannot. Klytaimestra upbraids her daughter for being outside alone and for so constantly going on about her situation. The tutor enters to tell Klytaimestra and Elektra the (false) tale that Orestes has been killed at Delphi. A stricken Elektra vows to take revenge herself. Chrysothemis appears to tell of offerings placed on the tomb of Agamemnon, but Elektra is convinced that they mark the death of Orestes. Finally Orestes enters with an (empty) urn supposedly containing his ashes. A recognition finally occurs, the token being their father's signet-ring, and with Elektra standing stage center Orestes and Pylades enter the palace and kill Klytaimestra. Aigisthos appears to learn more about the "death" of Orestes, but finds only the body of Klytaimestra and his own death awaiting him.

ANALYSIS: One approach will be that of "version," since we have the dramatic treatments of the same plot by Aeschylus (*Libation-Bearers*) and Euripides (*Elektra*). The relative dates of the two Elektras are an intriguing but ultimately unsolvable problem, although it now seems more likely that Sophokles' is the later version. Most interesting is the portrayal of the principal characters: the weakest Klytaimestra, an unpleasant and unfeeling Orestes, and an Elektra who keeps herself going with one aim: the return of her brother to wreak revenge. Sophokles seems to be giving us a study of an obsessed heroine, whose one hope is first dashed and then fulfilled. Does this Elektra have anything to live for once the murders are done? There seem to be no Furies in this version, although Elektra herself has been like a Fury to her mother, and Apollo is all but invisible. When props occur on the Greek stage, they are full of significance, none more so perhaps than the empty urn that Orestes carries, supposedly containing his own ashes. Sophokles reverses the order of the murders, making the death of Aigisthos the climax, and returns the locale to Homer's Mycenae.

Sophokles' *Philoktetes* (*Philoctetes*)

DATE: 409

COMPETITION: first prize

CHARACTERS: *Odysseus, Neoptolemos, Philoktetes, Merchant, Herakles*

CHORUS: *sailors from the ship of Neoptolemos*

SETTING: the deserted island of Lemnos

SYNOPSIS: The Greeks have been besieging Troy for ten years and discover that they cannot take the city without the presence of Philoktetes and the bow of Herakles. They (especially Odysseus and the sons of Atreus) had left him ten years ago on the deserted island of Lemnos, with an agonizing wound that would not heal. Neoptolemos, the young son of Achilles, and Odysseus are sent to fetch him. The youth would prefer to use force or to persuade Philoktetes, but Odysseus insists that only deception will succeed. Neoptolemos meets Philoktetes and hears how he has heroically prevailed for ten years over loneliness and pain, but still tells his false tale that he is fleeing Troy. A merchant enters with a lying story that Odysseus is on his way to Lemnos to fetch Philoktetes. Before they can leave, Philoktetes has a paralyzing attack of pain, and before he passes out, gives the bow to the youth, who promises to keep it until the hero wakes. Neoptolemos keeps his promise, and when Philoktetes revives, tells him the entire truth. Odysseus enters and escorts the youth (with the bow) away, but Neoptolemos returns, hands the bow back, and asks Philoktetes formally to come to Troy. Philoktetes refuses ("it is not the past I fear but the future"), and it seems that Neoptolemos will take him back to Greece; at this point Herakles appears, promising healing for Philoktetes and success for the Greeks.

ANALYSIS: In no other Greek play does character count for so much. We see two types of heroism: the traditional nobility of the man of action and the modern attitude that words are mightier than the sword. Neoptolemos is the young hero coming of age, who must decide where his priorities lie, but the central character is Philoktetes who shows how a true hero will triumph over adversity. To be sure, Sophokles does not make the case clear cut, since many will feel that his final refusal goes too far, that he is as extreme as those whom he detests. The ending promises a less than ideal future, since Neoptolemos is warned to avoid offending the gods when Troy falls – he will kill Priam at the altar of Zeus. The first and second actors play only one role each, and the third three very similar parts (Odysseus, Merchant, Herakles), and it is with difficulty that we accept Herakles as a true *deus ex machina*, as opposed to being Odysseus' last and final scheme. Dion of Prusa (ca. AD 100) acquaints us with earlier treatments of the story by Aeschylus and Euripides (431) and here we again encounter the issue of "version," for Sophokles makes considerable changes to the myth, including the presence of Neoptolemos on the mission and the fact that Lemnos is a deserted island.

Sophokles' *Oedipus at Kolonos* (*Colonus*)

DATE: produced posthumously in 401, written in 407/6

COMPETITION: unknown

CHARACTERS: *Oedipus, Antigone, Stranger, Ismene, Theseus, Kreon, Polyneikes, Messenger*

CHORUS: *men of Kolonos*

SETTING: the grove of the Eumenides at Kolonos, a village just outside Athens

SYNOPSIS: After many years of wandering the blind and accursed Oedipus and his daughter Antigone arrive at Kolonos, near Athens. Upon hearing from a stranger that he has reached the grove of the Eumenides (the Dread Goddesses), he realizes that he has reached the end of his journey. The chorus are at first appalled to learn that this is the cursed Oedipus, but after hearing his plea agree to let the king (Theseus) decide. Ismene, Antigone's sister, arrives unexpectedly, bringing news that Kreon has been sent to bring Oedipus back to Thebes – an oracle has declared that his presence will aid any city that possesses him – then Theseus arrives and grants Oedipus refuge in his kingdom. Kreon has already taken Ismene prisoner and carries off Antigone, leaving Oedipus alone. The chorus summon aid from Theseus, who rescues Oedipus' daughters and announces that a stranger from Argos wishes to speak with Oedipus. This is Oedipus' estranged son, Polyneikes, who asks his father to help him regain his rightful rule in Thebes, but a furious Oedipus rejects him and curses both his sons. Thunder now echoes through the grove and Oedipus then realizes his time has come. Only Theseus witnesses the final fate of Oedipus, who at last comes to his rest.

ANALYSIS: Sophokles' last play finally ends the story of the cursed Oedipus. The playwright has added unexpected elements to the story (the arrival of Ismene and Polyneikes, a blustering and arrogant Kreon). We see Oedipus go from the helpless blind man led by his daughter to the man who strides confidently on his own to meet his destiny. He will become a "hero," a mortal worshiped with honors and sacrifices, and we witness the change from suffering human to something more than man. Heroes in Greek myth are traditionally angry, and in his response to Kreon and then to Polyneikes he begins to assume this status. As with Philoktetes, we wonder whether his anger is too much, as his furious response will doom not only his sons but also Antigone. Kolonos was Sophokles' birthplace, and a magnificent choral ode celebrates the beauty of that place. The play continues the repeated theme of Athens as the place where suppliants and fugitives may find refuge, although in this play Athens is ruled by King Theseus, and is not the democracy it is elsewhere.

Euripides' *Alkestis* (*Alcestis*)

DATE: 438

COMPETITION: Euripides finished second (to Sophokles) with *Cretan Women, Alkmaion through Psophis, Telephos,* and *Alkestis.*

CHARACTERS: *Apollo, Thanatos (Death), serving-woman, Alkestis, Admetos, their son [Eumelos], Herakles, Pheres, servant*

CHORUS: *old men of Pherae*

SETTING: Pherae (a city in Thessaly), where Admetos is king

SYNOPSIS: Apollo has arranged that Admetos can avoid his death, if he can persuade someone else to die in his place. Only his wife, Alkestis, is agreeable, and the fatal day has now arrived. Death arrives to claim his victim. The dying Alkestis requests a favor of her husband: that he not marry again. He promises not only not to marry but to banish all entertainment and joy from his palace. After her death his friend Herakles arrives, expecting hospitality. Over the objections of the chorus, Admetos welcomes him, keeping secret the death of his wife. After a vicious interchange between Admetos and his father Pheres, whom Admetos had expected would die in his place, the funeral procession moves off. A drunken Herakles emerges, but sobers up rapidly when he learns the truth from a servant. Admetos returns from the funeral, realizing that he has made no good bargain in accepting Apollo's favor, that Alkestis in death is happier than he in life. Herakles returns leading a veiled woman, whom he hands over to a reluctant Admetos. She turns out to be Alkestis, rescued by Herakles by wrestling with Death for her life.

ANALYSIS: The principal problem is the nature of the play. It was produced in the fourth position and should therefore be a satyr-play, but there are no satyrs. Instead the background is that of European folk-tale, and although we get a carousing Herakles in the manner of satyr-play or comedy, the tone is at times tragic. How then should it treated, as tragedy, comedy, quasi-satyr-play, Euripidean experiment? Why does Alkestis die for her husband (duty, glory, love)? Does he deserve the happy ending that we seem to get? Admetos had a reputation for "virtue" in classical Greece. How "virtuous" is he in this play? He promises his dying wife that he will banish all joy and merriment from his palace, and ironically breaks this commitment when Herakles arrives. He makes a good point that he did not wish to add inhospitality to his other woes, but then spoils it by reminding the chorus that he is well treated when he goes to Herakles' home ("and Argos is a thirsty land"). Why does Alkestis not speak at the end? What sort of life will she and Admetos have in the future? One of the principal themes in the play is *charis* ("thanks," "debt," "reciprocity"), as characters repay the obligations that they have incurred.

Euripides' *Medea*

DATE: 431

COMPETITION: Euripides finished third, with his *Medea, Philoktetes, Diktys,* and *Harvesters* (satyr-play).

CHARACTERS: *Nurse, Tutor, Medea, Kreon, Jason, Aigeus, Messenger; the two sons of Medea and Jason* (silent)

CHORUS: *women of Corinth*

SETTING: Corinth

SYNOPSIS: Medea and Jason have arrived as exiles in Corinth, where Jason has decided to marry the king's (Kreon) daughter. Medea has sacrificed everything in her love for Jason (home, family), and is furious with him and with Kreon. To forestall her anger Kreon banishes her and her two children by Jason immediately from Corinth. The nurse and tutor worry about her state of mind, but when she appears to meet the chorus, she is marvelously cool and self-possessed. She pleads with Kreon and gains one day to arrange her affairs, has a violent scene with Jason, who tries to argue that he was only acting for the best, and then in a chance encounter with Aigeus (king of Athens) manages to arrange sanctuary with him. Then she announces her plan: to send a poisoned robe to Jason's new bride, and then to kill her children. The children are sent to the palace with the fatal gift, and then in a great scene Medea changes and re-changes her mind about killing the boys. Eventually her anger wins over her maternal love. A messenger announces not only the agonizing death of Jason's bride but also that of Kreon as well. Medea goes inside to kill her children, whose murder is heard off-stage. Jason enters to take his vengeance, but encounters Medea above the *skene* in the chariot of the Sun, with the bodies of her children.

ANALYSIS: Euripides' most powerful character, with so much against her: being a woman, a foreigner, and a witch. Yet she attracts the sympathy of the chorus and that of the audience for much of the play ("I would rather stand three times in the line of battle than bear one child"). Euripides seems also to have changed the plot in having Medea kill her own children. This must have horrified the ancient audience as they watched it unfold. Gods are very absent in this play – there is no *deus ex machina* at the end, only a powerful *femina ex machina*. Euripides presents a Medea who is essentially not at home in Greece, who changes from scene to scene (rational with the chorus, fawning to Kreon, furious with Jason, wise woman with Aigeus, very divided mentally in her great soliloquy, and vengeful Fury at the end). He has taken the witch of Greek legend, made her into a living, breathing human being for a time, before returning her to her status of demonic creature at the end. The play also explores human psychology and behavior, for while Sokrates said that "no one does wrong knowingly," Medea declares, "I know that I am about do something wrong, but my anger is stronger than my thoughts."

Euripides' *Children of Herakles*
(*Heraclidae, Herakleidai*)

DATE: 430 (?) – vv. 1026–44 *may* refer to the limited Peloponnesian invasion of Attica in 431.

COMPETITION: unknown

CHARACTERS: *Iolaos, Herald [Kopreus], Demophon, Maiden [Makaria], Alkmene, Servant, Messenger, Eurystheus; children of Herakles Akamas the brother of Demophon* (silent)

CHORUS: *Men of Marathon*

SETTING: the temple of Zeus at Marathon, which was part of Attica in antiquity and whose people are thus Athenian citizens. The setting may be Marathon, but Athens is always kept before us.

SYNOPSIS: The children of Herakles, led by an old and decrepit Iolaos (Herakles' companion on his labors) take refuge at the altar of Zeus at Marathon from their pursuer, Eurystheus, king of Mycenae. A threatening herald ("Kopreus") is driven off by a sympathetic chorus of Marathonians and by Demophon, the young and noble son of Theseus, now king of Athens. A battle is inevitable, and one of Herakles' daughters (often called "Makaria") offers her life as a sacrifice for victory. In the battle the forces of Theseus triumph with ease; Iolaos is miraculously rejuvenated, and even demi-gods fight for the cause of right. Eurystheus is captured after the battle, and his life is spared by Demophon. But Herakles' aged mother, Alkmene, orders his execution in a surprising change of character from pathetic old woman to vindictive Fury. Eurystheus goes nobly to his death, promising to protect Athens from invasion by the descendants of Herakles.

ANALYSIS: The play is generally criticized for loose structure and uninspired writing, perhaps missing a scene describing the death of the maiden or another at the end. The ending is unusual as the play veers from a simple opposition of good and evil to a vicious revenge perpetrated by the previous helpless Alkmene and condoned by the Athenian chorus. The drama plays upon two of Euripides' favorite themes, the suppliant-drama with Athens as the champion of the oppressed and the supporter of justice, and the motif of self-sacrifice, where a young person gives their life for a higher and nobler cause (Iphigeneia, Menoikeus, Polyxene). Contemporary events may play a role, since Sparta invaded Attica in 431 (the first year of the Peloponnesian War), and the Spartans claimed to be the ultimate descendants of the children of Herakles whom Athens is shown here as protecting. If this play belongs ca. 430, then there are strong propagandist resonances with contemporary events. Eurystheus begins the play as the persecutor of the children of Herakles and then enemy of Athens, but by the end he will become a protecting influence on Athens, while maintaining his hatred of Herakles and his descendants. Is Euripides' drama an attempt to reassess a myth in which Athens took pride (Lysias 2.11–16) in the light of current events?

Euripides' *Hippolytos*

DATE: 428

COMPETITION: Euripides won first prize (other plays unknown). Note that this is the second *Hippolytos*, an earlier version (now lost) was produced in the late 430s.

CHARACTERS: *Aphrodite, Hippolytos, Old Man, Nurse, Phaidra, Messenger, Theseus, Second Messenger, Artemis*

CHORUS(ES): *women of Troizen; huntsmen, companions of Hippolytos*

SETTING: the city of Troizen, across the Saronic Gulf from Athens, where Theseus was raised and where his son, Hippolytos, has grown up

SYNOPSIS: Hippolytos, son of Theseus and "the Amazon woman," devotes his life to the service of Artemis, goddess of purity and chastity and of the hunt. Aphrodite, goddess of sex and passion, to punish the youth has made his stepmother (Phaidra) fall in love with him. Hippolytos has a brief scene with his companions and with an old man, who advises him to respect all gods. Phaidra enters, leaning on her aged nurse, who eventually gets her to reveal her problem: Phaidra is in love with her stepson (very much against her will). The nurse, believing that the best remedy is "the man," informs Hippolytos of Phaidra's love for him. Horrified, the youth launches into a tirade against women. Phaidra fears that he will tell his father, and takes her own life, leaving a note accusing the youth of attempted seduction. Theseus enters and, upon reading the note, curses his son with death or exile. In a hotly charged scene between father and son, Hippolytos maintains his innocence, but does not reveal Phaidra's love for him. He leaves, followed by his companions, into exile. A messenger announces that Hippolytos' horses were frightened by a "bull from the sea," and that the youth has been dragged to his impending demise. The dying Hippolytos is brought on stage. The goddess Artemis appears, blames Theseus for killing his son, and promises vengeance on Aphrodite. The goddess leaves, while father and son exchange forgiveness.

ANALYSIS: A brilliant drama, and full of avenues to explore. Why did Euripides rewrite the play? What changes did he make? This is an example of what is called the "Potiphar's Wife theme," but in this play the usual features of a "Potiphar's Wife story" are reversed. Can we psychoanalyze Hippolytos as an illegitimate son, an outsider, with a fear of sexuality? What of the gods, who come off very badly? As often in Euripides, humans have a higher moral standard than the gods themselves – humans forgive at the end, gods cannot. Euripides is not saying that Love and Chastity are not gods, they are forces in the universe and in the human personality, but they are not the anthropomorphic spiteful gods of traditional myth. We can read the play in a structuralist manner, noting the opposition of the restricting city and the unrestraining wild, of indiscriminate sexuality and chastity resolved in monogamy. Much of the play is carried by its dominant imagery: beasts and the hunt, water (both fresh and salt), escape and flight.

Euripides' *Andromache*

DATE: uncertain, but 427–423 will not be far wrong

COMPETITION: unknown. The scholiast on line 445 suggests that its first performance was not at Athens.

CHARACTERS: *Andromache, serving-woman, Hermione, Menelaos, Molossos, Peleus, serving-woman [nurse], Orestes, Messenger, Thetis*

CHORUS: *women of the palace*

SETTING: the palace at Phthia

SYNOPSIS: Andromache, the widow of Hektor, the great defender of the Trojans, has been given as a victory-prize to Neoptolemos, whose father Achilles had killed Hektor. Back in Neoptolemos' home in Phthia, as his (unwilling) mistress she has borne him a son (Molossos), while his actual wife, Hermione, remains childless. While Neoptolemos is away in Delphi, Hermione and her father Menelaos plot to kill Andromache and her child. Andromache is enticed from sanctuary at the altar of Thetis (the sea-goddess who was Achilles' mother), and is about to be slain by Menelaos, when Peleus (Achilles' aged father) intervenes in the nick of time. Now it is Hermione's turn to be threatened, as her husband is still absent and her father has deserted her. She too is rescued, by Orestes to whom she was engaged before her marriage to the son of Achilles. They flee together. Later word comes to Peleus that his grandson, Neoptolemos, has been murdered at Delphi by Orestes and a band of thugs. It is his turn to despair, and he is consoled in his grief by the epiphany of Thetis, his goddess wife, who foretells the destiny of Andromache and her son and their own reunion as husband and wife.

ANALYSIS: The play clearly falls into three movements, each depicting despair and rescue. But how much unity is there? The title character, Andromache, is present only for the first movement. Do we then brand the play as "episodic"? There are some uniting themes: rescue, domestic disharmony, the absence of Neoptolemos (whom some see as the main character), a repetition of despair followed by rescue and relief. Menelaos, Hermione, and Orestes form a nasty trio of Spartan characters (in contrast to the true heroism of the Trojans and the Phthians) and the play expresses several anti-Spartan sentiments, which some find appropriate to the background of the early years of the War, but which are also part of the larger theme of heroism in this drama. The role of the gods has been questioned, for while Thetis may be that rare creature, a truly benevolent Euripidean god, Apollo has sanctioned the murder of Neoptolemos in his own shrine. Euripides expresses a familiar theme in this drama: the horror and futility of war, as the chorus sing of the plague "that has dripped bloody thunder" on both Greeks and Trojans alike.

Euripides' *Hecuba* (*Hekabe*)

DATE: mid-420s

COMPETITION: unknown

CHARACTERS: *Polydoros, Hecuba, Polyxena, Odysseus, Talthybios, Servant woman, Agamemnon, Polymestor; two sons of Polymestor* (silent)

CHORUS: *captive women of Troy*

SETTING: a region of Thrace opposite to Troy

SYNOPSIS: Troy has fallen to the Greeks, Hecuba and the other captured women have started their journey to Greece and have paused in the land of Thrace, where Polymestor rules. There Polydoros, Hecuba's youngest son, had been sent for safety but was murdered by Polymestor as soon as he had the news of Troy's fall. Polydoros' ghost speaks the prologue. The chorus inform Hecuba that the Greeks are considering whether to sacrifice her daughter Polyxena as an offering to the dead Achilles. Odysseus and Hecuba debate the fate of her daughter, Polyxena entering to say that she will die gladly rather than endure the life of a slave. Talthybios, the herald of the Greeks, describes how she died nobly, and Hecuba asks that she be allowed to give Polyxena a proper burial. A servant woman brings in the body of Polydoros which they have found floating in the sea, and, her grief now doubled, Hecuba asks Agamemnon to allow her to take revenge on Polymestor. Polymestor and his two sons are enticed into the women's tent, where he is blinded and his sons murdered. Agamemnon judges a final debate between Polymestor and Hecuba and finds for Hecuba. Polymestor predicts the imminent demise of Hecuba as Odysseus' ship returns to Greece.

ANALYSIS: A play that leaves an unpleasant taste, *Hecuba* is a product of the war, when values and ethics were in question. Some find the plot clumsy with two episodes each dealing with the death of a child of Hecuba, but it is held together by a dominant motif of *peitho* ("persuasion"). We witness Hecuba taking part in three debates, the first for the life of her daughter (which she loses), the second with Agamemnon over revenge (the decision of which is moot), and the third with Polymestor over the revenge she has taken (which she wins). It is more than a little ironic that her one "victory" justifies murder and blinding. Greeks are set against foreigners (Trojans), and their modern pragmatic ethics, by which loyalty and self-interest are used to justify the murder of Polyxena and the lack of action against Polymestor. Odysseus puts it well in his debate with Hecuba ("live with it!"). On the personal level we see a study of a tortured woman who eventually succumbs to vengeance and is little short of the madness predicted by Polymestor at the end of the play.

Euripides' *Suppliant Women* (*Suppliants, Hiketides*)

DATE: usually dated to 423–420

COMPETITION: unknown

CHARACTERS: *Aithra, Theseus, Adrastos, Theban herald, Messenger, Euadne, Iphis, Athene*

CHORUS(ES): *mothers of the Argive dead at Thebes; a second chorus of Argive boys*

SETTING: the temple of Demeter and Kore at Eleusis in Attica

SYNOPSIS: Not just the body of Polyneikes, but those of the Argive invaders lie unburied on the field before Thebes. The mothers of the dead are led by Adrastos, king of Argos, to the sacred shrine of the Mother and Daughter at Eleusis to ask Theseus to aid them in recovering the bodies for burial. They are met by Theseus' mother Aithra and then by Theseus himself. Initially Theseus rejects their request, as Adrastos has engaged in a war of aggression against Thebes, but he is persuaded by his mother, who has taken pity on her fellow-women in distress. A herald arrives from Thebes, warning Theseus not to intervene, and the two debate contemporary politics (monarchy v. democracy). Theseus leads the Athenian army off to Thebes. A messenger recounts the Athenian victory and the recovery of the bodies, but it has been a bloody and costly fight. The bodies of five of the Seven are brought back and a eulogy delivered by Adrastos, in which these traditional "villains" are portrayed as brave citizens and loving family men. Euadne, the wife of one of these, cannot live without her husband and leaps upon his funeral pyre, as her horrified father (Iphis) watches. The play ends with Adrastos thanking Theseus and promising Argive friendship with Athens, and the goddess Athene appearing to encourage the sons of the dead to further war with Thebes.

ANALYSIS: This tragedy has much in common with *Children of Herakles*, but here the world is gray, not black-and-white. The suppliants are not totally in the right, nor the adversary totally in the wrong. The herald makes telling points against democracy, the battle is not a walk-over with the gods helping, the Seven are not evil monsters but decent sorts, Athene appears to demand a treaty between Argos and Athens "in writing" and to promise even more war. The Athenians took great pride in their intervention on the side of international justice, but Euripides does what he can to dramatize this incident in shades of gray. In the early 410s Athens and Argos would strike a military alliance – this may provide some background to the play. In 424 Athenian dead after the battle against the Thebans at Delion lay unburied; this would have cast long shadows on a tragedy about Thebes and burial of bodies in the late 420s. At one point Theseus is described as "general" rather than "king," a strong echo of the Athenian political system of the 420s.

Euripides' *Elektra* (*Electra*)

DATE: in dispute – earlier critics assumed 413, but 420 or 419 seems better

COMPETITION: unknown

CHARACTERS: *Farmer, Elektra, Orestes, Old Man, Messenger, Klytaimestra, Castor; Pylades, Pollux* (silent)

CHORUS: *local countrywomen*

SETTING: a farm cottage in the Argive countryside

SYNOPSIS: After the death of her father, Elektra has been "married" to a farmer (who has not consummated the marriage) and lives in a cottage in the farthest reaches of Argos. Orestes and Pylades enter cautiously to spy out the territory – Apollo has told him to return with stealth and kill his mother. Pretending to be a messenger from her brother, Orestes is welcomed by Elektra and the farmer, who sends for an old man who knew Orestes as a boy. This old man effects the recognition of a rather hesitant Orestes in a scene that parodies the recognition scene in Aeschylus. The old man and Elektra plot how to get Aigisthos and Klytaimestra out of the palace and accomplish their murders. A messenger reports how Orestes and Pylades killed Aigisthos as he was offering a sacrifice and invited them to join his feast. Orestes returns with the body of Aigisthos, and with Elektra sees his mother approaching. He expresses his doubts about the oracle that has commanded matricide, but Elektra has none. A bitter confrontation between mother and daughter leads to Klytaimestra's entry into the cottage, where she is killed by Orestes and Elektra. Brother and sister emerge, stricken with guilt and remorse. The Dioskouroi (sons of Zeus and brothers of Klytaimestra) appear to declare that Apollo's oracle "was not a wise one" and to announce the future fate of the participants.

ANALYSIS: This play is one of the best instances of intertextuality (or version), since it depends on and responds to Aeschylus' earlier *Oresteia*. The setting is the countryside, not the palace; the plan is not how to gain access, but how to lure them out; the recognition-scene (whose authenticity has been questioned by some) all but laughs at that in *Libation-Bearers*. What sort of man (or woman) could kill their mother? Not a hero as in Aeschylus, but only a flawed and neurotically unstable antihero. Elektra suffers from a self-imposed martyrdom, Orestes is a coward who really doesn't want to be there, a hospitable Aigisthos is murdered at a religious occasion, and this Klytaimestra is almost sympathetic ("perhaps I was too hard on my husband," "I know you, my daughter, and forgive you"). Apollo's oracle is explicitly described as "unwise" by a demi-god, and when Orestes says in the debate with his sister, "I will not believe that oracle was right," he will be proved correct. Whether this play is later or earlier (more likely) than Sophokles' *Elektra* remains one of the great mysteries of the study of Greek drama.

Euripides' *Herakles* (*Hercules Furens, The Madness of Herakles*)

DATE: 416 or 414

COMPETITION: unknown

CHARACTERS: *Amphitryon, Megara, Lykos, Herakles, Iris, Lyssa (Madness), Messenger, Theseus; sons of Herakles* (silent)

CHORUS: *elders of Thebes*

SETTING: the palace at Thebes

SYNOPSIS: Herakles has married Megara, the daughter of the king of Thebes, and is now absent on his famous Labors; meanwhile a usurper, Lykos ("Wolf"), has seized power in Thebes and is preparing to kill Megara and her children. Megara asks for time to prepare herself and her children, and as she and Amphitryon (Herakles' stepfather) pray for aid from Zeus, Herakles returns, having completed the last of his Labors. When Lykos returns to take Megara in to her death, he is murdered (off-stage) by Herakles. All seems to have ended happily, but on the palace roof appear Iris (messenger of the gods) and Lyssa (Madness), sent by Hera to continue her wrath against Herakles. Lyssa is unwilling to assail Herakles who has been a defender of the gods, but does her work at the insistence of Iris. A messenger describes how Herakles has gone mad and killed his family. We see a tableau of Herakles amid the bodies of his wife and sons, and with the aid of Amphitryon he returns to sanity and the ghastly realization of what he has done. His friend Theseus, whom he rescued from the underworld, arrives to take the stricken hero to Athens.

ANALYSIS: Euripides has made major changes in the traditional plot-line: the placing of the Labors before the murder of his family, the reason for the Labors (to atone for his stepfather's guilt), four of the Labors have been replaced with feats that stress Herakles' protection of humanity, the entry of Theseus into the story. The greatest change is in the character of Herakles, who is not the gluttonous and stupid figure from comedy nor the brute from *Trachinian Women*, but a suffering servant, who has protected humanity and served the gods. The gods loom large over this play, not just the appearance of Iris and Lyssa and the wrath of Hera, but the acquiescence of Zeus and Herakles' insistence that the unflattering stories about the gods are "the wretched tales of poets – a god, if truly god, needs nothing." There is no hint of an apotheosis in *Herakles* – given what we see of the gods, why would Herakles want to be one? As so often in Euripides, mortal views about deity are higher than the reality. The play has been criticized for falling into two distinct episodes, but it is linked by the theme of friendship (something that only humans can appreciate) and by the heroism and pure humanity of its title character. This is one of Euripides' most innovative and powerful dramas.

Euripides' *Trojan Women* (*Troades*)

DATE: 415

COMPETITION: Euripides finished second to Xenokles, with his *Alexandros, Palamedes, Trojan Women*, and *Sisyphos* (satyr-play).

CHARACTERS: *Poseidon, Athene, Hecuba, Talthybios, Kassandra, Andromache, Menelaos, Helen; Astyanax* (silent)

CHORUS: *women of Troy*

SETTING: the city of Troy

SYNOPSIS: Troy has fallen after a ten-year war. The sea-god Poseidon, who favored the Trojans, is saying farewell to his ruined city. Athene, the great supporter of the Greeks, offended by the ill-treatment of her temple by one of the Greeks, asks Poseidon's aid in wreaking vengeance on the Greeks during their return. Hecuba and the chorus now rise, lament their fate, and wonder what will befall them. Talthybios, the herald from the Greeks, announces that they have been allotted each to separate masters, the virgin Kassandra to Agamemnon and Hecuba to Odysseus ("the worst lot of all"). Kassandra in the grip of prophetic madness is taken forcibly to her master. Then Hektor's despairing widow, Andromache, enters with her young son (Astyanax). Hecuba persuades her to live for her son, who may one day rebuild Troy – Talthybios reenters to announce that the boy must die. Menelaos appears to take vengeance on his wife Helen for starting the whole war. Hecuba and Helen debate the latter's responsibility, with Menelaos declaring in favor of Hecuba but postponing his revenge until they reach Greece. Finally the body of the young Astyanax is brought in for what burial they can provide. Hecuba and the women leave as the walls of Troy are brought down in flames.

ANALYSIS: All three tragedies of 415 are set at Troy within the context of the War. Did Euripides write a loose "Trojan trilogy" in 415? If so, were there connecting characters and themes? Do contemporary events provide a background – the Athenian massacre of the Melians in 416/5 and the preparations for the great Armada that will leave on an aggressive overseas campaign to Sicily? The two gods who speak the prologue are in fact the two national gods of Athens. "Victors write the history books," but this story is told from the point of view of defeated foreign women. On several occasions in the play Euripides suggests that the traditional story-line may not happen (Astyanax is usually killed on the night Troy falls, Helen may in fact die at her husband's hand). What unity is there in a play that seems to be a series of bleak and hopeless episodes? There is a natural rise and fall in each of the four episodes (hopes raised, hopes dashed usually by the entry of a male from the Greek army), and by the end Hecuba and the chorus realize what we know from the start, that the gods exist but they don't care.

Euripides' *Iphigeneia among the Taurians*
(*Iphigeneia in Tauris*)

DATE: 414–411

COMPETITION: unknown

CHARACTERS: *Iphigeneia, Pylades, Orestes, Herdsman, Thoas, Messenger, Athene*

CHORUS: *Greek women*

SETTING: the temple of Artemis among the Taurians (in what is today the Crimea)

SYNOPSIS: In the prologue Iphigeneia tells us that she did not die at Aulis, but was taken by Artemis to her temple among the Taurians, where she prepares for sacrifice any Greek males who arrive on that shore. Not all the Furies have left Orestes, and to rid himself of them he and Pylades have been sent by Apollo on a mission: to bring back to Greece the statue of Artemis from the Taurians. A messenger tells Iphigeneia that two Greeks (one named Pylades) have been captured on the shore. Orestes and Pylades are brought before her to be made ready for sacrifice, but in a clever recognition-scene brother and sister learn the other's identity and together they plan the theft of the statue and their escape to Greece. She informs Thoas, the local ruler, that one of these Greeks has polluted the statue of Artemis by touching it with his hands stained with a mother's blood, and it must be washed in the sea. A messenger tells Thoas that the Greek was really Iphigeneia's brother and that their ship is attempting to escape. Athene appears to prevent the pursuit, predicts the future for Iphigeneia, and finally resolves the conflict over Troy.

ANALYSIS: Euripides did not make up the story that Iphigeneia did not die at Aulis, but he is clearly writing a "sequel" to *Oresteia*, in which not all the Furies acquiesce in the verdict and Orestes must go on another mission for Apollo. The play makes a nice pair with his earlier *Elektra*, for where Elektra is bitter and spiteful, Iphigeneia rises above her fortunes and remains loyal to her family and to Greece, and where *Elektra* ends on an unpleasant note, the *IT* ends with "Orestes sailing home on a calm sea." With *Ion* and *Helen*, it belongs to the sub-genre described by Conacher (1967) as "Romantic Tragedy." The principal themes include the motif of sacrifice (Iphigeneia has gone from one altar of blood to another) and that of illusion. Orestes thinks falsely that his sister died at Aulis, while Iphigeneia has had a dream which she interprets (falsely) as meaning that her brother Orestes is dead. This leads to the questioning of oracles and to Apollo's role in the story ("Phoebus the prophet lied to us"), although the critique of the gods is not as severe as in other plays. A brother–sister doublet operates neatly in that as Orestes brings his sister back to Greece, Apollo arranges that his sister (Artemis, or at least her statue) is returned as well. Greek notions of ethnic superiority are punctured by Thoas' reaction to the news that one of the captives has killed his mother, "no barbarian could do that."

Euripides' *Ion*

DATE: late 410s – 412 is often proposed

COMPETITION: unknown

CHARACTERS: *Hermes, Ion, Kreousa, Xouthos, Old Man, Servant, the Pythia, Athene*

CHORUS: *Athenian servant-women*

SETTING: before the temple of Apollo at Delphi

SYNOPSIS: Kreousa, daughter of the king of Athens, was raped by Apollo and had a child by him. She exposed the infant, which was rescued by Hermes and taken to Delphi, where the boy has grown up as the temple servant of Apollo. Kreousa is married to a foreigner (Xouthos), but they are childless. They journey to Delphi to consult the god, and the first person she meets is the boy, her son by Apollo, but neither is aware of the other's identity. Xouthos, a gruff no-nonsense type, arrives, consults the oracle, and is told that the first person he meets "going out" (Greek – *ion*) of the temple is his son. This, of course, is the boy, who is now named "Ion." Kreousa finds out from an old man that her husband has been given a son by Apollo. She sings a marvelous song of grief and accusation, recounting her rape at Apollo's hands, and then with the old man plots to kill Ion. A messenger announces that Ion escaped the poison meant for him, that the old man was captured, and that Ion is on his way to take vengeance on Kreousa. She takes refuge at the altar of Apollo, and is rescued by the priestess of Apollo (the Pythia), who shows Ion the clothes and jewelry found with him as an infant. Kreousa recognizes these as her own, and realizes that Ion must be her son. Before Ion can ask the oracle about the false prophecy to Xouthos, Athene appears to straighten out the last wrinkles in the plot and to predict a glorious future for Ion as king of Athens.

ANALYSIS: *Ion* is an example of "Romantic Tragedy," tragedy with a happy ending, where the catastrophe is not realized but averted. The play is not without touches of humor: Hermes retreating to watch from the shrubbery, Kreousa relating her misfortunes as those of "a friend," the gruff Xouthos embracing the innocent boy who misunderstands his approaches. Can tragedy end happily? Are there hints of a more serious theme? Kreousa and her serving-women actually believe that her grandfather sprang from the earth itself. In this play Athenian ethnic purity leads to attempted murder. The gods fare badly in this tragedy: the plot does not proceed as Hermes has predicted in the prologue, Apollo gives a false oracle to Xouthos, and then Athene has to show up to "cover" for her brother. But not all agree with such an ironic reading of *Ion* – many see Apollo's handling of the action as essentially benevolent, and on one level the play does provide patriotic propaganda – Ionians (who include Athenians) are descended from a god (Apollo), while other Greeks have only human forebears. On the whole, however, the broad strokes of comedy do not completely cover the darker side of this fine play.

Euripides' *Helen*

DATE: 412

COMPETITION: result unknown – produced with *Andromeda*, and perhaps *Ion*

CHARACTERS: *Helen, Teukros, Menelaos, Old Woman, Messenger, Theonoe, Theoklymenos, Second Messenger, The Dioskouroi*

CHORUS: *captive Greek women*

SETTING: Egypt

SYNOPSIS: The play follows the line of Stesichoros' *Palinode*, that Helen did not in fact go to Troy. A phantom was substituted in her place, while the real Helen was spirited off to Egypt, where a lustful king (Theoklymenos) has been eyeing her. The War is over, Troy has fallen, and a Greek from the War (Teukros) meets Helen in Egypt, hears her story, and tells her that she is universally hated for her part in the conflict. Menelaos arrives, shipwrecked along with "Helen" on the coast of Egypt, and sees this woman "who looks just like Helen." Eventually he is convinced of her story, and husband and wife are joyfully reunited. But how to flee Egypt? Helen and Menelaos beg the king's wise sister (Theonoe) for aid, and with her assistance a plan is devised. Helen tells the king that she has just learned that her husband (Menelaos) has died in the shipwreck, and requests a ship to scatter his remains at sea. Menelaos and his sailors seize the ship and sail off into the sunset, while Helen's brothers (The Dioskouroi) forbid the Egyptian king to interfere.

ANALYSIS: Is this "tragedy"? Tragedy can have a happy ending, but here Euripides seems to cross the line into comedy. Like *Ion* and *Iphigeneia among the Taurians* this play belongs to what has been called "Romantic Tragedy." But unlike these plays where characters are in danger, there is little potential for tragedy here. Another matter of note is the change in Helen, from object of loathing (as so often in tragedy) to sympathetic heroine. What Euripides has done, it seems, is to change Helen into Penelope, waiting patiently (and chastely) for her husband to rescue her. One more serious theme is that of reality and illusion, for things in this case are not what they seem or what people think – the Helen for whom the Greeks fought at Troy is an illusion fashioned out of air, prompting the messenger to exclaim, "we fought for ten years – for nothing?," and when they meet the real Helen refuse to believe their eyes. Theone is certainly Euripides' creation and it lies with her whether Helen and Menelaos will return to Greece; in deciding, she will choose the plan of one goddess (Hera) over that of another (Aphrodite). Her mysterious comment that "the mind of the dead may not have life, but falling into the deathless *aither* it has deathless understanding" may reflect contemporary speculation on life after death.

Euripides' *Phoenician Women* (*Phoinissai*)

DATE: 411–408

COMPETITION: unknown

CHARACTERS: *Jokaste, Antigone, Tutor, Polyneikes, Eteokles, Kreon, Menoikeus, Teiresias, Messengers, Oedipus; Teiresias' daughter (silent)*

CHORUS: *a group of women from Phoenicia on their way to Delphi*

SETTING: Thebes, at the time of the invasion by the Seven

SYNOPSIS: Both Jokaste and Oedipus are still alive and in Thebes. Oedipus' sons have put their father away, but his curses haunt them, that they will share their inheritance with the sword. Eteokles has failed to yield power to his brother Polyneikes after a year's rule, as they had agreed, and the latter has arrived to besiege his own city at the head of a vast army from Argos. Jokaste attempts to reconcile her two sons but fails. Kreon and Eteokles on information taken from an Argive prisoner plot the defense of Thebes. Kreon and his son Menoikeus encounter Teiresias, who tells Kreon that only the sacrifice of Menoikeus to the War-god will save Thebes. Kreon immediately plans to send his son away, but Menoikeus goes off to leap willingly from the walls of Thebes to save his city. News comes of the encounters at the seven gates and the destruction of the enemy leaders and that the brothers will decide the issue in single combat. A later messenger tells not only of the brothers' mutual doom but of Jokaste's suicide over their bodies. Finally the aged and blind Oedipus appears and is sent into exile by the new ruler, Kreon.

ANALYSIS: On the level of plot, this is a bold retelling of the story, with typically Euripidean invention (the survival of Jokaste and Oedipus, the sub-plot of Kreon and Menoikeus). Study of the play is complicated by the intrusion of later material into the text (especially at the end, where themes from Sophokles' *Oedipus* and *Antigone* intervene – even the second half of the prologue where Antigone and her tutor view the Argive army may be suspected). What we do have is a dramatic study of a cursed family, with all the conflicts and loyalty that *philia* may engender. Eteokles is wrong to have kept the kingship, Polyneikes to have attacked his own city with a foreign army, but Jokaste loves them both. Meniokeus by his self-sacrifice shows how one man can save the larger community. The tragedy also displays a brilliant mingling of the images of human and the monstrous (the dragon, the Sphinx).

Euripides' *Orestes*

DATE: 408

COMPETITION: unknown

CHARACTERS: *Elektra, Helen, Hermione, Orestes, Menelaos, Tyndareus, Pylades, Messenger, Phrygian slave, Apollo*

CHORUS: *women of Argos*

SETTING: the palace at Argos

SYNOPSIS: The Argives are threatening to put Orestes and Elektra to death for killing their mother. Their one hope is that Menelaos (who has just arrived with Helen) will intervene on their behalf. Elektra has been caring for her brother, driven mad by his murder of his mother, but he awakes and suffers an attack of the Furies. Menelaos enters and is aghast at his nephew's condition and promises help, but Tyndareus (Orestes' grandfather) appears and, furious with Orestes, promises to speak for his execution. Menelaos decides not to intervene, leaving Orestes without hope. Pylades returns to Argos and rouses Orestes to make a defense to the assembly. A messenger reports to Elektra that the assembly has decreed that they must die. Orestes, Elektra, and Pylades plan to die but also to take Helen with them; they then decide to take Menelaos' daughter Hermione hostage – and thus may be able to escape. Orestes and Pylades go into the palace, Hermione is lured inside, and a Phrygian eunuch crawls over the roof and announces (in song) that Orestes and Pylades have tried to kill Helen, but that her fate is unknown. Menelaos arrives to find Orestes and Hermione on the palace roof, with Elektra and Pylades holding torches to burn the palace down. Apollo appears on the *mechane* and announces that Helen has been taken to dwell among the gods, that Menelaos is to rule Sparta, and that Orestes and Hermione will marry and live happily ever after.

ANALYSIS: In no other surviving play does Euripides push so boldly at the boundaries of myth. The Furies are not real, as in Aeschylus, but figments of Orestes' guilty conscience; the trial by the Argives and the presence of Tyndareus are clearly his inventions, as are the attempted murder of Helen and the abduction of Hermione. Tyndareus admits that his daughter Klytaimestra killed her husband, but asks why did Orestes not resort to the rule of law – thereby undermining all that went on in *Oresteia*. His most brilliant coup is the Phrygian slave, the marginalized foreigner who sings the messenger speech and who provides a bizarre, black comic touch to the end. Throughout the play Apollo and his command to Orestes are blamed for the situation, and his appearance at the end does little to restore faith in him ("I was afraid," remarks Orestes, "that I was hearing the voice of a demon"). These are not heroes, and although Orestes and Elektra do enjoy the audience's sympathy, they become vicious fiends by the end, and one can see how they could well have killed their mother. On a psychological approach Elektra and Pylades can be seen as projections of Orestes' own personality, his emotional side (which dominates the first half) and his rational side (which plans the events of the latter half). In many ways this is Euripides' most brilliant piece of theatre.

Euripides' *Iphigeneia at Aulis*

DATE: produced after Euripides' death (perhaps 405)

COMPETITION: won first prize with *Bacchae* and *Alkmaion*

CHARACTERS: *Agamemnon, Old Man, Menelaos, Messenger, Klytaimestra, Iphigeneia, Achilles, Second Messenger; Orestes* (silent)

CHORUS: *women of Chalkis, who have come to visit the camp*

SETTING: the Greek camp at Aulis

SYNOPSIS: To get the winds to take his ships to Troy, Agamemnon must sacrifice his daughter Iphigeneia to Artemis. He has written to his wife to bring Iphigeneia from Argos on the pretext that she will marry the young hero Achilles, but now sends the old man with another letter, telling Klytaimestra not to come. The old man is intercepted by Menelaos, and a furious argument results between the brothers, Agamemnon refusing to sacrifice his daughter and Menelaos demanding the expedition to retrieve Helen. A messenger announces the imminent arrival of Klytaimestra and Iphigeneia, and Agamemnon's great distress at his situation changes Menelaos' mind; he will no longer push for the sacrifice. But Agamemnon realizes that the army will insist on the expedition and that his daughter is doomed in either event. Klytaimestra and Iphigeneia are greeted by Agamemnon, and then encounter Achilles who knows nothing of the proposed marriage. The old man reveals all to them, and Klytaimestra begs Achilles to save her daughter. Husband and wife debate the matter bitterly, the army ("the mob") demand the sacrifice, and even Achilles is powerless to stop them. Iphigeneia changes her mind and is now willing to die for her country so that the Greeks may conquer Troy. She asks only that her mother not hate her father, and then leaves to die.

ANALYSIS: A bold retelling of the myth by Euripides, giving Iphigeneia a voice and putting Klytaimestra in a new light. Heroism is deflated: Agamemnon becomes a war-leader almost running for office, Menelaos can think only of his personal honor, while Achilles, the greatest of the Greeks at Troy, is reduced to a cocky young hero who cannot influence events. Aristotle found Iphigeneia's change of heart hard to accept, and indeed some scenes have a feel of melodrama or glorified soap opera (Menelaos' sudden change of mind, Achilles glorying in his own reputation, and of course Iphigeneia's patriotic declamation). But underlying it all is the sense of fatigue and despair – Greeks had now been at war with each other for over twenty years, and to talk of Greek unity must have left a sour taste in the mouth. Events are totally out of control, and only the mob has real power; the heroes seem to be watching events pass by them. More than any other extant Greek play, the text is in real doubt as lines, speeches, and whole scenes have been added, especially at the end where the "happy ending" cannot be the original that Euripides wrote, while the prologue is an odd mix of anapestic dialogue, broken by an iambic soliloquy. The most recent editor presents four layers of text, from genuine Euripides to certainly not by Euripides.

Euripides' *Bacchae* (*Bacchants*)

DATE: produced after Euripides' death (perhaps 405)

COMPETITION: won first prize with *Iphigeneia at Aulis* and *Alkmaion*

CHARACTERS: *Dionysos, Kadmos, Teiresias, Pentheus, Attendant, Messenger 1, Messenger 2, Agave*

CHORUS: *female followers of Dionysos from the East*

SETTING: the palace at Thebes

SYNOPSIS: The god Dionysos, son of Zeus and a Theban princess (Semele), has come to Thebes to bring his worship to his home city. For not believing in him, the women of Thebes have been driven from the city to the mountain, while Dionysos, disguised as a human priest, awaits the appearance of the king, his cousin Pentheus. The seer Teiresias and Pentheus' aged grandfather (Kadmos) have donned the apparel of the new god and prepare to join his revels, but are rebuked by Pentheus. The disguised Dionysos is brought before Pentheus and then imprisoned in the stables, from which he escapes with consummate ease, as lightning and fire destroy the stables. A messenger brings Pentheus news of the women on the mountain, who exist in harmony with nature until the men attempt to capture them, at which point they run riot over the hillsides and surrounding farms. Pentheus prepares to lead out his army, but when Dionysos asks "Would you like to see them on the mountain?," he falls under the spell of the god. In the next scene Dionysos leads him entranced and dressed as a female worshiper off to the mountain. A messenger reports how Pentheus was discovered by the women and was torn apart by his own female relatives. Agave, Pentheus' mother, arrives carrying what she thinks is the head of a young lion, in reality the head of her son. Kadmos brings her back to reality and the horror of what she has done. Dionysos appears to justify his vengeance and to announce the future fate of the characters.

ANALYSIS: Arguably, the greatest of Greek tragedies, and one that has been vigorously debated by the critics. Is this a late realization by Euripides of a "real" religion, or is it an attack on Dionysos as an essentially hostile force to civilization? At the end Dionysos is clearly a typical Euripidean deity ("gods should not be like men in their passions"), a god for whom personal honor is all. Or do we look primarily at Pentheus and see a disturbed young man who has repressed the essential liberating force that is Dionysos? Dionysos can be a deity of great blessings, as the chorus and other characters keep reminding us, but if rejected, can be a god of great destruction – a powerful force then in the life of humanity. Much discussion involves whether to take the scene with Kadmos and Teiresias seriously or as near-comedy – remember that Kadmos' piety stems from wanting a god in the family and Teiresias reminds one of a smooth-talking contemporary sophist. The plot-line by which Pentheus goes in disguise to the mountain and is killed by his own family is very likely to have been Euripides' invention.

Euripides' *Cyclops*

DATE: unknown, both 425 and 408 have been suggested with confidence

COMPETITION: unknown (a date of 408 would mean that it accompanied *Orestes*)

CHARACTERS: *Silenos, Odysseus, Cyclops (Polyphemos); Odysseus' men* (silent)

CHORUS: *satyrs*

SETTING: the cave of the Cyclops on Mount Etna (Sicily)

SYNOPSIS: A parody of *Odyssey* 9, *Cyclops* adds Silenos and satyrs to the encounter between Odysseus and the Cyclops. Silenos recounts how he and the satyrs in search of Dionysus were ship-wrecked and forced to serve as shepherds for the Cyclops. There is no wine or merriment in their wretched lives. Odysseus and his sailors arrive, seeking food and drink which Silenos offers to sell them from the Cyclops' larder. They are interrupted by the return of Polyphemos, who refuses their request for hospitality, threatens to eat the humans, and disavows any fear for the gods ("I sacrifice to the greatest of deities, my stomach"). The Cyclops takes Odysseus and his men inside the cave, from which Odysseus returns to describe the murder of two of his men and the horrible meal of the Cyclops and to report that he has gotten the Cyclops (who has never encountered wine) drunk. He asks the satyrs' help in blinding the Cyclops and effecting their escape. The drunken Polyphemos lurches on stage, we have the obligatory *Outis*-scene ("my name is Nobody"), and Silenos is carried off as the Cyclops' bed-mate. The blinding takes place off-stage, and Odysseus flees with his men and the satyrs. When Odysseus' true name is revealed, the Cyclops realizes that an ancient oracle has come true.

ANALYSIS: This is the only complete satyr-play that we possess, and we must be careful not to assume that all satyr-plays looked like this. It is a parody of epic (*Odyssey* 9) rather than tragedy; in the 430s the comedian Kratinos had done a comic parody of the same material but without satyrs. It can be instructive to trace the development of the Cyclops, from savage monster in *Odyssey* 9 (he eats his meat raw), to sophistic individualist in Euripides, to the monster in love (Philoxenos, Theokritos). Three worlds intersect in this play: civilized humanity, the anti-world of the satyrs, and the amoral brutality of the Cyclops. Ultimately it is a pleasant spoof of a more serious story, with liberation at the end, a liberation achieved through wine (in the last line the satyrs promise to "serve Bacchus forever").

[Euripides'] *Rhesos*

DATE: unknown – if by Euripides, then probably an early work (ca. 450)

COMPETITION: unknown

CHARACTERS: *Hektor, Aeneas, Dolon, Messenger, Rhesos, Odysseus, Diomedes, Athene, Paris, Charioteer, Muse*

CHORUS: *Trojan sentries*

SETTING: a Trojan outpost near the Greek camp

SYNOPSIS: The chorus wake Hektor to inform him that there is activity in the Greek camp. Hektor wishes to attack straightaway, but Aeneas cautions him to find out what is happening. Dolon volunteers to spy on the Greeks in return for the horses of Achilles as spoil of battle. A messenger announces the coming of Rhesos, king of Thrace, son of a river-god and a Muse, at the head of a powerful army. This invincible warrior has come to help the Trojans, but Hektor reproaches him for coming late in the war. Rhesos explains his delay and the two plan an attack for the morning which will be fatal for the Greeks. Hektor sends Rhesos and his men to a camping-place. Enter Odysseus and Diomedes, who have captured Dolon and are seeking to kill the Trojan leaders. Athene directs them to slay Rhesos and take his splendid horses as plunder. Paris arrives, looking for Hektor, but is deceived by Athene who adopts the guise of Aphrodite, Paris' protecting deity. A wounded Thracian charioteer crawls in, announcing the death of Rhesos and the theft of his horses and blaming this on Hektor. Hektor, however, sees this as the work of Odysseus, a suspicion that is confirmed by Rhesos' mother (a Muse), who enters with the body of her son, casts blame on Athene and Odysseus, and predicts the posthumous honors for her son.

ANALYSIS: Is this a play by Euripides? He did write a *Rhesos*, but even in antiquity there was a suspicion that this was not his work. If genuine (which one doubts), it may be an early work or possibly another play in the fourth position, Euripides again experimenting with drama. The last does contain a familiar establishment of a cult, but is rather harsh on Athens and Athene. On the whole, the quick pace and lack of any tragic depth argue against Euripides' authorship. The more likely conclusion is that this is an example of fourth-century tragedy, long on thrills and short on substance. A compelling argument has recently been made for Macedonian authorship in the third quarter of the fourth century. It does play well as drama, with brisk scenes and suitably theatrical posturings – but "melodrama" might be a better word than "tragedy." To be sure, there is a theme of heroism here: the impetuous and rather unsympathetic Hektor, the cocksure Dolon (complete with disguise of wolfskin), more than a little of the *miles gloriosus* about Rhesos, and the two Greeks, crafty Odysseus and blunt Diomedes ("you go horse-stealing; I'll do the killing").

Aristophanes' *Acharnians*

DATE: 425 – Lenaia

COMPETITION: Aristophanes finished first, Kratinos second with *Storm-Tossed*, and Eupolis third with *New Moons*.

CHARACTERS: *Dikaiopolis, Herald, Amphitheos, Envoy to Persia, Theoros, Dikaiopolis' daughter Euripides' servant, Euripides, Lamachos, Megarian, informer, Boiotian, Nikarchos, Servant of Lamachos, Herald, Derketes, Groomsman, Messengers; Pseudartabas, Thracians, eunuchs, pipers* (silent)

CHORUS: *men of Acharnae, a large community in Attica*

SETTING: the Pnyx at Athens; then the house of Dikaiopolis

SYNOPSIS: The war with Sparta is now in its sixth year. Dikaiopolis ("Just City") tries to persuade the Athenian assembly to discuss peace, but when they refuse, he sends Amphitheos to Sparta to negotiate a private peace. He incurs the wrath of the chorus, men of Acharnai, the largest community outside of Athens, who were strong supporters of the war. He deals with them by parodying a hostage-scene from Euripides' controversial *Telephos*, and delivering a major speech in which he blames both Athens and Sparta for an unnecessary and destructive war. He next encounters Lamachos (a general whose name means "battle"), a wonderful example of the swaggering soldier. In the second part of the play, we see the consequences of his private peace, as Dikaiopolis entertains visitors from enemy territory, including a Megarian who will sell his own daughters for food, and a Boiotian who wants to take home an informer packed up like a vase ("we don't have these at home"). Lamachos is summoned to deal with an enemy incursion, Dikaiopolis to attend a drinking party. The former arrives home wounded on a stretcher, while our hero is carried off drunk in the arms of music-girls.

ANALYSIS: There has been much discussion as to what extent this comedy should represent the personal views of the poet. Twice Dikaiopolis speaks for the poet himself, reminding the audience of what Kleon did to him last year, although others point out that Dikaiopolis adopts so many roles and speaks in so many voices that one cannot assume that he is Aristophanes throughout. One of the defining aspects of Aristophanes' comedy is his fascination with tragedy (Euripides in particular) and in this play he seems to be insisting on a serious role for comedy ("comedy too knows what is right") and to have coined a new term *trygoidia* ("wine-lees song") as a counterpoint to *tragoidia*. The humor is immediate and topical – five (and probably six) of the characters represent real Athenians. One of Aristophanes' strong-points is his creation of metaphor. The Greek for "treaty" (*spondai*) also means "drink-offering" and thus the three treaties brought back by Amphitheus are shown as "vintages," for five, ten, and thirty years, while the motif of the drinking party is carried on throughout the latter part of the comedy. Some regard Dikaiopolis' cause as undermined by an essential selfishness, but that is to read ancient plays with modern attitudes.

Aristophanes' *Knights* (*Hippeis, Equites, Horsemen*)

DATE: 424 – Lenaia

COMPETITION: Aristophanes won first prize, Kratinos second with *Satyrs* and Aristomenes third with *Sheath-carriers*.

CHARACTERS: *Slave 1, Slave 2, Sausage-seller (Agorakritos), Paphlagon, Demos*

CHORUS: *Athenian knights*

SETTING: the house of Demos

SYNOPSIS: Aristophanes creates an allegorical situation by which the city of Athens becomes a household, run by a crotchety old man named "Demos" ("the People"), with his slaves representing the politicians. A new slave (Paphlagon), who stands for the demagogue Kleon, has now taken over the household, and two other slaves discover a prophecy that he can be defeated only by an even worse slave, to wit a "Sausage-seller." Such a character opportunely happens by and with the aid of the knights, who formed the richest and most reactionary group in society, he takes on Paphlagon in two head-to-head encounters. The second encounter, the formal *agon*, is held before Demos, who will judge which of the two is the better benefactor of the people. The Sausage-seller is able to demonstrate that Paphlagon has been acting in his own interest, not in that of the people, and is awarded the victory. The Sausage-seller turns out to be a partisan of the glorious good old days of the victories over Persia, and rejuvenates Demos to his former self, while Paphlagon is banished to sell sausages at the city gates.

ANALYSIS: *Knights* is the first example of the "demagogue comedy," an entire play devoted to the attack of one popular politician, in this case Kleon. Comedy was certainly political before *Knights*, but it may be the case that the political part was incidental to the comedy as a whole. The name "Paphlagon" suggests "Paphlagonia," a region from which Athens drew some slaves, and also *paphlazein* ("to splutter" – Kleon had a distinctive speaking voice). Comedy unfairly depicts the demagogues as vulgar and illiterate members of the working class, whose citizenship could be disputed, who were dishonest and in politics solely to enrich themselves, who were exploiting rather than serving the people. The truth is more likely that they came from the commercial middle class, who made their money rather than inherited it, and who were moving into political life. Aristophanes clearly dislikes Kleon – they did come from the same deme – but one always wonders how much is sheer personal attack and how much comic exploitation of what the audience would take as a humorous stereotype. Still it is true that Aristophanes tends to portray the right wing favorably, especially the knights, and there are frequent hints that the people are easily deceived and misled by their leaders. The ending may be part of the comic fondness for a utopia in the past or represent a real feeling on the poet's part that things were better back then. Kleon is mentioned only once in the play, in a little choral song, where the chorus sing, "it will be the sweetest light of day / when Kleon is destroyed."

Aristophanes' *Wasps* (*Sphekes*, *Vespae*)

DATE: 422 – Lenaia

COMPETITION: *Wasps* finished second, Philonides first with *Precontest* and Leukon third with *Ambassadors* – *Precontest* may be by Aristophanes as well.

CHARACTERS: *Xanthias, Sosias, Bdelykleon, Philokleon, The Dog, Guest, Bread-seller, Complainant; Labes the Dog, Witnesses, music-girl, Karkinos and sons* (silent)

CHORUS(ES): *old men costumed as wasps, sub-chorus of boys*

SETTING: the house of Philokleon and Bdelykleon

SYNOPSIS: The slaves Xanthias and Sosias explain that the old man of the house, Philokleon ("Love-Kleon"), suffers from an addiction to jury service and that his son, Bdelykleon ("Loathe-Kleon"), has locked his father in the house to keep him at home. The old man tries various ruses to get out and eventually chews through the net to join his fellow jurors who are costumed as wasps. In the *agon*, father argues that jurors are respected and indeed feared in Athens ("we're the only ones that Kleon doesn't bite"), while the son demonstrates that they are just being used by the politicians. He convinces father to remain a juror, but at home, and judge domestic matters. The first case is the trial of a dog Labes ("Snatcher") who has wolfed down a cheese, prosecuted by The Dog from Kydathenaion. By a bit of trickery the old man is led to acquit a defendant for the first time in his life. In the final part of the comedy, the son teaches his father how to dress for and behave in polite society, and then takes him off to a drinking-party, where he insults the guests, steals a music-girl, and assaults a bystander on the way home. In the final scene the old man dances Karkinos and his sons into the ground and whirls his way off stage.

ANALYSIS: *Wasps* has three distinct themes: the jury-system, the demagogues such as Kleon, and a reversal of father and son. Those who see Aristophanes as essentially an anti-democrat will see this play not just as a spoof on the Athenians' known litigious behavior, but an attack on the core of the democracy which was the participatory jury-system. But Philokleon and the wasps are treated with fondness and good humor, and it is more likely that the satire of the comedy is aimed at the exploitation of the jury-system by the demagogues. Kleon had recently raised their pay and he and other popular politicians were wont to use the law-courts as a political weapon against their rivals. The dogs, Kyon and Labes, are thinly disguised politicians, Kleon and Laches, who were political enemies in the 420s. The chorus is another instance of Aristophanes' ability to exploit metaphor, for jurors sit in swarms and "sting" with their votes; therefore, let them be wasps. Athens is just like a wasps' nest, for there too are "drones" who do nothing – politicians. The reversal of father and son is very well handled ("just wait until my son dies; you see, I'm his only father"), although the final third of the play is only loosely connected to what goes before. Philokleon is a brilliant comic creation, the irrepressible jack-in-the-box, and some see Bdelykleon as a colorless spoil-sport, or worse a sinister anti-democrat. Yet Aristophanes all but identifies himself with the son, and gives him a grand send-off at the end.

Aristophanes' *Peace* (*Pax*, *Eirene*)

DATE: 421 – Dionysia

COMPETITION: *Peace* finished second, with Eupolis first with *Spongers* and Leukon third with *Phratries*.

CHARACTERS: *Two servants, Trygaios, child of Trygaios, Hermes, War, Riot, Hierokles, Arms Merchant, son of Lamachos, son of Kleonymos; Peace, Opora, Theoria various weapons-makers* (silent)

CHORUS: *farmers*

SETTING: the house of Trygaios; Mount Olympos; the house of Trygaios again

SYNOPSIS: The great idea of this play is that Trygaios flies up to the gods, not on Pegasos like Bellerophon, but on a gigantic dung-beetle. He arrives to find that the gods have deserted the world, leaving War in charge and Peace imprisoned in a cave. With the connivance of Hermes and the assistance of the chorus of farmers, he is able to draw Peace, represented on stage as a giant statue, out of her cave and thus put War to flight. Through Hermes Peace asks what has happened since she has been away. Trygaios is sent back to earth with Peace's handmaids, Opora ("Harvest") and Theoria ("Festival"), the former a gift for the Athenian Council, the latter for himself. Arriving back he deals harshly with a self-important oracle-monger (Hierokles) and those arms merchants who have profited from war, but will no longer. He celebrates his union to Theoria with a marvelous feast, at which two boys sing songs – the son of Lamachos the soldier sings martial verses from Homer, while the son of Kleonymos (who allegedly abandoned his shield in battle) sings a famous poem from Archilochos about throwing one's shield away, and surviving to laugh about it.

ANALYSIS: A comedy of high exuberance and sheer good spirits, *Peace* was produced only weeks before an actual peace between the Athenians and Spartans, ending their ten-year war. It reflects not so much the actual treaty but the expectation and good feelings that must have been in the air. The fact that Aristophanes' great foe, Kleon, had been killed over the winter will also have contributed to the buoyant spirit of the drama. Perhaps the most loosely structured comedy that we have of the eleven by Aristophanes, it begins with a brilliant parody of Euripides' *Bellerophon* and offers a new explanation for the start of the War, that 4th-c. critics mistook for historical fact. Even eight years after his death Aristophanes could not resist attacking Perikles for complicity in bringing on the War. Images of smells and odor dominate this comedy, from the disgusting smell of the dung on which the beetle feeds, to the ambrosial scent of the goddess and her handmaids, to the aroma of food cooking and the bouquet of good wines. There is no formal *agon* in this play – who would speak for War when Peace was imminent? – while the *parabasis* has mainly to do with drama, both tragedy and comedy.

Aristophanes' *Clouds* (*Nubes, Nephelai*)

DATE: the original *Clouds* was produced at 423-Dionysia – what we have is an incomplete revision ca. 419/8.

COMPETITION: in 423 *Clouds* was third – Kratinos first with *Wine-flask* and Ameipsias second with *Konnos*.

CHARACTERS: *Strepsiades, Pheidippides, servant, pupil 1, Sokrates, Stronger Argument, Weaker Argument, two creditors, pupil 2*

CHORUS: *clouds, costumed as women*

SETTING: Athens – the house of Strepsiades and the "reflectory" of Sokrates

SYNOPSIS: Strepsiades ("Twister") is a farmer who has married a wealthy aristocrat, and their son (Pheidippides) has run his father into debt because of his passion for horses. Strepsiades wants his son to go to the "reflectory" of Sokrates and there learn the argument that will get him out of having to pay his debts. The youth refuses and the old man must go himself. At the "reflectory" he meets certain of the pupils and Sokrates himself, suspended in a balloon, and the Clouds, the patron deities of the new learning. He agrees to be initiated into the mysteries of the school, but in a teaching-scene cannot learn or remember anything. Finally he compels his son to go, where the youth witnesses the *agon* between the Arguments, which the Weaker ("Wrong") wins and becomes the boy's teacher. In the final scene Pheidippides' new learning enables his father to avoid two creditors, but it leads also to a battle over poets and to the conclusion that in the new order children may beat their parents. At this point the Clouds reveal that they are instruments of the traditional gods, punishing men who go too far. In a fit of moral outrage Strepsiades burns down the "reflectory."

ANALYSIS: First and foremost, this is a partially completed revision and we do not know what went on in the original. An ancient source tells us that changes were made in the *parabasis* (where we have the revision complaining of the original play's poor showing), in the *agon* between the Arguments, and "where the reflectory is burned down." Thus one may not want to deal with this play in the same manner that one would a finished comedy. Then there is the Sokrates-problem. Apart from certain physical characteristics, the comic character is a deliberate distortion of the real Sokrates, who never taught in a school, taught for money, or gave instruction in science, grammar, or rhetoric. Does this indicate malice on the poet's part (as befits the hidebound conservative that some see as Aristophanes), or a joke that got away, or just that Aristophanes didn't know the difference between Sokrates and a sophist and didn't care? Plato in his *Apology* will blame the Athenians' prejudices against Sokrates on *Clouds*, but in his *Symposium* Aristophanes is part of the gathering of intellectuals. This is the only comedy in which the great idea is recanted at the end, and the hero made to take back his original scheme.

Aristophanes' *Birds* (*Ornithes, Aves*)

DATE: 414 – Dionysia

COMPETITION: *Birds* was second, Ameipsias first with *Revellers* and Phrynichos third with *Hermit*.

CHARACTERS: *Euelpides, Peithetairos, Errand-bird, The Hoopoe (Tereus), Priest, Poet, Oracle-seller, Meton Inspector, Decree-seller, two Messengers, Iris, Herald, Father-beater, Kinesias, Informer, Prometheus, Poseidon, Herakles Second Herald; Nightingale, servants, Triballian god, Basileia* (silent)

CHORUS: *birds*

SETTING: a deserted part of the world; later the city of Cloudcuckooland

SYNOPSIS: Two Athenians, Euelpides ("Good Hope") and Peithetairos ("Persuasive Companion"), have fled Athens to avoid politics and law-courts, and are seeking Tereus, a mythical human with Athenian connections, who has become a hoopoe. There Peithetairos has his great idea: to found a city in the clouds and intercept the worship and sacrifices of humanity to the gods, to starve the gods into submission. He persuades a hostile chorus of birds that birds used to rule the universe and can do so again. All are now onside and in the second part of the play, the new city ("Cloudcuckooland") is founded and sundry sorts of intruders arrive. All are dismissed, the passing goddess Iris is threatened with assault, and a messenger announces that Athens has become bird-crazy. Three more serious intruders are dealt with (a father-beater, Kinesias the poet, and an informer), before Prometheus enters to say that the blockade has put the gods in a bad way, that an embassy is on its way, and that Peithetairos must demand Basileia ("Princess") as his bride as part of the terms. The three gods agree to Peithetairos' conditions, and at the end of the comedy he enters in royal triumph as the new ruler in heaven.

ANALYSIS: Perhaps the most critically disputed play by Aristophanes, *Birds* is for some a fanciful escape from an unpleasant reality, a reaction to the campaign in Sicily, a sympathetic exploration of Athenian aspirations, a non-topical flight of wish-fulfilling fantasy, or a presentation of tyrannical megalomania, a black and ironic dystopia. Does Peithetairos achieve what any of us would want, to marry a goddess and become an all-powerful ruler, or is he a self-seeking tyrant with delusions of grandeur? Is the end of the play an upbeat fantasy or tinged with dark overtones? The birds which used to be free are now confined in a city, while Euelpides vanishes halfway through, leaving Peithetairos all the glory. Birds will never be harmed by humans ever again, promises Peithetairos, but in the scene with the ambassadors he is roasting birds "convicted of treason." But on balance it seems preferable to regard this comedy as a marvelous piece of fantasy, without investing it with any more serious and sinister overtones.

Aristophanes' *Lysistrate*

DATE: 411 – probably at the Lenaia

COMPETITION: unknown

CHARACTERS: *Lysistrate, Kalonike, Myrrhine, Lampito, Proboulos, Kinesias, Spartan herald, Spartan ambassador, Athenian ambassador, Athenian*

CHORUSES: *old women, old men*

SETTING: the Acropolis

SYNOPSIS: In order to bring the war to an end, all the wives of Athens (in cooperation with women throughout Greece) have taken over the Acropolis, seized the treasury, and have launched a sex-strike until the men cease from the fighting. A chorus of old men make their way up the steep slope of the Acropolis carrying large beams to batter down the women's gates. A chorus of old women easily deal with the old men, while Lysistrate debates with a *proboulos* (a current magistrate) on whether war is a woman's affair. In the second part of the play the sex-strike is going badly as the women "just want to get laid." Lysistrate rallies her forces, while Myrrhine seduces her husband and leaves him at a critical moment. A Spartan arrives in obvious sexual distress – things are just as hard at Sparta. The choruses of old men and women are reconciled, while Lysistrate reads the riot act to both Spartans and Athenians – they have a past history of cooperation and should be friends, not enemies. Athenians and Spartans sing each others' songs and harmony returns to Greece.

ANALYSIS: Sexual imagery dominates this play – the principal image is the erect male phallus, and the names "Myrrhine" ("Pussy") and "Kinesias" ("Rod") carry *double entendres*. It seems to be the first comedy with a dominant female character (certainly a politically active female) and, while it does exploit the male stereotype about women (fond of sex, wine, and gossip), there are moments of real empathy, especially in Lysistrate's description of how women are affected by war. A genuine harmony pervades the ending, between male and female, and between Athenians and Spartans. Some have seen the theme of peace with Sparta as essentially a fantasy, since no one in the aftermath of Sicily and the Spartan occupation of Attica could possibly suggest peace, but that is exactly what the oligarchs, who would take power briefly in 411, were proposing. Thus the play may shed light on Aristophanes' own personal stance. Beneath the impressive figure of Lysistrate ("she who breaks up armies") may be found the current priestess of Athene, Lysimache ("she who breaks up battles"), and the action is set on the Acropolis with its temples and shrines. Lysimache would be the best-known woman at Athens, known for herself and not as a man's wife, daughter, etc.

Aristophanes' *Women at the Thesmophoria* (*Thesmophoriazousai*)

DATE: 411 – probably at the Dionysia

COMPETITION: unknown

CHARACTERS: *Euripides, Euripides' relative (Mnesilochos), Agathon's servant, Agathon, Herald(ess), First Woman (Kritylla), Second Woman, Kleisthenes, Prytanis, Scythian policeman; Teredon (boy-piper), Artemisia (belly-dancer)*(silent)

CHORUS: *women celebrating the feast of the Thesmophoria*

SETTING: the Thesmophorion at Athens

SYNOPSIS: The Thesmophoria was a three-day festival attended only by women. Here they hold a meeting to discuss what to do about Euripides, who has been depicting them unfavorably in his tragedies. Euripides gets wind of this and with his relative asks Agathon (a tragic poet who looks like a woman, dresses like a woman) to infiltrate this meeting and plead his case. Agathon understandably refuses, and the relative allows himself to be singed, shaved, and dressed in women's gear. At the meeting, a close parody of the Athenian assembly, one woman is angry that Euripides has tipped off their husbands to their carryings-on, for another his "atheism" has robbed her of half her trade. Then the relative argues that women should be grateful that Euripides has not told the whole truth about them. In the furious uproar that erupts enters Kleisthenes, the only male allowed to attend women's gatherings, who tells the women that Euripides has sent a male relative to infiltrate their meeting. Unmasked and proven without doubt to be male, later bound to a plank and guarded by an uncouth barbarian, the relative engages in parodies from four of Euripides' tragedies (including his *Helen* from the previous year) to attempt to escape, but to no avail. Finally Euripides makes a deal with the women: he will refrain from abusing them if they release his kinsman. The policeman is distracted and the relative freed.

ANALYSIS: Arguably one of the wittiest of Western comedies, it has languished in critical obscurity, partly because literary parody is less appealing than out-and-out political satire and partly because the sex is "kinky," rather than the straight heterosexuality of *Lysistrate*. Just about every male in the play dresses up as a woman at some point, and gender is completely confused. Agathon is known also from the distinctive portrait of him in Plato's *Symposium*, while Kleisthenes is the arch-effeminate of Old Comedy. Of the plays parodied we actually have *Helen* and can thus examine directly how Aristophanic parody operated. Two of the other plays are recent, *Palamedes* (415) and *Andromeda* (412), and both seem to have distinctive visual moments that lent themselves to comic caricature. But *Telephos* is now thirty-seven years in the past, and clearly was a tragedy that stuck in the poet's and audience's memory. A South Italian vase (the Würzburg Telephos – figure 4.3) is now agreed to show a scene from this comedy. Also of interest is the close rendering of the Athenian assembly, at a time when the democracy was under threat and would soon be suspended by what we call the "Revolution of the 400."

Aristophanes' *Frogs* (*Ranae, Batrachoi*)

DATE: 405 – at the Lenaia; an extraordinary second performance has been dated variously to the same festival, the Dionysia of 405, the Lenaia of 404, or to 403, the year of the democratic restoration.

COMPETITION: *Frogs* won first prize, Platon second with *Kleophon*, Phrynichos third with *Muses*.

CHARACTERS: *Xanthias, Dionysos, Herakles, a corpse, Charon, Gatekeeper, servant-woman of Persephone, Plathane, Innkeeper(ess), slave, Euripides, Aeschylus, Plouton; Muse of Euripides* (silent)

CHORUS(ES): *frogs (unseen), the souls of initiates*

SETTING: the road to the Underworld, the house of Plouton

SYNOPSIS: Euripides and Sophokles have just died, and Dionysos, the patron god of drama, goes disguised as Herakles with his cheeky slave (Xanthias) to the underworld to bring back Euripides. His adventures along the way include a rowing-lesson with Charon, a singing-contest with a chorus of frogs, a hostile gatekeeper, a seductive serving-girl, two angry women, and being whipped in an attempt to distinguish the god from his human slave. After the *parabasis* (which contains some serious advice from the poet on contemporary politics), Dionysos finds himself judging a contest between Aeschylus and Euripides for the throne of tragedy, the winner to be brought back to Athens. The actual *agon* decides nothing, and after prologues are compared, choruses examined, a brilliant parody of a monody of Euripides performed, actual lines weighed, and questions about Athens put and answered, Dionysos is forced by Plouton to make a choice ("one is so good, and the other so *good*") and he chooses the one "in whom my soul delights," Aeschylus. An angry Euripides is dispatched with three of his own verses, and at the end Dionysos and Aeschylus return to Athens "to save the city."

ANALYSIS: Along with *Birds* this is Aristophanes' masterpiece, and can be approached from several critical angles: the main character is the god of the festival, the gathering of initiates form a "holy chorus," and for some Dionysos is in search of his identity. From the dramatic point of view, the comedy establishes the foundations of Western literary criticism (Euripides: "art for the sake of art," Aeschylus: "the poet as moral teacher / the poet has a duty to present what is proper"), and Dionysos seems finally to decide on personal preference. *Frogs* can be viewed as Aristophanes' most political comedy, not just in the *parabasis*, where a political amnesty and a complete change of leaders are proposed, but also at the end, where the final questions have to do with the political path for Athens, and Plouton asks that certain political leaders "get themselves down here as fast as they can." In fact all themes meet in a telling passage near the end, where Plouton asks Dionysos why he has come down to fetch a poet, and the god replies "to save the city." Set in the underworld, a comedy about the city and its leaders, the city and its cults, the city and its poets, *Frogs* is an elegant farewell to Athens' greatness.

Aristophanes' *Assembly-Women* (*Ekklesiazousai*)

DATE: 393–391.

COMPETITION: unknown

CHARACTERS: *Praxagora, various women, Blepyros, neighbor, Chremes, two men, Herald(ess), three old and very ugly women, Young Man (Epigenes Young Woman), Servant-girl*

CHORUS: *Athenian wives*

SETTING: before the house of Blepyros and Praxagora

SYNOPSIS: Praxagora ("Act in public") has organized a scheme that involves the wives of Athens. During the night they have appropriated their husbands' shoes, cloaks, and walking-sticks, put on false beards, and prepare to go to the Athenian assembly. Their plan: to propose and vote that power be handed over to the women. Blepyros, Praxagora's husband, needs to answer the call of nature and goes outside, dressed in her robes and slippers. Chremes brings news that the assembly seems to have been dominated by pale-faced cobblers (cobblers stayed indoors to work and thus were not sun-tanned) and has voted to put women in charge with Praxagora as leader. There is no formal *agon*, instead an explanation by Praxagora of how the new order will operate, in terms that remind one of Plato's *Republic* (which Plato wouldn't write for another twenty years), community of possessions, common parenting, gender equality. The episodes that show this great idea unfolding include two men bringing (or not bringing) their goods for the common pool, a young man who must have sex with an ugly old woman before he can have his young girlfriend (in the new order "they all shall equal be"), and an invitation to the inaugural dinner.

ANALYSIS: The signs of the decline of Old Comedy are present, principally in the decreased role of the chorus – no *parabasis* and some interludes are lost – and a sense of ennui and fatigue in the play. For the first time none of the characters represents a real Athenian. It begins well enough with a strong female lead with a significant name and a worthy great idea, but apart from the scene with the young man carried off by the three ugliest women in the world, loses its steam in the latter parts. For some critics this is an especially ironic play: how to save the city? – turn it over to women! Read in this way the latter scenes are the comedian's conscious attempt to undo his great idea. But it is more likely that Aristophanes has come up with a good comic theme, perhaps using some philosophic ideas and social theories which were in the air, added the reversal of gender roles (always good comic material), but not brought the whole thing off with the flair that he would in his earlier plays.

Aristophanes' *Wealth* (*Ploutos*)

DATE: 388

COMPETITION: the other four comedies were Nikostratos' *Laconians*, Aristomenes' *Admetos*, Nikophon's *Adonis*, and Alkaios' *Pasiphae*.

CHARACTERS: *Karion, Chremylos, Ploutos (Wealth), Blepsidemos, Penia (Poverty), wife of Chremylos, Just Man, Informer, Old Woman, Young Man, Hermes, priest of Zeus*

CHORUS: *old countrymen, from the same deme as Chremylos*

SETTING: the house of Chremylos in Athens

SYNOPSIS: Proverbially "Wealth is blind," for if Wealth could see and distinguish good men from evil, he would not go to the latter. The great idea for this comedy is that Chremylos and his slave Karion encounter the blind and filthy god Wealth and contrive that he regain his sight. Chremylos and his neighbor Blepsidemos are suddenly confronted by an angry female, Poverty, who argues in the formal *agon* that it is she who makes men virtuous through hard work and a lack of luxury. Poverty is dismissed and Wealth taken to the shrine of the healing-god Asklepios. He returns with his sight restored and everywhere just men (indeed all men as they realize that justice leads to prosperity) are becoming wealthy. The episodes involve an informer who has no one to accuse, an old woman whose young lover no longer needs her money, Hermes who is out of a job, and the priest of Zeus, also unemployed because all now worship Wealth. At the end Wealth is installed as the new controlling deity.

ANALYSIS: The trend to something other than Old Comedy is well under way by *Wealth* – notice three of the other four comedies are mythological burlesques, a popular comic sub-genre in the 4th c. The chorus have one song only, a parody of a poem by Philoxenos, and for the rest their interludes are marked with the entry *chorou* ("of the chorus"), most of the personal jokes are in the first part of the play, Poverty is a universal problem not just at Athens, and Karion has as much of the action as his master Chremylos – he is well on his way to the cunning slave of later comedy. Some discussion involves Aristophanes' own views, whether he has undergone a distinct change from his earlier "conservative" views, or whether (as with *Assembly-Women.*) the play should be read as ironic. Critics have not missed the fact that Poverty speaks second in the *agon* (the usual winning position) and that Chremylos does not so much win the debate as ride roughshod over Poverty. To many, this suggests that the entire second half of the comedy should be read as intentionally ironic.

Menander's *The Grouch*
(*Old Cantankerous, Dyskolos*)

DATE: 316 – at the Lenaia

COMPETITION: won first prize

CHARACTERS: *Pan, Chaireas, Sostratos, Pyrrhias, Knemon, Knemon's daughter, Daos, Gorgias, Sikon, Getas, Old woman, Kallippides*

CHORUS: celebrants of Pan – appear only between acts

SETTING: the shrine of Pan at Phyle, a remote part of Attica

SYNOPSIS: *Dyskolos* means "a bad-tempered man," in this case Knemon, an old farmer who lives with his daughter and hates people. His wife has now left him and gone to live with her son Gorgias (by a previous marriage). Sostratos, a city slicker from Athens, has fallen in love at first sight with the misanthrope's daughter and is trying to arrange matters with her father, who chases him and everyone else away. Daos, Gorgias' slave, reports to his master that someone is interested in his half-sister. Gorgias confronts Sostratos, but finding him a decent sort suggests that he pretend to be a hardworking farmer in order to impress Knemon. Unfortunately Sostratos spends all day in the sun doing backbreaking labor, and Knemon never comes by. Getas, the major-domo of Sostratos' household, arrives with a group for a picnic at the cave of Pan and attempts to borrow things from Knemon. Knemon's daughter has dropped a bucket down the well, and Knemon has fallen in attempting to retrieve it. When Gorgias rescues him, Knemon sees the error of his misanthropy, recants his ways, and entrusts himself and his daughter to Gorgias. Gorgias immediately arranges the marriage of his half-sister to Sostratos, while Sostratos reciprocates by convincing his father (Kallippides) to let Gorgias marry his sister.

ANALYSIS: New Comedy is comedy of the house, neatly packaged into five acts, with subjects of love and a happy ending. *Dyskolos* is an early effort by Menander, and is marred by too many characters (some appearing only once) and a weak final act, where two slaves torment an injured Knemon and force him to join the party. The play is dominated by two themes: a character-study of the bad-tempered misanthrope who sees the light and repents of his ways – his first scene is especially good, when he envies Perseus who could fly (and thus avoid people) and who had the Gorgon's head which turned men into stone ("if I had that, there'd be stone statues everywhere"), and the dichotomy between town and country, carried by Sostratos the young dandy from Athens with a good character and willing to suffer for the woman he wants. The publication of the text of the play (virtually complete) in 1957 was a major event in the history of Greek Comedy and thrust Menander into the forefront of critical study.

Menander's *Samian Woman (Samia)* or *Marriage-contract*

DATE: unknown – probably late in Menander's career (305–300)

COMPETITION: unknown

CHARACTERS: *Moschion, Chrysis, Parmenion, Demeas, Nikeratos, Cook*

CHORUS: not identified – the entry ⟨*chorou*⟩ appears in the text at v. 420

SETTING: the houses of Demeas and Nikeratos at Athens

SYNOPSIS: Moschion is the adopted son of Demeas, a wealthy Athenian merchant who, along with his neighbor Nikeratos, has been away for the winter. Demeas' "wife," Chrysis ("Goldie") the woman from Samos, has had a child which died, while Moschion has fathered a child secretly on Nikeratos' daughter. To direct suspicion away from Moschion and his girl, Chrysis has taken the child and pretended that it is her own, as all await the return of Demeas and Nikeratos. When the two arrive, they discuss a marriage between Moschion and Nikeratos' daughter, a prospect which Moschion welcomes (perhaps too readily). In the third act the complications arise. Demeas hears Moschion's old nurse talk of Moschion as the baby's father and thinks that Moschion has seduced (or rather been seduced by) Chrysis. He drives Chrysis into the street, where she takes refuge with Nikeratos. Moschion, informed by his father that he "knows all," cannot understand why his father is so upset, but Nikeratos, appalled at Chrysis' supposed infidelity, goes in to drive her out of his house, only to find his daughter nursing the child. Moschion puts Demeas in the picture, Demeas takes Chrysis back into his house, and an angry Nikeratos is placated by the prospect of a marriage-feast. In the final act a petulant Moschion threatens to run away and join the foreign legion, but is cajoled back to his own wedding.

ANALYSIS: This is Menander at his mature best. The comedy has far fewer characters than *The Grouch*, and each is drawn with sympathy and distinctiveness: Moschion as the adopted son who is anything but a hell-raiser, Demeas the old man who gets mad quickly, usually in tragic language, and Nikeratos, less bright who angers slowly but stays mad longer. The third and fourth acts are particularly good, when each of the principals thinks that he knows the whole truth, and they interact at cross-purposes and in witty and succinct language. The play provides valuable light on social customs of the late 4th c.: adoption, wedding arrangements, the Athenian household (Chrysis as a foreigner cannot be a "real" wife, but she is Demeas' wife in all but name), traveling merchants, hired chefs, the dependence of sons on fathers, etc.

A Note on Meter

With the exception of some passages in comedy (most notably *Women in the Thesmophoria* 295–311), where the official language of the Athenian assembly or legal formulae is parodied, Greek drama is written in verse. Behind the speeches of the actors or the songs of the chorus lie formal metrical patterns with distinct rules, rather stricter for tragedy than for comedy.

The Greeks did not use the stress meter that we are used to in English poetry, the formal pattern of stressed and unstressed syllables that creates a familiar and repeated rhythm. The iambic pentameter of Shakespeare, for instance, depends on five stressed syllables to the line

> The **skies** are **painted with** unnumber'd **sparks,**
> They **are** all **fire,** and **every one** doth **shine.** (*Julius Caesar* III.63–4)

More obvious are the opening lines to Browning's *How they brought the good news from Ghent to Aix*:

> I **sprang** to the **stirr**up, and **Jor**is, and **he**
> I **gallop'd,** Dirk **gallop'd,** we **gall**oped **all** three

with their powerful, if repetitive, anapests. Greek meter is "quantitative"; that is, it operates on a pattern of long and short syllables, much in the manner of musical notes (e.g., half-notes and quarter-notes). The pattern depended on the time taken to pronounce the syllable. A long syllable (–) took twice as long to utter as a short syllable (∪), and a long syllable did not necessarily receive the pitch accent of the Greek word.

The principal meter for both comedy and tragedy is the **iambic trimeter**, described by Aristotle (*Poetics* 1449a23–6) as the closest rhythm to normal speech, used for the prologue and most episodes. An iambic **foot** consists of a short + long [∪ –], two feet equal one **metron** (plural: metra) [× – ∪ –], where × denotes a syllable that can

be either short or long. Thus a trimeter (three metra) is so designated: × − ∪ − | × −
∪ − | × − ∪ −. For either foot of a metron a three-syllable unit may be substituted,
under rules that are tighter for tragedy than for comedy: ∪ ∪ − (**anapest**), − ∪ ∪
(**dactyl**), or ∪ ∪ ∪ (**tribrach**), thus creating a rougher pattern of meter that would be
noticeable in delivery. This technique is called "resolution," and we have pointed in
our discussion of Euripides how his increasing use of resolution in the iambic trimeter allows us to date his plays.

A longer iambic system is the **iambic tetrameter catalectic** ("catalectic" [ᴧ]
meaning that the last syllable of the line is missing), composed of four metra and
yielding the following scheme: × − ∪ − | × − ∪ − | × − ∪ − | × − − ᴧ |. It is used in satyr-
play and in comedy, both by the chorus and by participants in the *agon*
(e.g., Weaker Argument in *Clouds*, Euripides in *Frogs*). Comedy also employs systems
of **iambic dimeter**, both regular [× − ∪ − | × − ∪ −] and catalectic [× − ∪ − | × −
∪ ᴧ]. Often, but not always, the context is a formal song of abuse, as at *Acharnians*
836–59 or Eupolis fr. 99.1–22.

Aristotle (*Poetics* 1449a20–3) asserts that the **trochaic tetrameter** was the original
meter of tragedy, associated as it was with dancing. The **trochee** [− ∪] is the inverse
of the iamb and, like the iamb, two feet equal one metron: − ∪ − ×. The usual form
is a catalectic tetrameter, of this scheme: − ∪ − × | − ∪ − × | − ∪ − × | − ∪ − ᴧ. The
evidence seems to bear out Aristotle's assertion, since in tragedy this meter is found
in Aeschylus and then not until the late plays of Euripides. It carries a sense of emotional excitement and action. When choruses in comedy burst onto the scene, they
do so in trochaics (as at *Knights* 247). The epirrhematic sections of a comic *parabasis*
are normally in trochaic tetrameter. Trochaic metra allow the same sort of resolutions
as do iambic systems.

The **anapest** [∪ ∪ −] similarly employs metra consisting of two feet: ∪ ∪ − ∪ ∪
− and allows resolutions of two longs, a **spondee** [− −], or a **dactyl** [− ∪ ∪].
It occurs in both tragedy and comedy, in dimeters [∪ ∪ − ∪ ∪ − | ∪ ∪ − ∪ ∪ −] and
tetrameters, usually catalectic [∪ ∪ − ∪ ∪ − | ∪ ∪ − ∪ ∪ − | ∪ ∪ − ∪ ∪ − |
∪ ∪ − − ᴧ]. Choruses in tragedy often march on in anapestic dimeter, while in comedy
the anapestic tetrameter is used for speakers in the *agon* and the principal exposition
in Aristophanes' *parabases*. The anapestic tetrameter catalectic seems to have been an
elevated meter, suitable for arguments, grand statements, and declarations, and by the
ancients was called the "aristophanean." Other comic poets employed a variety of 15-
syllable meters for the *parabasis* proper. One of these, the eupolidean, was taken over
by Aristophanes at *Clouds* 518–62, where he attacks other comic poets, including
Eupolis, for the inferior nature of their comedy.

The **dactylic** or epic hexameter, which is the mainstay of all ancient epic, [− ∪ ∪
| − ∪ ∪ | − ∪ ∪ | − ∪ ∪ | − ∪ ∪ | − ×], is rare in Greek drama. Based on the **dactyl**
(− ∪ ∪), this meter allows only a resolution to a **spondee** (− −). This is the meter of
Homer, the Homeric Hymns, *The Voyage of Argo* (third century BC), and of oracular
pronouncements, and must have possessed the aura of grandeur and epic heroism.
This may well explain its rarity in drama. In comedy it does occur in parodies of
Homer or of oracles or speeches by a god or hero; *Frogs* closes with four solemn lines
in dactylic hexameters. An intriguing use of this meter in tragedy occurs at *Philoktetes*

839–42 when Neoptolemos rejects the chorus's advice to take the bow and flee – his argument is that "the god told us to take *him*." It is as if a god is speaking through Neoptolemos, this in a play which depends greatly on the proper interpretation of an oracle.

The meters of the choral odes, the *kommoi* between actor and chorus, and the monodies of the actor are complicated and beyond the scope of an introductory study. Some of the metrical schemes develop from what are called "lyric" versions of the above meters, others depend on a core unit of the **choriamb** [$-\cup\cup-$] with various embellishments at both ends. In the choral odes and *kommoi*, pairs of units will correspond formally in their metrical scheme, to the point where we may detect corruption in the ancient text where the meter does not correspond. One metrical unit, the **dochmiac** [$\cup--\cup-$, with the possibility of any long being resolved into two shorts], was especially associated with emotional intensity in tragedy, for example the entry of the terrified chorus of women at *Seven* 78–107, and when employed in comedy is very often used to create a tragic effect (as at *Birds* 1198–95/1262–8). We have already mentioned that the choral songs were written in a literary Doric dialect that would have given a different feel to their performance.

Glossary of Names and Terms

Aeschylus   the first of the three great tragedians (career: 498–456); seven plays have come down under his name.

Agathon   a tragic poet of the 410s and 400s, best known for his appearances in Plato's *Symposium* and Aristophanes' *Women at the Thesmophoria*.

agon   a formally structured contest between two antagonists, found in both tragedy and comedy.

anapest   meter based on the form [∪ ∪—]; see the appendix on meter.

archon   one of nine Athenian senior officials chosen by lot. The *archon eponymous* was in charge of the City Dionysia, the *archon basileus* of the Lenaia.

Aristophanes   the best-known and only surviving exponent of Old Comedy (career: 427–ca.385); eleven of his comedies have survived.

Aristotle   (385–322), philosopher and student of Plato, author of *Poetics*, an important early source for Greek drama.

aulos   a double-recorder (often misnamed "flute"), played to accompany the dithyramb and the sung parts of drama.

choregos   lit. "chorus-bringer," a wealthy Athenian (or metic for the Lenaia) who would sponsor the production of tragedy and comedy.

City Dionysia   the major Athenian festival honoring the god Dionysos, held in the month of Elaphebolion (late March).

comedy   "revel-song," introduced at the City Dionysia in 486, divided by the ancients into Old (486–ca.385), Middle (ca.385–ca.320), and New (320–250 BC).

dactyl   the grand heroic meter of epic poetry [—∪ ∪]; see the appendix on meter.

dithyramb   a large-scale choral song performed in honor of Dionysos, said by Aristotle to be the ancestor of tragedy.

eisodos   "way in," one of the two formal entrances on either side of the *orchestra*.

ekklesia   the Athenian assembly, composed of citizen males, which met on the Pnyx Hill.

ekkyklema   "wheel out," a large wheeled platform that could be rolled through the central door in the *skene* to display indoor scenes and dramatic tableaux.

episodes   the scenes, usually in iambic trimeter, involving the actors (and the chorus).

Eupolis   career: 429–411, one of the canonical three poets of Old Comedy, wrote fifteen comedies; only fragments survive.

Euripides   the third of the canonical three tragic poets (career: 455–407); nineteen plays have come down to us under his name.

exodos   "way out," the closing scene of a comedy or tragedy.

hypothesis   an ancient summary of a Greek play, often containing both a plot-line and the details of production.

iambic   meter based on the form [∪—]; see the appendix on meter.

kommos   a formal song between an actor (or actors) and the chorus.

komodoumenoi   real persons made fun of in comedy.

Kratinos   career: 545–423, one of the canonical three of Old Comedy, author of about twenty-five comedies, only fragments have survived.

Lenaia   ancient Athenian festival of Dionysos, held in the month of Gamelion (January).

Lykourgos   Athenian politician responsible for re-building the theater in the 330s.

mechane   "machine," a crane-like device that allowed performers to appear in the air or to enter aerially from behind the *skene*.

Menander   the best-known and only surviving exponent of New Comedy (career: *c*.320–290).

metic   *metoikos* in Greek, a non-Athenian resident at Athens.

monody   "song alone," a lyric piece sung by an actor alone, without the formal structure of a choral song (*stasimon*).

odeion   "singing-place," a covered auditorium for musical performances; the Odeion of Perikles was built next to the Theater of Dionysos in the 430s.

orchestra   "dancing-place," a round area at the foot of the slope on which spectators sat; this was the center of the dramatic spectacle.

parabasis   the formally structured part of an Old Comedy, where the actors have left and the chorus formally addresses the spectators.

parodos   "way on," the entry-song of the chorus.

Peloponnesian Wars   a series of conflicts involving Athens and her allies against Sparta and her league, the principal one lasting from 431 to 404.

Perikles   (494–429), the leading political figure of fifth-century Athens, in power almost continually from 461 to 429, responsible for the advancement of Athenian power and prestige and for the building program on the Acropolis.

Persian Wars   hostilities between Greece and Persia lasted for most of the classical period, but the formal wars consist of three unsuccessful invasions by Persia in 492, 490, and 481–479.

Phrynichos   career: 510–470, early writer of tragedy.

Plato   Athenian philosopher (429–347), student of Sokrates; in his dialogues (especially *Republic, Laws*) he put tight strictures on the role of poets in his ideal city.

polis   the ancient Greek term for "city-state."

satyr-drama   a short drama with a chorus of satyrs (half-human, half-animal followers of Dionysos); it followed the three tragedies and made fun of the serious themes and characters of myth.

skene   "tent," a formal structure behind the *orchestra* with a large central door, windows, and a roof that could be used as a playing-area (*theologeion*).

Sophokles   second of the canonical three tragic poets (career: 468–406); seven plays have survived under his name.

stasimon   "standing-song," sung by the chorus while in position within the *orchestra* and separating the action in the episodes. The usual form is a series of metrically responsive strophes ("turns") and antistrophes ("counter-turns"), finished with an epode. Sometimes referred to as a "choral ode."

stichomythia   the fast-paced and formal line-by-line response between two actors or between an actor and chorus.

strategoi   "generals," the ten annually elected political and military leaders of Athens.

Suda   an historical and literary encyclopedia of the ancient world, dating from the tenth century AD.

Syracuse   located on the east coast of Sicily and perhaps the leading Greek city in the early fifth century, it possessed an impressive theater and its own tradition of drama.

theologeion   "god speak," the roof of the *skene* which could be used for the appearance of gods or for any aerially raised scene.

Thespis   the traditional innovator of tragedy in 534.

tragedy   "goat-song," serious drama traditionally introduced in 534; in the fifth century each tragic poet would produce three tragedies, either together (trilogy) or as three unconnected dramas.

trochee   a meter of the form [—∪]; see the appendix on meter.

tyrant   a man who had made himself ruler, as opposed to an hereditary monarch (*basileus*, "king"); the term did not in itself carry the modern overtones of "tyrant."

Further Reading

The literature on a subject like Greek drama is immense. Critical studies vary from general introductions to rather more specialized treatments. The following is recommended as a basic reading list. Most of the secondary discussions will contain very useful bibliographies for further reading.

Texts

Oxford Classical Texts (Oxford: Oxford University Press)

Greek text only
Aeschylus edited by D. Page (1972)
Sophokles edited by H. Lloyd-Jones and N. G. Wilson (1990)
Euripides edited by J. Diggle, 3 vols (1981–94)
Aristophanes edited by F. W. Hall and W. M. Geldart, 2 vols (1906^2) – a new edition by N. G. Wilson is in preparation
Menander edited by F. H. Sandbach (1972)

Loeb Classical Library (Cambridge MA: Harvard University Press)

Greek text with facing English translation, introduction, and some notes
Aeschylus H. Weir-Smyth, 2 vols (1922)
Sophokles H. Lloyd-Jones, 3 vols (1994–6)
Euripides D. Kovacs, 6 vols (1994–2002)
Aristophanes J. Henderson, 4 vols (1998–2002)
Menander W. G. Arnott, 3 vols (1979–2000)

Aris and Phillips (Warminster)

Greek text, with introductions, facing English translation, and brief commentary

Aeschylus *Eumenides*, A. Podecki (1989); *Persians*, E. Hall (1996); *Prometheus*, A. Podlecki (2002).
Sophokles *Ajax*, A. F. Garvie (1998); *Antigone*, A. Brown (1987); *Elektra*, J. Marsh (2001); *Philoktetes*, R. G. Ussher (1990).
Euripides *Alkestis*, D. J. Conacher (1988); *Andromache*, M. Lloyd (1994); *Bacchae*, R. Seaford (1996); *Children of Herakles*, W. Allan (2001); *Elektra*, M. Cropp (1988); *Herakles*, S. Barlow (1996); *Hecuba*, C. Collard (1991); *Hippolytos*, M. Halleran (1995); *Ion*, K. H. Lee (1997); *Iphigeneia among the Taurians*, M. Cropp (2001); *Orestes*, M. L. West (1987); *Phoenician Women*, E. Craik (1988); *Trojan Women*, S. Barlow (1986).
Aristophanes A. H. Sommerstein, 12 vols (1980–2003)
Menander *The Grouch* (*Dyskolos*), S. Ireland (1995); *Samian Woman*, D. Bain (1983).

Oxford commentaries (Oxford: Clarendon Press)

Text, with scholarly introduction and commentary

Aeschylus *Agamemnon*, E. Fraenkel, 3 vols (1950); *Agamemnon*, J. D. Denniston and D. Page (1957); *Libation-Bearers* (*Choephoroi*), A. F. Garvie (1986); *Seven against Thebes*, G. O. Hutchinson (1985).
Sophokles *Trachinian Women*, M. Davies (1991).
Euripides *Alkestis*, A. M. Dale (1954); *Andromache*, P. T. Stevens (1971); *Bacchae*, E. R. Dodds (1960^2); *Children of Herakles*, J. Wilkins (1993); *Cyclops*, R. Seaford (1984); *Elektra*, J. D. Denniston (1939); *Helen*, A. M. Dale (1967); *Herakles*, G. Bond (1981); *Hippolytos*, W. G. Barrett (1964); *Ion*, A. S. Owen (1939); *Iphigeneia among the Taurians*, M. Platnauer (1938); *Medea*, D. L. Page (1938); *Orestes*, C. Willink (1986).
Aristophanes *Acharnians*, S. D. Olson (2002); *Clouds*, K. J. Dover (1968); *Wasps*, D. M. MacDowell (1971); *Peace*, S. D. Olson (1998); *Birds*, N. V. Dunbar (1995); *Lysistrate*, J. Henderson (1987); *Frogs*, K. J. Dover (1993); *Assembly-Women*, R. G. Ussher (1973).
Menander A.W. Gomme and F. H. Sandbach (1973)

Cambridge Greek and Latin Classics (Cambridge: Cambridge University Press)

Aeschylus *Eumenides*, A. H. Sommerstein (1989); *Prometheus*, M. Griffith (1983).
Sophokles *Antigone*, M. Griffith (1999); *Elektra*, J. H. Kells (1973); *Oedipus Rex*, R. D. Dawe (1982); *Philoktetes*, T. B. L. Webster (1970); *Trachinian Women*, P. Easterling (1982).
Euripides *Medea*, D. Mastronarde (2002).

Other commentaries of note

Aeschylus *Persians*, H. D. Broadhead (Cambridge: Cambridge University Press, 1960).
Sophokles *Ajax*, W. B. Standford (London: Macmillan, 1963).
Euripides *Cyclops*, R. G. Ussher (Rome: Edizioni dell'Ateneo and Bizarri, 1978); *Suppliant Women*, C. Collard, 2 vols (Groningen: Boema's Boekhuis, 1975); *Trojan Women*, K. H. Lee (London: Macmillan, 1976).

Aristophanes   *Frogs*, W. B. Standford (London: Macmillan, 1963).
Menander   *The Grouch* (*Dyskolos*), E. Handley (London: Methuen, 1965).
Fragments   The fragments of the Greek tragedians are collected in the series, *Tragicorum Graecorum Fragmenta* (*TrGF*), edited by G. Snell, R. Kannicht, and S. Radt, 5 vols (Göttingen: Vandenhoeck and Ruprecht, 1971→), of which all but vol. 5 (Euripides) have now appeared. The remains of lost comedy are found in *Poetae Comici Graeci*, edited by R. Kassel and C. Austin, 8 vols (Berlin/New York: de Gruyter, 1983→). The third volume of the Loeb Sophocles contains the fragments (with translation) of that tragic poet; C. Collard, M. Cropp, and K. H. Lee have produced the first of a projected two volumes on the major fragments of Euripides in the Aris and Phillips series (1995).

Translations

In addition to the translations provided in the Loeb Classical Library and the Aris and Phillips series, we would call attention to the following series.
D. Grene and R. Lattimore (eds.), *The Complete Greek Tragedies*, 9 vols (Chicago: University of Chicago Press)   **Aeschylus**, 2 vols (1953–6); **Sophokles**, 2 vols (1957, 1991²); **Euripides**, 5 vols (1953–6). A 3-volume abridgement containing 15 plays is also available.
W. Arrowsmith and H. Golder (eds.), *The Greek Tragedy in New Translations* (Oxford: Oxford University Press, in progress).
D. Slavitt and P. Bovie (eds.), *Penn Greek Drama Series* (Philadelphia: University of Pennsylvania Press, 1998→)   **Aeschylus** (1 vol.), **Sophokles** (1 vol.), **Euripides** (4 vols), **Aristophanes** (3 vols), **Menander** (1 vol.).
Oxford World Classics Series (Oxford: Oxford University Press)   **Aeschylus** (*Oresteia* only), C. Collard; **Sophokles** (*Elektra, Oedipus, Antigone*), H. D. F. Kitto; **Euripides**, 5 vols, R. Waterfield, E. Hall, and J. Morwood; **Aristophanes** (*Birds, Lysistrate, Assembly-Women, Wealth*), S. Halliwell; **Menander**, M. Balme and P. Brown.
Penguin Classics   **Aeschylus** (*Oresteia*), R. Fagles and W. B. Standford (1977); 2 vols, P. Vellacott (1973); **Sophokles** (Theban plays), R. Fagles (1984); 2 vols, E. F. Watling (1973); **Euripides**, 4 vols, J. Davie and R. Rutherford (1998→); **Aristophanes**, 3 vols, D. Barrett and A. H. Sommerstein(1974→); **Menander**, N. P. Miller (1987).
Focus Classical Library packs a great deal into one small volume: introduction, translation, useful notes, and bibliography.   **Sophokles**, R. Blondell (*Oedipus Tyrannos, Oedipus at Kolonos, Antigone*); S. Schein (*Philoktetes*); **Euripides**, D. Clay (*Trojan Women*); S. Esposito (*Bacchae*); M. Halleran (*Herakles, Hippolytos*); A. Podlecki (*Medea*); **Aristophanes**, J. Henderson (*Acharnians, Clouds, Lysistrate, Birds*).
Everyman's Classical Library has now published four volumes (two each for Aeschylus and Sophokles) of translations by M. Ewans, based on his experiences of production, with extensive theatrical notes.

Theater and Drama

P. D. Arnott, *Public and Performance in the Greek Theatre* (London: Routledge, 1989); M. Bieber, *The Greek and Roman Theater* (Princeton: Princeton University Press 1961²); E. Csapo and W. Slater, *The Context of Ancient Drama* (Ann Arbor: University of Michigan Press, 1995); J. R. Green, *Theatre in ancient Greek society* (London: Routledge, 1994); J. R. Green and E. Handley, *Images of the Greek Theatre* (London: British Museum Press, 1995); G. Ley, *A Short Introduction to the Greek Theater* (Chicago: University of Chicago Press, 1991); A. Pickard-Cambridge, *The*

Dramatic Festivals of Athens (Oxford: Oxford University Press, 1988²), *The Theatre of Dionysus* (Oxford: Oxford University Press, 1946); A. H. Sommerstein, *Greek Drama and Dramatists* (London: Routledge, 2002); J. M. Walton, *Greek Theatre Practice* (London: Methuen, 1980); D. Wiles, *Greek theatre performance: an introduction* (Cambridge: Cambridge University Press, 2000); P. Wilson, *The Athenian Institution of the* Khoregia (Cambridge: Cambridge University Press, 2000).

Tragedy

H. C. Baldry, *The Greek Tragic Theatre* (London: Chatto and Windus, 1977); M. Baldock, *Greek Tragedy: an introduction* (Bristol: Bristol Classical Press, 1989); R. G. A. Buxton, *Persuasion in Greek tragedy: a study of* peitho (Cambridge: Cambridge University Press, 1982); P. Easterling (ed.), *The Cambridge Companion to Greek Tragedy* (Cambridge: Cambridge University Press, 1997); S. Goldhill, *Reading Greek Tragedy* (Cambridge: Cambridge University Press, 1986); E. Hall, *Inventing the Barbarian: Greek Self-definition through Tragedy* (Oxford: Oxford University Press, 1989); M. Heath, *The Poetics of Greek Tragedy* (Stanford: Stanford University Press, 1987); H. D. F. Kitto, *Greek Tragedy* (London: Methuen, 1961³); A. Lesky, *Greek Tragic Poetry* (New Haven: Yale University Press, 1983); R. Padel, *In and out of the Mind: Greek Images of the Tragic Self* (Princeton: Princeton University Press, 1992); R. Rehm, *Greek Tragic Theatre* (London: Routledge, 1992), *The Play of Space: spatial transformation in Greek tragedy* (Princeton: Princeton University Press, 2002); W. B. Stanford, *Greek Tragedy and the Emotions* (London: Routledge and Kegan Paul, 1983); O. Taplin, *Greek Tragedy in Action* (Oxford: Oxford University Press, 1978); D. Wiles, *Tragedy in Action* (Cambridge: Cambridge University Press, 1997).

Satyr-Drama

M. Griffith, "Slaves of Dionysos: Satyrs, Audiences, and the Ends of the *Oresteia*," *Classical Antiquity* 21 (2002) 195–258; R. Krumeich, N. Pechstein and B. Seidensticker, *Das griechische Satyrspiel* (Darmstadt: Wissenschaftliche Buchgesellschaft, 1999); D. F. Sutton, *The Greek Satyr Play* (Meisenheim am Glan: Hain, 1980).

Comedy

E. Handley, "Comedy," in P. Easterling and B. M. W. Knox, *Cambridge History of Classical Literature*, vol. 1, *Greek Literature* (Cambridge: Cambridge University Press, 1985) 103–46; R. L. Hunter, *The New Comedy of Greece and Rome* (Cambridge: Cambridge University Press, 1985); G. Norwood, *Greek Comedy* (London: Methuen, 1931); F. H. Sandbach, *The Comic Theatre of Greece and Rome* (London: Chatto and Windus, 1977); O. Taplin, *Comic Angels* (Oxford: Oxford University Press, 1993); T. B. L. Webster, *Studies in Later Greek Comedy* (Manchester: Manchester University Press, 1970²).

Collections of Essays

Being neither whole monographs nor articles in the traditional journals, these papers are often hard for the student to locate. These collections may be volumes of essays honoring a distinguished scholar, the published papers of a conference, a thematic collection of new papers, or the republication of previously published articles on one theme or author. The following collections should provide a gold mine of useful and sometimes groundbreaking papers on Greek Drama.

M. J. Cropp, E. Fantham, and S. E. Scully (eds.), *Greek Tragedy and its Legacy: essays presented to D. J. Conacher* (Calgary: University of Calgary Press, 1986); B. Goff (ed.), *History, Tragedy, Theory: dialogues on Athenian drama* (Austin: University of Texas Press, 1995); S. Goldhill and R. Osborne, *Performance Culture and Athenian Democracy* (Cambridge: Cambridge University Press, 1999); T. F. Gould and C. J. Herington (eds.), *Greek Tragedy*, Yale Classical Studies vol. 25 (Cambridge 1977); A. Griffiths (ed.), *Stage Directions: Essays in Ancient Drama in Honour of E. W. Handley* (London: Institute of Classical Studies, 1995); I. McAuslan and P. Walcot (eds.), *Greek Tragedy* (Oxford: Oxford University Press, 1993); J. Porter *et al.* (eds.), *Crossing the Stages: The Production, Performance, and Reception of Ancient Theater*, Syllecta Classica vol. 10 (Iowa City 1999); R. Scodel (ed.), *Theater and Society in the Classical World* (Ann Arbor: University of Michigan Press, 1993); E. Segal (ed.), *Oxford Readings in Greek Tragedy* (Oxford: Oxford University Press, 1983); M. Silk (ed.), *Tragedy and the Tragic: Greek Theatre and Beyond* (Oxford: Oxford University Press, 1996); J. J. Winkler and F. I. Zeitlin (eds.), *Nothing to do with Dionysos? Athenian Drama in its Social Context* (Princeton: Princeton University Press, 1990).

Aeschylus   H. Bloom (ed.), *Aeschylus's The Oresteia* (New York: Chelsea House, 1988); M. H. McCall Jr. (ed.), *Aeschylus: a collection of critical essays* (Englewood Cliffs, NJ: Prentice-Hall, 1972).

Sophokles   H. Bloom (ed.), *Sophocles* (New York: Chelsea House, 1990), *Sophocles'* Oedipus Rex (New York: Chelsea House, 1988); T. M. Woodard (ed.), *Sophocles: a collection of critical essays* (Englewood Cliffs, NJ: Prentice Hall, 1966).

Euripides   P. Burian (ed.), *Directions in Euripidean Criticism* (Durham, NC: Duke University Press, 1985); M. Cropp, K. H. Lee, and D. Sansone (eds.), *Euripides and Tragic Theatre in the Late Fifth Century*, Illinois Classical Studies vols 24–5 (Champaign, IL 2000); R. Mitchell-Boyask (ed.), *Approaches to Teaching the Dramas of Euripides* (New York: Modern Language Association, 2002); J. Mossman (ed.), *Oxford Readings in Classical Studies: Euripides* (Oxford: Oxford University Press, 2003); C. A. Powell (ed.), *Euripides, Women and Sexuality* (London: Routledge, 1990); E. Segal (ed.), *Euripides: a collection of critical essays* (Englewood Cliffs, NJ: Prentice-Hall, 1968).

Aristophanes and Comedy   G. Dobrov (eds.), *Beyond Aristophanes: transition and diversity in Greek Comedy* (Atlanta: Scholars Press, 1993), *The City as Comedy* (Chapel Hill: University of North Carolina Press, 1997); J. Henderson (ed.), *Aristophanes: essays in interpretation*, Yale Classical Studies vol. 26 (Cambridge, 1980); H.-J. Newiger (ed.), *Aristophanes und die alte Komödie* (Darmstadt: Wissenschaftliche Buchgesellschaft, 1975); E. Segal (ed.), *Oxford Readings in Aristophanes* (Oxford: Oxford University Press, 1996), *Oxford Readings in Menander, Plautus, and Terence* (Oxford: Oxford University Press, 2001); J. Wilkins and D. Harvey (eds.), *The Rivals of Aristophanes* (London: Duckworth, 2000).

Aeschylus

D. J. Conacher, *Aeschylus. The Earlier Plays and Related Studies* (Toronto: University of Toronto Press, 1996); J. Herington, *Aeschylus* (New Haven: Yale University Press, 1986); S. Ireland, *Aeschylus* (Oxford: Oxford University Press, 1986); T. Rosenmeyer, *The Art of Aeschylus* (Berkeley: University of California Press, 1982); A. H. Sommerstein, *Aeschylean Tragedy* (Bari: Levante Editori, 1996); O. Taplin, *The Stagecraft of Aeschylus* (Oxford: Oxford University Press, 1977); R. P. Winnington-Ingram, *Studies in Aeschylus* (Cambridge: Cambridge University Press, 1983).

Individual plays: *Oresteia*, D. J. Conacher, *Aeschylus' Oresteia: a literary commentary* (Toronto: University of Toronto Press, 1987); S. Goldhill, *The Oresteia* (Cambridge: Cambridge University Press, 1992); A. Lebeck, *The* Oresteia: *A Study in Language and Structure* (Washington, DC: Center for Hellenic Studies, 1971); *Persians*, T. Harrison, *The Emptiness of Asia: Aeschylus' Persians and the History of the Fifth Century* (London: Duckworth, 2000); *Prometheus*, D. J. Conacher, *Aeschylus'* Prometheus Bound: *a literary commentary* (Toronto: University of Toronto Press, 1980); M. Griffith, *The Authenticity of* Prometheus Bound (Cambridge: Cambridge University Press, 1977); J. Herington, *The Author of the "Prometheus Bound"* (Austin, TX: University of Texas Press, 1970); *Suppliants*, A. Garvie, *Aeschylus' Supplices: Play and Trilogy* (Cambridge: Cambridge University Press, 1969); *Seven*, W. G. Thalmann, *Dramatic Art in Aeschylus'* Seven Against Thebes (New Haven: Yale University Press, 1978).

Sophokles

M. W. Blundell, *Helping Friends and Harming Enemies* (Cambridge: Cambridge University Press, 1989); R. Buxton, *Sophocles* (Oxford: Oxford University Press, 1984); G. Gellie, *Sophocles: a reading* (Melbourne: Melbourne University Press, 1972); B. M. W. Knox, *The Heroic Temper* (Berkeley: University of California Press, 1964); D. Seale, *Vision and Stagecraft in Sophocles* (London: Croom Helm, 1982); C. Segal, *Tragedy and civilization: an interpretation of Sophocles* (Cambridge: Cambridge University Press, 1981); A. J. A. Waldock, *Sophocles the Dramatist* (Cambridge: Cambridge University Press, 1951); C. H. Whitman, *Sophocles: a study of heroic humanism* (Cambridge, MA: Harvard University Press, 1951); R. P. Winnington-Ingram, *Sophocles* (Cambridge: Cambridge University Press, 1980).
Individual plays: *Ajax*, J. Park Poe, *Genre and Meaning in Sophocles'* Ajax (Frankfurt am Main: Athenäum, 1986), J. Hesk, *Sophocles* Ajax (London: Duckworth, 2003); *Antigone*, R. F. Goheen, *The Imagery of Sophocles'* Antigone (Princeton: Princeton University Press, 1951), G. Steiner, *Antigones* (Oxford: Oxford University Press, 1984); *Elektra*, L. MacLeod, *Dolos and Dikê in Sophokles'* Elektra: *An Ethical Study* (Leiden: Brill, 2001); *Oedipus Tyrannos*, R. D. Griffith, *The Theatre of Apollo: divine justice and* Oedipus the King (Montreal: McGill/Queen's Press, 1996), B. M. W. Knox, *Oedipus at Thebes* (New Haven: Yale University Press, 1957); *Philoktetes*, J. Park Poe, *Heroism and Divine Justice in Sophocles'* Philoctetes (Leiden: Brill, 1974).

Euripides

S. A. Barlow, *The Imagery of Euripides* (London: Methuen, 1971); A. P. Burnett, *Catastrophe Survived* (Oxford: Oxford University Press, 1971); D. J. Conacher, *Euripidean Drama: Myth, Theme, and Structure* (Toronto: University of Toronto Press, 1967), *Euripides and the Sophists* (London: Duckworth, 1998); C. Collard, *Euripides* (Oxford: Oxford University Press, 1981); H. Foley, *Ritual Irony: Poetry and Sacrifice in Euripides* (Ithaca, NY: Cornell University Press, 1985); J. Gregory, *Euripides and the Instruction of the Athenians* (Ann Arbor: University of Michigan Press, 1991); G. M. A. Grube, *The Drama of Euripides* (New York: Barnes and Noble, 1961[2]); M. Halleran, *Stagecraft in Euripides* (London: Croom Helm, 1985); K. Hartigan, *Ambiguity and Self-Deception: The Apollo and Artemis Plays of Euripides* (Frankfurt am Main: Lang, 1991); M. Lloyd, *The Agon in Euripides* (Oxford: Oxford University Press, 1992); A. Michelini, *Euripides and the Tragic Tradition* (Madison: University of Wisconsin Press, 1987); J. Morwood, *The Plays of Euripides* (London: Bristol Classical Press, 2002); T. B. L. Webster, *The Tragedies of Euripides* (London: Methuen 1967).

Individual plays: *Andromache*, W. Allan, *The* Andromache *and Euripidean Tragedy* (Oxford: Oxford University Press, 2000), P. D. Kovacs, *The* Andromache *of Euripides* (Chico CA: Scholars Press, 1980); *Bacchae*, C. Segal, *Dionysiac Poetics and Euripides' Bacchae* (Princeton: Princeton University Press, 1982), R. P. Winnington-Ingram, *Euripides and Dionysus* (Cambridge: Cambridge University Press, 1948); *Children of Herakles*, D. Mendelsohn, *Gender and the City in Euripides' political plays* (Oxford: Oxford University Press, 2002), G. Züntz, *The Political Plays of Euripides* (Manchester: Manchester University Press, 1955); *Hecuba*, D. Kovacs, *The Heroic Muse* (Baltimore: Johns Hopkins University Press, 1987), J. Mossman, *Wild Justice: A Study of Euripides'* Hecuba (London: Bristol Classical Press, 1999[2]); *Hippolytos*, B. Goff, *The Noose of Words* (Cambridge: Cambridge University Press, 1990), D. Kovacs, *The Heroic Muse* (Baltimore: Johns Hopkins University Press, 1987), C. A. E. Luschnig, *Time Holds the Mirror* (Leiden: Brill, 1988), S. Mills, *Euripides*: Hippolytus (London: Duckworth, 2002); *Ion*, K. Zacharia, *Converging Truths: Euripides'* Ion *and the Athenian quest for self-definition* (Leiden: Brill, 2003); *Medea*, W. Allan, *Euripides*: Medea (London: Duckworth, 2002), E. McDermott, *Euripides' Medea: the incarnation of disorder* (University Park, PA: Pennsylvania State University Press, 1989); *Orestes*, J. R. Porter, *Studies in Euripides'* Orestes (Leiden: Brill, 1994); *Rhesos*, W. Ritchie, *The authenticity of the* Rhesus *of Euripides* (Cambridge: Cambridge University Press, 1964); *Suppliant Women*, D. Mendelsohn, *Gender and the City in Euripides' political plays* (Oxford: Oxford University Press, 2002), G. Züntz, *The Political Plays of Euripides* (Manchester: Manchester University Press, 1955); *Trojan Women*, R. Scodel, *The Trojan Trilogy of Euripides* (Göttingen: Vandenhoeck and Ruprecht, 1980).

Aristophanes

A. M. Bowie, *Aristophanes: Myth, Ritual, and Comedy* (Cambridge: Cambridge University Press, 1993); P. Cartledge, *Aristophanes and his Theatre of the Absurd* (London: Bristol Classical Press, 1990); K. J. Dover, *Aristophanic Comedy* (London: Botsford, 1972); T. K. Hubbard, *The Mask of Comedy: Aristophanes and the Intertextual Parabasis* (Ithaca, NY: Cornell University Press, 1991); D. M. MacDowell, *Aristophanes and Athens* (Oxford: Oxford University Press, 1995); K. McLeish, *The Theatre of Aristophanes* (London: Thames and Hudson, 1980); G. Murray, *Aristophanes* (Oxford: Oxford University Press, 1933); K. J. Reckford, *Aristophanes' Old-and-New Comedy* (Chapel Hill: University of North Carolina Press, 1987); C. F. Russo, *Aristophanes, an author for the stage* (London: Routledge, 1992); R. G. Ussher, *Aristophanes* (Oxford: Oxford University Press, 1977).

Menander

S. M. Goldberg, *The Making of Menander's Comedy* (London: Athlone Press, 1980); J. M. Walton and P. D. Arnott, *Menander and the Making of Comedy* (Westport, CT: Praeger, 1996); D. Wiles, *The Masks of Menander* (Cambridge: Cambridge University Press, 1991); N. Zagagi, *The Comedy of Menander* (Bloomington, IN: Indiana University Press, 1994).

Women in Drama

S. Des Bouvrie, *Women in Greek Tragedy: an anthropological approach* (Oslo: Norwegian University Press, 1990); H. P. Foley, *Reflections of Women in Antiquity* (New York: Gordon and Breach

Science, 1981), *Female Acts in Greek Tragedy* (Princeton: Princeton University Press, 2001); N. Loraux, *Tragic Ways of Killing a Woman* (Cambridge, MA: Harvard University Press, 1987); L. McClure, *Spoken Like a Woman: speech and gender in Athenian drama* (Princeton: Princeton University Press, 1999); N. Rabinowitz, *Anxiety Veiled: Euripides and the Traffic in Women* (Ithaca, NY: Cornell University Press, 1993); R. Rehm, *Marriage to Death* (Princeton: Princeton University Press, 1994); L. Taaffe, *Aristophanes and Women* (London: Routledge, 1993); V. Wohl, *Intimate Commerce: exchange, gender, and subjectivity in Greek Tragedy* (Austin, TX, University of Texas Press, 1998); F. Zeitlin, *Playing the Other. Gender and Society in Classical Greek Literature* (Chicago: University of Chicago Press, 1996).

P. Easterling, "Women in Tragic Space," *Bulletin of the Institute of Classical Studies* 34 (1987) 15–26; J. Gardner, "Aristophanes and the Defence of the *oikos*," *Greece and Rome* 36 (1989) 51–62; J. Henderson, "Older Women in Attic Comedy," *Transactions of the American Philological Association* 117 (1987) 105–29, "Women in the Athenian Drama Festivals," *Transactions of the American Philological Society* 121 (1991) 133–47; M. Katz, "The character of tragedy: women and the Greek imagination," *Arethusa* 27 (1994) 81–103; F. Muecke, "A Portrait of the Artist as a Young Woman," *Classical Quarterly* 32 (1982) 41–55; A. Podlecki, "Could women attend the theatre in Ancient Athens?," *Ancient World* 21 (1990) 27–43; R. Seaford, "The tragic wedding," *Journal of Hellenic Studies* 107 (1987) 106–30, "Imprisonment of Women in Greek Tragedy", *Journal of Hellenic Studies* 110 (1990) 76–90; M. Shaw, "The Female Intruder: women in fifth-century drama," *Classical Philology* 70 (1975) 255–66.

Articles

Two bibliographical tools are available to the student searching for articles on Greek Drama in the journals: (i) *L'Année Philologique*, a yearly listing of the work done in all fields of classical studies, published in hard copy and available (by subscription) online (*www.annee-philologique.com/aph*) for the years 1969–2001 and (ii) TOCS-IN, an online site (*www.chass.utoronto.ca/amphoras/tocs.html*) that allows one to search the titles of journal articles since 1992 (in some cases before 1992) for names and significant terms.

The following are some significant articles in the field of Greek drama:
G. E. M. de Ste Croix, "The Political Outlook of Aristophanes," in *The Origins of the Peloponnesian War*, Appendix XXIX (Ithaca, NY: Cornell University Press, 1972); E. R. Dodds, "On Misunderstanding the *Oedipus Rex*," *Greece and Rome* 13 (1966) 37–49; J. R. Green, "On Seeing and Depicting the Theater in Classical Athens" *Greek, Roman and Byzantine Studies* 32 (1991) 15–50; J. Griffin, "The Social Function of Attic Tragedy," *Classical Quarterly* 48 (1998) 39–61; S. Goldhill, "Civic Ideology and the problem of difference: the politics of Aeschylean tragedy, once again," *Journal of Hellenic Studies* 120 (2000) 39–56; A. W. Gomme, "Aristophanes and Politics," *Classical Review* 52 (1938) 97–209; F. S. Halliwell, "Comic Satire and Freedom of Speech in classical Athens," *Journal of Hellenic Studies* 111 (1991) 48–70; N. G. L. Hammond, "The conditions of dramatic performance to the death of Aeschylus," *Greek, Roman, and Byzantine Studies* 13 (1972) 387–450; D. M. MacDowell, "The Number of Speaking Actors in Old Comedy," *Classical Quarterly* 44 (1994) 325–35; C. W. Marshall, "Comic Technique and the Fourth Actor," *Classical Quarterly* 47 (1997) 72–9; J. Park Poe, "The Determination of Episodes in Greek Tragedy," *American Journal of Philology* 114 (1993) 343–96; P. J. Rhodes, "Nothing to do with democracy; Athenian drama and the *polis*," *Journal of Hellenic Studies* 123 (2003) 104–19; S. Scullion, "'Nothing to do with Dionysus': tragedy misconceived as ritual," *Classical Quarterly* 52 (2002) 102–37, "Euripides and Macedon, or the silence of the Frogs," *Classical*

Quarterly 53 (2003) 389–401; R. Seaford, "The Social Function to Attic Tragedy: a response to Jasper Griffin," *Classical Quarterly* 50 (2000) 30–44; A. H. Sommerstein, "How to avoid being a *komodoumenos*," *Classical Quarterly* 46 (1996) 327–56; I. C. Storey, "Poets, Politicians, and Perverts: personal humour in Aristophanes," *Classics Ireland* 5 (1998) 85–134; O. Taplin, "Fifth-Century Tragedy and Comedy: a *synkrisis*," *Journal of Hellenic Studies* 106 (1986) 163–74.

THE ACTORS OF DIONYSUS

Since 1993 The Actors of Dionysus (www.actorsofdionysus.com) have been touring the British Isles, staging Greek dramas in a new English translation for modern audiences. Their performances are often accompanied by a lecture by the "local expert" on ancient drama, resulting in a small volume of essays published as the issues of a journal, *Dionysus*. These are pitched at the level of the student or the spectator coming to Greek tragedy for the first time, and can be very useful for the novice in understanding immediately what the issues of a particular drama are or what to look for in a production.

Vol. 4 (*Oedipus the King*); 5 (*Trojan Women*); 6 (*Medea*); 7 (*Elektra*); 9 (*Ajax*); 10 (*Antigone*); 11 (*Oedipus the King* – 2); 12 (*Hippolytos*); 13 (*Agamemnon*); 14 (*Libation-Bearers*); 15 (*Bacchae*).

Two collections of essays are also available: *Trojan Women* (2002), *Agamemnon* (2003).

Index

Play-titles enclosed in square brackets [. . .] denote lost dramas. Bold type indicates a particular study of an author or topic; for individual plays the bold type directs one to the play synopsis.

DATE DUE

DEMCO 38-296